Gillian Howard is an employment lawyer, broadcaster, and author, known as 'The Rottweiler with a Handbag' because of her fearsome reputation. She has been described as having nerves of tungsten or titanium. She never gives up for her clients and stands up to bullies, racists, sexists, and anyone professing hatred for minority groups and discriminatory views.

She has been instructed by several clients who were 'on the other side' and who do not want to find themselves up against her again.

This book is dedicated to

My late sister-in- law Judy Howard.
My late parents Alex and Margaret Howard.
My twin brother Charles and his partner Debbie and my nephews and nieces,
Gadi, Tali, Sharoni and Mickey.
My husband Barry and son Daniel, son Ben and his wife Aliza, grandchildren
Max, Nessia and Zoe.

Senior Rabbi David Mitchell and Ian, both of whom I call my 'Surrogate sons'.
Rabbi David is the most courageous, brilliant, kindest, talented young man I
have the pleasure to know and love. He has the utmost integrity. He stands up
against all forms of discrimination and unfairness. He is an inspirational leader
of the West London Synagogue of British Jews. He makes attending
Synagogue a joy and a privilege.

I was inspired to follow my career in employment law by the late Professor
Paul O'Higgins, Christ's College Cambridge, who made everything in my
career possible. I also dedicate this book to you Paul.

Finally, I dedicate this book to the many brave and courageous women who
have instructed me over the past 40 plus years, who have had the courage to
stand up to the base tyranny of and treatment by their employers and who have
trusted me to act for them and win.

Gillian Howard

Secrets and Lies – Tales of an Employment Lawyer

Austin Macauley Publishers™

LONDON * CAMBRIDGE * NEW YORK * SHARJAH

A CIP catalogue record for this title is available from the British Library.

ISBN 9781398486027 (Paperback)
ISBN 9781035805662 (Hardback)
ISBN 9781398497603 (ePub e-book)

www.austinmacauley.com

First Published 2023
Austin Macauley Publishers Ltd®
1 Canada Square
Canary Wharf
London
E14 5AA

Barristers who have acted for my clients

Human rights specialists Geoffrey Robertson KC, Edward Fitzgerald KC, Gemma Hobcraft, Doughty Street Chambers.

Public law and employment specialists Dinah Rose KC, Monica Carss-Frisk KC, Jane Mulcahy KC, Nick de Marco KC and Jane Collier, Blackstone Chambers.

Clinical negligence and regulatory law specialists, James Badenoch QC and Kieran Coonan QC (both retired, formerly 1 Crown Office Row); Professor Charles Foster, Green Templeton College, Oxford University and 4-5 Gray's Inn Square, medical law and medical ethics brilliant author, traveller extraordinaire, veterinarian, taxidermist, barrister and philosopher and most importantly our wonderful friend.

Employment Specialists Sir Patrick Elias (former Judge in the Court of Appeal); the late Adrian Lynch QC; Daniel Stilitz KC and Sir Akhlaq Choudhury KC (President of the Employment Appeals Tribunal) 11 King's Bench Walk (11 KBW); Mark Stephens (Gatehouse Chambers); Caspar Glyn KC, Tom Coghlin KC, Paul Epstein KC, Jason Galbraith-Marten KC, Claire McCann; Caroline Musgrave, Jennifer Danvers, Cloisters; Rebecca Tuck KC, Jane McNeill, KC, Eleena Misra KC and Hilary Winstone, Old Square Chambers.

SPECIAL MENTIONS

A special mention must go to Michael Beloff KC, a wonderful friend and former President of Trinity College Oxford, whose hospitality for over 10 years was so much appreciated. Inspired by him, our family became involved in a number of Societies and projects at Trinity College. Michael was the first guest speaker at the Annual Law and Literature lecture I sponsored in memory of my mother, which he agreed to host at Trinity College.

Another special mention goes to my friend and inspirational employment barrister, writer and broadcaster, Daniel Barnett of Outer Temple Chambers. We have worked together for many years with great pleasure on my part.

Finally, I make a very special mention to the wonderful broadcaster/presenter on LBC, Nick Ferrari, who has made me his 'go-to employment lawyer'. Over the years we have enjoyed and continue to enjoy some hilarious banter on his morning Breakfast Show.

SECRETS AND LIES
I will tell you some of the secrets of how I have won cases for my clients, sometimes in the face of seemingly hopeless odds.

I will also expose some of the lies and deceptions that I have faced from my opposition and how I made sure they didn't get away with it. I hope you enjoy this romp through my 40+ years' legal career.

THIS BOOK
Everything you read in this book is true up to a point. Bound by confidentiality, I have had to conceal the real names of the parties (apart from a few).

Some of the facts of many of these 'Tales' have also been changed to protect the identity of the protagonists for reasons of confidentiality and to protect the innocent and the guilty. I guess you could call those tales 'faction'.

As Eric Morecombe once famously said to Andre Previn, "I'm playing all the right notes...but not necessarily in the right order."

Where the cases have been reported either in the Press or published on the Government website I have been able say who was involved and exactly what happened and what was said and I have quoted from these newspaper and Law Reports.

However I have quoted accurately and verbatim in the cases where sexist, homophobic or racist language was used or behaviour was perpetrated by the miscreant individuals. It is only right that you should know what was actually done and said to my clients.

WARNING

Readers are warned they may be offended by the graphic and shocking descriptions of the sexual acts and language, racist and homophobic and anti-Semitic language and other appalling behaviour described in this book. I have not used euphemisms nor have I shied away from telling what and how it actually happened.

Some chapters contain descriptions of sexually lewd acts and sexual or racist language of a gravely offensive and obscene nature. This includes swear words and sexual, racist, anti-Semitic, Islamophobic, homophobic and other highly offensive language. It is there because that's what was actually said and done to my clients, shocking though it is.

Table of Content

Introduction: The Rottweiler's Tale   13

Chapter 1: In the Beginning…   18

Chapter 2: Abigail's Tale   23

Chapter 3: Alice's Tale   46

Chapter 4: Badra's Tale   63

Chapter 5: 'Bonking Billys' Tale   68

Chapter 6: Bianca's Tale   80

Chapter 7: Brigitte's Tale   100

Chapter 8: Bonnie's Tale   107

Chapter 9: The Bullies' Tales   117

Chapter 10: Colin's Tale   126

Chapter 11: David's Tale   133

Chapter 12: Derek's Tale   137

Chapter 13: Dirty Den's Tale   142

Chapter 14: Doctors and a Dentist's Tales   148

Chapter 15: Eddie's Tale   169

Chapter 16: Farid's Tale   182

Chapter 17: Faith's Tale   186

Chapter 18: The Fraudsters' Tales   193

Chapter 19: Gaynor's Tale   210

Chapter 20: Grace's Tale   227

Chapter 21: Gunilla's Tale   234

Chapter 22: Hannah's Tale   240

Chapter 23: Harriet's Tale   246

Chapter 24: Henrietta's Tale   252

Chapter 25: Iris's Tale   260

Chapter 26: Pauline's Tale   262

Chapter 27: Sean's Tale   270

Chapter 28: Kiaran's Tale   276

Chapter 29: Laurent's and Léon's Tales   283

Chapter 30: Miranda's Tale   288

Chapter 31: Nikki's Tale   291

Chapter 32: The Tales of Three Teachers   294

Chapter 33: Tomislav's Tale   302

Chapter 34: Xanthe's Tale   314

Chapter 35: 'Tales of The Unexpected'   323

Glossary   402

Introduction
The Rottweiler's Tale

"If I leave my clients better off than when I found them, I know I have done my job."

I have always had a passion, since a little girl, to stand up for anyone who has been bullied, fighting for the underdog—and winning. And nothing can scare me and no-one can bully me.

So, going into the law and finding employment law in its infancy, in 1974, giving rights to employees to be protected from unfair treatment at work when I graduated was perfect timing.

I was lucky that I first graduated just as modern employment law as we know it started. The infamous Industrial Relations Act 1971 introduced one good thing—unfair dismissal protection.

Sex and race discrimination legislation and the right to maternity pay and leave and rights of women to equal pay all followed in the mid-1970s. More recently the Equality Act 2010 consolidated all of the anti-discrimination legislation and introduced new protections, notably unlawful discrimination on the grounds of sexual orientation and gender reassignment.

I am still today battling for justice for women, ethnic minorities, workers with disabilities and members of the Lesbian, Gay, Bisexual and Transgender (LGBT) Community. Whilst the #MeToo, LGBT and Black Lives Matter movements have made huge strides to improve the treatment of women, the gay and transgender and the BAME communities, there is still a long way to go.

How I Got My Name

Many years ago, a client thanked me at the successful conclusion of her case and said, *"You really do deserve your name."* Intrigued, I asked what that was and she said, *"The Rottweiler with a handbag."*

A Consultant Physician, Dr Rob McNally, who had referred this client, had told her that was the name he had given me. I love it and am extremely happy to have it. It sometimes makes the other side quake in their shoes before they have even met me. I have even trademarked it to ensure that no-one else uses it.

I learnt early on in my career to bare my Rottweiler teeth and snap or even threaten to 'bite' the opposition where it hurts —more often this was the employer or their lawyers and it was often just enough to make them roll over and give in.

I have a soft and compassionate side however and I also been called *'the woman with the iron fist in the velvet glove'* and *'the woman with nerves, not of steel, but of Tungsten or Titanium'.*

What's in a Name?

The first Employment Judge I ever encountered, in 1974, was very old fashioned, dare I say a little misogynistic. When I introduced myself as *"Ms Howard"* he asked me whether I was 'Miss' or 'Mrs'. Not understanding why men get so hung up on identifying the single or marital status of a woman I repeated, *"I am Ms Howard."*

He muttered in a bad-tempered voice, *"I do not recognise that title in this Tribunal—and anyway I have no idea how to pronounce it."*

I immediately replied (thinking to myself 'what a silly, old fuddy-duddy he was'), *"Well think of 'Ms' rhyming with 'Fizz'."*

He looked at me, seething with anger, and told me to leave the Tribunal and to come back when I could apologise for my "unprofessional language."

Surprised he had taken such offence when all I had done was to give him the answer he had asked for, I walked out of the tribunal and walked straight back in. I said through gritted teeth, *"I am very sorry Sir, if you thought I was being rude"* and added, *"But I am still Ms Howard."* At that he gave up.

This is just one example of my willingness over the years to stand up to figures of authority if I felt they were abusing their position.

Bullies

I've encountered bullies in all shapes and sizes in my life but I have never let anyone get away with it, if I could help it.

I had been brought up by my father to stand up to bullies and he told me that the other side of a bully is a coward.

When I was at school, at the age of 9, there was a particularly nasty girl in my Class, Elizabeth Watson (that was her real name). Her father was a Black Shirt, an Oswald Mosley supporter and a 'Jew-hater'. Elizabeth had been bullying another Jewish girl in our class and had been calling her nasty names and was pushing and kicking her. I told Elizabeth to stop. She turned round to me and shouted, *"all you Jews should have died in the gas chambers and burned in the ovens."*

I didn't hesitate. I punched her in the stomach very hard and told her if she ever said anything like that again or even attempted to bully anyone else again she would get much worse from me and she wouldn't be able to sit down, her face would be not be the same shape ever again and she wouldn't be able to hold a pencil for a very long time.

She went straight to our form teacher and told her what I had done—to which the teacher said in a voice loud enough for me to hear, *"Oh No Elizabeth, Gillian wouldn't do anything like that. Now go away and stop telling tales."*

So when clients have told me they have been subjected to bullying at work or when solicitors on the other side have attempted to bully me—I know just what to do. Perhaps that's why I deserve my name *"The Rottweiler with a handbag"* or as one client called me *"A terrier with pink lipstick."*

21ˢᵗ Century Suffragette

Another client called me 'a 21ˢᵗ Century Suffragette' after I settled her case, two days before trial, for a multimillion dollar settlement (I am not allowed to say how many millions but it was lots). Her case features in this Book.

I often feel like a modern-day Suffragette, but I have always regarded my female clients who have stood up to sexism in the workplace to be modern day Suffragettes as well.

A Fashion Statement

I was once described by the Independent newspaper as *"providing the fashion moments"* during a lengthy tribunal hearing, in a sex discrimination case. This case is also described in the book. The description pleased me greatly. I always try to look my best and enjoy 'power dressing' as one rather cheeky male barrister told me, as he complimented me on my beautiful suit. My favourite clothes shop features below.

Insults

Sometimes disgruntled barristers and solicitors have tried to insult me—without success.

In the early 1980s a female barrister, on the other side, got very annoyed after she had lost the case for her client. She asked me a question that was meant as an insult—but it made me laugh and still makes me laugh and I had the last laugh.

We were both walking up Wimpole Street where I had my office after the case. I was wearing a beautiful Rena Lange black crepe suit with a red feather on the jacket, bought from my favourite Clothes Shop, "Helen", and Christian Louboutin shoes, carrying my Moschino handbag featured on my website and the front cover of this book.

This barrister looked me up and down and said, *"I know you will know the answer to this—where is Primark?"*

Without drawing breath, I looked at her, smiled sweetly and said, *"Oh yes I buy all my clothes there"* and pointed towards the shop "Helen", in those days in Thayer Street, now in George Street, in the West End of London.

This is where I have bought my beautiful clothes since coming to London in 1974. I said to this barrister, *"You will need to turn round and walk back down Wimpole Street. The Shop is on the right as you walk towards Wigmore Street but I think Primark has now changed its name to 'Helen'. Anyway that's where 'Primark' is."*

With my directions firmly in her mind, off she went. For all I know she is still wandering around the West End of London searching for Primark, looking now like Miss Haversham in "Great Expectations."

On another occasion a bad-tempered male solicitor, also having lost the case for his client, said to me, as we were leaving the Tribunal, *"You know who you remind me of—Mrs Thatcher—and you even have a handbag like hers."*

That was a real insult having been a lifelong Socialist. However, I smiled sweetly and said through gritted teeth, *"Thank you. That's one of the nicest compliments you could possibly pay me"* and walked off. His attempt to insult me had backfired on him.

"On the Game"—Promiscuous Me

I had never before been likened to 'ladies of the night' until I was a speaker at an employment law conference in 1996. The Chairman introduced me, to over 300 lawyers, by saying, *"I have the pleasure of introducing Employment Lawyer Gillian Howard. She has been on the game for many years."*

He was of course referring to my legal career and I believe he meant 'in' the game—a small but significant slip of the tongue. When the laughter died down, including mine, I got on with my lecture. At the end of my talk, I said, *"If anyone noticed that slip of the tongue when the Chairman introduced me—come and see me afterwards."* I walked off to much laughter.

I am on the Game

However, when I appeared in 'Roll on Friday', a satirical online legal magazine, 20 years ago, I realised that I had made myself sound on my website as if I was a lady of the night, offering *'a personal service available day and night'*.

Roll on Friday wrote, *"Glamorous lawyer of the week and this week's top legal website comes courtesy of Gillian Howard, employment law specialist and self-confessed 'rottweiler with a handbag'.*

"Her website features pictures of an accessorised attack dog and of her looking sexy in a ball gown in someone else's house. The rest of her website reads alarmingly like a card in a phone box, 'I offer a unique service...a very personal and dedicated service...I am very experienced. I make myself available day or night...nothing is too small to handle' etc.

"But to be fair, she's clearly got some proper skills given the long line of big-name cases she's won. And given her galactic rates, she charges a chunky £400 per hour, which increases to a profession-topping £800 per hour if she's contacted outside of working hours (9 am to 6 pm).

"Even Nigel Boardman doesn't manage that. Readers wanting to instruct her can get in touch here. Just do so before 6 pm."

Chapter 1
In the Beginning...

I had a lot to learn when I first started in practice.

Dean, Oh Dean!

In 1981, after I had opened my own practice, I was persuaded to represent Dean, who was being prosecuted in the Magistrates Court for a variety of criminal offences. Dean was Wayne's 15-year-old son.

Wayne was a Scrap Metal Merchant for whom I had acted in an unfair dismissal claim brought against him a year earlier.

Whilst it was an unfair dismissal because Wayne had sacked a thieving employee on the spot, Wayne charmed the Tribunal, persuading them that his thieving employee deserved no compensation.

The Appellant (as they were called in those days) was found to be 100% at fault for his dismissal and was awarded nothing, other than a basic award, equivalent to a statutory redundancy payment. As he only had two years' service it really was a basic award.

Wayne thought I had won the case for him and said I was the best thing since sliced bread. So when his son got into trouble a few months later, he asked me to represent him.

I told Wayne I did not do criminal work and I had never been to a Magistrates Court. That did not seem to matter to Wayne. I told him he should instruct an experienced criminal solicitor but he insisted I was the best person for the job and persuaded me to defend Dean at his trial. I never did this again.

One Saturday night, Dean had been arrested with three of his friends—all aged 15—when he was caught by the police driving a stolen car. Dean had been driving at over 100 mph round the Outer Circle in Regent's Park in Central London. The speed limit was then 30 mph (it's now 20 mph). He had no driving licence as he was under-age, nor was he insured and Dean and his friends were all drunk on beers and shots and high on 'spliffs' (cannabis).

The police had given chase to the car that Dean was driving round Regent's Park for over 10 minutes before the boys were caught. Dean had by then smashed the car into a lamp post and the car had come to an abrupt stop. It was a write-off.

Dean told me that when he heard and saw the blue lights behind him, he thought he could either try to outrun the police or stop and give himself up. Unfortunately, he chose the former and failed.

When the police finally caught him, Dean told the police officers he didn't know the car was stolen. He said he had met a 'friend', whose name he could not remember, in a pub, earlier that evening. This 'friend' had told Dean he could 'borrow' his car. Dean said he assumed it belonged to this 'friend' so he had 'borrowed' it.

When the officers told Dean to get out of the car and tried to 'cuff' him, he punched one of the officers in the face and tried to run away. He didn't make it.

When Dean was breathalysed, he was three times over the legal limit. I was surprised he could even stand up. The police found packets of cannabis in the pockets of all four boys.

Dean was arrested but the police let the other three boys off with a caution as they had been polite and compliant with the police. They were sent home in a police car. I can't imagine what their parents said to them when they arrived home in a police car.

Dean had continued being abusive to the police officers and was handcuffed, put into the back of the police car and detained in the custody suite at Holborn Police Station overnight.

Dean's case came up before the Magistrates the following Monday morning.

He was charged with numerous offences - taking and driving away a stolen car (TDA); driving without a licence; driving without insurance; driving three times over the legal limit; in possession of illegal drugs; obstructing the police in the execution of their duty; resisting arrest and assaulting a police officer. Quite a list.

I saw Dean on the Sunday morning in the police cells, before his hearing the next day. I told him to dress smartly for Court, to look at the Magistrates when giving his answers, to keep his answers short, admit everything he had done, to be very respectful about the Police and very remorseful about his behaviour. I told him to explain he had never done anything like this before and to promise that he had learnt a very valuable lesson and would stay out of trouble from now on. More importantly I told him not to chew gum in Court

His answer to all of this was *"Yes Miss."* This all fell on deaf ears as I was about to find out.

We got to Court the following day and Dean stepped into the witness box. After the prosecution had attempted to get him to tell the Magistrates what he had done, all he kept saying was *"no comment"*.

It was then my turn to ask him questions.

It was the first time I had ever been to a Magistrates Court and I imagined this was the same for Dean, so I started by saying to Dean, *"just take a couple of deep breaths Dean. You are in strange surroundings here…"* but before I could get any further, he shouted out in his cockney accent and cocky voice, *"Oh No Miss, I've been 'ere loads of times before."* He then smiled at the Magistrates into the bargain.

"I dare say" I said and my heart sank. This of course told the Magistrates he had a string of previous criminal convictions—something the Magistrates do not normally find out about until after the accused has been found guilty, if they are found guilty.

The Chief Magistrate looked sternly at Dean and asked, *"And what have you been convicted of son?"*

Dean replied, *"Oh last time it was 'buggery',"* or that's what we all thought he had said.

The Magistrate exclaimed, *"Buggery… How old are you son?"*

"Fifteen," replied Dean laughing, *"but it weren't buggery, Sir. It were burglary. Cor blimey you Magistrates 'ave got dirty minds"* and he looked around the Court as if he was expecting laughter and applause. There was a just sigh of relief all round and the Magistrates graciously ignored Dean's cheeky comment.

Dean then started to get into his stride. I asked him what the weather was like when he was driving the car round Regent's Park. I had planned to argue it had been pouring with rain and Dean had skidded rather than deliberately driving at 100 miles per hour. His reply was, *"tickle your arse with a feather."*

Puzzled and horrified at the same time I asked him to repeat what he had just said and he replied, *"particularly nasty weather"* laughed and then winked at me. Dean seemed to be treating this like an outing to a pantomime.

When I asked Dean when was the first time he had driven on a public road, he answered, *"When I kissed the teacher."* I thought that was odd but I let it go.

I then asked Dean why he had taken the car belonging to someone he didn't know? He answered, *"Money, Money, Money."* I thought that was also an odd answer but I still had not twigged.

I then asked him what did he do such a silly thing for. He answered he had done it because, *"It's a rich man's world."*

Yes you're probably ahead of me here but I still had not guessed what he was doing.

I asked him in which pub he had met this so-called friend who had said he could borrow the car. Dean answered, '*The Dancing Queen*'. I'd never heard of that pub so I asked him where that pub was. He said, '*Waterloo.*'

I didn't know there was a pub in Waterloo called The Dancing Queen.

I know I was very naïve—that's why I now stick to employment law.

I then asked him what he said to the police officers when he was finally caught in Regents Park. He said, *"I shouted SOS."*

By then I had had enough of his baffling evidence so I asked him if he had anything he wanted to say to the Magistrates in mitigation. He answered, *"Take a chance on me"* and *"Why did it have to be me?."*

Only then did I realise what Dean had been doing—answering my questions with Abba song titles. He was laughing as he gave me his answers.

When I collared him after the hearing he told me he had had a £20 bet with his other three friends who were in the car, that he could incorporate 20 Abba songs into his answers at the Magistrates Court and he had won the bet.

I don't remember much more but I do recall vowing to 'murder' Dean when we got outside the Court.

But I think the crowning glory to Dean's story and something I will never forget was this exchange during the trial. Dean had been chewing gum throughout giving his evidence despite my telling him to take the chewing gum out before we went into Court.

The Chief Magistrate had asked the Clerk to tell Dean to stop 'masticating'. The message to Dean, relayed by the Clerk was, *"The Magistrates have asked you to take your hands out of your pockets!"* How I kept a straight face I will never know.

Dean was found guilty of all charges but to my utter amazement he was only given a Youth Rehabilitation Order which entailed supervision by a member of

Dean's local Youth Offending Team; a fine of £200; a requirement to go for treatment for alcohol and drug abuse and to take part in a youth-offending behaviour and education programme.

His father was delighted with the result. Wayne told me he had been expecting *"Dean to be put away in Borstal for some time."* He added, *"You must have charmed them Magistrates."* He gave me a big hug and suggested he took me for a slap-up lunch, which he did.

What became of Dean you may be wondering? I never found out. Actually, I dread to think…

Chapter 2
Abigail's Tale

"Off with his testicles" I cried when Abigail told me what Philip had done to her.

Abigail worked for a global retail Organisation with an office in London, headquartered in the USA.

She had graduated with a first-class economics degree and was a qualified Chartered Accountant. She also had an MBA (Masters in Business Administration) from INSEAD in Fontainebleau, France. In addition she was an accomplished linguist, speaking fluent French, Spanish and Russian and a talented pianist.

Abigail had had one child during her 18 years' employment and had only taken six months' maternity leave. Her statutory right was to take one year. She was a dedicated, conscientious and very diligent worker.

She was in her mid-forties when she came to see me.

Philip, the Deputy Chief Executive had come from another global organisation specialising in IT. He was hired as the Deputy Chief Executive a couple of years before Abigail instructed me. He became her boss after a re-organisation a year before the incidents that led her to seek my advice.

Philip was a 52-year-old, 18 stone man, six feet four in height and an ex-Rugby International. He had a ruddy complexion from drinking too much over the years, had an over-inflated ego and self-image and an excessive sex drive.

Abigail was a petite, slim, young woman. She described herself as an introvert, who never drank alcohol and had been tee total all her life. She was a loyal, loving wife and mother. I would describe her as shy and rather unconfident when she first came to see me. That soon changed after she met me.

At the Department's Christmas party, Philip had been drinking pints of beer and shots of vodka before dinner. He drank at least two bottles of red wine with dinner. He had been making a fool of himself all evening, going up to girls in the gastropub, slobbering all over them, asking them to dance with him. They all said, "No."

There was a video of Philip during dinner, taken on someone's iPhone, singing into a microphone that he had grabbed from the Karaoke machine, rather the worse for wear. He continued making a fool of himself during the rest of the evening.

At one point in the evening he went up to Abigail, who was at the Bar getting a Coca-Cola, and said, *"Do you want to have sex? No. Well lie down 'cos I do."*

He then laughed and tried to kiss her. Abigail dodged his kiss and went back to sit with some of her colleagues.

By the end of the evening, Philip was very drunk. He staggered away from the bar to where Abigail was sitting and after making several incoherent suggestive comments to her, instructed her to remain behind after the party when everyone had gone home as he had *"something important to say"* to her.

She had just applied for promotion and was due to have her annual appraisal with Philip after the Christmas/New Year break, so she thought it would just be about work. She did as he instructed and stayed behind at the end of the evening.

The Bar staff were clearing up in another room and all Abigail's colleagues had left, when Philip suddenly lunged at Abigail. He forced himself on top of her, straddled alongside her, unzipped his trousers and said in a drunken voice, *"This is what you have been waiting for."*

Abigail struggled to get him off her but he was a brute of a man and she could not shift him. She screamed as loudly as she could and then bit him very hard on his lower lip when he tried to kiss her and kneed him between his legs as hard as she could.

Luckily one of the Bar staff heard her screams and came running into the Bar. By then Philip had managed to stagger to his feet, fumbled to zip up his trousers and left the pub, with his lip bleeding, clutching his private parts, howling in agony.

Abigail then ran down the stairs of the pub and ran as fast as she could all the way to the station, to catch the last train home, crying and very shaken.

During her train journey, at around ten minutes past midnight, Abigail started to receive texts from Philip. He sent similar texts the next day. Here are some of them:-

- *I really want to take you back and front.*
- *Can I ask you a personal question?*
- *Do you like your pussy licked?*
- *Would you suck my cock?*
- *I've wanted you for so long. I really want you.*
- *Can we meet tomorrow?*
- *I want to suck your tits.*
- *I want my cock right up you.*
- *We will have awesome sex*
- *I just to fuck you until you beg for more.*
- *I want to lick you all over when I have come all over you and fuck you until we come together. Then you can suck me off until I come all over you again.*
- *I will book a room in the hotel round the corner from the office the day after we all get back after the New Year.*
- *Come to me after work and put in your diary you are going to the cinema with girlfriends. I will authorise a half day off as a 'medical appointment' not holiday.*
- *I will book a hotel room send you a code—'It's tonight' to come up to my hotel room or 'Not tonight Josephine' if some reason I have a meeting and cannot make it.*

These disgusting sex texts kept coming even worse than the first ones. Abigail deleted the more disgusting ones but kept the ones above and forwarded them to her best friend, Deidre, a lawyer specialising in libel, the next day.

Abigail asked Deidre what she should do. Deirdre texted back, *"OMG I am gobsmacked—that dirty bastard. See an employment lawyer immediately and report the sick twat to his boss. He is disgusting and needs his balls cut off. That will stop him."*

Abigail took sick leave the following day as she could not bear to go back to the office where she would encounter Philip. She took a couple of weeks away from work to think what she should do next.

Deidre knew of me via another friend of hers and told Abigail to go to see me, which she did and she instructed me to act for her.

I advised Abigail to make a formal complaint about Philip's conduct so she sent in a formal grievance, drafted by me. Her employer started an investigation.

It was led by Bert, an inexperienced, junior HR officer - not really a suitable investigator for a serious sexual harassment complaint involving the deputy Chief Executive.

Bert made an introductory phone call to Abigail, before he formally interviewed Philip and her. Bert said several unfortunate things during this call to Abigail which came back to bite him.

"It's not like this took place on Company premises" he said first, implying that none of her allegations were any concern or the legal responsibility of the employer. Wrong.

He then said, *"the text messages could have come from anyone called 'Philip' ... I hope they are from Philip ... but you never know."*

The implication was that Abigail had somehow manipulated the texts to make them look like they had come from her boss, Philip.

This was a preposterous suggestion as Philip's iPhone could, and in fact was, analysed and of course the text messages were sent by Philip, the Deputy Chief Executive, from his iPhone.

Bert then said, *"normally in sexual harassment cases it is one person's word against another's and very rarely is the woman believed—they often make things up to get even when they haven't got promotion or they do it for more money. I'm not saying that's what you're doing. I'm just saying be prepared for that to be said to you."*

Bert then told Abigail that the grievance process might take *"at least six to nine months to complete"* - clearly trying to dissuade her from carrying on with her grievance.

Finally, when Abigail expressed her concerns about keeping her allegations confidential and asked what she could tell her work colleagues who would be potential witnesses, Bert's reply was, *"You can tell who you like what you like— you can put it on Facebook or on the side of a bus if you want to."*

Abigail was stunned because a major principle of the grievance and anti-harassment policy was that everything had to be kept strictly confidential. This was so that the alleged perpetrator and the complainant could be guaranteed confidentiality and a fair hearing and so witnesses could not collude.

All of Bert's remarks were entirely inappropriate and were potential acts of victimisation.

At Philip's formal investigation interview he denied everything that Abigail had alleged in her grievance. He said that Abigail had told him that she *"had the hots"* for him and *"really fancied"* him and *"wanted to fuck him."*

He alleged it was her decision to stay behind when everyone else had left the party - he hadn't asked her to. It was she who had first lent towards him and kissed him on the lips and put her tongue in his mouth. It was she who had become sexually excited, not him. It was she who had unzipped his trousers and had tried to arouse him and have sex with him.

Philip said they only stopped because a member of the bar staff behind the Bar at the time looked up and saw what they were doing. He said he had no idea who this Barman was or what he looked like.

He alleged they were both drunk and no sex act had actually taken place. If he meant that he didn't manage to have sex with Abigail that much was true but he had certainly tried.

Bert never investigated who, if any, of the Bar staff, had been working at the pub that night and may have witnessed some of what had taken place.

Worse still, Bert never attempted to track down the pub worker who, according to Abigail, had run into the bar after she shouted for help. None of this appeared to be important to Bert.

At her interview, Abigail told Bert that Philip had told a pack of lies. She was adamant that she was not drunk but that Philip was. She told Bert she was teetotal and had only been drinking Coca Cola and water all night. She said the incident had happened as she had described it and not as Philip had alleged.

She said no-one had been present in the Bar when he attempted the initial assault on her but one of the Bar staff had definitely run in when she screamed for help. She was sure this barman had seen Philip scramble to his feet and stagger out of the Bar. This same Barman was there when she ran out of the Bar and down the stairs, crying.

Abigail said she was extremely upset by Philip's texts and had sent some of them to Deidre the day after, asking her what she should do.

Abigail told Bert she had not texted back, telling Philip to stop or saying that she was disgusted by them because she was too scared. Philip was her boss and she had to be very careful how she spoke to him as he was responsible for her career and her salary. She was also worried about writing back to him on their work email as potentially others at the office could read them, including his secretary/PA.

The grievance process dragged on and on and after two and half months, there had not even been a grievance hearing for Abigail.

I decided we had waited long enough because in those days there was a three month time limit from the date of the alleged act of discrimination to issue tribunal proceedings. I issued proceedings for sexual harassment and victimisation naming the Company as First Respondent and Philip and Bert as Second and Third Respondents. Not only is the employer vicariously liable for acts of discrimination committed by their employees but the employees themselves are also personally liable.

The Company immediately instructed a senior HR Business Partner, Natasha, to make a decision on the grievance. She held a number of interviews, starting with Philip. That was entirely wrong because the person who lodges a grievance, in this case Abigail, should be interviewed first in order to get the details of their grievance. Then those details can be put to the alleged perpetrator, in this case Philip.

Natasha then interviewed Abigail and then went back to Philip allowing him to respond to Abigail's allegations. Natasha did not tell Abigail what Philip had said in his first interview and did not give Abigail any right of reply to what he had said in his second interview. But Philip was given the right of reply after Abigail had been interviewed – unfair or what?

Natasha did not interview Deirdre, to whom some of Philip's sex texts were sent, even though Abigail asked her to do so. Deidre had sent in an email saying she was a contemporaneous witness and was willing to assist.

Nor did Natasha ask for evidence from anyone who had been working in the pub that evening who may have heard Abigail's screams or witnessed Abigail running out of the pub in a very distressed state.

After I lodged the claim at the Employment Tribunal, the Company instructed a Nationwide Law Firm to represent all three Respondents.

Robin was an experienced Partner at this Law Firm. He sent me Philip's two sets of interview notes heavily redacted.

When I complained, Robin told me that the redacted sections *"had nothing to do with Abigail's grievance. They were Philip's personal data and would not therefore be disclosed."*

This was nonsense. The interviews with Philip were solely about Abigail's grievance so the whole of his interview notes should have been disclosed. They had nothing to do with his 'personal data'. The Bank had no right to hide any part of Philip's interviews.

By an amazing piece of 'magic' however, I managed to uncover the redacted sections. I had cut and pasted the redacted sentences from the interview notes into an email, ready to send to Abigail and lo and behold the black marking that had covered up the words disappeared. I could read every word that had been covered up. Well, what a find.

One of the redacted passages read, *"My bottom lip was bleeding badly because that bitch bit me very hard and she kicked me in the balls so hard I could hardly walk. She's a vindictive, lying whore. I could not go home to my wife as she would have asked me what on earth I had been up to, so I stayed overnight in a hotel. I rang my wife the next morning from the hotel and asked her to bring me some clean clothes and money to pay for the hotel. When I got home I told her I was slightly the worse for wear after the office party and was on my way to the station when I was beaten and robbed of my wallet and mobile phone so I could not call her and I decided not to walk any further and checked into a hotel."*

This was another lie. Philip had not been robbed of his wallet or phone nor had he stayed out all night. He went to the same rail station as Abigail. She saw him get onto his train. He had been texting those disgusting messages from his phone on the train after they had both left the pub. What he told Natasha was a fairy-tale.

Luckily I didn't need to complain to Robin about his redacted set of notes. I had already uncovered them. Nevertheless I wrote to say that none of Philip's grievance interviews could possibly be his personal data and therefore the Data Protection Act 1998 (as it was in those days) could not prevent the disclosure of the entire, unredacted interview notes. I said that the redacted sections were all disclosable in full but that I had in fact already uncovered all the redacted sections and knew what they said.

This is the kind of deception and lies that give lawyers a bad name.

After a wholly inadequate investigation, Natasha sent her written decision. She dismissed Abigail's grievance in its entirety. She said she had no idea who was telling the truth, *"It is one person's word against the other. I was not present at the alleged incident so I cannot make any decision about what happened."*

That was stating the obvious. Of course she wasn't there but it was *her* job to make a decision as to who was more likely to be telling the truth. Based on

29

the evidence she was supposed to determine who was telling the truth - either Philip with his self-serving denials, incoherent, inconsistent statements and barefaced lies or Abigail with her clear and truthful account.

Natasha had evidence to help her determine this. At the very least she had Philip's admissions at his first interview (initially covered up by Natasha) that Abigail had bitten his lip and kicked his 'balls'. That certainly was not consistent with Philip's story that Abigail wanted to have sex with him and had initiated the sexual encounter.

Abigail had also sent Philip's unsolicited sex texts to Deirdre and her replies were important and persuasive contemporaneous evidence.

In relation to the sex texts, Natasha held that *"because you never answered the texts that Philip sent on the night in question, you did not make it clear that they were unwelcome and unwanted. I cannot therefore find that the texts constituted sexual harassment. That means **you** were not sexually harassed in law. Philip was not aware you were finding his texts inappropriate or offensive or unwanted."*

The content of those texts would have offended any right-thinking person. There was no need to spell out in a Policy that when receiving disgusting sex texts the recipient had to respond to the sender that their messages were unwanted, otherwise the conduct and messages etc would be deemed to be welcome.

In any event the Company's disciplinary procedure made it clear that any inappropriate or offensive conduct or language such as racist language or language of a sexual nature were acts of gross misconduct for which summary dismissal could be a penalty.

Natasha concluded that Philip must have been encouraged by Abigail to think that she fancied him and wanted him.

At no point did Natasha offer a right of appeal to Abigail if she disagreed with the grievance decision.

However I did appeal the decision, citing the Company's grievance procedure and the ACAS Code of Practice on disciplinary and grievance procedures.

The entire grievance procedure was unfair. Junior members of HR with little or no experience of investigating sensitive harassment complaints are entirely inappropriate. They have no idea how to investigate sensitive harassment complaints. Bert was plainly out of his depth and Natasha was just incompetent and totally inept.

In a case as serious as this, the decision-maker should be very sure that the investigation carried out is as full and thorough as possible but both Bert and Natasha failed to do this.

The case of **A v B [2003]** requires employers to undertake an even more thorough investigation than they would normally do, where criminal acts are alleged. Her employer had really failed Abigail.

We lodged a lengthy and detailed appeal but that too was dismissed without even an appeal hearing. It was a paper exercise.

What was even more egregious was the fact that the covering email containing the appeal decision, in error, contained the trail of emails beneath it. They were to and from Robin, the Respondents' solicitor. He had drafted the original appeal decision and it had merely been signed off by the appeal manager.

In other words, their solicitor had decided to dismiss Abigail's appeal. It looked like a legal argument/submission suitable for a Tribunal, not a decision from an internal appeal. In any event it was not the lawyer's job to decide on Abigail's appeal.

Both the grievance decision and appeal found that no harassment had occurred. In fact, the appeal decision egregiously stated that Abigail only alleged she was 'upset' after the event and had stayed away from work because she was "embarrassed" at what had happened. It did not indicate Philip's guilt.

Abigail remained off sick with depression and anxiety and was referred to a clinical psychologist for Cognitive Behavioural Therapy (CBT). Her GP prescribed anti-depressants, tablets for anxiety and sleeping pills—all of which made her feel worse. Abigail was so shy she would not let her husband or her father read the sex texts or know many of the details of her grievance.

When I issued the tribunal proceedings, Abigail asked me what we would get from Philip if we sued him. I replied, *"His testicles—on a plate. Let's put it this way, he won't be wanting sex for a long time after I've have finished with him."*

I asked a forensic psychologist to be an expert witness at the tribunal, to give evidence about the texts Philip had sent Abigail. His conclusion was that Philip had most likely done this sort of thing before because of the words he had used and the confidence that he had clearly shown in his behaviour and his phraseology.

For example, Philip had said he would use a code word, *'It's tonight'* to confirm that Abigail should go up to his hotel room and *'Not tonight Josephine'* if he had to cancel. Our expert advised that in his opinion this was indicative that he was clearly familiar with sexually harassing women and inviting them to hotel bedrooms for sex.

Expert witnesses are allowed to give 'opinion' evidence as opposed to factual evidence. In this case the forensic psychologist's opinion about Philip was that he was probably a serial sexual predator who had done this sort of thing before. It was very powerful evidence in our favour.

In the employer's Grounds of Resistance, they denied that any harassment or discrimination had taken place. They argued that Philip's version of events had been believed after hearing 'all the evidence'.

They argued Natasha had decided, on the balance of probabilities, that it was Abigail and not Philip who had initiated their sexual encounter in the pub as she had waited until everyone else had gone home. She had therefore been a willing participant in what had happened. They also argued that Abigail had not responded to any of the text messages telling Philip she was disgusted or to stop so they concluded she had not been harassed or distressed by his texts or conduct.

The Respondents' lawyers argued that Abigail had merely felt embarrassment and remorse at being a willing participant, probably whilst drunk, if it was true she was unused to alcohol, and that had been her reason for bringing her grievance and the Tribunal claim.

Abigail had explained to Natasha why she had not dared to reply to any of his texts for fear that Philip might take that as encouragement or if she told him to stop because she found them offensive, he might say that she was being disrespectful to him. She told Natasha that she was acutely aware that her career, remuneration and bonus lay in his hands. He was her boss.

Abigail had pointed out in her grievance interview that she did not reply to Philip's invitation to go to a hotel room to have sex with him and that was evidence that his attentions were unwanted and unwelcome by her.

In relation to what Bert had said to Abigail at the start of the investigation, her employer stated in their defence that, *"his choice of words was unfortunate but his words were not discriminatory or victimisation. He was inexperienced and he would be undergoing equality training."*

The employer argued that he had not used those words *"because Abigail had made a complaint of sexual harassment (called a 'protected act'). He could have expressed himself better but those words could have been used to any complainant with any grievance."*

As a fallback position her employer argued its statutory defence (formerly in the Sex Discrimination Act 1975) that it had *"taken all reasonable steps to prevent"* Philip from committing the discrimination alleged. Of course the Bank had done nothing.

There was a weak and outdated harassment and equalities policy, no separate complaints procedure appropriate for handling complaints of harassment, they had done no training for managers on equalities or harassment and had no effective penalties when harassment was found to have happened.

If this defence had worked, her employer could escape liability and if the tribunal found in Abigail's favour that Philip had sexually harassed her, he alone would be found guilty.

The Company told Philip he had to instruct his own Barrister in light of their statutory defence but they defended Bert.

It was Abigail and me against two male barristers, one was a QC (Queen's Counsel in those days, now KC) and two male solicitors. I was not fazed at all. I said to Abigail, *"bring it on."*

Both Barristers representing the three Respondents looked very uncomfortable when they entered the Tribunal. The Judge and two lay members looked distinctly unimpressed as they said, *"Good Morning"* to the Respondents' barristers and solicitors.

The Judge had already read the pleadings before the start of the hearing. For the first two and a half hours the Tribunal panel read the witness statements and some of the documents, before Abigail was cross-examined.

It appeared to me that the Tribunal may have taken a preliminary 'view' as to who was more likely to be telling the truth. I gained the impression that it wasn't Philip or the employer or Bert.

I felt nervous for Abigail when she sat down at the witness table to be cross-examined. She was terrified and had wanted to pull out at the last minute.

However, I persuaded her to stick it out. I told her she had come all this way and had done all the hard work. I told her she was telling the truth and Philip was lying and it would be her turn to see him squirm—and squirm he did.

I gave Abigail some Rescue Remedy and literally pushed her out of the Claimant's waiting room and into the Tribunal.

I tell all my witnesses if they can answer "Yes"; or "No" or "I don't know" to questions in cross-examination, they should. They should also count slowly up to 5 in their head before answering the question and they should listen to the question very carefully and just answer what has been asked—and no more.

I told Abigail not to be tempted to agree if the Respondents' barristers started their questions with, "It's right isn't it?" or "I put it to you that x and y happened like this didn't it?"

Abigail did very well, controlling her nerves as she answered the questions put to her. I told her afterwards she was a star. She was telling the truth and that was obvious to see.

She told the tribunal she was a happily married woman with no love interest whatsoever in Philip. He was many years older than her. She had never been unfaithful nor had she ever been tempted to be unfaithful to her husband whom she adored. She certainly never fancied Philip nor had she ever told him she did.

She said she was teetotal and at the Christmas party had drunk no alcohol at all. She said she did not make up stories nor was she a compulsive liar or a fantasist nor had she wanted to get Philip into trouble. In fact, she had not wanted to make any complaint initially but he had continued to harass her after the Christmas party.

Making a complaint about his conduct was the only way she believed she could get him to stop. She said she had been encouraged to take a stand against Philip by her family and close friends.

She said she did not want anyone else to go through what she had gone through.

Abigail's first words to Natasha, recorded in the grievance hearing notes, were that she did not want Philip to get into trouble or for him to be dismissed. She said she felt awful and deeply embarrassed at having to report his assault on her and to share his text messages.

Natasha's response was a disgrace. She had replied, *"Well if you are telling the truth then Philip will of course be dismissed. It was your decision to report him so don't be so naïve. You must have known the consequences for him if you are believed. They are disastrous and he will lose his job."*

Abigail's evidence was that when Natasha had said that it nearly put her off continuing with her grievance.

When Abigail's cross-examination was over, there was no doubt in my mind that the tribunal believed her.

The next day it was Philip's turn to be cross-examined, by me and then the fun began—for our side that is. Somehow, I don't think it was fun for Philip and it didn't last that long but it was possibly too long for him.

My cross-examination went like this:

Me: *"Good morning, Philip. May I call you Philip?"* (He nodded)
"How would you describe Abigail?"

Philip: *"Well she's a liar. What more do you want me to say?"*

Me: *"A lot more. Would you agree with me that she is naturally shy, reserved and introverted?"*

Philip: *"If you say so."*

Me: *"Would you agree she is not a liar nor a fantasist and she would have no reason whatsoever to make up her complaints about you? You have never had cause to believe she tells lies have you?"*

Philip: *"If you say so."*

Me: *" She doesn't drink alcohol ever, does she? She was drinking Coca-Cola and water during the night of the Christmas party, wasn't she?"*

Philip: *"I don't know and you don't either because you weren't there, were you? So stop asking me these damn fool questions."*

He was starting to get very tetchy early on in his cross-examination. That was a good sign for us.

Me: *"You are quite right Philip I wasn't there. But believe me you would not have any balls left if I had been.*

"Now I'm sure your lawyer has told you—I'm here to ask the questions and you're here to answer them. Do we understand each other?

"It is Abigail's evidence that she had not been drinking alcohol that night because she never drinks alcohol. You have no evidence to disprove what she said, do you? In fact, there is no reference in your carefully worded witness statement that Abigail had been drinking any alcohol during the entire evening. So if Abigail never drinks alcohol and at the Christmas party was only drinking sparkling water and Coca-Cola all night she couldn't have been drunk could she?"

Philip: *"If you say so."*

Me: *"I do say so but please confirm this to the Tribunal—you accept that Abigail was not drinking alcohol during the Christmas party, nor was she drunk at any time during the Christmas party."*

Philip: *"If you say so."* (His record seemed to have got stuck).

Me: *"Perhaps you can tell the tribunal why you told the investigating officer, Bert, and Natasha, the hearing manager, that you and Abigail were both drunk by the end of the evening?"*

Philip: *"Well I may have been mistaken* (he then added) *but I don't think I was. I was under pressure when I said that. I'm not admitting anything to you. Stop trying to put words into my mouth you insolent bitch. I know what you're trying to do."*

Me: *"Yes Philip, I'm trying to get you to tell the truth. Now it's a pretty big mistake if, as the notes record and you have never contradicted these notes, you told Bert and Natasha that you and Abigail were both drunk by the end of the evening. That doesn't tie in with your witness statement is it?* **So were you lying then, when you spoke to Bert and Natasha, or are lying now? Which is it?** (My voice got considerably louder and I was almost shouting at Philip at this point.)

(Philip remained stunned and silent so I continued)

"Perhaps you can tell the tribunal how much you had to drink that night. Let's start with before dinner."

Philip: *"Well I had a couple of beers and vodka chasers before dinner."*

Me: *"And during dinner. How much did you drink?"*

Philip: *"Well there were three bottles of wine down our end of the table, for six of us, and most of the others weren't drinking much. Party poopers. So, I probably drank the best part of two bottles of wine with dinner. But that's nothing for me."*

Me: *"and after dinner—at the Bar?"*

Philip: *"I had a few rum and cokes. Probably 3 or 4."*

Me: *"Would you agree with me that you had drunk a lot of alcohol by the time you had finished dinner and you were certainly not sober by the end of the evening but Abigail was completely sober?"*

Philip: *"If you say so."*

Me: *"I do and I am asking the tribunal to note that you have repeatedly refused to answer my questions. I will be asking them to infer that you are agreeing with my propositions.*

"Would it be fair to say that out of the two of you, Abigail is far more likely to remember exactly what happened that night?"

Philip: *"If you say so…"*

Me: *"I do say so and you are not contradicting me so I will take that as a 'Yes'.*

"Let me ask you another question. Knowing the character of Abigail, on a scale of 1-10, '10' being very likely and '1' being highly unlikely, how likely is it that Abigail's recollection of that evening is clearer and more likely to be correct, rather than yours?"

Philip: *"I don't do guessing games so NO I will not be answering your question."*

He had the temerity to smile and wink at me and then smile at the Tribunal Panel, thinking this was a smart thing to do.

Me: *"You have already agreed with me that Abigail is naturally shy and introverted. I've put it to you that she never drinks alcohol and had not drunk any alcohol during the evening of the Christmas party and that she was sober and you were not. We will leave it there but I may come back to this a little later.*

"Let me turn to a different topic. Abigail is much younger than you, isn't she? You know she is happily married and that she has never shown any 'love' interest in you whatsoever? Will you agree to those propositions?"

Philip: *"Which of those propositions would you like me to answer first?"* (Philip was starting to get into stride now)

Me: *"In the order I asked them please"*

Philip: *"Well I am not agreeing with you and my answers are 'yes'; 'Don't know' and 'No'.*

"Yes - she is much younger than me but a lot of much younger women have found me attractive." (Philip winked at me again)

I gave him a look that could kill and said, *" Thin ice Philip. You are skating on very thin ice. 'Amber light', Philip. That's your last warning"* (my thanks to my good friend Suzanne for these quotes. She uses them on occasion to her husband Larry.)

Philip continued, *"I have no idea about her marriage happy or otherwise as she has never confided in me about her husband. I always had a sneaking suspicion she fancied me and I was right, because on the evening of the Christmas party she told me she fancied me and leapt all over me, unzipped my trousers and tried to have sex with me. I tried to fight her off but it was me who got injured."*

Me: *"That's interesting. So your story now is that she leapt all over you and tried to have sex with you? How did she manage that?"*

Philip: *"That was a figure of speech. She forced herself on top of me as I was sitting down finishing a drink. She unzipped my trousers and fondled me trying to arouse me but that didn't work. I tried to fight her off but I may have been a little sleepy as it was late in the evening. She tried her best to get me aroused but it didn't work."*

Me: *"So you are saying that <u>she</u> forced herself on top of <u>you</u> and tried to have sex with you and you tried to fight her off. Is that what you are saying? That's not what you told Natasha or Bert nor do you say that anywhere in your witness statement.*

"You described the scene to Natasha in your interview with her and said that you tripped and fell on top of Abigail, fell into her lap, and that it was an accident.

"But that's not how you describe this scene in your witness statement, is it? You do not say anywhere in your witness statement that you tripped and fell on top of Abigail or that she leapt on you, attacked you, unzipped your trousers and tried to arouse you.

"In fact your witness statement is entirely silent on how the alleged sexual assault happened. You merely deny that any sexual assault occurred. You give no description whatsoever of the incident about which Abigail has complained.

"And now, at this tribunal, you are giving us a different version of events, saying that Abigail lunged at you, leapt on top of you and basically tried to rape you. Is that what you are now saying?"

(Philip remained absolutely silent and offered no response).

Me: *"I am putting it to you that you have just made that up. Abigail did not force herself on top of you, neither did you trip and fall into her lap by accident neither did she try to have sex with you nor did you try to fight her off. What you have just said under oath isn't true is it? In fact, that was another lie wasn't it?"*

(I raised my voice asking this question)

(Philip remained silent).

"Just enlighten us – what do you say happened? I'm giving you a chance to say, on oath, what you say happened.

(He stared straight at me and said nothing.)

(I waited a long 15 seconds to make him feel even more uncomfortable and continued):

"Let me ask me another question whilst you try to lie your way out of that one.

"How likely is it on a scale of 1 to 10, '10' being very likely, and '1' being very unlikely, that Abigail would leap on top of you and force herself upon you, cold stone sober or according to you, drunk, unzip your trousers and try to have sex with you, in a public place?"

Philip: *"I don't have to answer that question do I?"*

(He was addressing his barrister who sat stony-faced.) He then asked his barrister, *"Please tell this Rottweiler to shut up about Abigail and the bloody Christmas party. I wish now I'd never gone."*

(Philip was by now very riled and very tetchy. That's how I like witnesses on the other side to get.)

The Judge intervened, *"Please do not address any comments or questions to your barrister. He cannot help you. You are on oath giving your evidence. My Wing Members and I will determine what are appropriate questions and you are being asked entirely proper questions and I am directing you to answer them."*

Philip snarled back at the Judge, *"Well I can't answer. OK?"*

Me: *"Well do try to answer my questions Philip. I put it to you that these are a series of ludicrous and wholly implausible stories that you have made up, to try to exonerate yourself from what you did that night or rather tried to do. You are not telling the truth to this tribunal, are you?"*

Philip: *"Are you calling me a liar?"*

Me: *"Well I didn't use that word —you did. But if you put it like that—YES. I am putting to you that you have been lying ever since that night and you are lying now.*

"So please now answer my question. On a scale of 1-10, what is the likelihood of Abigail behaving as you have described?

"Would you agree with me that it is '1' or probably a minus number?"

Philip: *"No I would not and how dare you call me a liar. If you can't keep a civil tongue in your head woman, I won't be answering any more of your questions. Bloody insolent woman. Do you know who I am? I'm telling you to shut up about that bloody Christmas party. I'm not answering any more of your damn fool questions."*

Me: *"Well I will be asking you more questions about the Christmas party and other matters. So I'm going to continue asking you questions. It will be up to you to decide whether to answer them or not. Saying 'If you say so' or you're 'not going to answer'—are not answers that will satisfy this tribunal. So I'm going to ask you more questions and I will expect you to answer them.*

"I don't mean to be disrespectful Philip (just about to be) *but you are no Adonis. You are very overweight and you are many years older than Abigail.*

"*I have put it to you that you have no evidence that she has ever told you she fancied you have you?*

"*So, I am going to put it you **again and perhaps you will answer my question this time**. It just isn't plausible—is it—that Abigail would say she fancies you and cold stone sober or even drunk would leap all over you, unzip your trousers and try to have sex with you in a public place, now, is it? We know that is a lie because you described the scene to Natasha and said that you fell on top of Abigail by accident and she kicked you in the balls and bit your lip.*

"*You remember – the section of your interview notes that your employer tried to conceal, saying it had nothing to do with the grievance, that it was your personal data and we could not see it.*

"*Kicking you in the balls and biting your lip doesn't sound as if Abigail was trying to make love to you now does it?*"

At that point I referred the Tribunal to our correspondence about Philip's redacted interview notes and how Robin, his solicitor, had tried to argue that that part of his interview had nothing to do with the grievance. The Judge scowled at Robin after reading this.

Philip: "*No comment.*"

Me: "*Philip, this is not a police interview under caution. I will give you one last chance to answer my question.*"

Philip: "*No comment—why can't you listen woman, or are you deaf as well as stupid and insolent? You probably put Abigail up to all of this. You lawyers are all ambulance-chasers after fat fees.*"

(I was loving this now. It was pure pantomime.)

Me: "*I can see the Judge has noted your refusal to answer my questions so I will move on to another topic.*

"*Why did you leave the previous Company that employed you with just under one year's service?*"

Philip: "*What the fuck has that got to do with anything? Listen I'm getting very fed up with your damn fool impertinent questions.*"

(Philip could see his Barrister glaring at him and realised he needed to answer my question.)

"*Well if you really want to know I resigned for personal reasons* (and then he muttered) *but actually it's none of your business you bloody bitch.*"

Philip glared at me as he said this and then smiled at his Barrister. That did not go down well with the Tribunal. The Judge and the wing members heard what he said and saw his gloating smile to his legal team.

The Judge intervened again and said, *"I'm not warning you again. Your language is abusive and disrespectful to Ms Howard and it is not acceptable. I have noted how many times I have had to warn you. If you want a break to steady your nerves, we can take a comfort break for 10 minutes but you are still under oath so you cannot talk to anyone about your evidence. I suggest you consider your behaviour and come back ready to answer the questions being put to you.*

"Please everyone come back in 10 minutes."

We then had a 10-minute comfort break and returned to the Hearing.

When Philip came back to the witness table, he continued to glare at me.

Me: *"Before the break I asked you about the reasons you left your last job. You said it was for 'personal reasons.' Please tell this Tribunal what those personal reasons were. Why did you leave your last job so abruptly with such short service, giving no notice as I understand and with no job to go to?"*

Philip: *"That's none of your bloody business and I refuse to answer your impertinent questions. That has nothing to do with this case. Has anyone told you—you really are a fucking bitch."*

Philip had by this time drinking copious amounts of water as he was sweating like a pig.

I just looked at the Judge and carried on.

Me: (My Rottweiler teeth were showing now) *"This Tribunal will be the judge of whether my questions are impertinent or not, so now please answer my question."*

The Judge intervened again, *"Philip—apologise to Ms Howard immediately. I will not allow language like this in my tribunal. If I have to warn you one more time I will not allow you to give any more evidence and we will strike out your defence and will find against you. You have been asked a simple question. There will be good reasons why you are being asked questions about why you left your last job so suddenly and I am directing you to answer."*

Philip: (turning to me) *"I've been told to apologise to you – so I apologise."* Then he turned to the Judge and asked, *"Why is she asking me?"*

The Judge said, *"You will find out soon enough. Now answer the question."*

The Judge showed considerable impatience in his manner and voice towards Philip —not a good sign for him.

Philip: *"Well there was an issue at work and I decided to leave because I was offered a higher paid and better job. I was bored in that job anyway if you must know. The Company I am employed in now had a role that suited my talents much better and I applied for it and got the job. I am well known in the industry and they said they were lucky to get me.*

"That's why I left my last job and that's all you need to know. I'm not answering any more questions about this subject."

Me: (with my Rottweiler teeth still gnashing) *"Well I have a few more questions about your last job and your last answer is not quite true is it?*

"You left your last employer without a job to go to and it took you ten months to find another job, so what you have just told this Tribunal isn't true is it? You didn't leave because you had a better job to go to, did you? You had nowhere to go.

"I must remind you, you are on oath and lying on oath is called 'perjury' for which you could go to prison.

"If you want, I can show you your LinkedIn profile that shows a gap of over ten months from leaving your last job and starting at this Company.

"So perhaps you will answer my question truthfully. You've already said there was an 'issue' at work so do tell us exactly what the 'issue' was."

(Philip remained silent and looked down at his witness statement and it became clear he was not going to answer).

Me: *"Let me help you out. I believe the issue concerned another young woman at your last employer, also many years your junior, whom you had also been sexually harassing. You were asked to leave rather than face dismissal. That's what happened wasn't it?*

"Please start telling the truth to this Tribunal about what happened at your last job because I know the whole story."

Philip: *"Well if you know the whole story why don't* ***you*** *tell the Tribunal. You seem to know all the answers. You are a frigging encyclopaedia of knowledge aren't you? I'm not answering any more of your impertinent questions. I'm out of here."*

At that he got up and stormed out of the Tribunal. The Judge and Wing members looked on in utter astonishment His barrister looked stony-faced. He knew what was coming next.

But what he and no-one knew was that I had no idea why Philip had left his last job. I was bluffing. I had no evidence as to what the issue was that had prompted him to resign without a job to go to. It was pure speculation on my part that he had done something similar there. I was relying on our forensic psychologist's expert opinion that Philip had harassed other women in the past.

His former employer had refused to disclose anything to me when I rang them. They said they could not tell me anything about Philip or the reasons for his departure for data protection reasons. I just guessed that it must have been the same sort of issue as Abigail's—and I must have guessed right.

I used my intuition that Philip did not want our forensic psychologist to give evidence.

Philip was not very bright or very canny. He could have made up anything that sounded credible about why he had left his last job without another job to go to—family illness, a family business in crisis, problems with his children etc. I would have not been able to challenge him because I had no evidence—but he clearly didn't know that.

His face was a picture when I asked him with some force and a knowing look to tell the Tribunal what this 'issue' had been in his former employment and why he had left there so suddenly with no job to go to.

Given the increasingly uninhibited way that Philip had been responding to my questions, I suspected that he may have been drinking alcohol at the witness table. He had taken what appeared to be a bottle of water with him to the witness table and was swigging it merrily through his evidence. He left it there when he stormed out.

I asked the Judge if I could take the bottle off the table and told him I suspected that it may actually be vodka or some other form of clear alcohol. I poured a little of this liquid into an empty glass and gingerly tasted it. I was right—it certainly wasn't water. It was neat vodka.

When I reported this to the Judge, there was another stony silence. The Judge asked his barrister for an explanation and announced this was contempt of Court. Philip's barrister said wearily he could not give any explanation and gave a fulsome apology to the Court.

He clearly had no idea that Philip had brought vodka into the tribunal. The Judge advised Philip's barrister that I would be asked if I wished to make an application to have his client's defence struck out and for our legal costs.

I made the applications and Philip's barrister made a feeble attempt to mitigate Philip's conduct in relation to the alleged harassment, his conduct during the hearing and in relation to my costs' application—without any success.

The Judge was having none of it. The Tribunal spent around 25 minutes deciding that Philip's defence would be struck out. In default, a decision of harassment and discrimination was made against Philip and he was ordered to pay substantial damages for injury to feelings.

The Judge also made an order for costs and that, as they say, was that.

Abigail's employer had nowhere to go. Their key witness had left the Tribunal and disappeared and there had been a finding of discrimination against him. The employer's QC asked for an adjournment so they could discuss settlement. They realised that their defence was now going to be hopeless.

Their QC asked me how I knew about Philip's previous employment history. I said, *"I have spies everywhere and I get to know these things. I haven't been called 'a witch' for nothing."* At that I smiled at him and said, *"Let's talk about the money now, shall we?"*

I negotiated a settlement in respect of all three Respondents for damages for injury to feelings – way above the 'Vento Band' limits. In addition, the employer agreed to pay all Abigail's legal fees and the fees for her CBT.

Abigail had not left her job and was still being paid her salary, despite Natasha's threat that her sick pay would stop, so Abigail had no loss of earnings.

There was a really happy ending—for Abigail, that is. A week after the tribunal, she received a phone call from her new boss, a very supportive woman, saying when Abigail was ready, she should come back to work and she would never have to see or work with Philip again.

Abigail asked what had happened to Philip but she was told that due to data protection reasons, she could not be told.

I looked up Philip's updated LinkedIn profile. It showed he 'left' this Company the day after the disastrous tribunal ruling and got a job working at a start-up as a sales consultant for a cyber security firm. He left there after 5 months.

He then went to a company as Head of Technology but only lasted just over a year there and left "for personal reasons" – either drinking on the job or another case of sexual harassment?

Justice really was done in this case because when Abigail returned to work, she had a very decent and supportive new female boss who promoted her within weeks of returning to work.

Abigail is thriving in her job, without having to work for a sex pest.

She now acts as a mentor to women and is an active member of a professional Women's Network Group. She also now mentors women who are being abused either at work or at home and acts as a 'buddy' for women, especially new young women starting out in their career at her own workplace.

And Abigail did a wonderful and touching thing when she received her damages. She gave a large donation to Cancer Research in memory of my mother who had died young of cancer. Abigail really is a quite amazing young woman.

Chapter 3
Alice's Tale

Alice's story is of one woman's fight against the odds. I am not using her real name even though her case was widely publicised.

Some of the details of this case are reported in the successful appeal in the High Court against a Restricted Reported Order.

Her tribunal case was also widely reported in the National and Local Press at the time.

Let me first describe Alice. She was (and still is) a hugely able, highly intelligent, conscientious hard-working woman. She was ambitious but had the greatest integrity and probity – unlike a number of the male Directors at the Council where she was employed at the time. What happened to her is a travesty.

Despite sex discrimination being unlawful for 23 years when I met Alice, she had been subjected to the most appalling sex discrimination by the Chief Executive (I will call him "Bernard" to protect the guilty). Alice had also been sexually assaulted by another senior officer of the Council at an away day.

Alice had been employed in a senior position for over ten years and had then been promoted to the role of Deputy Chief Executive the year before she came to see me.

She told me that Bernard had bullied her, threatened to dismiss her on numerous occasions and had treated her disrespectfully. She believed this was because he disrespected women.

There was at the time only one other woman in a Director position and she too had complained that she was not treated with any dignity or respect.

The disgraceful behaviour of some of Alice's male peers was worthy of dismissal yet either no disciplinary action was taken against them or they were allowed to resign rather than be dismissed and in some cases given handsome pay-offs.

In comparison, Alice, an innocent woman, was treated appallingly and threatened with dismissal—for standing up for herself and refusing to be bullied.

Alice told me that she had been sexually assaulted by a senior male Director who had been drinking all day, at an 'away day' to discuss strategy and 'blue sky thinking' (trying to find completely new ideas).

The miscreant Council officer was sitting next to Alice during lunch, when suddenly he had put his arms around her shoulders and against her will had stroked her breasts and right thigh. Another woman at the lunch had also complained that the same man had sexually assaulted her.

Another senior male officer was sitting across from both women at the time of the assaults and witnessed the assaults but when asked what he saw, said he saw nothing.

Bernard was informed of both assaults but he also did nothing about either.

The senior officer who had committed the sexual assaults was never disciplined or even spoken to and was later made redundant and given a large ex gratia payment.

It was also reported to Bernard that a senior Director (Mr X) was abusing his position by leaving work at lunchtime every Friday, returning to the office late on Monday morning. He lived outside London and liked to get home early and have a long weekend. This set a very bad example to his staff and was in effect 'stealing' his salary as he wasn't even working his basic contracted hours.

This Director merely received 'a warning' from Bernard not to leave early for the weekend in future and to make sure he was in at the normal start time on Mondays. No further action was taken against him.

Then there was another senior male Director, who was unaware of a massive fraud that had taken place in his department involving the unauthorised purchase and theft of computers and printers. The thefts cost the Council more than £400,000.

When this was discovered he was asked to leave the Council but received six months' pay in lieu of notice and was allowed to resign apparently blameless.

He even had the nerve to complain that he had no idea what had been going on in his department, so he could not see why he had to resign.

That was of course precisely why he had to leave. He **didn't** know what was going on in his own department. That was his job.

Alice, because of her position in the Council, was rightly concerned at the behaviour of these senior males and the *'get out of jail free cards'* they had received in contrast to the disciplinary action they deserved.

Her complaints about Bernard's discriminatory behaviour towards her were numerous.

For example, he had instructed her to sit next to him in the Senior Leadership Team (SLT) meetings and *"take the minutes."* It was not her job to take the minutes. There was a designated secretary, a man, who was the official note-taker at these meetings but he had been told he was not required to attend.

Bernard had never instructed any of Alice's male colleagues to sit next to him or take the minutes.

Bernard had threatened to dismiss Alice on several occasions when she had disagreed with him both in Council meetings and in private. He had ordered her *"to keep her mouth shut"* if she felt like disagreeing with him.

When she was appointed Deputy Chief Executive, she told Bernard she would *"speak up"* if she believed something was wrong or if she felt she had something to say. He clearly did not believe her or if he did, he tried to make sure she behaved like the *"male monkeys who obeyed the organ-grinder"* as Alice so graphically but accurately described her male SLT members to me.

On another occasion Alice alleged that Bernard had screamed and shouted abuse at her, and during her performance review meeting he had wholly unfairly denigrated her performance.

On another occasion he had lost his temper with Alice over some minor trivial matter and shouted at her she was a *"disgrace"*. He had also continually interrupted her during a Council meeting in the same month. The following day, after this Council meeting, Bernard threatened Alice with dismissal and threatened to remove her from her post as Deputy Chief Executive.

Alice also complained that Bernard treated her like a *"naughty schoolgirl"* and the Council had an *"an aggressively male culture."*

After these incidents Alice came to see me. I told her that as another professional woman I would act for her pro bono, which I did throughout the entire case. I was incensed at her treatment and determined to try to get some justice for her.

I advised her to put in a formal grievance about Bernard's discriminatory treatment of her, the assault by the senior male officer at the away day about which no action had been taken and about how miscreant male Directors, in contrast to her, were favourably treated.

Alice told me that by the summer of the year in question, her relationship with Bernard had deteriorated to the point of no return.

She described a letter that he had sent her, (read out as part of the evidence at the tribunal hearing) complaining about her behaviour and setting out her alleged faults. None of his allegations were true but it was his way of trying to bully, intimidate and punish her.

At one point in his letter Bernard suggested that Alice may need to be *"re-energised"* by seconding her to *"another public body."* Sub-headings in this letter included *"undermining me"*, *"belittling the achievements of others"* and *"persistent pursuit of self-interest above other considerations."*

Then it all kicked off. As soon as Alice lodged her formal grievance about Bernard, he removed her from her statutory functions and those as Deputy Chief Executive. In other words he victimised her for making a complaint of sex discrimination.

Her grievance was heard and then quickly dismissed by a fellow male Director (A) obviously briefed by Bernard. (A) made a finding of no sex discrimination or harassment or bullying. He decided that there had only been *"a clash of personalities and that Alice was at fault for disrespecting Bernard and disobeying his instructions on numerous occasions."*

He also held that the sexual assault was a one-off incident and the man involved had stopped when Alice had made it clear to him that his conduct was "unwanted".

This Director (A) also held that Alice *"was unable to accept the authority of or respect the instructions given to her by Bernard her line manager."*

Funny that—those were the very words used by Bernard to Alice when he suspended her from her role as Deputy Chief Executive.

We then issued proceedings for sex discrimination, sexual harassment and victimisation against the Council as the First Respondent and Bernard as the Second Respondent. At this stage Alice was still at work albeit not on her normal duties as ordered by Bernard.

The Council immediately instructed a major Law Firm to represent both Respondents. This Firm's legal team consisted of a male partner, two male associates and a male trainee. They also instructed a QC and a junior barrister to represent them in the tribunal.

Alice had just me to represent her. That was six against one – but that never fazes me.

Bernard did not want the Council or his name to be made public before the local elections. The 15 day hearing had been listed in an Industrial Tribunal (as they were called then) right in the middle of the local elections that May.

The QC persuaded the then Regional Employment Judge to grant a Restricted Reporting Order (RRO) giving anonymity to the Council, Bernard, other male members of SLT and to Alice.

Until the promulgation of the decision, which could be several months after the hearing, none of those individuals could be identified in the media. This would have been months after the local elections.

The purpose of an RRO is to prevent the identification of *"any person affected by or making of an allegation"* of sexual misconduct or a sexual offence. Its purpose was not to assist or cover up the wrongdoing of Council officials at a politically sensitive time.

The local and national newspapers wanted to publish details about this case as the hearing was going on but it would not be a story without being able to identify the Council or the names of the Council officials involved.

The Daily Mail offered to pay for a QC to seek to quash this decision in the High Court. We accepted. The brilliant Geoffrey Robertson was instructed.

The application before the High Court was successful. Mr Justice Keen quashed the RRO in relation to the names of the Council and the Chief Executive, Bernard and all of their witnesses.

Mr Justice Keen held he was not satisfied that the Council was a *'person affected by'* the allegations. He also ruled that while the Chief Executive might experience some embarrassment at being identified, this was outweighed by the 'public interest' in reporting the case.

The restriction on identifying the Council and Bernard was ruled to be unreasonable and not within the relevant Tribunal rules. Mr Justice Keen made it clear that the Regional Employment Judge's approach to the exercise of her discretion was *"wrong in law."*

The newspapers were now free to report the case, naming the Council and Bernard and all their witnesses but not Alice, who was to continue to remain anonymous under the terms of the RRO.

During the disclosure process, the solicitors acting for the Council and Bernard, sent a young trainee, Peter, to inspect our documents. I had 'a cunning plan' (as Baldrick in Blackadder, a TV series, used to say). I would do some 'promiscuous bundling' and 'documentary carpet bombing'.

These two phrases had been used Mr Justice Turner in *Griffiths vs The Secretary of State for Health [2015]* as an example of deliberately over-sized trial bundles.

He quoted the Civil Procedure Rules on the parties' duty of disclosure of documents and stated that *"these rules impose a duty upon the parties to help the court to further the overriding objective and this duty is not fulfilled by promiscuous bundling and documentary carpet bombing."* (see the Glossary for more detail on the origins of these phrases).

While Alice was out of the office for the day, I asked a young legal trainee to get from the store room as many lever arch files as she could find and place them round the room. Only one or two of these files were actually relevant. The trainee was able to fit 78 lever arch files, neatly piled round the floor and on the shelves in Alice's office.

Peter arrived and took one look at the files and said to me, *"Wow where do I start?"*

I replied, *"Why not start by having a cup of tea and some chocolate biscuits?"* I had brought with me a plentiful supply. He gratefully accepted.

When he had finished his tea and biscuits, he asked me again how he should go about starting reviewing all the documents.

I suggested he go back to his Firm and tell them he couldn't possibly read 78 lever arch files on his own and he should ask his supervising Partner for some assistance.

We never saw Peter again.

The Council's solicitors had also done some promiscuous bundling themselves. Their disclosure consisted of 18 files of largely irrelevant documents. Whilst they brought these 18 lever arch files to the tribunal, I made a core bundle of the documents that were relevant and to be relied upon by all the witnesses. This consisted of only 1099 pages in one large lever arch file.

It has been, and still may be the practice of some lawyers, to draft witness statements for their witnesses and just get the witness to sign it. This is extremely unwise, as Bernard found out to his cost.

It is perfectly sensible for lawyers to guide witnesses as to what is needed in their statement or even do a first draft and then to speak to them about the draft and "proof" the witness.

This may involve the lawyer asking questions to clarify what the witness has written or has meant when it is not clear or to add things that are relevant that have been omitted and delete irrelevancies. It is also important to ensure that witnesses are giving consistent evidence and if their evidence is not consistent, to explain why one witness differs from another.

The purpose of a witness statement is for the witness to tell the Court/Employment Tribunal in their own words what happened, what they saw, heard or know about.

It goes without saying that the witness must tell the truth and must (obviously) understand every word in their witness statement. I try as far as possible to advise the witness to use their own words as long as they make sense and are acceptable English.

It was such a pity for Bernard that his solicitors had not appreciated these niceties and that he did not understand his evidence. It did lead to some amusing cross examination for me and considerable embarrassment for him and his lawyers.

Money appeared to be no object to the Council. Their solicitors hired the official Court transcription Service, Wordwave International Ltd, to transcribe each day's witness evidence. At the time (in the 1990s) the cost for Wordwave was £900 plus VAT a day and the hearing lasted three weeks—a hefty £13,500 plus VAT.

The Judge allowed Wordwave to make a transcript of the evidence given every day of the trial, on the condition that he and I were given a copy of the transcript the following morning, by 0900 am, so we could read it before the next day's evidence started.

The national and local press had a field day during the hearing. On the morning of the third day the Independent newspaper reported Alice's evidence. The headlines read:

"Fondling, fraud and feminism—just another day at the Council." It was all very New Labour, New Women, New Broom. But then something very old Labour occurred: they had a falling out and a pretty dramatic one at that. Now they are the worst of enemies. How do we know? Because, in that great Old Labour tradition, they are tearing each other to bits in public.

The setting is equally old-fashioned: an industrial tribunal in ..... London. There, for the past week, Alice has been spilling the beans on fondling, fraud and huge pay-offs at the council.

The attack is ferocious and, because of Alice's seniority, extremely damaging, especially at a council that prides itself on its equal opportunity policies.

She accuses the council and Bernard of sexual discrimination and victimisation. She says he treated her like a "naughty schoolgirl" and that the town hall has an "aggressive male culture."

She claims her job was put on the line over trivial matters while men who had committed serious sins were let off lightly. The heart of her case revolves around two letters from Bernard last summer that threatened her job: "The tone resembles nothing so much as an irate headmaster wagging his finger at a naughty schoolgirl who has dared to disagree with him."

She is speaking from Room 11 of the Tribunal building and the audience is a pretty rich one.

First there is Alice, who, when not at the tribunal, is still at work in her office that lies directly above Bernard's. I figure she makes about £320 per day.

She looks a local government version of the City superwoman Nicola Horlick. She is one of the very few senior women to have brought a sex discrimination suit, a trend that is growing, according to the Equal Opportunities Commission.

She did so because she couldn't face herself in the mirror if she had just "slunk away." She is a 41-year-old mother of two who graduated from Oxford in philosophy and modern languages, trained as a .... She is ambitious and not afraid to say so.

The Rottweiler with a Handbag, as she is known, is acting for Alice. Her questions are precise and, occasionally, deadly. In addition to being an expert on employment law, she provides the tribunal's fashion moments.

One day last week she was wearing beautiful black jet earrings and a stunning black designer suit with a Moschino T-shirt underneath with "This T-shirt has no Sense of Humour" written on the front.

The tribunal, which began earlier this week, is scheduled to last two more, and the Council has admitted it will cost £300,000 to half a million pounds. If Alice wins, that figure could double.

Whatever the judgment, the Council will lose big time when it comes to their reputation. The picture that emerged last week was of an organisation that was at war, obsessed with petty rivalries, secrecy and pub gossip.

*At one point, when asked if she had criticised a certain person, Alice's voice rose: **"At this Council everybody is criticising everyone else 24 hours a day."***

Easy to see why the Council applied for, and won, a gagging order. The High Court overturned it earlier this month.

[There were more extensive quotes from Alice's Witness Statement.]

Expect much more of the same over the next few weeks, although the cast of characters will be expanded on. Among them is Y, the son of a Labour MP. He is an assistant Chief Executive and Alice has previously claimed he was allowed to be "extremely rude" to her by Bernard.

We will also hear more from Council Leader, C, who was drafted in late last year to try and resolve the battle. He offered "marriage guidance" in the form of a trip to ACAS. Alice thought not.

Instead, she made the Council an offer to settle including asking for an apology from Bernard, that her role be taken out of the Chief Executive's department, that she be treated respectfully and as a professional, like the male officers and that she receive a small sum in compensation and costs.

The Council and Bernard declined, especially over a "finding of fault" against Bernard.

She was offered the post of Director of Leisure and Community Services, which would have meant a drop in salary and status.

It was an offer that she could—and did—refuse. And that's how some of the most highly paid people in Britain found themselves in Room Y last week with the gloves off.

And there are more embarrassing battles to come with two further sexual discrimination cases being brought against the same Council due this year. I wonder what Blair's Babes will have to say about that.

I was in fact acting for one of those other women. We sued the Council again and won, the following year. This time the Council had no Leading Counsel or expensive lawyers on their side – and they still lost.

After Alice and several of our witnesses had given evidence and had given a very good account of themselves, one morning, before the start of the hearing, the Judge called the Council's QC and me to his Chambers. He said he had something rather sensitive to ask and hoped we would co-operate with his request.

Our witness the day before was a Councillor and a rather beautiful woman. She had supported Alice during her career at the Council. This Councillor had had a little banter with the Judge at the start of her evidence. He had asked her what name he should call her because she had said at the start of her evidence that no-one called her by her real first name except her mother when she was cross with her. She asked the Judge to call her by a nickname that everyone used. The Judge agreed to do so.

At one point during her evidence this witness could not find a document in one of the trial Bundles and the Judge had leapt down from his chair, to show her where she should be looking. He looked as if he enjoyed this immensely and he lingered a little longer than was necessary at her side.

At another point during the day, our witness had asked the Judge if she could take the Trial Bundles off the witness table as she was finding she had no room for her witness statement.

The Judge had allowed her to do so but it had come out in the transcript as him saying, *"Of course (X),* ***you can take everything off now if you like."***

The Judge asked if we would agree to have that sentence removed from the transcript. We all had a good laugh and of course agreed for those words to be struck from the record.

I could just imagine the headlines – Judge tells beautiful witness to *"you can get them all off...."*

It was then the turn of the Council's witnesses to give evidence. Bernard went first and I started my cross-examination. It all went to plan with no surprises on the first day. I had already prepared my cross examination for the next day.

So I started my cross examination on the second day. Bernard had alleged that Alice had written *'acerbic'* memos to him and the Leader of the Council (C). Even though emails were in standard use in workplaces by 1998, memos were still being written as an means of internal communication and they were circulated in the internal mail system.

Bernard's witness statement read, *"Acerbic memos were sent by the Claimant. They were in my view unnecessarily impertinent and disrespectful both to me and to C, the Leader of the Council, in their language, tone and content.*

"We are servants of the Council and this disrespectful behaviour to the Leader from Alice continued, despite my warnings to her over and over again to be compliant, respectful and obedient to Council Members. She was supposed to serve the Council Members and to be respectful to them as well as to me, her line manager. She found it impossible to do either."

I searched the Trial Bundles for these acerbic memos. To be fair I found a few that could well have fitted this description. However there were no page references to any of these documents in Bernard's witness statement. I suspected that maybe he had not identified the ones that I had spotted so I took a risk.

I asked him to point out the '*acerbic*' memos in the Bundles that he had referred to in his witness statement. His face went blank.

He stared at me and said nothing so I asked him for a second time, *"Please identify in the Trial Bundles which memos you say were 'acerbic'. You refer to my client writing 'acerbic memos', at paragraph 50 of your witness statement, but you have not given any page references so where we can find them in the Trial Bundles?"*

After the third time of asking he finally replied, *"You lawyers with your fancy words. Why are you asking me? I didn't write this witness statement. I'm not a lawyer. How should I know what 'acerbic' means?"*

I asked him, *"Well who has written this witness statement if it wasn't you?"*

He replied, *"My solicitors of course. What do you think they're being paid for? They are charging a fortune. One of their juniors drafted this for me and asked me to read it, approve it, sign it and send it back to him. I didn't have time to read it. I just signed it and sent it back. They were supposed to be preparing this case for me so that's what they were doing."*

He then added, *"Wake up girl and don't be so naïve."* That didn't go unnoticed by the Judge.

Bernard then started smirking and smiling at me as if this was funny but soon the laugh was on the other side of his face.

There was a sharp intake of breath from many people in the room. The Judge glared first at Bernard and then at his solicitors.

Now knowing that Bernard had no idea to what he had just confessed, I asked my next question, *"Well since you have admitted that you don't know what 'acerbic' means, despite the fact that you have sworn on oath you are telling the truth, the Tribunal will take a note of that and I will move on."*

(He looked relieved but not for long.)

"I take it you know what the rest of your witness statement means so let me ask another question. What was 'disingenuous' about Alice's conduct, to which you refer in paragraph 57 of your witness statement?"

He gave the same answer. *"Look I know what you're doing. You're trying to make me look stupid. I don't know what 'disingenuous' means OK."* He added, *"You had better ask all these questions to my solicitor. They will know what they meant."*

I'm afraid I could not resist saying *"No I'm not **making** you look stupid......"*

I didn't need to *make* Bernard look stupid—he was stupid.

I just stopped myself in time from saying that. When I looked up at the tribunal panel I could see them stifling their laughter thinking, I presume, that I might be adding those words to my retort to Bernard. I'm not that impolite or tactless but I knew most people in the tribunal were thinking the same as me.

I pushed on and asked him to tell me what he meant by saying that Alice's manner was *"supercilious"* and *"egregious"*?

The Judge then intervened and turned to me and said: *"We've got your point. To use a football analogy Ms Howard, you have already won 3:0. There is no need to win 5:0."*

"Oh Yes Sir, with respect there is" I replied. *"I'm an Arsenal supporter so I always want to win 5:0."*

I could see the lay members of the Tribunal suppressing their laughter but I took the hint and moved on to another topic.

In fact, if Bernard had understood the words of his witness statement, he could have pointed to at least three or four 'acerbic' memos and all the other negative things that he had alleged Alice had written and done. He couldn't, because he didn't understand basic English.

In one of the memos Alice had written to Bernard, after he had warned her never to disagree with him, she wrote, *"I am not a sycophant or a clone and if I need to disagree with you, I will. I am not like those 'Yes men' and 'nodding donkeys' with whom you surround yourself nor am I a member of your 'boys' club'. By the way neither is the Director of .... whom you also try to bully. I shall stand firm and say what I believe to be right. I will not be bullied or censured by you."*

I was expecting Bernard to point to those documents but he did not. Luckily for me he did not have a clue what "acerbic" or "egregious" or "supercilious" meant or for that matter what much else in his witness statement meant.

The junior solicitor who had actually written his witness statement was semi-illiterate himself. I had a good laugh at some of the spelling mistakes and malapropisms that littered this witness statement.

At one point Bernard's witness statement described Alice as a *"loose Canon"*! I put my hands together and looked up to heaven.

It did not go very well for Bernard. He started sweating profusely, asking for more water and several comfort breaks. During these breaks he was not allowed to speak to anyone as he was still giving evidence under oath, so no-one could help him understand his evidence.

When we reconvened after one of the comfort breaks, I asked him why he had not asked any of the other, male members of SLT, to sit next to him and take notes at their meetings.

Bernard then winked at me. He had gone back into misogyny mode and said, obviously thinking this was funny, *"Why do you think? I would much prefer to sit next to a pretty girl than any of those men. I'm not gay you know. Alice smelt so nice. I loved her perfume—not like men who sweat so much. And women do love to gossip don't they and I wanted to hear it all. Anyway, they make far better note-takers than men. Most women have been to secretarial school—haven't they?"*

He then looked at me and said, *"Pity you didn't go. Perhaps if you had gone to secretarial school instead of filling your head with all this feminist nonsense someone might have wanted to give you a job or marry you. I see you're not married."*

Bernard laughed and looked round the hearing room for everyone's appreciation of what he thought was a joke. No-one was laughing. That also went down like a lead balloon. I wasn't wearing a wedding ring but I was in fact married to a man with the surname as me. That has infuriated me because I was never going to change my surname and no-one believes me. I had also taken a touch typing course when I was a student.

I replied to Bernard, *"my marital status or whether I have done a secretarial course has nothing to do with you or this case so I will move on.*

"I will ignore those sexist remarks to me—luckily, I have never had to work with you. Your transcription service has noted down word for word what you have just said.

"Let me ask you another question and see if this time you can take this litigation seriously.

"Do you accept that you never spoke to the male members of SLT in the same overbearing, bullying or sexist manner in which you spoke to Alice?"

Bernard asked, "What do you mean? Sorry I don't understand your question."

I replied seething with suppressed anger, "Well let me put it in words of one syllable so that even **you** will understand. You never threatened any of the male directors with dismissal even though a number of them had committed acts of serious misconduct or had shown themselves to be thoroughly incompetent - did you? And I will ask you again why you didn't ask any of your male SLT members to sit next to you, gossip with you or take the notes?"

He replied as I hoped, "Of course not. What a ridiculous suggestion. We chaps talk about men's stuff. Men don't gossip. We have a good laugh when we are having a beer. We talk about football and men's stuff.

"If my fellow directors do anything wrong we discuss it in the pub like gentlemen and sort out the problems over a beer or two.

"Anyway men don't go to secretarial school unless there's something wrong with them. How many men do you know who have been to secretarial school?

"It would be insulting to my male colleagues to ask if they had any gossip to tell me. Of course, they don't gossip. It's a 'woman's thing' isn't it? You're being ridiculous."

He then stared at his QC looking for approval but she had dropped her head and I was sure she was inwardly sighing, hoping this cross examination was coming to an end soon. It didn't.

I continued, "Bernard, do you accept that you treated Alice, one of only two senior female Directors at the Council, differently than her male colleagues?"

Back came the answer I wanted, "Of course I treated her differently—she is a woman, isn't she?" and then Bernard added gratuitously "I was always afraid she would start crying.

"You feminists are all the same—hard on the outside and 'pussies' on the inside—if you know what I mean (and he winked and laughed—no-one else laughed).

"Perhaps you hadn't noticed but men and women are different? I think secretly you feminists want to be a man and you're all jealous of us.

"Anyway, I always felt I had to tread on eggshells when I was speaking to Alice. She would get upset over any little thing. I think the song 'Why can't a woman be more like a man' sums it up for me."

I stood there with my mouth open. I felt like saying actually the song by Ella Fitzgerald 'These foolish things' (adding 'that you are saying') comes to my mind about you - but decided against it.

At that moment he must have remembered what his solicitors had told him to say because he tried to correct himself, *"What I mean is Alice and I clashed on lots of things. It was a clash of personalities—that's all it was"* and then add these gratuitous words, *"I put it all down to her jealousy."*

I don't believe his lawyers told him to say that. I'm sure that was totally 'off script'.

I was intrigued to hear why Bernard thought Alice was jealous of him so I asked, *"What do you mean you put it all down to 'her jealousy'? What was Alice jealous of?"*

He replied, *"jealous of me and my job. The only reason I can think of for Alice lodging a grievance against me and bringing this case is she's vindictive and jealous. She wants my job and wants me out of the way—probably egged on by feminists like you."*

I let that answer sink in and then put it to Bernard, *"Would you agree with me that there is not a shred of evidence that Alice ever showed she was jealous of you or your position and there is possibly an easier way to get promotion and getting rid of your boss, than bringing a grievance and then suing in a Tribunal at a public hearing?"*

He did not have an answer so he just shook his head and said, *"whatever— Have you finished with me?"*

"Not quite yet" I said and carried on until I had finished all my cross-examination. The rest of his cross-examination went equally badly for Bernard.

It was very telling that the Tribunal had no questions for him. It seemed to me they had already made up their minds about his shambolic evidence.

His QC decided not to ask any questions in re-examination. She couldn't take the chance that by asking him to clarify some of his appalling answers it would reveal even more ignorance about the meaning of his witness statement and his misogyny and the risk he might keep putting his foot in it. His QC seemed relieved to see him leave the witness table.

The Council's other witnesses fared no better.

One of the Councillors who also gave evidence against Alice, branded her a 'troublemaker' and someone who *"just didn't fit in."*

I put it to him, *"Do you agree with me that Alice did not 'fit in' with you and your beer-swilling, sycophantic male colleagues, some of whom behaved really badly, who worked in a male clique? Is that what you meant?"*

He went silent. He had put his foot right in it. The senior leadership team were all white, middle-aged males, apart from Alice and one other female Director.

Alice and her female colleague certainly were different from their male colleagues. They were highly principled and professional, devoted to their jobs and to the community whom they served.

These men covered up for each other's wrongdoing. There was no place for intelligent, independent-thinking women like Alice.

I asked, *"Would you agree that Alice is a principled and clever woman, who clearly did not "fit in" with you or your male colleagues?"*

This Councillor went silent and shrugged his shoulders and merely repeated what Bernard had said, *"Well women are different from men and Alice certainly didn't fit in with the rest of us men on SLT."*

Their QC's cross examination of Alice did not go well. Her first question was about some Committee minutes that recorded that the SLT had discussed Alice's new contract before she started her new role as Deputy Chief Executive.

Alice was asked why she had felt it appropriate to draft and then comment on the terms of her new contract, at the SLT meeting, when she must have known she had a conflict of interest.

Alice stared at the QC and replied in a slow, dignified voice, *"Of course I did not draft or comment on the terms of my new contract. I would have been conflicted. One of my staff drafted the terms, with Bernard. I left the Committee Room when my new contract was being discussed by SLT."*

The QC didn't know what to say next and ploughed on with her other questions.

The Tribunal then went part-heard after a three week hearing and was re-listed for several months later. But there was no need for another hearing.

The Judge made scathing comments at the end of this hearing about the damage that the Council, Bernard and their other witnesses had done to their reputation. He said no such thing about Alice.

The Judge added 'win or lose' the damage to the reputation of the Council and their witnesses could not be undone.

He told their QC that he did not expect to see them again at his tribunal and made a strong recommendation to the Council to settle the case before the next hearing, the following November.

The Council did settle the case for a substantial sum. Alice then resigned and went off to a new job.

Worse was to come for the Council after they settled Alice's case. Their legal bill for the three-week hearing came to just over £450,000 (this was in the late 1990s). The District Auditor ordered a public enquiry into this expenditure.

As the Leader of the Council entered the Enquiry, it was reported to me by a friendly Councillor who was there, that the Leader had punched the air and shouted, *"Burn the Witch and Kill the Bitch."*

I will never know whether I was the witch who should burn or the bitch who should die.

In light of the enormous legal fees for this case, when I next saw the Council's solicitor whom I knew rather well, I asked him, rather tongue in cheek, if he would name a staircase in their new offices, *"The Alice.... Golden Staircase."* I reckoned the fees charged to the Council would have easily paid for it.

Not ever having met the Leader (Mr C) - he was not called as a witness at the tribunal - one of Alice's colleagues rather cruelly described to me what he looked like. She said he was a despicable man, with lips that looked like *"two slugs mating."*

I pictured him, punching the air and shouting his abuse about Alice and me, with those disgusting fat pouting lips. My imagination ran riot.

Chapter 4
Badra's Tale

"Are you circumcised?" I asked Roger, a brilliant scientist and a future Nobel Prize-winner.

This was my first question to him in my cross examination at the London North Industrial Tribunal in Woburn Place (as it was called and where it was located in those early days), when I sued him and his employer, a Scientific Research Institute, for sexual harassment.

The case involved Badra, who was employed as a lab technician in Roger's laboratory. A few months before the Tribunal hearing, she had come to see me, very distressed.

She told me she was divorced, she was Muslim and a mother of two school-age children. She said that her boss, Roger, had been sexually harassing and sexually abusing her from the start of her employment.

By the time she came to see me, she had been off sick for several months.

She told me two years earlier, she had gone for an interview for the job of lab assistant at Roger's laboratory. He had offered her the job at the end of the interview—without requiring any references or interviewing any other candidates.

He said to her that he could offer all sorts of benefits. He would give her paid time off to study for a degree in biochemistry once she had been at the Institute for a year. She had said at her interview that this was her dream. He said she could come in later than the normal start time of 08.30 in the mornings so she could take her children to school, leave early in the afternoons (15.00) to collect them from school and he would let her take off all the school holidays with pay and that would not count as annual leave —BUT—and there is always a BUT— she would have to do certain things for him in return.

Badra said it all started in the car park of the Royal Free Hospital in Hampstead, North West London, in her first week at work.

Roger and Badra were waiting in the car before attending a lecture. He put his hand up her skirt and "twanged her suspenders" and then made some dirty suggestions about what they could do after the lecture—have sex in the car. It then very quickly became much more sinister.

He insisted she had sex with him whenever he wanted it otherwise, he said, he would dismiss her and give her a bad reference. He would only demand sex in the laboratory during working hours to hide his disgusting behaviour from his wife.

Badra told me she felt degraded and disgusted but at the time she did not have two years' service so if she lost her job, she thought she could not sue for unfair dismissal. She was the sole breadwinner and told me she could not afford to be sacked.

At the time she was unaware that she could have sued for sexual harassment and discriminatory constructive dismissal for which no service is required.

She told me she was under severe duress to comply, unwillingly, with his sexual demands over a period of nearly two years.

I asked her very sensitively why she was complaining about him now. She said it had all come to a head a few months earlier after he had asked her *"to do something so dirty and disgusting I wouldn't even have done it with my husband."*

Stunned and horribly embarrassed I quickly moved on to my next question— without asking her what the dirty and disgusting thing was?

When I got home and told my husband what a client (anonymous of course) had told me, he asked, *"so what was so dirty and disgusting that she wouldn't have even done it with her husband?"* I replied I was too embarrassed to ask. *"You never ask the right questions"* he quipped, not for the first or last time.

I found out what the "thing" was when Badra prepared her witness statement for the tribunal hearing.

Roger had asked her to have sex with three of his male friends while he watched. Roger was going to film them performing sex acts on her. He then said he wanted to have sex with her while his friends watched and filmed them.

He described it as his friends *"playing golf with Badra, three holes"* and his friends *"could each choose which hole."* This was utterly disgusting. I had never heard of such degrading talk before or since. I must live a rather sheltered life – thank goodness.

Badra said she was utterly appalled and disgusted at what he had asked her to do — and so was I.

Armed with what she had told me, we sued her employer and Roger personally, for sexual harassment.

They both denied everything in their defence, including the claim that Roger had required Badra to have sex with him, that he had asked to do that 'dirty and disgusting thing' with his friends or that he had threatened to dismiss her if she didn't do exactly what he asked.

I already knew the answer to my first question to Roger, *"Are you circumcised?"* I knew he was because Badra had told me. She had seen him naked on many occasions and she had had to give him oral sex when he demanded it.

When I asked if he was circumcised the entire tribunal went deathly quiet. He then responded, *"that is absolutely disgusting and it is impertinent and irrelevant and none of your damned business."*

I replied, *"it is very much my business and it is not a disgusting, irrelevant or impertinent question. It is highly relevant. We are all waiting for your answer."*

While he was staring at me saying nothing, I asked, *"Are you Muslim or Jewish?"* He sneered, *"No I am not. Do I look Muslim or Jewish?"* I smiled and thought he is a racist as well as sexist pig and was about to ask him the question, *"What do Muslims and Jews look like? Or are you just stereotyping both religious and racial groups?"* but decided not to.

I then asked, *"Have you ever had sex with Badra?"*

He replied with another arrogant sneer, *"No I have not. I'm not that desperate. If I want sex I can get it without having to ask a junior member of my staff. I don't even fancy her. She is so very plain and unattractive and too fat for my liking. You would have to be desperate to want to have sex with her."*

I said, *"Well I'm going to put to you that you did have sex with her on numerous occasions. So I will ask you again, are you circumcised?"*

Roger replied, *"and I've already told you, I'm not answering your impertinent and irrelevant question."*

I then said, *"Well actually you are right — you don't have to answer my question because I already know the answer — you are circumcised. Badra has* told me you are because she has seen you naked when you were having sex with her. She couldn't have guessed that. It is unusual for a non-Jew or non-Muslim to be circumcised and you have just confirmed you are neither.

"So, unless you are prepared to deny that you are circumcised, I will invite this tribunal to accept that you are.

"I don't want to sound crude but Badra would know if a man is circumcised, having been married to a Muslim and her evidence has been very clear - you are circumcised."

At this point, Roger went bright red and stood there with his mouth opening and shutting but no words were coming out. Then he managed to splutter, "I am going to ask my lawyer if I have to respond to this utter garbage and I am saying nothing from now on."

Before his barrister could intervene or say anything, I said, "Well that's your choice but I will invite the Tribunal to draw an inference from your refusal to answer my questions. I will ask this Tribunal to take your refusal to answer my question 'are you circumcised? as a 'YES'— unless you swear on oath that you are not. I will ask you one more time. Are you circumcised or not?"

Roger remained completely silent. I let him sweat, in silence, while I counted silently to 10 very slowly. That's a long time when you're in a tribunal being asked a question you do not want to answer. That silence seems like hours.

The tribunal waited patiently for his answer but no answer came.

I eventually broke the silence and said, "Well I will ask the tribunal to believe Badra's uncontradicted evidence on this question—unless of course you would like to prove otherwise."

There was an audible gasp around the Tribunal and I could see the female Judge looking at me with terror on her face.

I said to Roger, "Guilty as charged and as you aren't denying that you are circumcised, I will ask the tribunal to draw their own conclusion. I will now to turn to another topic."

The Judge looked mightily relieved that that line of questioning was over. Badra whispered to me, "Thank goodness Gillian. I thought you were going to say 'Well get it out then and let's see for ourselves' "—as if I would….. It had crossed my mind for a fleeting moment.

In further cross-examination Roger continued to deny having any sexual involvement with Badra, denied ever offering her inducements to have sex with him or threatening dismissal if she didn't.

He denied ever having said he wanted to film her having sex with his friends. He added gratuitously, *"I never been unfaithful to my wife. I love her and would never cheat on her."*

Oh dear… she was in the tribunal listening to this.

The Tribunal didn't need to hear any more from Roger. I finished my cross-examination and his barrister had no re-examination and the tribunal had no questions for him. The Judge then released Roger as a witness.

The tribunal spent less than an hour deliberating and found in Badra's favour. They ruled that she had been subjected to the most horrific sexual harassment and abuse and invited both of us to go outside and agree on compensation.

We negotiated a great settlement for Badra but she would have to leave the Institute. That's what she wanted.

They agreed to give her a very good reference and an agreed reason for leaving with no job to go to. That was enough of a financial cushion so that Badra did not have to work again until she had recovered from this trauma and was well enough to find another good job.

Justice doesn't always go to those who deserve it. Roger was given a peerage for his services to Science and five years later won the Nobel Prize for his cutting-edge medical research.

After retiring from the Science Institute, Lord Roger as he was now, was appointed President of an Ivy League University in the USA. Sometimes it appears that there is little or no justice in the world.

Chapter 5
'Bonking Billys' Tale

It always makes for an interesting case when there's sex, fraud and lies—on the other side, of course. We had it all in the tale of 'Bonking Billy'. Not only was the employer in this case a 'Bonking Billy' but he was also a cheat, liar and fraudster.

"Bonking Billy" (otherwise known as Mark) was one of the most loathsome men I have ever met in my long, legal career. He stupidly allowed his lawyers to put forward one of the most ill-judged defences I have ever heard. This was in the early 1980s.

Mark died several years ago but his legacy lives on. Those who were badly treated by Mark still remember this loathsome man.

Even after 30 years, after one of the most dramatic tribunal cases I have been involved in, one of the lay members on that Tribunal still remembers it. He met me in the same Tribunal many years later. He said, *"I still remember that case you were in all those years ago. That was one of THE stand-out cases for me. You were magnificent. How are you? Glad to see you are still in practice."*

Mark had started a travel agency with a sleeping partner but after a few years he bought out his partner. Many years later he sold it to a global organisation for millions.

It was a very successful travel agency, with its head office in Mayfair in London and an office in Los Angeles. Mark had cultivated celebrity clients all over the world as well as other wealthy corporate and individual clients. He would arrange first-class business travel and luxury bespoke holidays. He had a lucrative agreement with BA for first class and business tickets at a discount.

Mark was not a nice man. He was mercurial, bad-tempered, controlling, money-mad and thoroughly nasty – and they were his good points. Over the years, he had become a multi-millionaire—but he was mean, oh so mean.

If he liked you that was fine, until he believed you had done something he didn't like and then he vented his anger and revenge in equal measure.

If he believed a member of staff had done something wrong, even if they hadn't, or if they had done something to annoy him, he would sack them on the spot. He never asked questions or allowed anyone to tell him what had actually happened.

He had a very nasty temper. Oh, and did I mention, he had fallen out with his daughter, son and son-in-law-law from whom he was estranged for some of his life. He didn't even go to his mother's funeral.

He also fell out with longstanding and loyal friends. He was also a terrible womaniser. As I say those were his good points.

His gamble to cross Barbara and me was very ill-judged, which he learnt to his cost.

Barbara had been a loyal employee for 15 years when Mark dismissed her on the spot without telling her what she was alleged to have done or allowing her to have a hearing with a representative present or an appeal.

She was the first member of staff to stand up to him and sue him when he dismissed her.

Barbara dealt with some of his high net worth, celebrity clients and they loved her. She didn't earn a fortune and her bonus payments over the years were modest but she loved her job and the work and enjoyed the company of her colleagues and clients.

One day Mark called Barbara into his office and dismissed her without notice or pay in lieu. Shocked, she asked, *"Why?"* but he merely snarled, *"You know why. Now get out."*

Barbara was absolutely distraught when she came to see me. A mutual friend, Ruth, who had also worked for Mark and had also been dismissed by him several years earlier for doing absolutely nothing wrong, introduced Barbara to me.

Barbara told me the timing of her dismissal was very odd. Two weeks earlier she had informed Mark, that she would no longer get involved in the practice of *'folding back'* that he required some of his staff, including Barbara, to do.

"Folding back" worked like this. Holiday Insurance forms came in a pack of numbered carbonised forms. A form would be physically folded back but left blank and left in place.

The forms were consecutively numbered. Each form was supposed to be completed, in the order in which they appeared, adding the date on the form when it was completed, at the time of booking a holiday when the insurance was supposed to be taken out. The form gave the date and details of the holiday and details of the client and the insurance premium paid.

The client was supposed to pay the premium when booking the holiday, at the same time as the form was completed, so that the insurance was taken out before the risk of cancellation had occurred.

If the form had been folded back and left blank and the holiday had to be cancelled for some reason before the end of that month when the forms were sent off to the insurance company, the form could be folded back open and completed, making it look as though it had been completed on the earlier date put on fraudulently by the agent. It then looked as if it had been completed before the risk had occurred. This was of course a fraud on the insurance company.

The client would then be able to claim for the cost of the aborted holiday. Mark ordered his staff to do this for his favoured friends and family.

Barbara had told Mark two weeks before her dismissal, that she was terrified the insurance company, upon which the fraud was being perpetrated, would find out and they would all be prosecuted.

Barbara has been advised by the brother of a friend who was a criminal lawyer, that she could be prosecuted for aiding and abetting and being an accomplice to this fraud. The penalty could be prosecution, a criminal record and possibly a prison sentence.

She begged Mark to stop ordering her to be involved in this practice and said she was refusing to do it anymore.

A few weeks before her dismissal, Barbara had booked a holiday to Spain during half term for Mark's daughter and granddaughter. This was a time when he and his daughter were speaking. Mark ordered Barbara to ensure that she "folded back" an insurance form for her daughter and granddaughter.

He had shouted at Barbara, *"Do it and shut up"* when she protested. He was in a fit of rage when Barbara argued with him and upon threat of instant dismissal, Barbara very reluctantly did as she was told.

As luck would have it, Mark's granddaughter caught chicken pox two days before they were due to go on this holiday. He ordered Barbara to fold back the insurance form, complete it, backdate it and send it off to the insurers. Mark was claiming for the entire cost of the aborted flights and hotel.

With him standing over her, albeit protesting and very reluctant, Barbara did as she was ordered to do, 'folded back' the form, completed his daughter's details and sent it off with all the other forms at the end of that month.

The insurance company then paid Mark (he had actually paid for this holiday) for the entire cost including the flights and the hotel.

Barbara's protest to Mark would now constitute 'whistleblowing' but this was many years before the Public Interest Disclosure Act 1998 so there was no special legal protection for whistle-blowers if they were dismissed.

By a cruel coincidence, Barbara was dismissed just after Mark had received divorce papers, served at his office, by his first wife. She cited adultery, unreasonable conduct and mental cruelty. As Barbara was friendly with his first wife, Mark believed, quite wrongly, that Barbara must have told her about some of his recent affairs with various women and that had prompted his wife to start divorce proceedings.

After Mark dismissed Barbara, he told her work colleagues that she had been dismissed because she *"gossiped about my private life."* He used the words, *"That's women for you—gossips, greedy and vindictive. That's the last time I employ a woman."* Nice man......

Barbara instructed me to sue Mark's Firm for unfair dismissal, which I did.

She was entitled to a written statement for the reason for her dismissal so his lawyers, aggressive West End lawyers, alleged that Barbara had been dismissed for *"gossiping and disclosing confidential information to external third parties."*

I requested Further and Better Particulars of the alleged *"gossiping and breach of confidential information."*

The Further and Better Particulars stated that Mark believed that Barbara had *"disclosed personal information to his first wife about his private life which was confidential information."*

Of course it wasn't confidential business information for which he could have lawfully dismissed her if she had leaked that kind of information but in any event Barbara hadn't disclosed *anything* to his wife—but that didn't matter to Mark. He thought she had done and that was good enough for him. 'Shoot first and ask questions later' must have been his motto.

It had actually been one of Mark's ex-mistresses, who had informed Mark's wife about their affair, after it had ended very acrimoniously. She told his wife about several other recent affairs.

Mark had to have a 'fair' reason for dismissing Barbara and had to have followed a fair procedure to satisfy an Industrial Tribunal (as it was called in those days) that the dismissal was fair.

Disclosing information about his extra marital affairs to his wife, even if true which it was not, would not have qualified as a 'fair' reason to dismiss Barbara.

It came out in the tribunal hearing that his other reason for dismissing Barbara was because she had told him she would no longer be prepared to be involved in his instructions to 'fold back' insurance forms. Mark's lawyers referred to this as "*Barbara's refusal to carry out a lawful and reasonable instruction'*.

That was of course nonsense. Mark's instructions to perpetrate a fraud was neither lawful nor reasonable.

After Mark's daughter's holiday was cancelled and the insurance company had paid Mark in full for the aborted holiday, Barbara told him that she intended to report him and herself to the insurers. That caused Mark's temper tantrum and his diatribe to Barbara, ending with him shouting that she was *"sacked"* and to get out of the office and never come back.

Mark had been having affairs for years with women both in his office and women he met outside the office.

It must have been for the money because it certainly was not for his looks, sophistication, charm, intellect or his scintillating company. As Mrs Merton once asked Debbie McGee, *"What was it about the Millionaire Paul Daniels that first attracted you to him?"* That was the question I would have asked these women about what attracted them to Mark?

Sylvia was a good friend of Barbara. She came to see me when I was preparing Barbara's case. Sylvia told me that she had ended her affair with Mark rather acrimoniously, one month before Barbara was sacked. I heard all the gory details. Sylvia was a good sort and said she would give evidence at the tribunal about her affair, how it ended and what he was like to work for, the practice of folding back, why she was dismissed and about the other women he had affairs with and then dumped.

I thought that would make for an interesting case so I made sure the Press including the Travel Press were at the tribunal hearing – and they were.

Things did not go well for Mark from the start of the Hearing. On the first morning I was handed some more documents by his legal team. I cannot believe that his solicitor could have read these documents. The documents were correspondence from the hotel in Spain, which had been booked for his daughter and granddaughter. Out of "goodwill", the hotel had reimbursed Mark for the full cost of the room and pre-booked meals.

Mark was their first witness. Cross-examining him, I asked him if the insurance company had refunded him for the entire cost of his daughter's and granddaughter's holiday, including the flights and the hotel. He replied they had.

I waited while this sank in and then asked why he had failed to notify the insurance company that the hotel had reimbursed him for part of the monies for which they had already paid him and why he had not repaid those monies to his insurers.

He retorted, *"I'm not answering your questions. They have nothing to do with Barbara's dismissal."*

I said, *"I beg to differ. Fraud lies at the heart of this case. You instructed Barbara to ensure that she 'folded back' the insurance form for your daughter's holiday and you then ordered her to fold it back open and fill out the form with an earlier date, after the risk had happened.*

"You then compounded your fraud by receiving two amounts of compensation for the same loss and did not inform or repay the insurers."

He glared at me and said, *"Of course I didn't tell the insurance company that the hotel had paid me as well. What do think I am—a fool?"*

"Oh no, not a fool," I replied and couldn't help myself, I added, *"you're just a bully, adulterer, fraudster, cheat, liar and thief."*

I could see the tribunal panel staring incredulously at him, trying not to laugh at my riposte to him.

I then asked him if he would tell the tribunal about the practice of *'folding back'.*

Mark had no qualms about doing this. He explained how it worked and ended his little speech by saying, *"this is common practice in the travel industry."*

It appeared he was oblivious to the fact he was describing a criminal offence and appeared to be proud of getting away with serious and multiple acts of fraud.

That was until the Judge spoke. We had the very good fortune that our Judge in this case was Judge Donaldson, the brother of Sir John Donaldson, the President of the then infamous National Industrial Relations Court (NIRC).

Our Judge Donaldson drew himself up very straight, took a deep breath and said in a voice that caused a frisson around the room, *"Mr....., I happen to be a non-Executive Director of a major insurance company and what you have just told me is FRAUD and you have perpetrated this fraud for years instructing and requiring your staff to do your dirty work for you."*

Now that was a real bonus for Barbara and me. Sometimes one of the parties gets lucky and Barbara did in this case. We got Judge Donaldson as our Judge.

Mark called two of his female members of staff to give evidence. Valerie gave evidence about the practice of 'folding back' and confirmed everything Barbara had alleged in her pleadings about it.

The other witness, Jacqui, who was Mark's PA, gave untruthful evidence that Barbara had actually been sacked for wasting work time, gossiping to staff about her inability to get pregnant again. She had had a new partner for five years and according to Jacqui, Barbara had talked nonstop about her failed fertility treatments. According to Jacqui, Barbara wasted much of her work time disrupting her work colleagues, talking about her infertility problems and crying in the Ladies.

This was something that was very private and personal to Barbara and which Barbara had not gossiped about to anyone else at work. She had confided only in Jacqui about her infertility issues. Barbara thought she could confide in Jacqui but instead Jacqui gave this 'bitchy' evidence which wasn't true. Barbara did not tell anyone else at work about her infertility and worked hard and often long hours. Jacqui did not impress the tribunal one bit.

Things only got worse for Mark when his evidence was finished and I called Barbara to give evidence.

Barbara explained how terrified she had been when Mark had ordered her to commit fraud on the insurance company and how devastated she was when he sacked her. She said she will never understand his vindictiveness towards her after her long and loyal and devoted service.

She felt disgraced and humiliated and ashamed at being sacked. She could not sleep at night knowing that, under duress, she had been committing fraud and would possibly not get another job.

Barbara said she was also very alarmed when the hotel in Spain reimbursed Mark for some of the costs paid out by the insurers. Mark forbad Barbara from informing the insurance company that the hotel had reimbursed the majority of the costs of the holiday. The insurers had already paid Mark for the costs of the hotel.

Barbara said she had not disclosed any confidential information about Mark's private life to his first wife and had no idea why Mark should think she had done.

Barbara also wept when I asked her about the evidence given by Jacqui about her infertility problems. The tribunal looked very sympathetically at Barbara and glared at Jacqui who was cosying up to Mark in the tribunal. They clearly hated Jacqui.

Barbara's testimony was very powerful. She told the tribunal she had been a single mother for many years and had brought up her daughter largely on her own. She said she needed the job but knew right from wrong and hated participating in the fraud. She said she was mortified and hugely embarrassed at being summarily dismissed after 20 years' service.

I had asked our other witness, Sylvia, to wait in the Applicant's waiting room (Claimants were called Applicants at that time) until we were ready for her to give her evidence—so that Mark would not know she was at the tribunal. I wanted this to be a little surprise for him – and it was – a nasty surprise.

This was at a time, before witness statements were in use, so the evidence of every witness was given by examination in chief – the witness answering questions put by their lawyer, to give their evidence.

Witness statements were introduced in Employment Tribunals in England and Wales years after this case so Mark had no idea before the hearing who we were calling to give evidence.

At the appropriate moment the Clerk brought Sylvia into the Tribunal. I heard Mark hiss to his fancy West End lawyers, *"What's she doing here?"*

I answered, *"You will soon find out"* and gave him a wink and a quizzical grin.

After Sylvia had sworn on oath to tell the truth, I asked her whether she had had an affair with Mark whilst working for him. She said she had, for over a year, but then she had ended it and he had sacked her on the spot. I asked her why she had ended her affair with him.

She held up a gold cigarette lighter and said, *"this is why I ended our affair. This is what he gave me for Christmas that year - a gold cigarette lighter."*

I asked her what was wrong with that—to which she turned to look at him and said, *"Apart from the fact that that bastard knew I didn't smoke, the card inside the box read 'To my darling Mark. For the best sex ever, from your ever-loving Suzie'."* Whoops!!!

Sylvia went on, *"The cheap, lying bastard had passed on a gift to me that he had received from another of his lovers. He had not even opened the gift first. He didn't even bother find out what was in the box, which was a gold cigarette lighter, useless to me, or that it had a card written to him inside, from another of his conquests, bragging about the wonderful sex they were having."*

He turned to his barrister and snarled, *"Get her off."* I snarled back, *"Oh No, not yet...I haven't quite finished with Sylvia."* My Rottweiler teeth were gnashing.

I asked Sylvia if she knew about any other affairs that he had had. *"Oh yes"* she said, *"I understand that his wife got fed up with his philandering, lying and cheating, sleeping with girls in the office and his meanness to her. His wife knew about some of his affairs and the amazing presents he gave his lovers. She got nothing—not even a birthday present. Mark used to say to her 'you've got everything—what else do **you** need?'"*

"Is there anything else you would like to add?" I asked.

"Yes," said Sylvia, *"He takes his mistresses to the South of France where he has a Villa and a luxury Sunseeker Yacht. He installs his lovers in a Suite at the Hotel Carlton for the summer when his wife is staying in their villa. He says he and his lover are 'working'. Of course they aren't. They are sneaking around, sleeping together at the Carlton that he is paying for. He is a complete and utter bastard.*

"He even takes these women to his wife's favourite restaurants and he lets them order her favourite dish, lobster. His wife once found the restaurant bills in his jacket pockets and she was hopping mad.

"Of course he sacked me when I finished our affair and told me not to even think of suing him as he would instruct the best lawyers in London and I would never win and he would then sue me for his legal costs.

"As it happened, I had a friend who was also in the travel business who is an honest and decent person and she gave me a job the week after I was sacked, so I didn't need to sue Mark."

Sylvia then added, *"there have been other women who have worked for him with whom he has had affairs and then he's sacked them. I could name some of them if you like."*

At that everyone stared at this loathsome man. Judge Donaldson intervened, *"that won't be necessary thank you Sylvia"* and turned to me and asked a rhetorical question, *"You don't have any further questions for this witness do you Ms Howard?"*

I took the hint and said I had no further questions. Not surprisingly Mark's solicitor had no questions for Sylvia. They wanted to get her out of the tribunal as soon as possible.

The Judge said he had a few questions for Sylvia. He asked her about the practice of *'folding back'* and told her she would not get into any trouble. She told him exactly what this was and how the staff were terrified to do it but Mark ordered them to do it and they dare not refuse under the threat of instant dismissal.

Sylvia was then released as a witness but sat at the back of the Tribunal to listen to the rest of the case and the decision.

The Tribunal didn't take long to deliver their decision—Barbara's dismissal was unfair with no contributory fault on her part.

Judge Donaldson seeing how scared she was when giving her evidence on the practice of 'folding back' reassured her in his Judgement that she would not be getting into any trouble nor would she be reported to the authorities or the insurers and thanked her for being so frank and honest. He did not give any such assurance to Mark. Judge Donaldson ruled that Barbara had been placed under severe duress to participate in the fraud of 'folding back' and eventually had said she wasn't doing it anymore and would be self-reporting to the insurance company —and was then unfairly dismissed for saying so.

They also dismissed Mark's nonsensical and false allegations that Barbara had disclosed confidential information and that was the reason he had sacked her.

It was clear that the Tribunal panel had thoroughly enjoyed Sylvia's colourful evidence about Mark's sexual history.

Barbara was awarded substantial compensation for future loss of earnings and lost bonuses and all her legal costs. Mark was so angry at the decision he stormed out of the tribunal hearing room and slammed the door in his solicitor's face as he ran after him. Mark was not pleased with his solicitor's performance.

Barbara told me afterwards that she hoped with the passing of time, any new employer would give her a job. Now that she had a Tribunal decision in her favour, she could tell any prospective employer that she had been unfairly dismissed and had not been dishonest.

Over one year had passed since Barbara's dismissal, before the tribunal hearing took place and without a reference and having to tell prospective employers that she had been dismissed for alleged gross misconduct after 20 years' service, she had not been able to find another job.

She had made 96 job applications in that time, had been interviewed for five jobs and had been rejected by all five employers.

Mark's meanness cost him dear.

With the compensation that Barbara received she was able to afford to marry her lovely partner, John, with whom she had been living for the past few years. Ruth, Sylvia and I were all invited to the wedding. We drank a toast to Mark and thanked him, in his absence, for paying for the wedding.

His marriage to his first wife ended in an expensive divorce, with her taking him to the cleaners. That hurt.

Jacqui was at that time of Barbara's tribunal case, Mark's PA. She was a pretty blonde who had also been having an affair with Mark for years.

After Mark's divorce, Jacqui eventually moved in with him, left and then divorced her lovely husband and several years later, Jacqui married Mark. I hear their marriage was not made in heaven.

By then Mark had sold his business and had, for a short time, been a consultant, on an initial three-year contract with the new owners, American Express. That had not worked out because the first time he went abroad on business, he was not given permission to travel first class. He had to go economy. He went mad, lost his temper, flew into a terrible rage and walked out tearing up his contract as he went.

He opened another travel business in St John's Wood, with a new partner, Jenni, but that partnership also soon fell apart when Mark argued with her over a business matter. Mark ranted and raved at Jenni and soon after bought her out and ran the business as the sole director.

He later closed this business and his former offices are now a supermarket.

Not being able to claim everything off expenses, he was not nearly so generous to Jacqui.

History often has a habit of repeating itself. After Jacqui and Mark got married, he got himself another mistress—a young girl, Siobhan, who worked for him in this new travel business—yes, you've guessed it—as his PA.

As Oscar Wilde once said, *"A man who marries his mistress leaves a vacancy."*

When Mark and Jacqui went down to his villa in the South of France, Mark installed Siobhan in a hotel near his villa. With history repeating itself again, Mark took Siobhan to Jacqui's favourite restaurants and bought Siobhan lobster, caviar, Dover sole and champagne— all Jacqui's favourite foods and drink.

Jacqui also found the bills in a pocket of one of Mark's jacket but she knew how to deal with this deceit unlike his first wife, who just got mad.

'Don't get made, get even" was Jacqui's motto. So she took his Platinum AMEX Card and spent a fortune on herself, buying beautiful jewellery, designer clothes and handbags and shoes to make up for his meanness and deceit. Now, that's was one smart lady with great style.

Mark died several years ago. I have no idea who turned up to **his** funeral.

Chapter 6
Bianca's Tale

If Bianca's case seems familiar then you will have seen it featured in the BBC 2 one-off drama, *"Sex, the City and me."* It was first shown on TV on 17 June 2007. It has been repeated several times over the years.

Lucy Mangan in the Guardian wrote, *"So, it turns out that life is not so funny in a rich man's world, after all. 'Sex, the City and Me' (Sunday, BBC2) was a one-off drama about the rampant sexism and female victimisation that goes on in the testosterone money-soaked world of banking."*

I was the legal adviser on the programme and gave the scriptwriter details of Bianca's and Brigitte's cases (Brigitte's case is featured in the next Chapter). Their cases were combined and to a point fictionalised. They featured as the joint 'heroine' in the programme.

The lead actors in the drama were the brilliant actors Sarah Parrish, playing Bianca's/Brigitte's part, the brilliant Sarah Lancashire, playing Ruth Gilbert, the lawyer, my part (but portrayed as a cardigan-wearing smoker and of course sharp as a tack), and the very talented and handsome Ben Miles (one of my heart throbs) played Paul, Bianca's/Brigitte's boss.

I was invited to the recording. The first scene in the first draft of the script was pure fiction. It was of Paul in bed with the Bianca/Brigitte character, having very energetic and rather graphic sex.

I told the Director that they could not possibly include such a scene. It wasn't true as neither woman had ever had sex with their boss. More importantly, their husbands and families would be mortified if this was how the programme opened, portraying their wives and daughters as loose women. I understood why it would make great TV though.

The Director agreed to cut that first scene but only after I had already offered to rehearse the scene with Ben Miles. My offer was rejected and that scene was cut.

The programme started with a scene in an Investment Bank in the City of London with the Bianca/Brigitte character working at her Desk.

This programme was and still is an excellent and accurate portrayal of the struggle women had and still have, when they decide to sue their employers for sex discrimination – particularly women in the City. In both Bianca's and Brigitte's cases I had to fight 'slightly dirty' to beat their cheating employers and devious lawyers. I played them at their own game and let's just say they came second.

Bianca worked in the Front Office, in M&A and Corporate Finance, at an American Investment Bank, in their London office. She was a Cambridge Alumni with Master of Business Administration (MBA) from Wharton Business School of the University of Pennsylvania, one of the most prestigious Business Schools in the world. She was the most senior woman in their London office.

Her issues started when, in the year she instructed me, Human Resources (HR) had, by mistake, a rather big one, sent her the entire spreadsheet of all the bonus awards for the London Office, instead of just her bonus number.

When Bianca saw the spectacular seven-figure bonuses paid to her male peers (other Heads of Desks) and more junior male colleagues and her pathetic bonus award in comparison, she came to me for advice. She told me that she had always suspected that she had received much lower bonuses than her male colleagues but never had any proof. Now she did.

Her suspicions had been sort of confirmed the year before, when one of her male peers had come out of his bonus meeting, waving his bonus letter shouting, *"my wife can now buy the house in Eaton Square that she had always wanted."*

That clearly signalled a multiple seven figure bonus and it had really annoyed Bianca because she knew she had earned significantly more in revenues compared to that man, the year before, but she had received a ridiculously low bonus in comparison.

I told Bianca that she first had to exhaust the internal grievance procedure before we could issue legal proceedings. I warned her if she did, she would be *"putting (her) head above the parapet and (she) would most likely get it shot off."*

I asked her to go away for a couple of weeks and think about it and come back to see me if she wanted to take this further.

She came back a week later and told me she had decided to pursue this. She wanted to put in a formal grievance complaining of sex discrimination.

She told me after 17 years' loyal and diligent service at this Bank she expected to be treated fairly and equitably, in terms of her bonus and career progression, with her male colleagues. She told me that at the age of 52 she had worked for over 25 years in the City of London and it was time for her to *"stand up and be counted."*

I said, *"OK—I'm your woman. Leave this to me."* I drafted her grievance and sent it to Human Resources (HR).

I used to call Bianca during the working day with my code words, *"It's Auntie Gill. Do you have a moment to speak?"* Bianca would then tell me she was busy and she would call me back. Within 30 minutes or so she would go out of the building for a coffee and call me on her mobile from the coffee shop. That way we could stay in touch. This was one of my 'tricks of the trade'.

Calls on the trading floor are all recorded, under the rules of the former Regulator, the Financial ServicesAuthority (FSA), (now the Financial Conduct Authority - FCA). No-one on the trading floor has a direct line. All calls go through the switchboard so that they can be recorded. This is to ensure that the client's instructions are being faithfully carried out and so that Bank staff are not breaching any FSA Rules or the Bank's internal Rules—for example the 'Insider dealing' rules or manipulating LIBOR.

For the same reason, no-one on the trading floor is allowed to use their own mobile phone to make or receive any calls. They may only use their landlines with the calls being recorded.

This way I avoided having the content of my calls with my clients listened to and recorded.

I have always wondered if the Banks ever got suspicious about who this *'Auntie Gill'* really was. She seemed to be everyone's Auntie who would always be phoning their niece or nephew during working hours to speak to them. Any employer reading this – take note.

Bianca's employer, much to their regret in hindsight I am sure, allowed me to accompany Bianca to her grievance hearing. The HR Director, Miranda, chaired the hearing.

One of the things that Miranda kept saying from the start of the hearing was *"we do not believe this ...;we do not believe that; we want to know this, etc."*

Eventually, intrigued who this Royal "we" was, I asked to whom Miranda was referring when she used the pronoun "we".

She replied, *"The Bank of course. I am speaking on behalf of the Bank."*

"Oh I'm so sorry" I said, *"I thought you were an impartial, independent person determining the grievance. I had no idea you were representing the Bank, Bianca's employer, in this grievance."*

I then said, *"Bianca would like to know why Axel Schmidt (Axel), an employee on her Desk who reported to her, received a bonus of $2,500,000 this year and she only received $X. Bianca did deals earning fees of $78,000,000 last year and he did not do one single deal last year."*

"Ah," said Miranda. *"Well I can explain. He has a unique skill."*

"What is that?" I asked. I could not wait to hear her answer.

"He speaks German," said Miranda.

I waited for what seemed like minutes but was probably only about 10 seconds and said, *"Apart from the fact that around 130 million people speak German, he **is** German."*

Everyone went silent. It clearly hadn't dawned on Miranda how daft that sounded.

What she may have meant was that before recruiting Axel, the Bank had no contacts or presence in M&A in Germany. He had boasted at his interview the year before, that he had many contacts and could introduce new clients to the M&A Division of the Bank. However, despite his boasts he had not done one single deal or introduced one successful contact to the Bank that year.

Nevertheless, the Bank still felt it appropriate to pay him his 'guaranteed' bonus of $2,500,000 for doing no deals. When I eventually saw his contract, the guaranteed bonus was dependent on bringing in a minimum of $500,000 revenue but he had not earned the Bank a single penny during the entire year.

The grievance hearing ended. It had been a farce. Not surprisingly, Bianca's grievance was dismissed as having *"no merit."* No reason was given.

Bianca then appealed. I told her to covertly record the appeal hearing as I was not allowed to attend that hearing and I didn't trust this Bank. The recording was dynamite as we were to find out when we had the recording transcribed. I will describe what we found in the Bank's version of their notes later in the

Chapter but for now just know it was also 'dynamite'. Her appeal by the way was dismissed.

A week after the grievance appeal was dismissed and while I was on holiday, my phone rang and it was Bianca. She started the call with a nervous laugh, saying four words *"I've just been fired."* I thought she was joking - she wasn't.

She told me Mike, her Head of Desk, had called her into his office and told her she *"didn't fit in with the Bank's ethos and way of doing things."* He offered her a very modest settlement to leave the Bank. She had refused his offer. He told her she was very foolish and promptly fired her.

Most egregiously, after Mike had told Bianca she was fired, he said, *"take that mask of death off your face."* Those were sexist words. Women wear make up on their face as a kind of mask. Mike would never have used those words or anything similar to a man if he had just fired a man for no good reason.

I issued proceedings in the Tribunal against the Bank and Mike, for sex discrimination, victimisation and discriminatory unfair dismissal. Then the fun began.

A common 'trick' mainly used by employer's or defendant's lawyers is to overload the Claimant with thousands of irrelevant documents. The Claimant and their lawyers then have to plough through and read many thousands of documents to try to find the relevant ones.

This takes a huge amount of time and money and the hope by the other side is that relevant documents (and often unhelpful documents to the employer/defendant) will get missed.

This practice of *"promiscuous bundling and documentary carpet-bombing"* and has been severely criticised by the Judiciary.

The lawyer for this Bank (Robert) must have thought they were being very clever because they disclosed 18,450 pages of documents in 18 lever arch files. I do not believe they ever thought I would read all their disclosure—well, Bianca and I did.

We read or scanned the documents in every file. Many of the documents were duplications, with long chains of emails, repeated over and over again. These comprised several thousands of pages.

Similarly, there were thousands of pages of irrelevant tables of revenues going back several years before the year we are suing for. The files also contained hundreds upon hundreds of irrelevant emails to and from HR and Mike stretching over ten years.

We sorted out the repetitions and got rid of all the irrelevant documents and reduced the documents down to one core bundle, comprising 1054 pages.

One of the emails buried in the 18 lever arch files had been written just after Bianca had put in her grievance. It was from Mike to the Chief Executive, William Jr 111.

It was a tirade of abuse about women in the workplace being ungrateful and unreliable, thinking they deserve the same rewards as men. He likened Bianca to such women and ended by saying how disloyal she was, lodging her grievance about her bonus, for which he said she should have been grateful, with the added insult written at the end of his email, *"Is she deaf and stupid?"* She was neither and those words came back to haunt him.

At quite a late stage in the proceedings, Bianca asked me if I had seen any of Mike's meeting notes in his notebooks. I said *"No, they haven't been disclosed by the Bank."* We then realised that the Bank had not disclosed any of these notebooks.

Bianca told me that Mike always made notes of every meeting he attended and every call he made or received. He always brought these notebooks to meetings.

Bianca told me he even joked about these notebooks calling them *"My Book of Lies"* and there were many of these notebooks.

He kept the latest ones with him at all times and once, when he left them in a meeting room and someone had picked them up in error, he fled back in a terrible panic to retrieve them. He then went ballistic until he found the person who had them.

I was sure there must be some 'golden nuggets' buried in his notebooks so just a few weeks before the tribunal was due to start, I urgently requested disclosure of the notebooks from the Bank's solicitor, Robert.

At first he denied that any notebooks actually existed. I insisted they did. He then took instructions and admitted I was right and disclosed photocopies of five notebooks with some of those pages redacted but with many pages missing altogether. I suspected there was 'dynamite' hidden under the redacted passages and on the missing pages.

Original pages must never be torn out of documents. Copies are supposed to be made and anything that is strictly not relevant is permitted to be redacted on the copies, i.e. blanked out.

The Somerset Red and Black notebooks disclosed to me stated on the front that there were '50 pages'. I did a simple count of the first notebook disclosed and there were only 26 pages.

When I complained to Robert that 24 pages had actually been torn out, at first, he denied it. When I told him to count the pages in the first notebook, he then had to admit that pages had been torn out and agreed this should not have happened. He discovered that HR had torn out the pages which they said were entirely irrelevant. Luckily, they hadn't thrown them away.

The redactions on the pages disclosed to me had been done by placing post-it notes over paragraphs which HR decided were not relevant. I was then sent photocopies.

Robert admitted that HR should not have done the redactions as they were under no ethical or regulatory duty to do this honestly. Only lawyers should redact documents.

Robert told me that HR had confirmed to him that what had been redacted was not relevant to Bianca's case so they would not be disclosing the entire, unredacted, original notebooks for me to inspect. I had every right to inspect the original documents 'untouched by human hand'.

I had to think of a way for me to see exactly what had been redacted and what had been written on the torn-out pages, so I became a little imaginative.

I was sure the Bank's HR staff were lying and failing to disclose documents that was helpful to us and unhelpful to them—exactly what the Civil Procedure Rules (CPR) on Disclosure say the parties mustn't do. They have to disclose documents helpful to the other side even where they are unhelpful to them.

I needed to get hold of these unredacted 'Books of Lies' and the torn out pages to see exactly what had been written about Bianca after she had sent in her grievance. I did not trust HR and, as it turned out, I was quite right not to trust them.

I knew if I applied for an Order for specific disclosure for the entire unredacted 5 Books of Lies and the torn out pages, Robert would object, declaring that all the relevant pages for this case had been disclosed. No Judge would go behind such a declaration from a solicitor because they are supposed to tell the truth.

I actually believed that Robert relied on his client to tell him the truth and that he had no idea what was underneath the post-it notes or on the pages that had been torn out. How foolish....

My issue was how was I to get these notebooks to see what was under the post-it notes and on the pages that had been torn out?

So I had to use my ingenuity. Unbeknownst to Bianca, I hired a private investigator (PI) whom I had used several times before. It was lucky he had been an undercover officer in the Met Police for 15 years so knew how to deal with situations like this. I asked him to get me copies of all the pages in the five (5) 'Books of Lies' that had the post it notes on them. I asked him to lift up the post-it notes and copy what was underneath them and copy the loose, torn out pages. I told him they would be somewhere in the HR office. I asked him if he could do this. He said 'Yes'. I said I did not want to know how he did it.

One week later I received an anonymous brown envelope through my letterbox with copies of the complete pages of the notebooks and copies of the torn out pages.

A few years later I asked the PI how he had done this. *"Simple'* he told me. *"I watched the cleaners go into the Bank for several evenings and noted when they started their shift at 10 pm. I got talking to one of them. I asked if I could substitute myself for him the following night. I told him I could not say who I was or why I needed to access the Bank for* **'reasons of national security'** *and explained I was working* **'undercover'***. I told him he would not get into any trouble and I could pay him for the evening that he wouldn't be working.*

"He agreed, telling me he had 'always wanted to be a spy'. I let him think I must be MI5 and told him I would meet him the following evening. He gave me his security pass and told me where I could find the HR Office. I slipped him 'a brown envelope' and went into the Bank dressed as a cleaner, with the other cleaners, using his security pass. No-one even asked who I was.

"I went straight to the HR office and found Miranda's Desk. The five original notebooks and torn out pages were in the bottom drawer of her unlocked desk. I was surprised what lax security there was. I noted there were no CCTV cameras anywhere,

"I photocopied the pages, after lifting up the post-it notes and copied them and the torn out pages, put the post it notes back on each page and returned the notebooks and loose pages to the drawer where I had found them. Then I joined the rest of the cleaners as they were leaving the building and no-one was any the wiser."

I was amazed at the lack of security this Bank had and that Miranda did not even lock her desk drawers and was very pleased with the PI's work.

As soon as I had received these documents I rang Robert and told him that I had just received an anonymous brown envelope with the unredacted 'Books of Lies' and the torn out pages relating to Bianca's case.

I said I was shocked at what I had discovered. His clients had dishonestly withheld critical evidence that was harmful to their case and helpful to ours in flagrant breach of the rules of disclosure in the CPR. What had been concealed was dynamite.

Under one of the post-it notes was a note of a meeting with Mike, Miranda, (the HR Director) and the Chief Executive, William Jr 111. This was held the day after we had had the grievance meeting with Miranda.

The notes revealed that Mike had said to William Jr III, talking about Bianca, *"Let's get rid of her now. She is thoroughly disloyal and a serial complainer. She got a bonus but it's never enough for these women. They all want equality but when it comes to it they go off and have babies, taking years of maternity leave and get paid for it, while we men stay at work and work for their salary.*

"That's inequality for men not inequality for women. May I have your permission to sack her after we dismiss her grievance? Her grievance is a complete waste of time. We know what to do—we can pay her off. All she wants is money anyway. I suggest offering her a maximum of $x."

The notes recorded that William Jr III agreed and had told Mike to *"do what you have to do."*

Mike dismissed Bianca and offered her a very modest payoff which she refused.

Did either of them really think that all women are interested in is money and that they are happy to be paid off and lose their jobs and their careers, after raising a serious issue such as sex discrimination and equal pay? If these men thought that then they were very much mistaken and very naïve.

I told Robert I would be making an application to have his clients' defence struck out under the rules of the Tribunal, for their *'unreasonable conduct'* in deliberately concealing evidence that was harmful to their case and helpful to ours.

He accused me of somehow obtaining these documents by nefarious means and said he wanted the envelope and the documents to be tested for fingerprints. I told him he was very welcome but mine would be all over the envelope and documents because I had opened the envelope and had inspected the documents. I suspected that my PI would have used gloves so his prints would not be found.

Anyway Robert didn't have a clue how I had obtained these documents and the cleaner who had been bribed kept very quiet.

Robert asked me several times where I had got these documents from. I said I had *"a theory but it is just a theory"* and I didn't like to speculate so I told him I would rather keep my thoughts to myself.

I asked him if **he** had any ideas about who had slipped me these documents but he clearly had no idea although he said he suspected I had had a hand in getting them. I said if he wished to tell that to the tribunal when I made my strike out application, he could go ahead. That seemed to shut him up.

I told Robert in no uncertain terms that there had been thoroughly dishonest disclosure, in breach of the CPR. He knew only too well what the Rules required and no tribunal would forgive such dishonesty even if Robert had no idea what HR had done.

Because the employer is in possession of the majority of documents, it is even more important in litigation that the Claimant is given full and frank disclosure of all the relevant documents, because documents often win cases.

The failure to disclose these notebooks came back to bite this employer.

Then something very strange happened. A week before the tribunal hearing, the manager of Bianca's retail Bank rang her to advise her that there had been a security breach in relation to one of her bank accounts.

After twelve unsuccessful attempts to pass through security, someone impersonating Bianca had got past the last security question on the 13th attempt, even though they had given the wrong answer. This question was what was the location of Bianca's local Nat West Branch?

Bianca had moved house since leaving the Bank and her local Branch was no longer the one still listed in the Bank's records. This **was** Notting Hill, where she used to live. She had moved since being sacked.

Nevertheless, the imposter got through security on the thirteenth attempt giving "Notting Hill" as the wrong answer.

The call centre operator on this 13th attempt had been a man. All the other call centre operators had been women. I'm saying nothing.

The Bank account about which the impersonator was enquiring was known only to Bianca and her employer as it was the account into which her salary and bonuses were paid. That account was not even known to her husband.

Even more bizarre, the impersonator had asked what payments had been made **into** the account. They did not ask to withdraw any monies or whether there had been any withdrawals, so the caller was not a thief. The impersonator specifically asked about whether any payments had been made to Bianca by another investment bank in London.

Suddenly, a week before the tribunal hearing, Robert disclosed **their** grievance appeal notes. I was shocked. The Bank had falsely noted that Bianca had said she had already secured a conditional job offer with another Bank as she was disgusted with the way she had been treated. The notes falsely stated that Bianca had said she intended starting with her new employer the following week.

This was of course complete fiction. Bianca had said nothing of the sort.

I then disclosed the recording that Bianca had made and our transcript, to Robert, with a very fierce note about the Bank's wholly dishonest notes written by his client. I had absolutely no reaction or response from Robert. What a surprise.

Mike had believed, quite wrongly and quite inexplicably, that Bianca had secured another job with another Investment Bank shortly after being dismissed.

If this had been true, Bianca would have 'mitigated her loss' and her loss of future earnings would have been extremely limited although she would still have been able to claim for unequal bonuses over past years.

She would never have been awarded the amount of compensation we were claiming for future loss of earnings from age 52 to 60, when she would have retired. Mike believed she had not disclosed this 'new job'.

They were quite wrong. Bianca had been completely honest. No monies had been paid into this account because she had not been able to get any new job in the 15 months from the date of her dismissal to the date of the tribunal hearing.

So here was a deliberate deception by the Bank's HR department and was I glad I had instructed Bianca to covertly record her appeal hearing. Sometimes I have to indulge in a bit of skullduggery when the other side is thoroughly dishonest and cannot be trusted.

After this security breach had been discovered by Bianca's personal Bank, I said to her that I hoped they were truly sorry and that they had made a gesture of goodwill by offering not to make any bank charges for the following year.

She smiled and told me that her personal Bank was Coutts and they did not make bank charges on current accounts as long as they stayed in the black. I then realised that customers to be eligible to open an account in this exclusive Bank had to place a rather large cash sum in their current account to start with. I said rather weakly, *"Oh yes I had forgotten."*

Suing your employer in the City is bad enough, but winning means you are known forever as a 'serial litigator' and not just a 'troublemaker' but a 'successful troublemaker'. No employer wants to hire that. There is normally no going back to the financial world.

Since February 2017 employers can look up cases online and see who has sued who.

Since February 2017 employers can look up cases online and see who has sued who. All Employment Tribunal and Employment Appeal Tribunal decisions are published on the Government websites—

https://www.gov.uk/employment-tribunal-decisions and

https://www.gov.uk/employment-appeal-tribunal-decisions.

Prospective employers can easily look up the names of Claimants to see who have sued their previous employers.

At the time of this case Tribunal decisions were not published on any website. Nevertheless, the grapevine in the City was vicious—everyone knew everyone's business. The City of London's financial markets still leak like a sieve. There are no secrets. Bianca's prospective litigation was well known in the City.

Two working days before trial, on the Thursday, Robert rang me, at 11 am, with an offer to settle. He told me it was their first and final offer and I had to accept it by 12 noon and my client had to sign a Settlement Agreement by midnight that day. He said otherwise he would see us in the tribunal the following Monday.

Being very polite I thanked Robert and asked him to put all that in writing, which he did.

Bianca begged me to accept it as it had been described as their *'first and final offer'* but I said, *"No, let's wait and see."* I had a second sense about this case.

I did phone our QC to tell him about the offer. *"I advise you to take it"* he said. *"This isn't an easy case and even if we win, there's no guarantee the Tribunal would award anything like the offer you have just received."*

I replied, *"If this was an easy case I wouldn't have needed to instruct a QC"* and with that I put down the phone and decided to ignore his advice. I'm not known as 'the Negotiating Queen' for nothing.

The art of negotiation is knowing the psychology of the other side better than they know you; holding your nerve; having a second sense for when a final offer really is a final offer – in other words, knowing the 'tipping' point over which the other side will not go; and, as I had in this case, having a lucky break and inside knowledge.

The minutes ticked by and Bianca was getting more and more nervous. Then I had a stroke of luck. At around 1pm my phone went. A voice said, *"You don't know me but I work for the Bank I believe you are suing. You acted for my sister 15 years ago and you would not charge her and neither she nor my family have ever forgotten your kindness.*

"So you may find this information useful. Mike has just asked me to re-book his skiing holiday for him and his family for next week. I thought you would like to know. He won't be in the country next week. Is that helpful?"

I said, *"That is amazingly helpful and that's all I need to know. I can't thank you enough."* With that the caller rang off.

I genuinely had no idea who this was. I couldn't remember to whom this caller was referring when she spoke about her sister from 15 years ago but I was thrilled with this information. Mike had to attend the hearing as he was the Second Respondent and the Bank's key witness. It was he who had decided on Bianca's poor bonuses year after year and it was he, who had dismissed her.

I realised he must have instructed their solicitor to settle the case to ensure that it did not go ahead the following week. That was why I had had the call that morning from Robert. The Bank was not going to fight this case.

The clock ticked by. Bianca was getting more and more jittery. She asked me to ring back and accept the Bank's offer, even though it was way past their deadline of 12 noon. I asked her to be patient because that was not their 'final' offer and I was sure that Robert would phone me again.

As I was saying this, my phone rang and it was, as I had predicted, Robert. He said, *"I'm ringing to reopen the channels of communication."*

"Oh No" I said, *"You can't do that because you wrote to me that if we didn't accept your first and final offer by 12 noon today, it would be taken off the table and there would be no more offers and no further negotiations."*

"Oh" he said rather nervously, *"You don't have to believe everything I write."*

I replied, *"Ah well, that's where I've been going wrong all these years. I have, until now at least, always believed what a solicitor has written."*

There was a very nervous silence. Robert then started pleading with me, *"I'm trying to negotiate with you."*

"Ah," I replied, *"well, that's where we differ—because I am not."*

I'm not called a Rottweiler for nothing. It is not a good idea to upset me when I'm acting for any Client who has been badly wronged.

Bianca had been sacked for doing nothing more than standing up for her rights. We had been deceived during the disclosure process and had it not been for some slightly unorthodox action on my part, we would never have got hold of those notebooks. It was also a stroke of genius that the anonymous caller happened to be the sister of a former client of mine who had had the decency to let me know Mike would not be in the country the following week – the week of the tribunal.

And now the Bank's lawyer was trying to 'persuade' me into accepting an offer to settle for far less than our claim was worth. That's not how you win me over. I will not allow my clients to be bullied into settling when the other side is in deep trouble even though they didn't know that I knew what trouble they were in.

Robert knew he was defeated. He sighed and said he would take instructions and would call back—and he did, 30 minutes later (at 3.30pm). We reached an agreement on part of the compensation but I told him that I had not finished. I asked if his client wanted confidentiality. Robert said of course they would. I then said, *"Well that will be another \$xxxxx"*. He agreed.

I also said that Bianca wanted all her share options to be paid as part of the compensation as they would have vested in the next three years. They agreed to that as well. We settled the case that Thursday evening one working day before trial.

To celebrate Bianca's success I had a t shirt made for her. On the front it said, *"I may be deaf and stupid"*. On the back it said, *"But I am rich."*

After Bianca's case settled we both went to the tribunal hearing of one of her female colleagues. She had also brought a sex discrimination claim against the same Bank a few months later. She had not been allowed to return to her job after her maternity leave but the Bank had never offered to settle her claim.

Bianca wore my t shirt at the tribunal.

This other woman was represented by another lawyer. They were unaware of Mike's 'Books of Lies' and those notebooks had not been disclosed in this case by the Bank yet again.

We had found plenty of material in those notebooks about this colleague of Bianca's that would have been very useful to her at her hearing but as documents obtained in a case are strictly confidential, I could not disclose them to her lawyers.

After the case was settled, Bianca could not get another job anywhere in the City. Every time she got down to the last two candidates, as if by magic, the job was given to the other candidate. This always happened after references had been taken up.

So I decided to ring Mike and find out what he was saying about her. I told him a little white lie. I said I was considering Bianca for a role and I wanted a little background about her first. I had my notebook to hand to write down every word he said. I asked him to speak slowly as I wanted to make notes and he was very obliging.

"Well," he said, *"I wouldn't touch her with a bargepole. She's a troublemaker and a serial litigator."*

I nearly blurted out that Bianca has only ever sued them once, but managed to stop myself in time.

He went on, *"She is wholly unsuitable for future employment anywhere. You can't trust her. She's a traitor and deeply disloyal. You don't know when she will knife you in the back. She sued us for millions. We had to pay her off with a huge settlement* (he actually named the figure).

"She's devious too and she will do the same again to you. She is a poisoned chalice. I wouldn't employ her if I were you. We certainly wouldn't ever employ her again. She was jealous of her male colleagues who were better than her and got paid more than her - that's all it was."

Oh dear, I thought—this man (Mike) has 'foot in mouth disease' and what about the confidentiality that the Bank had insisted upon? He had just disclosed the actual sum in settlement to me. And wasn't what he had just said about Bianca slander?

I then told Mike who I was and that I had made a contemporaneous, verbatim note of what he had just said to me and that he had just slandered my client and breached the non-disclosure agreement (NDA) that both parties had signed.

He spluttered and asked me what I wanted. I told him, *"Stop badmouthing Bianca, give her an honest and fair reference and pay her another $x for that wicked slander and the defamatory references you've been giving her, denying her multiple job opportunities."* He agreed without blinking an eye.

I will not put up with bullying or unfairness.

One week after Bianca put in her grievance, she was informed that she had won the IFR Award for M&A Deal of the Year. These awards are given by the International Finance Review (IFR) and are the equivalent of the Oscars in the Financial world. The awards are given to the person who did the best deal in a particular category within the financial institutions throughout Europe.

The Awards were presented every year, at a prestigious dinner, at the Grosvenor House Hotel in Park Lane, Central London, with invited guests from the world of finance in the UK and abroad.

The Public Relations (PR) Officer of the IFR had telephoned Bianca to tell her the good news about her Award and told her she could invite 9 guests to make up a table. I was one of Bianca's invited guests.

When Mike heard that Bianca had won this Award and was going to collect it, he was furious. He decided that he would accept the Award not her. He telephoned the IFR's PR officer to tell her there had been a change of plan and he would be collecting the Award not Bianca.

The PR Officer then rang Bianca the day before the Award Ceremony to tell her that Mike had now instructed her that he would be collecting the Award. Bianca was annoyed but quite sanguine about it. She told me she couldn't do anything about it. Well, I thought, if **she** couldn't, **I** could.

I was so incensed that I rang the PR Officer on the morning of the Award Ceremony to tell her that there had been yet another change of plan. We were reverting to the original plan of Bianca collecting her Award. I asked the PR Officer to make sure that Bianca's name would be called out and not Mike's.

She confirmed that Bianca would collect the award. Mike had no idea what I had done.

During the evening, I could see and hear Mike from our table, which was next to his. During dinner, he had been boasting about collecting the Award and had even discussed which side of the platform he should walk up and what he would say.

The news crews were there filming the event for the following day's news bulletins in the UK, USA and Asia, and for the IFR magazine.

When the Editor of the IFR announced the winner of the award for M&A deal of the Year, not listening to the name that had actually been called out, Mike rose from his chair with a huge, smug smile on his face and started to walk towards the platform, waving at financiers and bankers as he went. Soon that smug smile was wiped right off his face.

As Bianca caught up with him and overtook him, she whispered, *"Not you, Mike —you didn't listen. It was my name that was called out not yours. It is my Award so I am going to collect it—so sorry if that wasn't your plan."* With that, she walked up the steps to the platform and Mike was left standing looking the fool that he was.

His face was a picture. He had a look of utter astonishment and then embarrassment. He just stood there as he watched Bianca go up to the platform and collect her award. He then had to walk back to his table looking rather foolish while the audience was clapping for Bianca.

Being a little naughty, I had already briefed some of the press about what was going to happen so they caught Mike on camera looking utterly embarrassed. His photo appeared in the next IFR Journal looking totally bemused alongside Bianca, looking totally professional.

However, as soon as Bianca came down from the platform, Mike stood up from the table, patted her on the head, snatched the Award from her and said he was taking it back to the office to display it for the entire team to see.

It was a personal award given to Bianca and not to her department. It was not Mike's award or his decision where it should be displayed, although Bianca had planned to display it in the Department.

But it never found its way back to the office. A couple of years later, Bianca learnt that it had ended up in Mike's son's bedroom. Apparently it looked very like a replica of the FA Cup. His son was a keen football fan and was delighted to have it.

Unfair or what? That award was Bianca's.

This case does have a happy ending. Bianca got fed up chasing jobs in the City and then being rejected from job after job at the last hurdle so she enrolled on a Cookery course for a year.

She then got herself an agent and a publisher and wrote three bestselling cookery books. They all went to the top of the Sunday Times nonfiction best sellers list for weeks. She is now a very popular cookery author.

The Course Leader of the Cookery course was so impressed with Bianca that a few year later he asked her to come back as a guest lecturer for a term, which she did. She has also appeared in numerous popular cookery programmes on TV.

She never went back to the City and the financial world is the poorer for it.

A few years later, Mike called me. He asked me if I remembered him. I said of course I did. He told me, *"We had terrible advice in Bianca's case."* I replied, *"Yes you did —but you didn't have to take it."*

He agreed with me and then asked me if I would act for his brother, who was a whistle-blower at a major financial institution. I said *"of course"*.

During the year following Bianca's case, six women from the same Bank, came to me for advice about how they had been treated. None of them had been allowed to return to their jobs after taking maternity leave. These women were just paid off.

I rang Mike to ask why his Bank had so many discrimination cases and why managers felt they could refuse with impunity to allow women to return after their maternity leave.

He told me that each Head of Desk was given 'a black hole account' (as he called it) which provided them with funds to manage and pay for 'risk'.

The managers could choose to spend their black hole account budget however they liked. If they chose to spend it paying out compensation to women whom they refused to allow back to work after their maternity leave, that was their choice.

In other words it was a pot of gold that their managers could spend to discriminate against working mothers. I could hardly believe my ears. I thought I had heard it all.

Mike and I did end up 'good friends' until he retired from the Bank. In fact, he even joked that there should be a notice on the Bank's Notice Board with my office address saying *"The Rottweiler's Office this way"* pointing to Wimpole Street. He was kind enough to recommend me to several other women who had issues with their employer—but not at his Bank.

Bianca came back to me for help four years later. She rang me and told me she had been locked out of the screen when she tried to sell her shares that had now vested. These had been granted as part of her settlement.

When she rang the relevant department at her former employer, they said they knew nothing about these shares and they would not give her any login details.

I rang the Bank's solicitor (Robert had retired so I spoke to the new Head of the Employment Department), and told her about our 'little problem'. She came back five days later to say the problem had now been fixed. No-one had told the staff in the relevant department that Blanca had been granted these shares or that she could sell them when they vested. The solicitor said Bianca was now free to sell her shares and she was sent the login details to access the relevant screen.

Only now there was another 'little problem'. In the five days that had passed, the share price had fallen and Bianca had suffered a loss of thousands of dollars. When I told the solicitor what had happened, she tried to brush this aside and told me there was nothing she could do about it.

I disagreed. I said that due to her client's error, Bianca had suffered a loss. This was a breach of the agreement we had reached four years earlier and if we did not receive compensation in the amount she had lost, by the end of that day, we would sue for damages for breach of contract in the County Court.

I said I would append the confidential Compromise Agreement to our Particulars of Claim and I would invite members of the Press to read our pleadings and see the settlement that the Bank had had to pay Bianca for her sex discrimination claim.

At that this solicitor seemed to "wake up." She said she could not get a cheque round that afternoon but would do her best to get one *"in the next day or so"*.

I said that wasn't good enough and if we did not receive a cheque by 5 pm that afternoon, we would have to issue proceedings the following morning. I said her client shouldn't have a problem—they were a Bank after all.

At 4.55 pm that afternoon a courier arrived at my office, with a cheque for the amount we had asked for. Amazing what can be done when an employer tries a little harder.

The Retail Banks had all closed by the time the cheque arrived but I wanted that cheque by close of play that day so that Bianca could bank it at 9 am the following morning. I could not trust her former employer to delay payment any longer.

A few years later, the Judge in the case which Bianca and I had attended and sat at the back of the tribunal, met me at a Chamber's Christmas Party. He asked me what the writing meant on the front of the t shirt, *"I may be deaf and stupid"*, that he had seen Bianca wearing. The Judge could of course only see the front of her t Shirt.

I said, *"Ah, it repeated what Bianca's boss had said about her. On the front of the t shirt it said, 'Is she deaf and stupid?' That's what Bianca's boss had written about her, But on the back of the t shirt I had the words added 'But I am rich'. That's all that I can tell you. Bianca also had a run-in with the same Bank as in your case, but we didn't need to bother the tribunal with our case."*

The Judge nodded. He knew what I meant.

Chapter 7
Brigitte's Tale

Brigitte's case was the other case that formed the plot of the BBC2 drama 'Sex, The City and Me'.

Brigitte was dismissed because she committed the 'crime' of getting pregnant. In the financial world, that was and possibly still is, 'a crime'.

Brigitte introduced herself to me in a very unconventional way. One Friday afternoon my phone rang and I heard a voice sobbing at the other end, saying, *"Please tell me I don't have to go back to work this afternoon."* I asked gingerly, *"To whom am I speaking?"*

She told me her name was Brigitte and she was a Japanese Bond trader for an Investment Bank in London. She had been given my number by her father-in-law who was very friendly with my parents.

Brigitte is American by birth but had lived in Japan for many years as a child so speaks fluent Japanese. She went back to live in New York City when she was 16, graduated at Columbia University and then got a job in an American Investment Bank in New York for several years. She then moved to London and joined another Investment Bank.

She is now a very successful venture capitalist raising funds from investors mainly for start-ups run by women.

Brigitte had been at lunch on the day she called me, 23 years ago. She had come back to her desk in the afternoon and one of her colleagues had shown her a couple of Bloomberg messages. They had been sent by her boss, Nick, to his boss, Ahmed.

That Friday morning Brigitte had informed Nick that she was three months' pregnant. She had been trying for months to get pregnant and had suffered two miscarriages the previous year. Nick had not looked at all pleased when she told him her news. The week before, he had boasted at a dinner, at which Brigitte had been present, *"I never employ pregnant women on my desk."*

In this Bloomberg message Nick had written to his boss, Ahmed, that Friday lunchtime, *"Brigitte's just told me she's pregnant. Fuck - these bloody women. Let's fire her and it will end a sticky situation."*

Ahmed had written back, *"Yea do that. Brigitte is a real pain in the arse at the best of times but pregnant... she will be a double pain in the arse and we won't be able to touch her. Bloody women and their urge to have babies. Next time make sure they're all sterilised or post-menopausal before they come to work for us."*

Brigitte had printed out these Bloomberg messages and kept them as evidence.

Instant Bloomberg is a chat tool used by many investment banks. It captures chats between traders and Bankers as well as crucial deal details and sends them directly to the trading platform. Through Instant Bloomberg, messages can be passed very quickly and easily to colleagues and trading partners.

I advised Brigitte to go home and get an emergency appointment with her GP to get signed off sick. She was far too distressed to remain at work. She went straight to her GP and he signed her off work for the next four weeks.

Two weeks later, Nick sent Brigitte an email saying she was at risk of redundancy. He had no idea she had read or had taken copies of his Bloomberg messages about her.

Four weeks later, on the day before she was due to return to work, Brigitte received a dismissal letter, saying her role had been made redundant and her last day at work was that day and she would be paid in lieu of notice and her statutory redundancy pay. This was of course utter nonsense. Her role was not redundant—it was smokescreen to cover up a discriminatory dismissal for being pregnant. It is automatically unfair to dismiss a woman because she is pregnant or for any reason related to her pregnancy. There is no defence and there is no minimum service requirement to bring a claim for pregnancy discrimination.

I called the copies of those Instant Bloomberg messages our "smoking gun" and "golden bullets."

I issued proceedings against the Bank for pregnancy discrimination and unfair dismissal and against Nick personally for pregnancy discrimination. Their defence continued to purport that the dismissal was for redundancy and had nothing to do with Brigitte's pregnancy.

During the process of disclosure of documents to the Bank's lawyers, I sent copies of the Bloomberg messages that Brigitte had printed off. The Bank had failed to disclose these to us as they should have done.

Luckily I sometimes don't need to rely on the other side's 'honesty' in the disclosure process.

The Respondents made a feeble attempt to explain the words *'it will end a sticky situation'* saying it referred to arguments that Brigitte had had with Nick over certain deals, the previous year. They added that things had come to a head this year over one particular deal and that determined her role should be made redundant. This was absolute nonsense, of course.

The case started at the London North Industrial Tribunal at Woburn House.

Brigitte took the first day to read out her witness statement (in those days witness statements were read out. Now they are pre-read by the Tribunal).

Her witness statement was very compelling. The Tribunal Panel kept giving Nick long, cold, hard stares. He was oblivious to their glares and must have thought they were approving of him because he kept smiling back at them throughout her evidence.

All in all, Bianca gave a very credible account of how she had been treated. She referred to the difficulties she had had keeping a baby, with two late miscarriages the year before with the dreadful loss of two unborn babies at late stages of her pregnancy. She knew the second unborn baby that she lost at 20 weeks had been a girl.

Brigitte was 38 years of age by the time of the tribunal hearing and said in her statement she feared that her last pregnancy had been her last chance to have a baby.

She told the Tribunal about the dinner, the week before she told Nick she was pregnant and what he had said about *"never employing pregnant women on (his) desk."*

She read out the Bloomberg messages between Nick and Ahmed and explained the distress of reading them—that she was to be fired for getting pregnant. She referred to the fact she had suffered another miscarriage the week after she was dismissed.

Happily, she got pregnant again shortly after the last miscarriage and by the time of the tribunal hearing she was seven months' pregnant and was having a healthy pregnancy. She went on to have a lovely little boy and 18 months later had another little boy. They are now 20 and 18 years of age.

Before even cross-examining Brigitte, the Bank's QC asked for an adjournment to settle the case.

It is unusual for a case to be settled midway through the hearing when the Respondent's Counsel has not even cross examined the Claimant and when the Respondent has not given their evidence. But that's what happened in this case.

We went back and forth trying to settle on a figure that we said was acceptable. I kept telling their QC, now a High Court Judge, that their offers were 'insulting' and she should go back to her client "and get real."

Eventually, we negotiated a substantial settlement and a written apology for the way that Nick had treated Brigitte.

When we were leaving the Tribunal, Nick came up to Brigitte and held out his hand and said, "I am really sorry." I snapped back, "Sorry for what? Sorry you got caught?"

With that Brigitte and I walked away—Brigitte much richer than she was before.

Nick left the Bank shortly afterwards. After getting jobs in two other Banks in London within short succession and 'leaving' both jobs with less than one year's service, he went back to USA where he had originally come from.

We heard Nick got into trouble with some not very nice people back in the States. He got a job with a private Bank that had allegedly been laundering money for some Russian Oligarchs but had failed to give them their funds when they asked for them.

One night a dumper truck full of cow dung was thrown all over the front porch of Nick's home on the shores of Lake Michigan. Nick then received a rather sinister message that this was only the start and that if he wanted to keep his family alive, he had better get them their money. We never heard the end of that story.

Sadly, as a result of the World Financial Crash in 2008, the Bank where Brigitte had worked went out of business very suddenly leaving thousands of their staff without their last month's salary and no notice they had lost their jobs. They turned up for work one morning to find the Bank locked up and security guards outside.

I have become very good friends with Brigitte. Although I am just about old enough to be her mother, she calls me her "sister." I have sometimes performed duties for her that are not strictly 'legal'. By that I don't mean they are illegal.

One day Brigitte rang me to ask me to come with her to look at a house she was thinking of buying. The vendor had said that Brigitte was to view the property on her own. She did not want Brigitte's friends or family trooping round her home. Brigitte asked if she could bring her 'interior designer'—me. The vendor agreed.

As I walked into this house, which had not been touched for about 50 years, I started my spiel. *"Oh,"* I said, *"Just give me this house—I know exactly what I want to do with it. This entrance hall could be amazing."*

I went around the house with Brigitte and the vendor, making it up as I went along. I said I would take walls down here and there. We would add a large extension onto the back of the house and build a conservatory. We would put a swimming pool in the garden and a deck with a barbecue.

We would make a basement with a gym, sauna, cinema and laundry room.

I would put in a beautiful cloakroom in the hall, using black granite, mined only in Russia, containing fossils millions of years old. I said *"this could only be mined in the month of November"* sounding very knowledgeable. (My thanks to Mark Evans of Mark Nicholas Design Ltd for this information.) This was of course 21 years before the war in the Ukraine.

I said we would hang Murano glass lights and bespoke lighting everywhere. I would put in a new top of the range Hacker kitchen, with black sparkling granite surfaces, a large island, sub-zero fridge/freezer, a range cooker and a Quooker hot and cold filtered and sparkling water taps (all from Mark Nicholas Designs).

I said I would put in underfloor heating everywhere so we would not see ugly radiators.

Upstairs I said I would make the whole of the first floor a huge Master bedroom with two bespoke walk-in wardrobes, his and hers bathrooms with infra-red radiators, Villeroy and Bosch whisper baths and Japanese toilets with heated seats. I would put a TV in all the rooms, including the bathrooms, hidden behind mirrors. It really did sound convincing. Even I was convinced.

We then went into the garden and I said I knew exactly which landscape gardener I would use - Mark Enright —the best there is.

When it came time for us to leave, the vendor turned to me and said she would like to hire me as <u>her</u> interior designer for the house she had just bought and asked for my business card. In shock horror, I shrieked, *"No you can't."*

She looked at me as if I was mad but I recovered quickly and said, *"What I mean to say is I am retiring after this job and going to live abroad. This is my last job. But thank you so much for asking."* With that 'little white lie', *"we made our excuses and left."*

Brigitte needed my assistance again a few years later. She rang me in real distress. She told me that the day before, on the very rare occasion that she had ever gone to the dry cleaners to drop off some clothes (usually her husband did this), she had seen the wife of the owner behind the counter, wearing her Tiffany gold and diamond earrings.

Brigitte told me that she had lost those earrings about six months previously and despite searching high and low at home, she could not find them. She had no idea what happened to them.

When she saw the owner's wife wearing them at the dry cleaners, Brigitte realised that she must have put the earrings into a jacket pocket and had given the jacket to her husband to be dry cleaned six months earlier—forgetting the earrings were still in the pocket.

The owner's wife must have found them in the pocket before putting them in the dry-cleaning machine and had decided to keep them for herself.

The odds of Brigitte going into the shop and finding the owner's wife, Mrs Khan, serving in the shop and wearing those earrings, were millions to one.

Brigitte very rarely took her clothes to the dry cleaners and Mrs Khan very rarely served in the front of the shop. She was normally in the back, out of sight, sorting and organising the dry cleaning and the laundry.

Her husband had taken that particular day off and Mrs Khan was 'manning' the shop. To cap it all, she had decided that morning to put on Brigitte's diamond earrings. That's what you call 'fate'.

Brigitte wanted to know how she could get her earrings back? That's what she had rung to ask me. I had the perfect plan. I told Brigitte, *"Leave it to me."*

We went to the shop the following day. Mr Khan was serving as usual behind the counter. I told him that Brigitte had been in two days earlier, dropping off her dry cleaning when she had seen his wife wearing some glorious diamond earrings. I asked him where he or his wife had bought them. He said he had no idea and did not know what earrings we were talking about.

I described them and asked if he would bring them to the shop the following day and we would come back with a camera and photograph them so that Brigitte could get similar ones made for herself. This was before smart phones with cameras.

Mr Khan did as we asked. We went back the next day and he showed us the diamond earrings. I took several photos including the posts of the earrings and asked where his wife had got them. He said he didn't know. I believed him.

I told him I knew where *she* hadn't got them from—Tiffany in New York—because Brigitte had bought them there when she worked for an investment bank there. I said they had cost approximately $10,000 and I showed him the engraving on the posts of the earrings - "BLK" (Brigitte's initials). Tiffany engraves the purchaser's initials on its expensive jewellery.

For one terrible moment, I thought that perhaps the initials on the earrings were those of Mrs Khan. The "K" in the engraving "BLK" could have been Mrs Khan's initial. Brigitte's maiden name was 'Kellmann'. However the initials were not Mrs Khan's.

I told Mr Khan that we had evidence that the owner of these earrings was Brigitte and not his wife and we had the receipt.

I asked if he or his wife had ever been to Tiffany's in New York. Mr Khan said, "No." I asked if his wife's first names began with a 'B' and an 'L'. He said 'No'.

I told Mr Khan that his wife must have found these earrings in Brigitte's jacket pocket when the jacket was brought in for dry cleaning six months earlier and instead of returning the earrings, his wife had kept them for herself.

I explained that this was technically theft and we could call the police but we would not do that if he handed over the earrings to Brigitte now. Shocked, Mr Khan handed them over immediately without saying a word.

Brigitte then asked for her dry cleaning and to my horror asked how much she owed him. I mouthed, *"You shouldn't have to pay for your dry cleaning. Tell him to void the ticket"* but she ignored me.

Mr Khan also said nothing and Brigitte handed over the money for her dry cleaning and left the shop without saying another word. The earrings were clasped tightly in Brigitte's hand. Another happy ending.

Chapter 8
Bonnie's Tale

"You're nicked"

"We are the taxman and you're nicked" was what Nigel heard, a year after he had dismissed my client – and it could not have happened to a nicer man.

This is the tale of Bonnie, Nigel's PA, who got the better of him, when he treated her very badly and unfairly dismissed her after 35 years' service. His stupidity and greed, involving a large tax and VAT fraud on his part, got him into big trouble.

Nigel was a very successful haute couture dress designer. He was famous for designing spectacular evening dresses and bespoke men's suits and tuxedos. He became a worldwide phenomenon. There was nobody to touch him. He really was the best.

He made clothes for members of our Royal Family, several UK Prime Ministers and their wives or husband, Presidents and Prime Ministers and their wives worldwide, crowned Kings and Queens, Princes and Princesses all over the world and for celebrity clients. He was the 'go to' designer of men's and women's clothes.

He branched out designing beautiful bespoke handbags, shoes and one-off pieces of jewellery using precious stones and coloured diamonds. Later in his career he designed and made the most beautiful theatrical and film costumes.

Bonnie had worked at the same French Couture House as Nigel when they were both 15 years of age. Nigel had started as a junior machinist, at first just stitching on buttons. As he learnt his trade he started designing clothes and moved onwards and upwards.

Bonnie moved from a seamstress to become the secretary/PA to the Chief Designer. Nigel was promoted to Chief Designer at the age of 24. Bonnie was a great organiser and had done a touch-typing course in her spare time. When Nigel was promoted to Chief Designer he inherited Bonnie as his secretary/PA.

When Nigel was 27, he heard about a bomb site in Central London that was ripe for development. The Couture House for which he worked needed bigger premises but they decided not to buy the site. So Nigel persuaded one of the other designers to leave and become his partner. They both left the Couture House after persuading a Bank to lend them the money to buy the site.

They developed the site, built a large workshop and showroom and bought all the equipment and sewing machines needed for an upmarket, bespoke business for Couture clothes and later jewellery, handbags and shoes.

They hired top designers and experienced needlewomen. Bonnie left the Couture House to join Nigel to become his PA/'Girl Friday'. She served him loyally and faithfully for 35 years.

After a year Nigel bought out his partner due to differences as to how to run the business. Nigel was much more 'commercial' than his partner.

Nigel knew exactly what the rich and famous wanted—something bigger and better than the last person and they didn't care how much it cost. They wanted exquisite, bespoke clothes and one-off designs. They also liked to be wined and dined. Nigel was good at that as well. He knew a brilliant Events Organiser, Linda C and she is the best in the business. She would organise fabulous dinners and parties for Nigel's clients.

Nigel knew many influential theatre designers and film producers and won lucrative contracts over the years to design and make beautiful costumes for the theatre and film world.

Celebrities vied for Nigel's outfits. One Celebrity had his 40th birthday party in Monte Carlo, for which Nigel had designed and made the clothes and jewellery for his entire family. This Celebrity flew Nigel out to attend the party and hired the band 'Red', to play for an hour, at a cost of €1,000,000. This Celebrity with more money than sense, paid Nigel a total of over €500,000 for the dresses, outfits and jewellery. Afterwards, this Celebrity was heard to say, *"that was damn good value."*

Anyway, Bonnie was devoted to Nigel until he turned on her.

Bonnie had had a very unhappy marriage when she was young. She had divorced her husband many years before. Her elderly mother was fit and well until the year Bonnie came to see me, when she sadly had a stroke and needed a full-time carer.

Bonnie employed a carer four days a week after her mother had her stroke which left her bedridden unable to speak or move her left side. Bonnie needed to take Fridays off to look after her mother when the carer had another elderly person she looked after.

One Thursday evening Bonnie asked Nigel if she could take Fridays off from the following month to look after her bedridden mother. Fridays were normally very quiet in head office and Nigel often let the staff go home at lunchtime.

Nigel flew into a terrible rage and shouted, *"If you don't want your fucking job, you can fuck off out of here. Clear off then. There are plenty of good people out there who would love your cushy number. Damn cheek, coming in here asking to work part-time. If I <u>wanted</u> a part-time PA, I would <u>get</u> a part-time PA.*

"How do you think I built this business into what it is today? Not by working part-time that's for sure.

"If your mother needs a fucking babysitter, tell her to fucking pay for one. You're not her fucking carer or her fucking unpaid babysitter. Make your choice—her or me. Now fuck off and get out of my sight."

Bonnie burst into tears and ran out of the office and went home. She told her brother, Edward, what had happened and the abuse that Nigel had given her. Edward told her to calm down and go back to work the next day. Edward knew Nigel had a terrible temper but that he would probably forget all about it the next day. Edward told Bonnie, *"He can't function without you."* That much was true.

When she arrived at work the next day Nigel said, *"What are you doing here? You resigned last night and I accepted your resignation. I told you to choose between being an unpaid babysitter for your mother, or me. You told me you had made your choice. I've already informed the rest of the staff you resigned and you no longer work here. Now get your stuff and get out now. You are technically trespassing."*

Shocked to the core, as were the rest of the staff, Bonnie left.

Bonnie had heard of me through her best friend Gloria for whom I had acted several years before. Gloria said, *"The only person who will get the better of Nigel is 'The Rottweiler with a Handbag'. Go and see her."* She was so right.

Bonnie came to see me and told me exactly what had happened. I told her that Nigel had unfairly dismissed her, had unlawfully sexually harassed her as well and had committed *'associative disability discrimination'*. I said I would sue him for unfair dismissal, sexual harassment and associative disability discrimination, which I did.

Nigel went to one of the most aggressive Firms of litigators in London. His defence was a fairy tale. According to Nigel, Bonnie had gone into his office at the end of the Thursday in question and had said, *"This will come as a shock but after working for you for 35 glorious years I have decided to retire so I can look after my mother."*

Nigel alleged he had tried to persuade her to stay, even offering to allow her to work 4 days a week and take Fridays off, but she had said her mind was made up.

According to the fairy tale Nigel told his lawyers, Bonnie said *"I am resigning. I'm retiring from work."* Nigel claimed he had kissed her and said she would be very much missed and he didn't know how he would run his business without her. That last statement was true—he couldn't run his business without her but now he had to.

According to this 'fairy tale' Bonnie had allegedly said, *"No-one is indispensable. I will help you find someone to replace me."*

During the first few weeks after issuing proceedings I received nasty, aggressive letters from Nigel's solicitors. They threatened to apply for an Order for wasted costs against my Firm for bringing what they described as *'vexatious and abusive claims made only to extract money out of the Respondent'*.

I made it clear to these solicitors that Bonnie was an entirely honest person, who had been brutally treated after many years of loyal service. I then made a 'Without Prejudice save as to costs' offer to settle.

Bonnie had decided to try to find a part-time job but she was finding it very difficult even to get an interview. In those days prospective employers asked for the age of the applicants and Bonnie told me she had made over 100 job applications had not had even one interview in the space of six months.

My offer to settle was met with the most laughable response—that I was trying to 'blackmail' Nigel under s.21 of the Theft Act 1968.

Blackmail is a very serious criminal offence defined as demanding payment or another benefit "…with a view to gain for himself or another or with intent to cause loss to another, (a person) makes any unwarranted demand with menaces; and for this purpose a demand with menaces is unwarranted unless the person making it does so in the belief:

    a) that he has reasonable grounds for making the demand

    b) that the use of the menaces is a proper means of reinforcing the demand."

I had done no such thing. This was just a pathetic attempt to "scare" me and make the case go away. Nice try but it didn't scare me in the least. Nigel's solicitors clearly didn't know how this Rottweiler worked.

I told Bonnie that these were bully boy tactics and that I never responded well when the other side started to behave like this. I told her that she would be believed, not Nigel and he would be 'sorry' he ever started with me.

She then 'spilt the beans'. She was so incensed at his lies, that she told me about some of the skeletons in his cupboard.

Nigel had managed to get even wealthier than he should have done, by cheating the Inland Revenue of tax and VAT for years.

She told me he had two sets of books and did deals with many of his clients. He would agree with the client to issue an official bill for half the cost of the dresses, jewellery or outfits. They would be charged for and paid 'on the books'. The rest would be paid in cash with a 20% discount to the client—reducing the VAT the client would have to pay as well as reducing the income tax and Corporation tax Nigel would have to pay.

He had stashed the cash in a secret Swiss Bank Account which only he and Bonnie knew about.

The clients were very happy being charged only half of the costs, on the books, and the rest discounted in cash. The cash was of course never declared to the Revenue by Nigel. As he had told Bonnie over and over again *"everyone's happy."* Well, that was not quite true because the taxman wasn't.

Nigel had instructed Bonnie to take home both sets of books including the only copies of the 'fraudulent' paperwork, for 'safekeeping'. She had for years reluctantly done as he had ordered her to do.

She took home every month all invoices received and paid. This included the details of the tax and VAT that had been under-reported to the Inland Revenue as well as the details of what the clients actually paid in cash. She left no copies of these fraudulent transactions in the office. She also kept the only copies of his Swiss Bank Statements—again as she had been ordered to do by him. Nigel trusted Bonnie so it was not very clever of him to fall out with her.

She had complained to him over the years that she felt very uncomfortable knowing what he was doing and being involved in this deceit. He had always ignored her protests.

Two weeks before Bonnie asked for Fridays off, she had told Nigel she was not going to be involved any more in his fraudulent activities and would no longer be the keeper of his false sets of accounts or the evidence of his Swiss Bank account. She said that if he didn't stop this practice, half on the books and the rest in cash, she would report him to the taxman as she would not any longer be prepared to be complicit in his tax evasion.

She told him she was returning all of his paperwork that she had in her flat. She added she had become even more concerned about hiding Nigel's money as his second wife had started divorce proceedings. The Court had ordered full disclosure of all his assets on what is called a Statement of Means. This Order also allowed his wife's forensic accountants to come to the office and take copies of Nigel's accounts and an image of the hard drive of his computer.

Nigel had ordered Bonnie to show the accountants only the 'official' accounts i.e. the false accounts with the reduced income. She was instructed not to disclose the cash deposits including details of his Swiss Bank account, showing hundreds of thousands of Euros. He told her to hide the computer with the full accounts in her house.

Nigel ignored all of Bonnie's protests about the double accounting and cheating the Revenue and his second wife.

He batted Bonnie off on this last occasion when she protested, saying, in his very patronising way, *"Don't be so naïve Bonnie. Everyone does it. You don't get rich by declaring every penny to the taxman and you wouldn't earn what you do, nor get your lovely Christmas bonuses if I had to declare every penny. And that bitch of a wife I married won't be getting a penny more than I have to pay her if I can help it. So, go home and don't worry your pretty little head about this anymore."*

I always love it when clients tell me about the skeletons in cupboards.

I wrote back to Nigel's solicitor, Chris, telling him that new information had come to light which had just been disclosed to me by my client and that I would be amending our pleadings.

I wrote that I was preparing to add a claim for whistleblowing as Bonnie's dismissal was clearly connected with her whistleblowing. Indeed, I said I was convinced that this was the real reason that Nigel dismissed her. He had used Bonnie asking for Fridays off as the pretext to dismiss her.

Rather than putting the details of this amended claim in writing, I telephoned Chris on a Friday afternoon and told him what we intended to add to our pleadings.

I said my client had just disclosed to me that she had told Nigel two weeks before she was dismissed that she would no longer go along with his tax fraud and that if he did not self-report to the Revenue, she would inform them and his wife's divorce solicitors about his real earnings. I said we believed that this was the real reason for Nigel dismissing her.

Chris started to say that Nigel had not dismissed anyone, that Bonnie had resigned voluntarily but I shut him down very quickly.

I told Chris to drop that argument. I said that Bonnie had so far delayed sending the information she had to the Inland Revenue and to his ex-wife's accountants and lawyers, but she would be doing so the following Tuesday (three calendar days after my call). I said nothing about what settlement we wanted as that could have amounted to blackmail. One has to be so careful and sensitive in these matters.

Chris rang me back at 0900 am the following Monday and said he had instructions to settle but any settlement would have to include very strict confidentiality terms and no amendments to the pleadings. I knew what he meant.

Settlement agreements cannot prevent anyone from reporting wrongdoing to the authorities. However, Bonnie was prepared to sign the agreement, agreeing not to report Nigel if he agreed to self-report. Chris said he would..... Hm – I doubted it but there it was.

Chris also said Bonnie would be required to return all the copies of Nigel's accounts and his computers, as part of the deal. I said she had already done this.

The settlement was very generous. We also negotiated a very good reference and an agreed reason for Bonnie leaving after 35 years.

Nigel promised in the Agreement to self-report his true earnings for the past six years and to disclose to his second ex-wife's lawyers his true earnings. I was very doubtful that he would do this but it was the best we could do.

We then withdrew the tribunal claim without any amendments to our pleadings and the details of the settlement were kept strictly confidential. This was before on the ET1 Claim form it asked, as it now does, *"If your claim consists of, or includes, a claim that you are making a protected disclosure under the Employment Rights Act 1996 (otherwise known as a 'whistleblowing' claim), please tick the box if you want a copy of this form, or information from it, to be forwarded on your behalf to a relevant regulator (known as a 'prescribed person' under the relevant legislation) by tribunal staff."*

Within a month of receiving the settlement, Bonnie received an hilarious phone call from Jim, a supplier of many of Nigel's expensive fabrics and leathers. Jim asked Bonnie if Nigel was *"ill, had lost his mind or had had a personality transplant?"*

Nigel had paid his bill within days of receiving it. In the past this supplier had had to threaten to sue Nigel for payment and it would take months for Nigel to pay Jim.

Bonnie told Jim she had an idea about why Nigel was now paying his bills in a timely fashion rather than being sued but left it at that.

There were two postscripts to this story.

The first happened a year after this case settled. Barry and I attended a wedding at a luxury hotel in Central London. The bride and bridal party were wearing clothes designed and made by Nigel's Couture House. So were some of the guests. Nigel was also a guest at the wedding.

Nigel was "working the room" schmoozing with some of the guests who were clients of his or potential clients when he suddenly saw someone on my table whom he knew. He came up to talk to them and greeted them like a long-lost friend.

My back was turned towards the person sitting on my right when Nigel spotted this acquaintance, who was sitting on my left.

After a couple of minutes this acquaintance said to Nigel, *"I don't know if you know my friend Gill Howard? She's an employment lawyer known as The Rottweiler with a Handbag"* I turned round to greet a smiling and then not so smiling, in fact terrified-looking, Nigel.

I said, *"No I don't think I have had the pleasure of actually meeting you in person, Nigel. So good to meet you at last."* The irony was lost on everyone at the table except Nigel.

Nigel's face was a picture. He stared at me for a few seconds while it sunk in who I was and then he ran... So fast that he tripped over a guest's handbag (ironically one designed by him), which was lying on the floor by her chair. Nigel tripped and fell flat on his face. The ground was a good place for Nigel to end up—he probably wished the ground would swallow him up. Nigel was not seen again that night.

If that wasn't bad enough for Nigel, he had another nasty shock. It had nothing to do with Bonnie or me. It's what you call Karma. We heard about this from a friend of Bonnie's.

Around a few months after our case against Nigel settled, he received an invitation to a Dinner for the Award of Business Person of the Year. Nigel was notified that he was one of the nominees.

The London Chamber of Commerce hosted these Awards. There were around 200 guests at this particular Dinner that year.

After pre-dinner drinks and canapés the guests were ushered in for dinner. The Master of Ceremonies (MC) took the microphone and announced that all the guests had been specially invited to the Dinner but they were not guests at the Business Person of the Year Awards.

He was in fact the Chief Inland Revenue Inspector from the High Holborn Office and the other gentlemen standing around the room were Inland Revenue Inspectors. He said that each guest had been handpicked to attend this "dinner" because they had been investigated for under-reporting their income and corporation tax and PAYE and NICs for their staff.

Nigel had been under surveillance for months. Inspectors had watched clients going in and out of his premises in Mayfair in London. They entered the building with a warrant and seized his diaries and accounts, which showed the details of the clients and the clothes, handbags, shoes and jewellery that they had ordered and details of wholesale costs of the fabrics etc and the costs charged on and off the books to the clients.

They also took away a list of his staff and all the payroll details and found that some had been paid in cash *"off the books"* and some had been paid partly on the books and had been paid additional cash off the books, thus not paying the correct PAYE and national insurance contributions.

This had all happened when Nigel was in Los Angeles for several months, designing the costumes for a major film production.

The Revenue was then able to calculate what the profit margins would have been and what tax should have been reported. They used a formula to calculate what should have been declared. They estimated that Nigel had been grossly under-reporting his Income and his Corporation Tax on his tax returns and had been defrauding the Revenue for years.

They also calculated what PAYE and NICs should have been paid. As the employer is responsible for collecting PAYE and NICs and paying both the employer and employee share to the Revenue, Nigel had to pay both the employer and employees' share of the PAYE and NICs unpaid over the past 6 years.

The other 'guests' at this so-called dinner were also in the same position as Nigel. They were from different industries such as top-end catering, private cosmetic dentistry, private cosmetic surgery etc. These individuals were all under investigation for under-reporting their income.

The Chief Revenue Inspector then said, *"We will offer an amnesty from prosecution and fines and interest if you come up to the top table and we reach a deal about how much tax we will be asking you to pay."*

Nigel was almost killed in the rush.

It turned out the Revenue calculated Nigel owed them a seven figure sum going back over the past 6 years. Luckily for him they didn't go back a further six years. He was given 24 months to pay this overdue tax with no penalties or interest to pay.

His ex-wife heard about this 'Dinner' and went back to Court to reopen her divorce settlement. The Court ordered Nigel to pay considerably more to his ex-wife than he had originally paid to her. Nigel was hit with a double whammy.

Chapter 9
The Bullies' Tales

I acted for a boy who was the victim of appalling bullying and racism at an elite boys' public school. I will call this school St Stephens (not its real name).

I also acted for a boy who **was** the bully. He was a pupil at another elite boys' public school. I will call this school Broadway College (not its real name).

It was very interesting how differently both boys were treated by their respective Headmasters. The Headmaster at St Stephens eat your heart out. The Headmaster at Broadway College was brilliant.

Winston's Tale

Winston was the victim of merciless and cruel bullying at St Stephens—and not just by some of the boys. His Housemaster was also, I believe, a bully and a racist. This was over 20 years ago. I would hope things have changed at this School now.

Winston was a brilliant child. He was born in the USA. Both his parents were originally from Nigeria. They had emigrated to the USA before Winston was born. His parents were both doctors working at the John Hopkins Hospital in Baltimore, Maryland.

Winston was sent to St Stephens as a boarder at the age of 13. He was not like the other boys. He had a very high IQ of 149. Apart from his ethnicity and being a genius, he had a number of medical problems which made him different from the other boys.

He was allergic to the wool used in the School Uniform so he was exempt from wearing the regulation trousers and jacket. He was short sighted, wore thick spectacles and did not play any field Sports because he had medical conditions that made it impossible. However, he was a brilliant cox for the rowing team. The Cox does not row. They face forward, towards the bow and steer the boat and coordinate the power and rhythm of the rowers. Winston also mentored and coached the young rowers.

Two aristocratic boys, sons of Lords, Miles and Archie, were horrid bullies. They called Winston nasty names including *"Odd Ball"*; *"Four Eyes"*; *"Merchant Banker"* (cockney slang for wanker); *"Blackie"*; *"nig nog"* and *"wog."*

They made his life a misery. In Winston's first week at St Stephens, Miles and Archie had dangled him by his ankles out of the top floor window of their House and told him to *"climb back up like a monkey."* Winston was terrified out of his wits.

At age 15, after only two academic years, Winston went straight up to the Sixth Form as he had passed 13 GSCEs, all with straight A*s.

Miles and Archie continued bullying him and calling him names. They were in the same House.

His parents made a formal complaint about these two bullies. After making these complaints, Winston was not elected to be a Prefect when they went up to the Sixth Form.

Prefects were allowed to wear their own suits (not school uniform) and had special privileges others did not. They had a prefects' common room and were allowed into the town in free periods and at weekends.

Winston was not elected to be a Prefect despite having many recommendations from other teachers and votes from most of the other boys in his Form.

Unbeknownst to Winston or his parents, his Housemaster had the right of veto and had used it in Winston's case.

His parents asked his Housemaster what was the reason for their son not being elected to be a Prefect. His Housemaster refused to tell them.

His parents then appealed and the School set up an Appeals Committee made up of two Governors and chaired by a former Head Boy and now member of the House of Lords – not what you would call an independent Panel.

I attended the appeal hearing on behalf of Winston accompanied by his mother, Dorothy.

The Headmaster, Dr Small, and the Housemaster, Mr Watson, were also present at the hearing.

They were all seated as we walked in. No-one stood up or shook our hands. Dr Small did not introduce himself nor did he invite us to sit down or offer us any refreshments.

I went up to him, shook his hand and introduced Winston's mother, Dorothy and myself. Dr Small gave me a very limp handshake, still sitting down and averted his gaze. He made a very poor first impression.

I then asked if I could address the Appeal Panel with our grounds of appeal and then ask questions of Mr Watson.

I started by saying that Winston had been described by some of his teachers as:-

a) *"Popular in the House."*

b) *"Always reliable, I can always expect him to carry out his prefectorial duties effectively in the evening without prompting from me."*

c) *"It is good to see that Winston finishes in the top spot in most of his subjects."*

d) *"Enjoys the company of his peers and other boys around the House…and this has opened up a new circle of friends."*

e) *"No-one could ever accuse him of passing up the opportunities that are presented to him."*

f) *"Is an intellectually gifted student and the possessor of a fine and lively mind."*

I said Winston should have been a very strong contender to be elected as a prefect having regard to his outstanding academic record and the recommendations he had received.

I said it was baffling why, with such an outstanding academic record and such glowing recommendations, Winston had failed to impress his Housemaster, Mr Watson, who had the final veto on who should be a Prefect. We were still none the wiser after the Appeal Hearing.

I knew that the criteria for being elected a Prefect included the total number of distinctions; absence of any disciplinary record and "exceptionally distinguished academic record."

I argued that the Panel must accept that Winston's academic record was exceptional. He had been attending tutorials at a University near the School, for his Science 'A' levels because his teachers at St Stephens could not teach him any more. Winston knew more than they did. He had also given a brilliant lecture to the Archaeology Society.

His Form Master had also observed that whilst *"some of his peers shirked their form duties, Winston was punctilious about them."* This should have impressed those determining his suitability for Prefect.

Mr Watson had written a number of offensive statements about Winston. He seemed oblivious to the insulting and racist content of his letter. He had written that Winston *"came from a very different background from that of many of the other boys"* and he was *"unpopular and isolated from the other boys."*

The latter statement was completely untrue. No evidence was ever produced to substantiate this slur.

When I pointed out that the first reference was racist, Mr Watson interrupted me and told me that the reference to Winston's *"very different background"* was to his *"previous schooling in America"* and had *"nothing to do with his race."*

I told the Panel that this comment had quite clearly nothing to do with his previous Schooling. The ordinary, natural meaning of Mr Watson's words was quite clear. It was a reference to his racial and ethnic background and social class as he was born of modest Nigerian parents and had been brought up in America.

I said that if reference been made to the *"very different background"* of Princes William and Harry, this would not have been referring to their previous Prep School but rather to their parentage and social class.

I suggested that an American-born boy of Nigerian parents was rare at St Stephens and that Mr Watson was drawing the distinction between the white, English aristocrats, the English elite from the privileged classes, from which many of the boys came, and a black, American boy who had come from more humble parentage.

Equally, when Mr Watson made reference to Winston as *"a flatfooted American"*, I said that it was not made in any proper contextual sense as Mr Watson, ex post facto, sought to explain.

He said it was merely a factual description about Winston's lack of sporting ability. He said it was a statement that he would make about any boy.

I said that was not true. I said it was clearly written in a derogatory sense and was in no way an attempt to distinguish his sporting achievements. There was no need to refer to Winston as 'a flatfooted American'. I said using 'flatfooted' as an adjective to describe him was wholly inappropriate. His flat feet were not relevant in distinguishing what he could and could not achieve on the Sports field.

Nor was there any need to refer to him as an '*American*' distinguishing him from the English boys.

If there was any need to distinguish Winston's sporting achievements, then all that needed to be said was that whilst he was unable to participate in field sports, he excelled at coxing the rowing team and at coaching and mentoring rowing for the younger boys.

In any event I said that this reference to his health conditions was a breach of medical confidentiality. I said that it was noticeable that no-one had the good grace to accept this and to apologise for the distress that this had caused.

I said I did not believe that any other recommendations written by Mr Watson discussed the boys' medical conditions.

I asked him to show us any other recommendations, redacted to conceal the boys' identities, written by Mr Watson, where he had made references to **their** medical conditions. He refused to do so. I thought "guilty as charged".

I argued he had made these derogatory remarks in an attempt to demean and diminish Winston's achievements, based on his race, colour and ethnic background. I argued that Mr Watson had written comments which could be regarded as racist. At the very least I said that it was unfortunate wording and that he needed to explain his use of this wording. It seemed to me to be inexplicable and indefensible in the circumstances.

Furthermore, I said that we inferred from comments made by two members of the Appeal Panel that they were unaware of the evidence that Winston's mother. Dorothy, had discovered.

It had been reported to her that Miles and Archie had overpowered another new boy and had used duct tape to cover the boy's eyes, ears and mouth and had bound his hands behind his back. They had left him in a locked cupboard for over an hour. It must have been a terrifying experience for this new boy.

Miles and Archie had not just been rehabilitated but had been rewarded with two of the highest offices in their House, that of House Captain and Games Captain.

I said that for Mr Watson to say that these two bullies *"were appropriate role models for the younger boys"* was nothing less than farcical.

I said he was being thoroughly disingenuous when he suggested that he had asked Winston and other younger boys in the House whether they 'objected' to Miles and Archie being elected to positions of House and Games Captain.

Even if this were true, which I doubted, Winston and the younger boys would hardly have felt confident enough to say *"Yes I object"* when Mr Watson asked them such a question.

He had appointed two nasty bullies as House Captain and Captain of Games. Their conduct, I said, was reprehensible and at the very least their rehabilitation should have been demonstrated over a substantial period of time, before any honours were heaped upon them.

I added that even if it were demonstrated that they had corrected their behaviour and that it was one-off conduct on their part, which it wasn't, to reward their behaviour so quickly after the bullying complaints from Winston's parents, by making them House Captain and Captain of Games, beggared belief.

Given that Miles and Archie had bullied other boys, as well as Winston, and had been seen to be quickly rewarded with high and prestigious office, I said that it was little wonder that those perpetrators felt comfortable continuing to bully the boys. They were clearly no role models to any of the other boys in the House.

I said that refusing to accept the recommendations in favour of Winston being made a Prefect, by an existing Prefect and the rowing coach, because they did not use the correct form, should *never* have been used as the reason for not taking their recommendations into account.

I also said I was appalled at the conduct of some of the current Prefects. They had posted photographs of themselves on Facebook, wearing their school hats and school uniform "for a joke", drinking in the local town. They were very easily identifiable.

The excuses put forward by their Housemaster for this behaviour were a) it may not have been on a school night, (in spite of many of the photos having the occasion listed as the first meeting of the Prefects that Academic Year, on a school night); b) it may have been someone over 18 who had bought the under-18 year olds drinks; or c) perhaps they were eating as well as drinking.

I said it was not worthy of their Housemaster to make up such ludicrous explanations.

Someone aged 16 or 17, accompanied by an adult, can drink, but not buy, beer, wine or cider with a meal at a licensed premises (except in Northern

Ireland). These boys were drinking vodka shots and were photographed drinking from bottles of red wine.

The Housemaster should have said on the face of those photographs, it was clear that many of these Prefects who were under-age, were drinking, and that this was worthy of investigation. He should have said that action would be taken as this was illegal, under-age drinking - hardly behaviour worthy of being prefects.

I argued that the Appeal Panel should pay regard to the description of Winston as 'exceptional' and he should be allowed to become a Prefect.

It may not surprise you to know that our appeal failed.

The Headmaster also denied that there was any bullying at his School. He said they had recently done an anonymous survey on bullying and 98% of the boys who had answered said they had never seen or been the subject of bullying.

Well I wanted to know about the 2% who said there was bullying going on.

I replied that most of the boys were probably afraid that there was some identifying number or feature on the so-called anonymised form that could identify them so they were probably too frightened to answer honestly.

Winston got so fed up with the elitist and racist culture at the School, he left midway through his 'A' level year and went back to the USA to finish his studies there.

The Bully's Tale

In contrast to Winston's case, I was asked to act for a bully, Conor, who went to Broadway College (not its real name). The attitude and conduct of the then Headmaster, Bernard Levitt (not his real name), could not have been more different from that of the Headmaster at St Stephen's.

Mr Levitt is an impressive man, over 6 foot tall, handsome and very charming.

When we met, he was wearing red braces, an expensive, white, handmade shirt, silk tie and beautiful Saville Row suit. He really looked the part.

He greeted me at the door with a delightful smile and the words, *"Ah, the Rottweiler with a handbag. Delighted to meet you."*

He had obviously looked me up on my website. He had done his homework. He ushered me into his Study and offered me a seat and a cup of tea.

"What are we going to do with this boy then?" he asked me.

Conor's parents were American, both with high flying jobs. His father was a banker and his mother, a consultant in paediatrics, working in a major Teaching Hospital. From my dealings with Conor's father I reckoned he had bullied Conor.

Conor was the leader of a gang of boys who had regularly terrorised the new boys. Conor and his gang had done some terrible things to several new boys that year, in what Conor had described as an "initiation ceremony."

One new boy had told his parents after the first (Michaelmas) term that he would not return to school after the Christmas holidays.

After much persuasion he told his parents that in their first week at School, he and several other new boys had been stripped naked by Conor and his gang. These bullies then stuck the hose of a hoover between their buttocks and up into their rectum.

They were badly hurt and bleeding but they were told by Conor if they reported their injuries to anyone, much worse would happen to them. In any event Conor told them they wouldn't be believed and he and his friends would deny everything.

I admitted that this conduct was very shocking and understood that Conor could not remain at the School nor go unpunished but I said this was his GCSE year and if he was expelled before he was able to take his GCSEs it would harm his future career.

Mr Levitt offered a solution. Conor would not be permitted to return to his House. He would be moved to a special Boarding House reserved for boys with behavioural issues or learning difficulties. He would not be allowed to do any lessons or revision classes with the rest of his class nor eat his meals nor do his Prep with the other boys.

His behaviour would be closely monitored and if stepped out of line even once, he would face expulsion.

He would receive one to one teaching and revision lessons from his teachers and would take all his meals at the new House and do his Prep there, on his own, supervised by a teacher. He would be allowed to take his GCSE examinations and would then be asked to leave the School voluntarily without expulsion on his record.

His mother had sourced another School in the USA to which he could be moved after his examinations had finished. This was an ideal solution.

I accepted this kind offer on behalf of Conor's parents and thanked Mr Levitt for his compassion and humanity.

Mr Levitt has since left Broadway College to go to a prestigious role elsewhere in the education field in the UK. That School lost a brilliant Headmaster.

Chapter 10
Colin's Tale

Men in positions of power, who should know better, can sometimes be tempted into sexual relationships with more junior, colleagues and then things can go very badly wrong.

Occasionally, and in rare cases in my experience, the junior colleague has ulterior or selfish motives. They may wish to manipulate the more senior colleague to their own advantage or at least try to and sometimes that can lead to blackmail or false allegations of rape or sexual harassment.

'Pillow talk', preventing breaches of confidential information, risk of potential blackmail, false allegations of sexual harassment or even rape, seeking unwarranted advancement or more money, are some of the reasons why some employers in the UK ban or restrict consensual relationships at work.

Even where the relationships start as consensual, they can easily 'morph' into something more sinister - into allegations of sexual harassment or worse, rape —as Colin was to find out to his cost.

Statistics show that more than 50% of couples meet their partners at work and that is not surprising. More than 50% of the waking time is spent at work and many friendships are made at work so it is not surprising that many employees meet their partners at work.

But some employers put in safeguards. In schools, Colleges of Further Education and Universities, relationships between teacher and pupil are strictly forbidden even if the student is over the age of 16. Of course any sexual or improper relationship with a child under the age of 16 is a criminal offence.

Many employers require the couple to report their relationship and if one party is managing the other or they are working together, one or other is often required to move out of the same department to a different department or division or even to a different location.

I am always happy to act for anyone who has been falsely accused of sexual harassment or any other form of sexual misconduct if they have been victims themselves. I will fight for the underdog.

Colin was one of them. This happened to him 17 years ago but it is one of the stand out cases for me as an example of where things went very badly wrong – for the man. This case was not however about a younger woman who took advantage of the older man. Colin was a man in his early fifties and the other person concerned was a younger man.

Colin had been newly-appointed as the Chief Executive of one of the largest global sportswear Companies. It had a London office, a large factory in the North of England and a headquarters in Chicago, USA. He had worked for this Company for 24 years and was a member of the Europe-wide Board of Directors.

Colin was gay but had not 'come out' at work. He had always kept his sexuality secret. He had a long term (male) partner and had never been unfaithful to him during their twenty years together until disaster struck for Colin.

Samuel (Sam) was a much younger, junior colleague, who was also gay and who had been quite public about his sexuality. Colin had noticed Sam as he was a very attractive young man who was openly flirtatious. Apart from saying 'Hello' when Colin saw Sam in the office, they had had nothing to do with each other until one fateful day.

On that day Sam had come in to Colin's office in tears, complaining that he had been constantly overlooked for promotion by his boss, had just received a wholly unmerited poor appraisal, with the lowest rating possible and had not been awarded any salary increase or bonus for the past three years.

He complained to Colin that his boss warned him that the next stage would be his dismissal for unacceptably poor performance. He said his boss knew he was gay and his boss was openly homophobic.

Sam must have guessed at Colin's sexuality and that was why Sam went to confide in him.

Sam said that his boss had said a few unpleasant things about gay men within his earshot, including, *'gay relationships are not natural'; 'I wouldn't want a gay man working for me'; 'I wouldn't want a son of mine turning out to be gay'.*

Sam asked Colin if he could help him and asked him if he would meet him for a drink that evening, after work, to discuss his concerns. He told Colin he greatly admired him and believed that he understood his 'issues', unlike HR.

He said he had had an informal chat with the HR Director who dismissed his concerns with the words, *"You are talking nonsense. I would be careful what you say about your boss. It's slander and he will not hesitate to sue you if you make those allegations about him again."*

Colin should have directed him straight back to HR to make a formal grievance. He could have even suggested that Sam made covert recordings of his boss making homophobic remarks to prove the allegations but instead Colin fell hook, line and sinker for Sam's 'sob story' and flattery and agreed to meet him for a drink after work.

This Company had rules about consensual relationships at work. Anyone working in a senior management position (above that of team leader) had to report any consensual relationship with another member of staff to the HR Director or in Colin's case to the Board and the Chairman to whom he reported.

Directors were prohibited from any consensual relationship, unless one or other of them either moved to another office or left the Company.

This prohibition included socialising outside work with any work colleague, save at an official company function unless sanctioned by the Board.

The reason for this was because senior managers and Directors held highly confidential information about staff including salaries and future bonuses, career plans, disciplinary and grievance cases, trade secrets such as future products and services, client lists and potentially new clients, five year plans, budgets, gross income and profit margins etc.

Colin and Sam had a drink and then a meal that evening at an expensive restaurant in a swish hotel on the Thames, which Colin paid for. He then offered Sam a lift home in his car. Sam accepted the lift and asked Colin up to his flat for a nightcap. Colin readily agreed.

Colin described to me what happened when they got up to Sam's flat. They had several more gins and tonics and Sam put on some pornographic gay videos. While they were watching these videos Sam started kissing Colin passionately on the lips and started fondling him until Colin was fully aroused. Sam then led Colin into his bedroom and undressed him and gave him a blow job.

Sam then handed Colin a condom and they had sex three times that night. Colin went to Sam's flat on two more occasions over the next couple of weeks when they repeated what had happened on that first night.

Sam then asked Colin to organise a promotion and a pay rise for him. Colin told Sam he could not help him get promotion or a pay rise, that he would have to make a formal complaint about his boss to HR and appeal his appraisal rating. Sam then made his move.

He told Colin that he had secretly video-recorded their love-making and he wanted £5000 and a pay rise and a promotion, otherwise he would sell his story and the videos to a Sunday tabloid newspaper and inform the Chairman and the Board that Colin had raped him and Colin would be ruined.

Colin refused to be blackmailed so Sam put in a formal grievance to the HR Director, that Colin had sexually assaulted and raped him in Colin's office.

Sam alleged that Colin had promised he would get him a pay rise and promotion if he agreed to have sex with him. Sam said that in the office, after work one evening, when he refused to have sex with Colin, Colin had overpowered him and forced himself on Sam and had raped him.

Sam said he had been powerless to stop Colin who was 6 foot 3 inches tall and was very strong. Sam was a much smaller, much slimmer, young man.

Luckily for Colin he had texted Sam after their first night of passion at his flat, saying, *"that was unexpected. Hope to find myself in your bed again soon (with an explicit emoji)"* Sam had texted back with an emoji of a smiling face.

Sam's allegations were not believed by the HR Director so Sam then reported the alleged rape to the police.

Colin was then arrested. He and I attended his interview with the Chief Constable of a major Police Force, who led the investigation.

There was a two-way mirror, with other officers watching and listening to the interview and it was recorded. It was held under the Police and Criminal Evidence Act 1984 (PACE).

Colin was first given the police caution, *"You do not have to say anything but it may harm your defence if you do not mention when questioned something which you later rely on in court. Anything you do say may be given in evidence."*

He was told they were investigating an allegation of male rape (they referred to it as sodomy) and that if he was charged and found guilty, he would receive a lengthy prison sentence and would go on the Sex Offenders' Register, probably for life.

I advised him to co-operate with the investigation and to tell the truth to the police and not to say, *"No comment."* It was all very scary.

Colin followed my advice and told the police what had happened – that he and Sam had had consensual sex on three occasions in Sam's flat. Unbeknownst to Colin, Sam had secretly filmed their consensual love-making and had then attempted to blackmail him, demanding £5000 from Colin and favours at work, to keep quiet. When Colin refused to be blackmailed, Sam made this false report to the police that he had been raped in the office.

Colin's 'grilling' lasted over four hours.

The Police then spent the next six months investigating Sam's allegations. His lies of being raped at the office were exposed by Colin's phone records and the swipe cards used to get in and out of the office.

The police tracked Colin's mobile phone using triangulation. It was tracked to a mast near to Sam's flat on the date and time he alleged he had been raped in the office. The swipe cards showed that Sam had left at the normal time of 5.30pm on the night he had alleged rape in the office and Colin had left even earlier than Sam to go to a dental appointment.

Sam always maintained that he had never invited Colin back to his flat and he had never agreed to have sex with him.

Colin was also able to show by the text he had sent Sam after their first sexual encounter that he had been at Sam's flat when they had had consensual sex. Sam was never able to explain his smiling emoji response to Colin's text after their first night of sex '*in your bed*'.

The examination of the data from the phone mast near to Sam's flat confirmed Colin's account that he had been to that flat on three different occasions on the evenings that he had always claimed.

After six months the Crown Prosecution Service (CPS) concluded there was insufficient evidence to charge Colin and the matter was "NFA'd"—No Further Action taken.

After Sam's grievance had been dismissed by the HR Director, Sam resigned with no notice and brought a claim in the Tribunal, for constructive dismissal and sexual harassment against the Company and sexual harassment against Colin.

Colin had to have separate legal representation (me), because the Company pleaded their statutory defence as an alternative defence, that it had taken all reasonable steps to prevent the act of harassment taking place – if it did take place, which was denied.

This was an appropriate case for a Restricted Reporting Order (RRO) because it involved allegations of sexual misconduct. The name of the Company and the names of Colin and Sam were made the subject of the RRO. The Press would have no story during the trial itself because they were unable to name the parties.

However because the RRO is posted on the door of the tribunal, the Press buzzed round that tribunal like bees round a honey pot. Allegations of male rape by a Chief Executive of a well-known Global Company were a rare, juicy news story.

The Press and TV and radio reporters turned up on the first day of the hearing in droves and took copies of Sam's witness statement.

He had made all sorts of outlandish and false claims to try to bolster his tribunal case. For example, he alleged that Colin had bought him his favourite aftershave, as a present, because Colin had allegedly said, he *"wanted to smell Sam coming down the corridors."* This was untrue.

Sam had in fact asked Colin to buy this particular aftershave for him when Colin went through duty free on his holiday abroad. Sam said he would pay Colin for it, which he did with three £20 notes.

Luckily Colin had kept Sam's text message asking him to buy the aftershave in duty free, giving the name of the aftershave and the price and his offer to pay for it.

This was not a sensible thing for Colin to do but he wasn't thinking straight nor had he any idea what Sam would make up if Colin didn't get him the promotion and pay rise he wanted or pay him his blackmail money.

After Sam had given evidence on the first day of the Tribunal and despite it being a tissue of lies, the Company halted the proceedings and made Sam an offer to settle, a payment of his notice pay only. He agreed and withdrew his Tribunal claim.

Nevertheless the newspapers reported (mentioning no names) the graphic details of the alleged rape with the headlines *"Chief Executive sodomised me claims junior male. I was forced to leave the job I loved."* The reports concluded that after one day of a three week tribunal the Company halted the case and paid a 'substantial' settlement to the unnamed Claimant.

There were no names given in the newspapers because of the RRO but Colin and the senior executives of his Company knew who the Press were talking about.

Although neither the police investigating the alleged rape nor the Company believed Sam's allegations and Colin was not prosecuted, his reputation was shot to pieces. He had breached the Company's consensual relations policy and had potentially brought the Company into disrepute. He was told to resign, which he reluctantly did.

I negotiated a fair settlement for Colin. He was allowed to keep his shares, as a 'good leaver' but he had to leave the job that he loved—his reputation in tatters. After 24 years' service he left without a farewell party or a thank you for his loyal service with just the standard reference with his employment dates and job title. At least he kept his pension.

He told his partner what had happened and he forgave him.

Luckily for Colin he was offered the role of Chief Executive Officer of a worldwide Charity, through a very good head-hunter, just one month after resigning. He has been gainfully employed ever since. As far as I know he has never done anything like that again. As the saying goes 'Once bitten, twice shy'.

Here was a classic case of why policies restricting or banning consensual relationships at work are there to protect both parties involved. If things turn sour there can be serious consequences for both parties – and not just a broken heart.

Chapter 11
David's Tale

David was the Marketing Director of a global retail Company. I describe him as a *"Walter Mitty"* character, with delusions of grandeur and a criminal mind - but actually he was just a common thief.

David managed to embezzle over £1,000,000 from his employer over a period of three years until he was caught. He spent some of his ill-gotten gains on expensive cars, designer watches, gambling, expensive dinners, lavish holidays and 'Miss Whiplash'. The rest, as the saying goes, he just frittered away.

Lindi St Claire or 'Miss Whiplash' as she was more commonly known, was in those days possibly the most famous prostitute/dominatrix to the rich and famous. She worked from the mid-1970s until her bankruptcy in 1992 when the Inland Revenue prosecuted her for tax evasion.

She was a voluminous woman, who wore rubber and leather outfits and was into sadomasochism, including whips and torture on her willing clients. She described herself as an *'extrovert nymphomaniac who loves her work'*. David had been one of her regulars for over two years. She wasn't cheap—she charged several hundreds of pounds per session.

David was eventually caught embezzling the Company because he got careless and underestimated a canny lady.

He was going on holiday. His secretary had resigned and had left, so a temp was employed. He told this temp that if any correspondence addressed to him personally came for him while he was away, she was not to open it or to give it to anyone else. She was to put it in a large brown envelope and leave all this correspondence unopened in his desk drawer.

She didn't think that sounded right and became suspicious so she reported this instruction to the Managing Director. He gave instructions that all correspondence addressed to David was to go straight to him.

When David's letters were opened, several of the envelopes contained large amounts of cash, with cryptic notes saying similar things, *"Here's your share. Just let me know when you want me to do another 'marketing report' again."*

I was asked to investigate who these people were and why they were sending large amounts of cash to David in registered envelopes, to his office, and what these cryptic notes meant.

I started my investigation by going through all the marketing reports in David's office, over the past three years.

I found that they were all false, with cover sheets purporting to be a marketing report. Inside, they were telephone directories, Yellow Pages, A-Z road maps and other publications. They were certainly not marketing reports.

I went to one of the addresses that appeared on the front of one of these reports. It was a disused garage in Willesden. The man whose name was on the envelope was traced from a cheque made out to him in an amount less than £50,000. The cheque had been signed by David. David had been the sole signatory on cheques under £50,000.

The recipient of the cheque had then banked it and had withdrawn the amount on the cheque in cash and after deducting his 10% cut, had sent the rest of the cash to David, while David was away on holiday.

I discovered the author of another fake Report, who had also been sent a cheque for a fake marketing report. He was a farmer named Giles, living in Kent.

I went to Giles's farm and asked him how he knew David and why he was sent a cheque for a 'report' which was in fact an A to Z road map of Great Britain with a false front cover.

I told Giles he could be charged with the criminal offence of conspiracy and aiding and abetting but I offered him a deal. If he told me what was going on, we would not press charges against him. I said part of the deal was that he would have to agree to be a prosecution witness and a witness for the Company in any civil claim for restitution.

He quickly confessed. He told me he was an old schoolfriend of David's and he had allowed his name to go on fake marketing reports which were to be sent direct to David. David had told him to bill the Company and send the invoice direct to him.

David would then send Giles a cheque for the amount invoiced (always under £50,000) and Giles would bank it and take out the cash. He would keep 10% for himself and send the rest of the money in a registered envelope to David, at the office, marked '*Private and Confidential. To be opened by Addressee Only*'.

Giles said he had been doing this off and on for the past three years and said that other friends of David's had been doing the same thing. David had told them they wouldn't get caught.

I asked Giles to give me the names and addresses of those friends whom he knew had been doing the same as him.

Because David had been a sole signatory on cheques below the value of £50,000 no-one at the Company had known or suspected anything.

Forensic accountants were called in to trace the money that David had stolen over the past three years. It amounted to over £1,000,000.

The police were then called and when David arrived back from holiday he was arrested at the office and charged with theft and fraud. He was remanded in custody. Bail was refused as he was deemed to be a flight risk.

He was found guilty at his criminal trial at the Old Bailey and was sentenced to the maximum term of ten years in prison.

Counsel for my client had already applied in the civil courts for a Mareva Injunction to freeze his assets. Only a small amount in cash was ever recovered in various bank accounts belonging to David and his wife. Whatever assets were found, were sold. This included a Porsche and a new Range Rover and a number of expensive designer watches.

When David found out that his collection of cars had been sold, he seemed more upset about that than being sent to prison.

The case hit the headlines in the very popular News of the World. There was a huge spread on its front and inside pages. It was still in existence at the time.

It was the only time I ever featured on the front page of the News of the World.

There was a photograph of Miss Whiplash and David. The article reported that, "*Marketing Director spends over £100,000 of the Company's cash on Miss Whiplash.*"

The paper reported on the civil case to recover whatever assets David had. They also reported his criminal trial at the Old Bailey when he had been sent down for ten years.

My name was in the newspaper as I was part of the legal team in the civil case to get restitution of the Company's money and in his hopeless unfair dismissal claim.

On the Sunday morning that these photographs and the report appeared, several judges and barristers rang me to tell me they had just read about 'my case' in the News of the World.

When I asked what were they doing buying the News of the World, none of them apparently had – no, not one of them.

One Judge had '*found the newspaper on the train*'. One QC had been '*shown the story by his neighbour*'. Another QC had '*read the headlines in his local newsagent*'. A solicitor had '*seen the newspaper on a table in the pub that morning*'... Funny that...

The excuses were numerous. Amazing—apparently no-one actually bought the News of the World.

Chapter 12
Derek's Tale

Stealing from your employer is never a clever thing to do but stealing tobacco at the docks bound for the bonded warehouse was very foolish, as Derek was to find out to his cost.

Derek worked as a 'lasher' down at the Docks. A 'lasher' is responsible for securing and releasing the equipment on board a ship that secures containers for safe transportation.

Derek's employer is a Company that loaded and unloaded container ships that docked at the port.

Derek and his accomplice were caught stealing crates of cigarettes from containers which had been left unloaded at the dockside, apparently abandoned. They should have been sent straight to the bonded warehouse.

Derek's employer had had thefts from containers from time to time. Alcohol and tobacco products, which were due to be sent to the bonded warehouses, were the most frequent target of such thefts. The men would unload the containers onto the dockside before moving them to the bonded warehouse and sometimes the containers would be broken into and some of the contents stolen.

As alcohol and tobacco products were high worth, taxed goods, they were the targets of thieves and there was very tight security around the dockside.

There were CCTV cameras scanning the docks and the yard and security guards on duty 24 hours. Every employee had to show their ID security pass and sign in and out when they came on duty and when leaving the site. There were spot checks of vehicles leaving the site and personal searches of the men when leaving the docks.

The police and customs officers would also make spot checks on the Docks, particularly when there had been a tip off that contraband or drugs were being smuggled out of the docks.

Around midnight one night a white van was spotted on the dockside. Derek was in the driver's seat. He had another member of staff in the passenger seat.

They were both caught on CCTV getting out of the van and opening the door of a container that had been left on the dockside, unlocked.

The cameras recorded them stuffing Gauloises cigarettes from the container into the back of their van. Neither Derek nor his companion were on duty at the time.

They had managed to drive in when the security barrier was temporarily raised and the Security Guard had popped into his office to make himself a cup of tea. It was known he did this at a particular time most nights.

Derek and his passenger were stopped at the security gates trying to leave as the gates closed just missing the bonnet of their van. The van was searched and the boxes of Gauloises cigarettes were found.

Both men refused to say anything when questioned by the security officer as to why the cigarettes were in their van or what they were doing on site when they were not on duty. The police were called and the men were arrested and subsequently charged with theft.

An internal investigation took place and four other men who had unloaded the container from the ship and had left it on the dockside unattended and unlocked that evening, were also the subject of gross misconduct hearings.

Along with Derek and his co-conspirator, all six men were summarily dismissed, on my advice, for theft and/or aiding and abetting the theft, conspiracy to steal and breaching company rules concerning the unloading and storage of bonded goods. I was instructed by Derek's employer to advise them.

The evidence against Derek and his colleagues was overwhelming. Derek and his colleague were seen on the CCTV footage loading the cigarettes from the container into the back of the van.

Derek argued at his disciplinary hearing that he had no idea what he was loading into the van. He said all he had been asked to do was to drive a van that night at midnight and *"load some stuff into the van for some mates."*

The problem for Derek was that the word *"Gauloises"* was printed on the boxes of cigarettes and the outside of the crates. We could see on the CCTV that Derek was actually looking at the crates as he carried them into the van. He took 30 packs of cigarettes out of one of these crates for himself. He was seen stuffing them into his rucksack that he had brought with him.

After we received his claim for unfair dismissal, I wrote to him explaining that he had a hopeless case, that a perfectly fair procedure had been followed and that he had committed gross misconduct which justified his summary dismissal. His union refused to act for him at his internal appeal or for his Tribunal claim.

I explained to Derek that a tribunal would inevitably find his dismissal to be fair and that if he did not withdraw his claim, we would seek all our legal costs incurred in defending the case. I explained that could be a significant sum of money because we would instruct an expensive barrister.

My letter to Derek read:

By courier and recorded delivery and first-class post
      Without Prejudice save as to costs and subject to contract

Dear Derek
RE: YOUR TRIBUNAL CLAIM, CASE NO: XXXXX

I am acting for your former employer, in the above Tribunal claim, in which you are alleging that your dismissal was unfair. I note you are not legally represented nor is your union representing you.

I must therefore advise you to take urgent independent legal advice.

Your local Citizens' Advice is less than 2 miles from your home. The address and telephone number are ADDRESS AND PHONE NUMBER

There is also the Free Representation Unit (FRU) which can be contacted at the address written here - FRU ADDRESS AND PHONE NUMBER

I must advise you that in our view your case is hopeless and is bound to fail with little or no prospect of success.

Your failure to withdraw your claim voluntarily, as this letter invites you to do, will lead to an application by us to strike out your claim and/or a deposit order as your case lacks any chance of success and is entirely without merit. A costs application will be made against you if this case goes to trial and you lose.

You were seen clearly on CCTV driving a white van and stealing cigarettes from the dockside. The footage shows you taking these cigarettes from the container and packing them into your van.

You and a colleague had driven onto the dockside at midnight on ..... Date. You were not on duty at the time and you did not have permission to be on site with or without the van.

You had not signed in nor had you notified anyone that you were coming to the Docks. In fact, you "snuck" into the docks when the barrier was left open and unattended for a few minutes.

The cigarettes that you were seen stealing had been unloaded from the ship and were bound for the bonded Warehouses. They had been left unattended by your four of your colleagues who were also dismissed.

Your explanation that you were just loading the van for a friend and had no idea what you were loading is not credible.

The word "Gauloises" was clearly marked on the outside of the boxes. You were seen taking 30 packs of Gauloises and stuffing them into a rucksack that you had brought with you.

Your rucksack was found in the back of the van stuffed full of these cigarettes. 500 packs of cigarettes were found neatly stacked at the back of the van that you had placed there.

You were suspended with the colleague who was with you in the van. The others who were involved in this theft with you were also suspended. All six of you went through the full disciplinary procedure with your union representing you. You were all dismissed after lengthy disciplinary hearings.

You were the only person who appealed your dismissal and your appeal failed. You are the only one to bring an unfair dismissal claim. Your union has refused to represent you.

Bringing such a hopeless claim is a shocking waste of taxpayers' money and that of your employer, especially with all the evidence of your wrongdoing that my client has.

The legal test for determining whether a dismissal is fair in law is the BHS v Burchell test and your employer will be able to show they satisfy that test.

They will show that they had a genuine and honest belief in the reason for your dismissal; that they had reasonable grounds to sustain that belief and that they carried out as thorough an investigation into the matter as was reasonable in all the circumstances of the case.

The tribunal also asks itself this question, *"Did your employer's decision to summarily dismiss you fall within the band of reasonable responses that any reasonable employer could have adopted?"*

Stealing in most, if not all, workplaces is regarded as gross misconduct and gives an employer grounds for summary dismissal. Stealing bonded goods is particularly reprehensible and extremely serious and lying about it afterwards has compounded your offence.

You know that the colleague who was with you in the van and the other four men involved in this theft have all admitted their guilt and have implicated you. They have all stated that you were in on this theft and stole some cigarettes for yourself.

In these circumstances I am giving you the opportunity to withdraw your claim within the next 7 days with no Order as to costs.

I repeat I urge you to take independent legal advice on the contents of this letter.

If you fail to withdraw your claim and if our application for a strike out is successful, or if this goes to trial and you lose, we will seek all our costs against you. That could amount to over £20,000.

I trust you will take some urgent legal advice and will revert to me with your decision by ... Date.

Yours sincerely
Gillian S Howard

Derek promptly wrote back to me and withdrew his case. He thanked me for not seeking our legal costs to date.

All six men were prosecuted and all pleaded guilty at a very late stage. The Judge at the Crown Court in Southampton gave the men short shrift. He said their crimes were a shocking breach of trust. The cigarettes on the open market were worth nearly £500,000.

The Judge held there were no mitigating circumstances and gave the men no credit for their late guilty pleas. He said a lengthy prison sentence would hopefully deter others who might be minded to do what they had done. They were all sent to prison for 18 months and each fined £5000.

Chapter 13
Dirty Den's Tale

Dennis or 'Dirty Den' (as I called him to myself) was once the very respectable Director of Housing at a major Council in the North of England. He had 24 years' service in Local Government.

Dennis used to instruct me regularly to advise him on employment law issues—of which he had many and several very serious ones.

All sorts of scams had taken place over the years in the Housing Department including staff putting in false claims for housing benefits for homeless families who did not exist and stealing the benefits for themselves. Over 20 members of staff were found to be involved in that racket. They were all dismissed and several went to prison.

So nothing should have shocked me but this did.

One evening Dennis's wife rang me very distressed to tell me that her husband was in serious trouble. That afternoon he had been suspended from work for alleged gross misconduct.

When I enquired exactly what he was alleged to have done, his wife said Dennis would tell me himself.

He came to the phone and said he had been accused of allowing a friend to 'rent' the Council Chamber during the evenings and weekends. He told me that he had been unaware at the time the friend had asked him, what the Council Chamber was going to be used for.

I asked Dennis to come to my office so I could take proper instructions. When he arrived he looked a shadow of his former self.

He told me he had first met Tony, the friend involved, when their sons joined the same preparatory school. Dennis didn't know at the time that Tony was head of the so-called 'local Mafia'.

Tony was a particularly nasty man, dealing drugs, pimping prostitutes and masterminding an extortion racket on local shopkeepers and traders. He was also suspected of organising several murders of members of rival gangs and Asian shopkeepers who refused to pay him protection money.

Dennis initially knew nothing of Tony's reputation or about his criminal activities. Dennis and his family had been invited several times to stay with Tony during the school holidays in his villa in Crete.

Dennis told me that he unfortunately had a gambling addiction and had got into considerable debt with the local casinos. He said he was being threatened if he didn't repay his debts, his wife and children would receive a visit at their home to 'persuade' him to pay up. Dennis owed over £500,000 and had no way to repay these gambling debts.

Dennis asked Tony if he could help him. Tony suggested that if he could 'rent' the Council Chamber 'out of hours', no questions asked—Dennis could then earn enough money to pay off his gambling debts. Tony said he would pay Dennis a percentage of the profits from the activities taking place in the Council Chamber.

When Dennis asked how the profits would be made, Tony told him from the 'adult' videos. He apparently assured Dennis that the adult videos were soft porn and not that bad.

Dennis only found out later that they were the worst kind of hard core porn videos, using animals and children and one was actually a "snuff" video.

Tony sold these videos at a vast profit in strip clubs and sex shops all over the UK and abroad. This was before the internet and online sales.

On the basis of Tony's false promises about the nature of these films and Dennis's desperation to pay off his gambling debts, he agreed to Tony's 'offer'.

Under-age girls and boys, animals and porn stars would come and go in and out of the Council Chamber, late at night and at weekends, making hard core porn videos and worse.

Several senior members of staff and Councillors found out about this 'enterprise' and used to come to watch the pornographic recordings and buy copies. Dennis's secretary, Marilyn, even starred in a couple of the porn films.

It was a cleaner who had blown the whistle. She had come into the Council Chamber, unexpectedly, late one evening when the filming was in full swing and had nearly fainted with horror. She reported what she had seen the next morning to the HR Director. Unfortunately for Dennis the cleaner recognised him, so she reported she had seen him at the filming. He was immediately suspended pending an investigation.

Dennis asked me to act for him at his gross misconduct disciplinary hearing. Of course, I said '*Yes*' but I could not think of much of a defence but I said I would do my best.

I advised Dennis to admit everything and resign, to avoid being dismissed for gross misconduct but he said he couldn't do that.

The Council had already said if he resigned before the hearing, they would hold the hearing anyway in his absence and would record that they would have dismissed him for gross misconduct had he not resigned.

The facts leading up to the disciplinary hearing and the circumstances leading to his resignation would be included in any future employment reference and this would then render him ineligible for his Local Government pension.

The rules about Local Government pensions were that if an officer is dismissed for gross misconduct, they lose their pension. The rules also state that if an officer of the Council resigns before a gross misconduct hearing and the hearing goes ahead and it determines the officer would have been summarily dismissed, he will still lose his pension. So resigning would have been no advantage to Dennis in respect of retaining his pension. He had 24 years of accrued pension.

I told Dennis to go sick and get a doctor's letter confirming he was mentally too ill to attend and participate in any hearing. The letter stated that Dennis was so traumatised he would not be able to understand what was being put to him or be able to give me coherent instructions. I said that I would attend in his place.

At his hearing, in Dennis's absence, before the personnel sub-committee of Councillors, I made a full confession on his behalf.

In mitigation I argued that he was seriously mentally ill and had been placed under severe duress when his family was threatened with their lives if he did not pay his gambling debts.

The threats included the torture and murder of his wife and children. Dennis saw the only way out was to allow Tony to 'help him'.

I said Dennis was desperate and had acted totally out of character. Until this time he had an exemplary record.

I said that initially Dennis had no idea what Tony had intended to use the Council Chamber for—that is until the first video shoot. I said it had actually given lucrative employment to Dennis's secretary, Marilyn, who was a single mother and needed some extra cash—now that was chutzpah I admit.

I named several Councillors whom I said had enjoyed watching these videos being made and had bought some of them. Those Councillors all denied everything—naturally.

I also added that Dennis had been assured by Tony that no children or animals would be used in the making of these films and Dennis was horrified to discover that they were.

I said Dennis bitterly regretted his actions but he had shown real insight into what he had done and how wrong his actions had been and that he would work especially hard to make amends. He wanted to show his sincere remorse for what he had done. He asked me to throw him on their mercy and give him a second chance.

That all went down like a lead balloon.

Dennis was duly summarily dismissed, in disgrace, for numerous offences of gross misconduct. He lost his pension as well as his job.

Before we had a chance to appeal the dismissal, Dennis was arrested and charged under the Sexual Offences Act 2003 and the Obscene Publications Act 1959 for aiding and abetting and conspiracy. He was remanded in custody.

Tony meanwhile had fled to his villa in Crete. Greece had no extradition treaty in those days so Tony could not be brought back to the UK for any trial.

Dennis was advised by his criminal lawyers, very badly in my view, to plead 'Not guilty'.

At his trial at the Old Bailey, the Jury found him guilty on all charges. The Judge took a very dim view of Dennis's conduct and his "not guilty" plea.

Despite my evidence of his good character, at his sentencing, two months later, the Judge ruled, *"You were in a senior and trusted position. There can be no justification or excuses for your conduct. You abused your position and the trust that the Council in the most shocking manner and you let down the ratepayers who placed their trust in you as a senior public official.*

"You have let down those vulnerable innocent children and animals who were abused mercilessly for your own personal gain.

"You have let down all those people who depended upon you to house them and keep them safe.

"You have let down your family who will now have to live with the disgrace and shame that this prosecution and the guilty verdict will bring to you and to them. You have ruined a lifetime's public service.

"You deserve the most serious punishment I can give you. The Jury found you guilty of these heinous crimes in less than two hours. Your 'not guilty' plea did you no good and your plea in mitigation was nothing less than a travesty. You have shown little or no insight into the seriousness of what you did.

"You are partly responsible for these dreadful crimes. I will make sure that society is protected from you and that you receive the punishment you deserve.

"Rather than admit what you have done, you have sought to blame your gambling as your pathetic excuse for what you did—I will call it a pathetic excuse because that is what it is.

"I am sentencing you to five years in prison and fining you £20,000. You will also go on the Sex offenders Register for life. Take him away."

With that, Dennis was led down the steps to the cells to start his sentence.

His wife had to sell their house to pay the fine and her future living costs. She divorced Dennis soon afterwards. His sons refused to have anything to do with him and neither his ex-wife or sons ever visited him in prison.

Dennis was sent first to HM Prison Belmarsh in South London. This is a Category 'A', High Security men's prison where some of the most dangerous and notorious prisoners are sent.

When I visited Dennis there, he was too traumatised to tell me what some of the other prisoners had done to him—I could only guess. He had cuts and bruises all over his body, two swollen and very bruised eyes and his right arm was in plaster. Even though he had been put in a separation wing for 'nonces' (sex offenders), some heavies in the prison got to him in the showers.

He had been a man larger than life in all senses of that word but he had lost over two stones in weight by the time I saw him a couple of months after his trial.

Luckily for him, after one month, he was transferred to Hollesley Bay Open Prison in Suffolk (known colloquially as Holiday Bay Open Prison). He spent the rest of his sentence there running literacy classes very successfully for the prisoners who could not read or write.

I visited Dennis only once more at the Open Prison.

He called me after his release on parole, after serving two years in prison. I then lost touch with him.

He was put on the Sex Offenders' Register for life and found it impossible to rent anywhere or to get another job. He ended up first living in a half-way house and then on the streets. What a bitter irony.

I learnt years later that Dennis had died of a drugs overdose in 2010, a sad end.

Chapter 14
Doctors and a Dentist's Tales

Sometimes doctors and dentists do things that get themselves into trouble. In two cases in which I was instructed the doctors were accused of sexual misconduct. In the third case, the doctor was accused of making fraudulent misrepresentations on application forms for Consultants' posts.

In the fourth case my client had written 13 private prescriptions for diazepam, for someone not his patient and had used the notepaper of a private Hospital at which he had not worked for many years.

The dentist for whom I acted made one error in a long career. No-one had died or was maimed. Two brilliant Counsel prevented him from being struck off the dental Register unable to practise dentistry. They saved his career.

Doctors and dentists accused of negligence can be sued for damages by the patient concerned. If they are accused of gross professional misconduct they may be reported to their regulatory bodies.

The General Medical Council (GMC) regulates the fitness to practise of doctors. The General Dental Council (GDC) regulates dentists.

The ultimate punishments are being prosecuted, sent to prison and being struck off the Register for life.

That would mean the doctor or dentist would never be able to practice medicine or dentistry again.

In cases of convictions for sexual offences, the offender would be put on the Sex Offenders' Register often for life.

The GMC

In the next series of tales, all four doctors were reported to the General Medical Council (GMC) before 2012, when the procedures for professional misconduct changed. The changes followed the implementation of the Human Rights Act 1998 —Article 6, the right to a fair trial.

The dentist I acted for was luckier. The Human Rights Act 1998 had just come into force.

Prior to the implementation of the Human Rights Act, the GMC procedures for an initial screening of a complaint and final determination offended the principles of natural justice and could be gravely unfair.

Sometimes the same person who was the Initial Screener, determining whether there was a prima facie case, was also the Chair of the Fitness to Practice or Professional Misconduct Panel, deciding the ultimate fate of the doctor. That is now seen as unacceptable. The same person who makes an initial finding should not then go on to hear the evidence and make the final decision.

In 2012, after the implementation of the Human Rights Act 1998, the Medical Practitioners Tribunal, a separate body from the GMC, was set up to determine the fitness to practise or professional misconduct of doctors. This provided a satisfactory separation of powers ensuring that an independent body determines the ultimate fate of the doctor concerned.

There are rules of conduct which all doctors and dentists are either required or expected to follow. These are set out in the GMC's "Good Medical Practice" and the GDC's "Standards and Guidance for dental practitioners."

Where the Guidance uses the word "must" that is a mandatory rule. Where they use the word "should" that indicates recommended good practice.

The GMC's rules include an absolute prohibition on a doctor having any intimate or sexual or improper emotional relationship with a patient.

The relationship between a doctor and their patient must have that necessary boundary.

The rules state, *"You must not pursue a sexual or improper emotional relationship with a current patient.*

If a patient pursues a sexual or improper emotional relationship with you, you should treat them politely and considerately and try to re-establish a professional boundary. If trust has broken down and you find it necessary to end the professional relationship, you must follow the guidance, 'Ending your professional relationship with a patient'.

You must not use your professional relationship with a patient to pursue a relationship with someone close to them. For example, you must not use home visits to pursue a relationship with a member of a patient's family.

You must not end a professional relationship with a patient solely to pursue a personal relationship with them."

Dr 'Groper'

'Dr Groper' was the name I secretly gave Dr Jane, the doctor in this first case. The reason will soon become obvious. She didn't have affairs with patients. She allegedly committed sexual acts upon them or attempted to do so or acted in a most improper manner in front of and not to only patients but also to doctors, nurses and medical students whom she was supervising.

She was and still is a well-respected and successful physician. She had a private practice in the heart of Central London. At the time she instructed me she had just resigned from her post at a major teaching hospital in London, as a Consultant in Orthopaedics, specialising in shoulders.

She came to see me after she had been reported to the GMC by two female patients and a male patient, for alleged sexual misconduct.

The female patients complained that she had fondled their breasts during their medical examinations. The medical conditions of these patients did not necessitate any examination of their breasts.

The male patient complained she had asked him to take off all his clothes and had then examined his private parts. After she had done this, he realised that this completely wrong, got dressed and left the consultation room, without waiting for her diagnosis or treatment plan.

All three patients sued Dr Jane for damages. Their civil actions in respect of these alleged sexual assaults were settled out of court by her professional insurers, the Medical Protection Society (MPS).

However, the settlements could not prevent the complainants from reporting her to the GMC. It would be against public policy for any person to be prevented from making a complaint to a Regulatory Body or from reporting potentially criminal conduct to the police. So the agreements could only settle their civil claims.

The agreements clearly stated that the settlements were made without any admissions of any wrongdoing by Dr Jane and all the allegations were denied. The terms of the settlements were to be kept strictly confidential.

The complainants then reported Dr Jane to the GMC and she faced gross professional misconduct proceedings.

Dr Jane could have been represented at her GMC hearing by the MPS but she told me she had no faith in her medical insurers.

She said she had heard that I was a "Rottweiler" and she needed me to represent her. In fact, she told me that the MPS lawyer had advised her to "plead guilty."

She told me that the complainant (in the end only one woman agreed to give evidence at the GMC) had lied about what she said Dr Jane had done to her.

Dr Jane told me that the complainant's description of how, when she was standing in front of Dr Jane, she had allegedly put her hand down the Complainant's blouse and inside her bra and had then fondled her breast, was a physical impossibility.

From her description it certainly sounded as if it could have been a physical impossibility. Dr Jane offered to show me how impossible this manoeuvre would have been but I rapidly declined her offer and said I believed her.

Then we had some real luck. A Hospital Secretary sent me all of this Complainant's NHS medical records, with a covering letter written and addressed to me. The secretary had meant to send these records to the GMC's solicitor but she obviously got confused as to who was acting for the GMC and wrote to me instead.

The rule is that if it is obvious on the face of the documents that a lawyer has received documents meant for the other side, this is clearly an error. The lawyer must not read them and should return them to the sender. If the lawyer has read the documents, they must recuse themselves (stand down).

However, the covering letter was not addressed to the GMC's solicitors. It was addressed to me and had been put in an envelope with my name and address. So, on the face of it I was the intended recipient. Our QC advised that I could read the medical records and could then send them to him.

What these medical records showed was that the Complainant had an obsession about her breasts. She had had two breast augmentation operations on the NHS and she was still not satisfied with their size. In fact, she had made a complaint to the NHS Hospital and then to the GMC about her plastic surgeon.

The records also revealed that this lady also had a criminal record for theft and common assault. Shortly after being discharged from hospital, after the second operation, she had started an argument with a customer in a queue in Iceland Frozen Foods and had then hit and injured this customer.

She was then caught leaving the shop without paying for her goods.

She argued she was still suffering from the effects of the operation and had been in great pain. Her surgeon had written a medical report seeking to mitigate and excuse what she had done. Her 'excuse' for the assault and forgetfulness in paying for her shopping and her aggressive conduct towards another shopper, was, according to her surgeon, her *"pain and its effect on her mental health following the operation."*

She was not believed by the Magistrates and was found guilty and given a six-month suspended custodial sentence and 100 hours' Community Service.

These medical records were all relevant regarding her credibility, if we were allowed to use them. I felt much more optimistic about getting Dr Jane off after I had read these records.

However, my optimism fell to rock bottom when a week before the hearing, the GMC solicitors disclosed a rather large file to me. In it were documents that revealed that Dr Jane had been struck off the GMC Register ten years earlier for sexually assaulting a male patient and a female nurse. She had been restored to the Register five years later.

She had also been the subject of numerous complaints at the teaching Hospital where she had worked. Male and female medical students, nurses and two consultants had complained that she made inappropriate remarks to them of a sexual nature, had tried to fondle the women's breasts and had been seen 'playing with herself' in the Theatre prep room, in front of them. It had also been alleged that she had offered to give "blow jobs" to the male students and doctors.

She denied all of these complaints at the time but as a result she had received disciplinary warnings and as a precaution, the Hospital insisted that she had to have a chaperone present when she examined all patients. She was also banned from supervising any medical students.

Eventually, just before she instructed me, she resigned from the teaching Hospital after they had received yet more complaints of a similar nature against her. She was allowed to resign and a disciplinary hearing never took place.

When I asked her what these latest complaints were about and for what she had been struck off the Register ten years earlier, she said, *"I can't remember."* I didn't believe her but that was not the point.

Her previous conduct could have been devastating for the case before the GMC but our brilliant QC knew exactly what to do.

Before the start of the first day of the hearing, he took the GMC Counsel, Sasha, to one side. He asked her how she intended to use the file disclosed to us the week before and whether she would be referring to Dr Jane's previous misconduct and earlier erasure from the GMC Register.

Sasha said that once our QC had cross-examined the Complainant and had attacked her character, she could then bring in the "similar fact" evidence about the character of Dr Jane, including all her previous disciplinary issues and the earlier erasure and restoration to the GMC Register. These are the rules of evidence.

Our QC told Sasha that he would not be attacking the Complainant's character so if Sasha attempted to bring into evidence anything in that file, he would seek an immediate stay of the GMC proceedings and would appeal to the Privy Council. The Judicial Council of the Privy Council (JCPC) was where appeals from the GMC and GDC used to go before they were transferred to the High Court on 31 December 2015.

Our QC told Sasha that the Privy Council would allow his appeal and her name would then forever be associated with losing an important legal precedent concerning disclosure of documents, from the highest Court in the land. As an alternative she could agree to withdraw the file that had been recently disclosed to us and agree not to use it.

She did as our QC suggested, choosing the latter course of action and agreed she would not adduce the file into evidence unless he attacked the character of the Complainant.

On the second day of the hearing Sasha was delayed in the traffic and was late. It was well known that she rode a motorbike and wore leathers. On this particular day she rushed in to the GMC hearing room in her leathers, carrying her crash helmet and apologised to the Panel for being late. The Chair was seen to smile and was heard to say, *"I do love to see women in leather—so sexy."*

Sasha then went to change and returned in her smart black suit and high heels.

Our QC tiptoed around the Complainant's character but managed to goad her into referring to her two breast augmentation operations on the NHS, her complaints about her plastic surgeon and her *"trouble with the police"* and, as she put it, *"those biased Magistrates."*

Our QC was then able to question her fully about what we had found in her medical records, namely her obsession with her breasts and her complaints about her plastic surgeon. Our QC accused her of being a serial complainer about doctors and lying on oath in the Magistrates' Court.

In other words, he attacked her character and her credibility but was permitted to do so under the rules of evidence because she had introduced these issues herself. Under the rules of evidence, Sasha was still not permitted to adduce the previous conduct of, or character evidence about, Dr Jane.

Our QC also got the Complainant very muddled as to how Dr Jane had actually allegedly groped her breast, and which breast Dr Jane had allegedly groped, given that she was standing opposite her patient at the time. A patient's left-hand side appears to be the right-hand side to the person standing opposite.

Doctors and nurses are well aware of this potential confusion and are trained to use the term *'the patient's left or right hand side'*. They ask the patient where possible, to touch the side of the body or face to which they are referring.

Our QC got the Complainant totally confused, accusing her of changing her evidence from *"it was the left breast"* to *"it was my right breast"* on at least four occasions. She then got very angry and started shouting and swearing at our QC calling him an *"f.....ing, lying bastard"* and worse. She made a very poor impression on the GMC Panel.

In the end she was made out to be a calculated and professional liar, repeatedly making false allegations about respectable doctors.

Our QC painted Dr Jane as a "saint" and to be fair she was a very good, caring Orthopaedic specialist, loved by many of her patients.

Several of Dr Jane's professional colleagues and patients were called to give character evidence. They all testified that Dr Jane was a most moral, upright, expert, professional and caring doctor. Her patients declared she was a *"life saver."* They all confirmed she was a woman *"above reproach."*

They said she exhibited the highest ethical standards, had never conducted herself improperly to them and they trusted her implicitly. According to them she was universally loved and admired. They proved to be very credible witnesses.

Dr Jane was then called to give evidence but poor Sasha could not cross examine her about any of her past misdemeanours or her previous erasure from the Register ten years earlier. When asked why she had resigned from the NHS teaching Hospital Dr Jane said it was *"to concentrate on my private practice and my research."*

Sasha had prepared her cross examination on the basis of being able to ask Dr Jane about all the evidence in the file so she had very little to put to her other than a rather weak accusation that she had groped the Complainant's breast—to which Dr Jane said very firmly that she had not done so and denied any misconduct.

Sasha only had the Complainant's very confused evidence to put to Dr Jane, which had sounded incredible.

Dr Jane presented herself superbly well and I could tell the GMC Panel was impressed by her.

The Panel did not need long to dismiss all the complaints. The Chair of the Panel said some very flattering things about Dr Jane and some rather unkind things about the Complainant.

Not knowing any of the background the Chair said, *"Dr Jane is a doctor of impeccable character, an excellent surgeon who had dedicated her life to caring for patients who are in considerable pain and distress. She has an exemplary record. We have heard character evidence from several of her patients and professional colleagues who have testified to her integrity, professionalism and the highest standards of conduct.*

It must have been a great strain on this doctor and her family, being falsely accused of sexual misconduct. The Panel is unanimous. We have no doubt that the allegations are untrue and they are dismissed. We have concluded that the complainant has been malicious in making these complaints.

We did not believe the evidence of the complainant and did not find her to be a credible witness. On every occasion where her evidence conflicted with that of Dr Jane, we believed the evidence of Dr Jane.

We would like to thank Dr Jane for the respectful and measured way in which she gave evidence. She must have been under considerable strain for the past ten months but we are pleased to say she is free to continue practising medicine. The complaints are dismissed in their entirety."

At that Dr Jane's 'wife', who had been sitting at the back of the room for the five days of the hearing, collapsed.

Because the English legal system is adversarial and not inquisitorial, litigation is a little like a game of tennis. The better 'player' wins on the day.

The Judge, or in this case the Chair of the GMC Panel, is often merely the umpire. Winning sometimes has very little to do with 'justice' or the truth.

To thank our QC and me, Dr Jane very generously treated us to tickets at the Royal Opera House and a slap-up dinner.

Dr Jones

I acted for another consultant physician, Dr Jones, but in his case, the outcome was very different.

He had been found by a nurse, one evening, in his office in a private hospital, on top of one of his female patients, having sex. His patient was positioned like a dog on all fours with Dr Jones on top of her having vigorous sex. Dr Jones had a whip with sharp spikes in his hand wearing only a black leather face mask, a leather belt and black thigh length leather boots.

He was heard shouting, *"Bitch, take that"* as he whipped his patient. He froze when the nurse came in. She exclaimed, horrified, *"What on earth are you doing?"*

She reported Dr Jones to the Medical Director the next morning and Dr Jones was immediately suspended.

During the investigation, it was discovered that he had enrolled this woman as his NHS patient, getting her an NHS number, so she could be treated by Dr Jones free of charge. Payment was sexual favours.

Dr Jones had also written several NHS prescriptions for some expensive drugs for this patient. Dr Jones was not her NHS doctor so this was a criminal offence.

There wasn't much I could do for Dr Jones.

He had been suspended from both the NHS Hospital at which he worked and from all the private hospitals where he undertook his private practice.

Whilst suspended he only received his NHS Salary. He earned nothing from his private practice which practically disappeared overnight.

I turned up at the GMC Hearing in Manchester with our QC but Dr Jones was nowhere to be seen. We could not contact him and the message on his mobile phone said, '*this number is no longer available*'.

The hearing continued without him and he was struck off the Register. I later discovered that he had fled the country and was practising medicine in Australia. His patient/lover had gone with him and his wife had divorced him. Apparently, no-one in Australia bothered to check his GMC status in the UK and as far as I know he is still in practice in Australia.

Dr Alasdair

A joke amongst doctors is that the definition of an alcoholic is *"someone who drinks more than their doctor."*

Well, I had a client who fitted that description perfectly—only he *was* the doctor.

Dr Angus was a GP whom I had known for some time. He asked me to act for a friend of his, Dr Alasdair, who was a locum Consultant at an NHS Hospital.

Dr Alasdair had been reported to the GMC by a private Hospital where he had worked eight years earlier, for using their notepaper to prescribe drugs on multiple occasions, to someone who was not his patient.

The NHS Hospital that employed Dr Alasdair as a locum consultant at the time he instructed me, had suspended him for this alleged professional misconduct.

A sharp-eyed pharmacist had telephoned the private Hospital asking whether they justified the high dosages of diazepam that had been prescribed by Dr Alasdair, 13 times in one year. He had written these prescriptions for the same 'patient', on the headed notepaper of this private Hospital, where he had worked eight years previously.

The prescription was for someone living at the other end of the country from the Hospital. This 'patient' was in fact Dr Alasdair's cousin who had the same surname as Dr Alasdair. He was not his patient. His cousin was addicted to diazepam and Dr Alasdair had been feeding his habit.

The GMC Guidance states it is inadvisable for a doctor to prescribe medication for close relatives or close friends. Under the Guidance: *"Prescribing for yourself or those close to you"* the Rules state

67 *Wherever possible, you must avoid prescribing for yourself or anyone you have a close personal relationship with.*

68 *If you prescribe any medicine for yourself or someone close to you, you must:*

   a) make a clear record at the same time or as soon as possible afterwards; the record should include your relationship to the patient, where relevant, and the reason it was necessary for you to prescribe;

    b) *follow the advice on information sharing and safe prescribing in paragraphs 27 to 33 and 53 to 58.*

69 *You must not prescribe controlled drugs for yourself or someone close to you unless:*

    a) *no other person with the legal right to prescribe is available to assess and prescribe without a delay;*

    b) *emergency treatment is immediately necessary to avoid serious deterioration in health or serious harm.*

If the doctor is not the regular prescribing doctor, such as their GP, the GMC Guidance states that the doctor: "should ask for the patient's consent to:

    a) *contact their GP or other treating doctors if you need more information or confirmation of the information you have before prescribing, and*

    b) *share information with their GP when the episode of care is completed."*

Dr Alasdair had not followed any of the GMC Guidance. In any event it was illegal to use the headed notepaper from a hospital where he no longer worked.

I arranged for both doctors, Drs Angus and Alasdair, to come to see me one evening, at 7 pm, at my home office.

Dr Alasdair arrived an hour early, around 6.00 pm, just as I had arrived home. I invited him into our sitting room and offered him *"a cup of coffee or tea or perhaps a glass of wine?"*

He said he would love a glass of wine so I brought in a bottle of Rioja and three glasses, intending that his friend and I would join him. I poured a glass for Dr Alasdair and within a matter of twenty minutes or so the bottle of wine was empty. Dr Alasdair had been helping himself and had drunk the lot.

When Dr Angus arrived at 7 pm he asked me to wait in the hall and told me not to offer his friend any alcohol because he was an alcoholic. My face fell. I said I just had and in fact he had drunk an entire bottle of wine but I was now warned.

When we both sat down, Dr Alasdair picked up the empty bottle and said, *"What about another? That was very good wine. Why don't both of you join me in a glass."*

I replied, *"I'm so sorry, that was the last bottle."* Half joking I said, *"You've drunk us dry."* and we carried on with our meeting.

Fifteen minutes later, at around 7.15 pm, my husband, Barry, arrived home. He is a wine connoisseur and had passed the Sommelier examination with distinction. He has an extensive wine cellar.

He put his head round the door of our sitting room to say, *"Good evening"* and noticed the empty bottle of Rioja on the table. He turned to the two doctors and said, *"Good choice, that is a very fine Rioja. I hope you enjoyed it. I can see the bottle is empty. Can I get you another?"*

I replied quick as a flash, *"No, that was the last bottle of wine in the house. We will stick to water or coffee."*

My husband laughed and said, *"Well you must have got through my wine cellar at a rate of knots because there were over 800 bottles there this morning."*

I replied, *"Oh you are funny"* and turned to the doctors and said, *"We don't have a wine cellar but I know Barry would love to have one. It is his dream to have wine cellar with 800 bottles of wine. That was in fact the last bottle of wine we have in the house."* I glared at poor Barry and physically pushed him out of the door.

Out of earshot I told him that Dr Alasdair was an alcoholic, of which I was unaware until his friend had arrived fifteen minutes earlier. Barry then popped his head round the door as if nothing had happened and asked innocently, *"Anyone for a cup of tea?"* I said, *"No thanks, we're fine"* and beckoned him out of the room.

The GMC pursued the case against Dr Alasdair and sent a 'Rule 7' letter, setting out the allegations of theft of Hospital property, improper prescribing of medication for a person not his patient and failing to notify their GP.

I responded to the GMC with a letter of abject apology on behalf of Dr Alasdair, making excuses for what he had done. I said he had inadvertently picked up the notepaper of this private Hospital and had not realised what notepaper he was using when he wrote the prescriptions. I said he had been under extreme stress at the time. His marriage was falling apart and he was not well.

His cousin had pressurised Dr Alasdair and begged him to prescribe the diazepam and had threatened to commit suicide if Dr Alasdair didn't do as he had asked.

Dr Alasdair decided to resign from his locum post at the NHS Hospital and promptly got another locum consultant post at a private hospital in another part of the country. I will never know if they ever asked for a reference from his last employer or asked Dr Alasdair about any on-going GMC proceedings.

The GMC investigation went completely quiet and we heard nothing more. I heard from a Legal Assessor at the GMC a few months later, who did some digging for me. The GMC had lost the papers regarding the complaint against Dr Alasdair, so no further action was ever taken. I call that 'a win'.

Dr Ali

Dr Ali was another very lucky doctor who escaped the worst punishment from the GMC because of the skill and eloquence of our brilliant QC.

Dr Ali was a Pakistani national who had qualified in Pakistan and then came to the UK to take his Fellowship exams at the Royal College of Surgeons. He held a number of posts in UK hospitals and at the time I met him he was a Senior Middle grade doctor in a Hospital in the Midlands. Senior Middle Grade is the equivalent of the former grade of Registrar.

Dr Ali had been caught making, allegedly, untruthful claims on his application form for a consultant's post at an NHS Hospital in the South of England. Mr Mark was the Consultant who had interviewed Dr Ali and it was Mr Mark who discovered that Dr Ali had in fact made numerous untruthful statements on his application form.

In fact, researching 13 of Dr Ali's previous application forms for consultants' posts over the previous three years, Mr Mark discovered they all contained the same 'false representations'.

The untruthful statements ranged from alleging he had won a Gold Medal for research (he had not won any Gold Medal), to having held a locum Consultant's post for six months, on nights, in his particular speciality, when he had in fact only done so for three nights as a locum whist the Consultant was off sick.

Numerous other statements on these application forms were also untrue including holding a postgraduate qualification in tropical medicine.

Mr Mark had checked some of the statements made on his application form and found them to be untrue. He then reported Dr Ali to the GMC.

Dr Ali received a Rule 7 letter alleging Gross Professional Misconduct—fraud and false representation. A person makes a false representation when they dishonestly make a statement, knowing the representation was or might be untrue or misleading with an intent to make a gain for themselves.

Dr Ali was called to a Professional Misconduct Hearing in Manchester where most of the GMC hearings used to take place.

I instructed a brilliant defence QC specialising in criminal law and sent him all the papers. We then went to see him for a conference (con) before the GMC hearing.

At the start of the con our QC said to me, *"I do not want to hear from our client. I will tell you how I see it."*

He then told us what I can only describe as a fairy story. When he stopped speaking, I asked him, *"Do you have the same papers as me?"*

He said he would not be calling Dr Ali to give evidence so this meant he could not be cross-examined by the GMC's Counsel. Thank goodness for that I thought.

Amongst Dr Ali's papers was a Diploma in Tropical Medicine from a University in the Midlands but something did not look right about it. Our QC asked me to check its authenticity with the University but if I received a negative answer he did not want to know. I was merely to leave out the Diploma from the documents that we would disclose to the GMC.

The Diploma turned out to be false. The University had no record of Dr Ali studying for this Diploma and confirmed that the Diploma that I had, had been forged. Dr Ali had no explanation when I asked him about it.

In any event this Diploma was cited on all 13 application forms for which Dr Ali had been charged with fraudulent misrepresentation, so the GMC could, if they had been diligent, have checked it for themselves. However, the GMC did not check it and it never made its way into the documents.

We went up to Manchester for the 10-day hearing. I felt very worried for Dr Ali and wondered what our QC was going to say to get him off. I need not have worried.

The GMC's Counsel was Sasha, the same Counsel who had represented the GMC in Dr Jane's case.

Sasha took me aside before the start of the first day of the hearing and said she was very worried that we would not finish in 10 days as she intended to spend at least one and a half days cross-examining my client. She said that she had two witnesses and we had ten. She thought we were calling Dr Ali as one of our ten witnesses but in fact we had only nine witnesses and most would be giving very short evidence. We were not calling Dr Ali but she did not know that.

I told her not to worry. I said our QC was very experienced and had worked out a timetable and we would finish in 10 days. I said most of our witnesses would not be long giving their evidence.

I wasn't telling her that she would not be spending **any** days cross-examining our client as he wasn't being called as a witness.

She could not call Dr Ali as her witness because he was the accused and she was representing the other side, the GMC. If the accused is not called by their Counsel, that witness cannot be cross examined. You cannot cross examine your own witness. Sasha had assumed we would call Dr Ali, as the accused, and she would then be able to cross examine him. How wrong she was.

It was essential to the GMC's case that Dr Ali was called as our witness, so then Sasha could tear him to shreds.

The GMC Panel appeared to be stacked against us. The Chair was a former Head of the Crown Prosecution Service (CPS). One of the wing members was a Professor of Medical Ethics and the other wing member was the Deputy Chief Constable of the Suffolk Constabulary. I feared they would all know dishonesty when they saw it.

I should not have worried. Our silver-tongued QC had a flowing, compelling and seductive way of speaking. He had a great line up of witnesses for Dr Ali and wicked cross-examination for the Consultant, Mr Mark, the GMC's 'whistle-blower'.

Our first witness was a Professor of Communication and Ethics from Oxford University. He ran a course for undergraduate medical students and postgraduate doctors on how to complete application forms for hospital jobs and how to make the best case of their skills and qualifications. Medicine is very competitive and most doctors have a reputation for downplaying their talents and achievements.

He was a compelling witness. He explained how doctors only in rare cases made 'improvements' (as he called them) to their skills, qualifications and experience. His course focussed on getting that balance just right and making the best case for the job applicants. Dr Ali had had no training on how to complete application forms so had had no guidance on how to do this.

Sasha had no cross-examination for this witness.

Then our QC called a linguistics expert. He explained how someone whose native language is not English, like Dr Ali, may not understand the nuances of the English language.

When asked to explain this, he used the example of Dr Ali stating he had won a 'Gold Medal' for Medical Research. A Professor of Medicine had won the Gold Medal. Dr Ali had assisted this Professor with some of the experiments and the making of some slides. Dr Ali, it was explained, may have believed that he too had "won" the Gold Medal as he had been part of the Professor's team.

Similarly, Dr Ali had acted as a locum consultant for several nights over a period of six months. He had been standing in for a consultant, who had been off sick for three nights. Dr Ali, it was explained, had misunderstood that part of the application form where it asked about his 'experience as a locum consultant'.

Dr Ali had written that he had been "a locum Consultant, on nights, *for* a period of six months" when what he had meant was, he had been a locum consultant on nights *"during"* a period of six months. This was a subtle but important difference.

Our QC then called three of Dr Ali's fellow doctors and four former patients, all of whom gave evidence as to his excellent character and his great care, skill, kindness, probity and devotion to his profession. He was universally liked and respected by his fellow medics, nurses and patients.

Our QC then told the Panel that was the end of our case. Sasha looked daggers at me and mouthed, *"What about your client? When is he giving evidence?"* I just shook my head as if I didn't know what she was going on about.

Then came the nail in the coffin for the GMC. Mr Mark, the Consultant who had "shopped" Dr Ali, was in for a real annihilation.

During the course of giving his evidence, Mr Mark had used the expression *"those people"* pointing to Dr Ali, when answering a question about the ethnicity of doctors of whom Mr Mark had experience writing false application forms.

The first question our QC asked Mr Mark in cross examination was, *"You were asked a question by Miss Sasha about how many application forms you have seen in your career and in particular how many false application forms you have seen. You said you had seen a considerable number of forms with* falsehoods over the years and they were mainly from foreign doctors. You then pointed at Dr Ali and said, 'often from those people'."

"Yes, I did" said Mr Mark with an arrogant sneer—nail in the coffin number one.

"Perhaps you could explain to whom you were referring by 'those people'?" asked our QC.

Not realising the trap that had been set for him, Mr Mark then started on a racist rant, "You know, all those foreign doctors who come to the UK and falsify their qualifications. Those people do not have the same standards of truth and honesty as we do in the UK.

"I've read the GMC Annual Reports as well as using my own experience. Most of those dishonest doctors who are reported to the GMC are foreigners. You know — Indians and Pakis — they are only one better than the Nigerians.

"Nigerians are the worst but all these foreign doctors are thoroughly dishonest – well most of them anyway. We don't want those kind of doctors practising medicine here."

There was an audible gasp from everyone in the hearing room.

By the time our Counsel had led him up and down the garden path this Consultant was "toast." Mr Mark's credibility was totally destroyed. Our QC tapped his nerve and he became a ranting racist.

The Panel hated Mr Mark. It helped that the Professor of Medical Ethics was also from Pakistan.

But the other panel member and the Chair were also appalled at Mr Mark's racist tirade. To be fair so was the entire room including Sasha. I do not believe that she had expected that from her witness.

Our Counsel's closing speech was a masterpiece of eloquence.

He explained that Dr Ali's father was a well-known and very successful Professor of Surgery in Pakistan, who had very high expectations of his son. Dr Ali felt he could never live up to his father's expectations and was never given any encouragement or praise for what he had achieved.

Dr Ali had not appreciated the nuances of the English language and had unwittingly given inaccurate answers on the application forms but they were not knowingly wrong or false and his conduct should not be held to meet the high bar of 'fraud' or 'false misrepresentation'.

Our QC said that Dr Ali was devastated and very ashamed at having been brought before the GMC. He had understood what he had done wrong and was determined to show his remorse and would take all possible remedial steps.

He would undertake intensive English language lessons as soon as the hearing was over. He had already completed a course on Medical Ethics by the time of the GMC hearing. Our Counsel had recommended that he should do this when we first met.

The Panel was invited to give Dr Ali the second chance he deserved. Our QC said he would work hard to show the faith the GMC had in him was well placed. Our Counsel's final sentence still makes me laugh to this day. His submissions concluded, ***"I want you to look at this as one single incident."***

Even I, with my 'O' level Maths, knew that 13 false application forms over a period of three years could never amount to *"one single incident."* That's the magic of brilliant advocacy for you.

The Panel must have felt sorry for Dr Ali or completely seduced by our Counsel's brilliant eloquence or both because they ruled that although Dr Ali had *"made errors"* on his application forms *"they were not fraudulent or deliberately misleading nor did they amount to false misrepresentation"*—and they hadn't even heard a word out of Dr Ali's mouth.

The Panel accepted that he had placed himself under considerable pressure and stress to achieve his medical qualifications. They held it was his lack of understanding of the nuances of the English language that had led him to make these errors.

They held that through his Counsel he had clearly demonstrated insight into what he had done and he had shown sincere remorse and was most unlikely ever to repeat this conduct.

On that basis they ruled that Dr Ali was at very low or no risk of repeating the conduct. He had already taken remedial steps to overcome his *"sub-optimal conduct"* as they called it.

He was given a warning and a three-month supervision order but was not suspended or erased from the Register.

Sasha was speechless and walked out at the end of the hearing without even saying "Goodbye" to me. She was fuming.

That was two defeats within the space of 12 months. Oh dear. Just goes to show that when you instruct the best—you get the best.

A Dentist's One Mistake

This is yet another example of where this time, two brilliant Barristers (James Badenoch QC and Dinah Rose KC) won the case for our client, Marcus, a well-known, private dentist practising in Harley Street, Central London.

Marcus's wife first called me after he had been suspended from practice at a General Dental Council (GDC) hearing. I had not acted for him at this Hearing. Solicitors instructed by his professional insurers had represented him.

Marcus had been charged with making a serious mistake (gross negligence) in the clinical care of a private patient. He was then in his late fifties. He ran a highly successful private dental practice specialising in advanced restorative dentistry.

He had trained in restorative aesthetic dentistry for three years in the USA and was considered to be one of the best implant specialists in the UK.

He had never before been sued or referred to the GDC.

The patient, Mrs H, had paid Marcus thousands of pounds to have implants fitted throughout her mouth as she did not want any dentures. Most of her teeth were rotten. Marcus's care plan included the requirement that Mrs H had to come every three months for dental hygiene sessions as her gums were in a shocking condition but she had failed to attend any hygienist appointments.

Instead of refusing to continue to treat her, Marcus carried on with his work on her implants. That was his mistake.

One Bank Holiday Mrs H had a raging infection in her mouth and called Marcus but he was abroad and did not pick up her call. She was admitted as an emergency to the Edgware General Hospital where an inexperienced Houseman extracted all her teeth.

Heartbroken and very, very angry, Mrs H sued Marcus for professional negligence and reported him to the GDC as unfit to practise. The civil action was settled by his professional indemnity insurers but at the GDC Fitness to Practise Hearing he was suspended.

Marcus's wife told me about several serious procedural irregularities that had occurred at that GDC hearing. For example, new evidence, never disclosed to Marcus's solicitors, was adduced at the hearing by the GDC's Counsel and Marcus's solicitors had no chance to rebut it.

In addition, the President of the GDC had acted as the Preliminary Screener and had then been the Chair of the Professional Conduct Committee (PCC) making the final decision about Marcus's conduct. This was a breach of Article 6 of the Human Rights Act 1998, the right to a fair trial.

Natural justice requires that there are independent parties—an investigator, a prosecutor and a Judge.

The person who originally investigates a case at the GDC is the Preliminary Screener and they should never sit at the Professional Conduct Committee (PCC) stage to make the final decision.

This had happened in Marcus's case but his solicitors were not made aware of this until after the hearing.

Luckily the Human Rights Act 1998 had been passed and it applied to all public bodies including the GDC.

The final nail in the GDC's coffin was that after the Professional Conduct Committee (PCC) had delivered its verdict but before the Panel made their decision on the penalty, Marcus's solicitor asked if he could present testimonials from other dentists and former patients. The President of the PCC refused to admit this evidence.

At that stage and before a final decision had been made, we sought a stay of any further proceedings and appealed to the Privy Council.

The appeal at that time went to the Judicial Committee of the Privy Council (JCPC) which sat in 9 Downing Street. The JCPC is the highest court of appeal for a number of Commonwealth countries, crown dependencies and United Kingdom overseas territories.

On the day of our appeal there were many cases in front of us waiting to be heard before ours.

All appeals from the Commonwealth countries that still have the death penalty go to the Privy Council. I can still picture the look of sheer desperation on the faces of those barristers defending their clients on Death Row, as they made their appeals.

When it came to our appeal, James Badenoch QC told the Judges that our client was a man who had an impeccable record and had never made a mistake in 35 years of practice, until this one. The penalty of suspension and erasure, depriving this man of his profession, had to be an error of law, offending the principles of natural justice.

Dinah Rose (now KC) made submissions that Marcus's rights at his GDC hearing, breached the Human Rights Act in numerous ways. She cited all of them.

Both Counsels' advocacy was a masterpiece of eloquence and brilliance.

We then had to wait three months before the Privy Council gave their decisions on the appeals they had heard that day.

Dinah told us that they would merely announce one word concerning the appeal—*"dismissed"* or *"allowed."*

There was a long line of Barristers in front of us. They had been fighting to save their clients from the death penalty. All I could hear was *"dismissed"*, *"dismissed"*, *"dismissed."* I could only imagine their agony.

Then it came to us and we heard the one word *"allowed."* We were overjoyed.

The written Judgement of the Judicial Committee of the Privy Council in **……..** *v GDC (PC)* reads, *"There were 52 testimonials from patients of the appellant and 16 from professional colleagues who have either referred patients to him, often very difficult cases, or had connections in practice with him in some other way.*

"Together with the testimonials that were before the PCC, they comprise a large and solid body of testimony to his customary skill and dedication as a specialist dentist.

"There is force in a submission in the case for the appellant, submitted by Mr Badenoch QC and Miss Rose, 'That for every professional man whose career spans, as this appellant has, many years and many clients, there is likely to be at least one case in which for reasons good and bad everything goes wrong—and that this was his, with no suggestion that it was in any way representative of his otherwise unblemished record.'

In the opinion of their Lordships to erase from the Register or suspend the appellant from practice would be neither necessary nor just. This is an exceptional case where the right to practise should not be interfered with despite a finding of serious professional misconduct.

They will humbly advise Her Majesty that the appeal ought to be allowed to the extent of replacing the erasure by an admonition. The respondent Council should pay the costs of this appeal."

Marcus's suspension was quashed and he was able to go back to his Practice. The GDC had to pay all his legal costs for the appeal.

That was one of the most satisfying cases I had dealt with. Justice was served.

Chapter 15
Eddie's Tale

This was the case of Eddie Daniel who said, *"I don't know why I'm here, Guv."* It was also the case where I got into hot water with the Serious and Organised Crime Command of the Metropolitan Police, after the tribunal case was over.

This is a case where I would not allow injustice to go unchallenged. I never take 'No' for an answer and where I see a miscarriage of justice I am determined to put that right. This time it was for the employer.

This is a reported case so real names are being used. The details of the tribunal and appeal are reported in the Employment Appeal Tribunal decision. I have spared the embarrassment o the First Employment Tribunal Judge by not naming them.

Mr Daniel was an illiterate electrician's mate. The fact that he was illiterate is relevant to his story. He had worked at the docks in East London for 14 years for a corporate client of mine. His job was a maintenance assistant and it included routine tasks such as assisting the qualified electricians. Over the years, he had learned about repairing electrical plug sockets and rectifying other minor electrical faults.

He was on duty during an Easter Bank Holiday weekend when only essential maintenance was being done on site. There was a skeleton maintenance crew of 23 men on duty over this weekend.

However, a number of managers had gone into Head Office over the Bank Holiday weekend to do some work.

At around 2.35 pm on Easter Saturday, one of the managers, Geoffrey Brown, had been walking along the corridor in the office block and saw Alf Boyle's office door close from the inside. Geoffrey had seen Alf leave his office and drive off from the car park an hour or so earlier so he knew that his office should have been empty.

Curious, Geoffrey opened the door and found Mr Daniel hiding behind the door. Geoffrey asked him what he was doing. Mr Daniel said that at around 2pm that afternoon he had been working on his computer joystick in the electrical workshop when he got a call *"to go to Alf Boyle's office."*

When Geoffrey asked Mr Daniel why he had been asked to go to Alf's office, he said, *"I don't know why I'm here Guv."*

Geoffrey thought that sounded odd and asked him how long he had been waiting. He said, *"about 40 minutes Guv."* By this time, it was 2.40 pm. Geoffrey asked who had made the call but Mr Daniel said, *"I have no idea."*

At the time Geoffrey accepted at face value what Mr Daniel had told him and said as no-one was obviously coming, he should leave the office block and report to his supervisor.

Mr Daniel left the office block but went straight home, without first reporting to his supervisor as he should have done.

When Security did a routine check of the offices early the following Tuesday morning, they found the desk drawers in Alf Boyle's office had been forced open and £23 of charity money was missing. It had been locked in a drawer in his office for safe-keeping. His secretary had been collecting money for the local Hospice.

When Geoffrey heard about the break-in, he reported to Security that he had found Mr Daniel in Alf Boyle's office over the weekend and thought his story about why he was there sounded questionable.

Mr Daniel was called in by one of the Security Officers and asked to explain what he had been doing in Mr Boyle's office on Saturday afternoon. Mr Daniel's explanation also did not satisfy the Security officer so he was suspended. A full investigation was then started.

Mr Daniel was formally questioned by John, Head of Security. Mr Daniel told him the same story that he had told the Security Officer and Geoffrey. He had received a call in the electrical workshop, around 2pm, whilst working on his computer joystick. He didn't recognise the voice of the man who had called him and the caller did not say who he was. He said he was told to *"go to Alf Boyle's office"* but added the caller had told him, *"to wait for an electrician."*

The internal call logs of all four phone extensions in the electrical workshop were checked between the times of 11am and 3pm on that Easter Saturday. The logs revealed that no calls had been made or received during those times.

Mr Daniel did not have a mobile phone so the call could not have been made to him on a mobile phone. No external calls could be made on these extensions unless a passcode was used to get a line out. Only the senior managers had passcodes.

In any event the call log system operated by the Company showed all *internal* calls made or received, from every extension. No internal incoming calls had been logged on the system.

Mr Daniel was asked whether he knew who had called him or whether he recognised the voice of the caller. He repeated he did not.

He was asked if he had anything else to say about why he was in Alf Boyle's office. He repeated that he hadn't recognised the person who had called him. He had only been told to go to Alf Boyle's office and '*wait for an electrician*'. Other than that he said he had no idea why he had been asked to go to this office.

As part of their investigation the Company wanted to ask all 23 men on duty if any of them had made that phone call to Mr Daniel. This was a highly unionised workforce and it was believed that the men might not be willing to tell the Head of Security or a manager. It was considered far more likely that if anyone <u>had</u> made the call they would be prepared to tell Jason, the Works Convenor.

Jason was therefore asked to interview the 23 union members on duty that weekend. He was to ask them if they had made that call. He was told that management did not need to know the name of the person and no disciplinary or other action would be taken against anyone, if they admitted to Jason they had made the call.

Jason was told that mere confirmation to management that a call had been made to Mr Daniel in the terms he alleged, would be sufficient to exonerate him from suspicion of the theft.

However, after an hour of questioning all 23 men, no-one admitted that they had made the call, not even when offered anonymity and amnesty from any disciplinary action.

Alf Boyle was also interviewed and asked if he had reported any faulty electric sockets in his office. He said he had not and that as far as he was concerned everything was in perfect working order. This was checked and confirmed.

The superintendent in charge of the essential maintenance was also asked whether any electrician had scheduled any maintenance in Alf Boyle's office that weekend or whether anyone had asked for this to be added to the essential works schedule. The superintendent replied there had been no request at any time for any electrical repairs of any kind to be carried out in Alf Boyle's office.

This was a full and thorough investigation of the matter and should have satisfied the third limb of the **BHS v Burchell** test—that, at the stage the employer has formed a reasonable belief in the guilt of the employee, the employer has *"carried out as much investigation into the matter as was reasonable in all the circumstances of the case."*

The Company then held a disciplinary hearing at which Mr Daniel was charged with the suspected theft of £23 from Alf Boyle's office, over the Easter Holiday weekend. This was potential gross misconduct for which summary dismissal was one possible outcome.

The hearing was conducted by the late and much lamented Andy Weir (Andy), the HR Director and a former shop steward. Andy had been poached by management to become their HR Manager and then HR Director.

Andy had the trust of the men and knew exactly how things worked in the Docks having been a dock worker for many years.

Mr Daniel told Andy at the disciplinary hearing, for the first time, never mentioned at the two investigation meetings, that in the past he had been *"the butt of practical jokes"* by the other men. He then suggested that the men might have thought it would be funny to tell him to go to stand in Alf Boyle's office to wait for someone who was never coming.

When asked what other practical jokes had been played on him in the past and when they had happened, Mr Daniel was unable to say. His union representative, George, looked distinctly unimpressed with Mr Daniel's story.

Andy put to Mr Daniel that his story did not ring true. He was found hiding behind the door in the office. If he had been waiting for someone and had no idea who it might be, he would not have been hiding behind the office door and certainly not when he heard footsteps approaching. The natural thing to do when hearing advancing footsteps would have been to open the door, not close it, and step out of the office into the corridor to see who was coming.

The description of Mr Daniel by Geoffrey was that Mr Daniel had been *"hiding behind the door"* and that he had *"closed the door when he heard (Geoffrey's) footsteps in the corridor."*

Mr Daniel denied he was hiding behind the door or that he had closed it when he heard someone coming along the corridor. When Andy asked if Geoffrey was lying, Mr Daniel said '*Yes*'.

That didn't go down well. Andy had to decide, on the balance of probabilities, was it more likely than not that Mr Daniel was the thief and had been in Alf Boyle's office for nefarious purposes? Or was Geoffrey Brown lying about what he saw?

Andy found Mr Daniel's explanations wholly implausible. Andy decided that it was beyond the balance of probabilities—in other words—he was 'sure' that Geoffrey Brown's version was the truth. Mr Daniel had been in the office block to search for and steal money and that he was the most likely person to have stolen the £23 charity money from Alf's office.

Andy decided Mr Daniel should be summarily dismissed for theft – with no notice or payment in lieu of notice.

Mr Daniel was about to lodge an appeal against his dismissal when 'a miracle' occurred. Before his appeal hearing could take place, his shop steward, George, received an anonymous, handwritten note in an envelope containing a postal order for £23.

It had arrived at the Union office a week after Mr Daniel's dismissal. The note read, *"I am very sorry. I stole the money. Please do not blame Mr Daniel. I am returning the money. Here is a postal order for £23."*

Andy was asked by the union to ***review*** his original decision and postpone the appeal hearing, to which Andy agreed.

Mr Daniel attended the review meeting with George and the full-time union official, Mr Gordon.

As Mr Daniel could not read or write, Andy knew that the note could not have been written by him. Nevertheless, Andy took the view that this did not clear Mr Daniel's name. Andy still had reasonable grounds to believe that he was the thief.

Andy took the view that the note could have been written by a member of Mr Daniel's family, a friend or a workmate so Andy did not change his decision and Eddie remained dismissed.

Mr Daniel did not appeal as he was offered to do but immediately issued a claim to a Tribunal for unfair dismissal.

His union refused to represent him at the Tribunal. They too did not believe him. Andy was told, off the record, they would not support a thief or a liar.

I represented the Company and Mr Daniel came to the tribunal with his girlfriend, Tracey, acting as his 'representative'.

She asked very few questions of our witnesses. The Judge took the part of Mr Daniel's advocate and she asked most of the questions of our witnesses. There is absolutely nothing wrong in doing this. In fact it is the duty of the Judge to do so, where a Claimant is not legally represented - but what was wrong was the fact that *this* Judge was putting the questions in such a way so as to suggest the answers. That is not part of the Judicial Oath.

We had a most unreasonable and irascible Judge hearing this case. She was well known for her rudeness to the parties and her short temper and she was one of the most appealed against Judges in her day.

As I walked into the Tribunal with my five witnesses, she said to me in a voice which sounded as if she was already in a bad mood, *"If you think I am going to listen to all your witnesses, Ms Howard, you can think again."*

I replied, *"Madam, I have five witnesses and they will all be giving their evidence on oath in this case. It will be your choice whether or not to listen to them"*—not a good start.

She then said, *"And what's all this rubbish?"* as she tipped the trial bundles onto the floor.

I replied, *"They are not rubbish Madam. They are the trial bundles with the documentary evidence to which my witnesses will be referring when giving their evidence. However, I have made a note of both of your comments."*

She was true to her word. She appeared not to listen to the evidence of our witnesses. She tut-tutted, drummed her fingers loudly on her desk, looked bored, looked out of the window and yawned throughout the time my witnesses were giving their evidence.

She was supposed to take verbatim, longhand notes of every word of the evidence given but I could see she took only a few notes. I thought at the time if we needed her notes for an appeal, that was good for us.

After my witnesses had finished giving their evidence she asked them questions to clarify aspects of our defence. There was nothing wrong with that either as the Judge must make sure both parties are on an even playing field and Mr Daniel was not legally represented.

It was then my turn to cross-examine Mr Daniel. He said he had been unemployed for 18 months since his dismissal. However, I noticed he was wearing what looked like a very smart Armani suit, crocodile skin leather shoes, a very expensive designer watch and he was 'dripping' with gold jewellery. He was clearly not short of money.

He clutched a bottle of white medicine and said that it was for the ulcer that we had given him caused by the stress of being dismissed and unfairly labelled a thief. This Judge sympathised with him and told him to ask for as many comfort breaks as he needed. She then scowled at my witnesses who were now all sitting at the back of the tribunal.

I started my cross-examination by asking Mr Daniel about the tools that he had taken with him when he went to the office block.

I asked, *"Tell me about the tools you had with you…"* but before I could finish my question, this Judge butted in, *"You have never said you had any tools with you Mr Daniel did you? You were waiting for a qualified electrician. I dare say you believed he would bring the necessary tools with him, didn't you?"* She stared at him clearly willing him to answer *" Yes."*

I was asking my question because the drawers of the office had been forced open with a screwdriver. I was sure that Mr Daniel would have had a tool bag with him and would therefore have had the opportunity to 'jemmy' open the drawers with a screwdriver.

Taking his lead from the Judge, he smiled at me and said, *"That's right—I didn't 'ave no tools with me. As the Judge 'as just said, I was waiting for an electrician. I thought he would bring his own tools with 'im. So, it couldn't have been me who jemmied open them drawers, could it?"* He laughed as he said this.

He was streetwise enough to know what I was hinting at, picked up on what the Judge had said and dodged my question.

Most of his answers to my questions were *"no comment."* I had to remind him more than once that he was not in a police interview, being questioned under the Police and Criminal Evidence Act 1984 (PACE)—about which, by the way, he seemed very knowledgeable.

I reminded him that he was now giving evidence on oath at a Tribunal at which he was claiming he had been unfairly dismissed. My exhortations to answer my questions fell on deaf ears and I got very little out of him.

When the evidence was over, this Judge and the wing members took less than an hour to rule that it was an unfair dismissal. This Judge ruled that my client did not conduct a sufficient investigation and they failed to hold an appeal hearing.

What more by way of an investigation we could had done remains a mystery to this day. And it was Mr Daniel's choice not to take up the offer to appeal.

The Judge held that Andy Weir had reviewed his own decision and that was unfair. He had failed to carry out any appeal hearing so Mr Daniel never had any chance to appeal to an independent person. An appeal hearing is part of a fair procedure.

But the fact that Mr Daniel did not have an appeal was not the fault of my client. His union had asked for the 'review' meeting, which he was given. Mr Daniel chose not to appeal after his review meeting but to go straight to the Tribunal (without the support of his union).

This Judge held that the Company did not have *"any proof"* that Mr Daniel had stolen the money and he *"had just been in the wrong place at the wrong time."* That, she said, *"warranted only an informal warning."* She awarded him the maximum compensation allowed at the time.

Being the suspicious and rather cynical person I am, I suspected who the anonymous note-writer might have been, having seen the interplay between Mr Daniel and Tracey. I went up to Tracey after the case had ended and congratulated her on her win.

I said I had not taken down a note of the compensation that Mr Daniel had been awarded and asked her if she would kindly write down the figure on a piece of paper for me, with Mr Daniel's address, so I could send him a cheque.

That piece of paper went straight down to a forensic document laboratory, with the original, anonymous note.

The writing on the anonymous note returning the money was found to be an almost perfect match to the handwriting on the paper written and given to me by Tracey.

We appealed the decision to the Employment Appeal Tribunal (EAT). I instructed the brilliant, late Adrian Lynch QC.

The appeal was on the grounds that the Judge had made serious errors of law, had used the wrong test to determine whether the dismissal was fair or unfair, had in effect put herself in the shoes of the employer and held what she would have done faced with the same facts. Her decision also failed to explain to the losing party why they had lost—an essential element of any Judge's decision.

This is the important ruling of the Court of Appeal in *Meek v City of Birmingham* [1987] IRLR 250. That Court held that *"The reasons given by Employment Judges .... are to tell the parties in broad terms why they lose or, as the case may be, win."*

Our Judge, for example, had ruled that my client had not undertaken an *'adequate investigation'* but she had not explained why it was *'inadequate'*.

My client had had two fact-finding meetings with Mr Daniel as part of their investigation, asking him what he was doing in Alf Boyle's office that Saturday afternoon.

They had had all the phone extensions in and around the workshop checked to try to see if any calls had made. There were none.

Geoffrey Brown who had discovered Mr Daniel in Alf Boyle's office had been interviewed and a statement taken from him.

All the men on duty were interviewed by their Works Convenor asking if any of them had made the alleged phone call.

The Maintenance Superintendent had been asked whether there had been any planned or unplanned maintenance on the electrical sockets in Alf Boyle's office over that weekend.

Alf Boyle was interviewed and asked whether he had reported any faulty electrical sockets.

The EAT, without any difficulty, ruled that the Judge's decision should be overturned as it continued several fatal flaws and errors of law.

At the end of its damning Judgement of her decision, in *Tate & Lyle Sugars Ltd v Daniel [1995] UKEAT 928942510*, the EAT remitted the case to a fresh and newly constituted tribunal with the words, *"It is quite clear that it would be embarrassing for this Tribunal to be asked to reconsider the matter in the light of our criticisms."*

The Employment Appeal Tribunal held that, *"The Tribunal should have set out exactly why it was wrong for Mr Weir to reach his conclusion on the material which he had and they seem, as was said to us, to have been addressing themselves very little to what Mr Weir had in his mind at the time and very much more to what they found to be the truth of the situation, having heard the evidence of some of the protagonists, at any rate.*

The Tribunal had held that 'At the time of dismissal the Respondents could not have had a reasonable belief in the truth of the facts, as certain other information only came to his notice after the dismissal had been made'.

..... We accept the employer's submission about this, this was a complete non sequitur.

The question is whether Mr Weir had proper material at the time, material on which he could reasonably form the belief that he said he did, and to say that other information only came to his notice after the dismissal had been made, indicating that he could not have had a reasonable belief in the truth of the facts that he ascertained, is completely illogical and shows that every question relating to the reasonableness of his belief is being begged in the thought process of the Tribunal.

They should, of course, have asked themselves, first of all, "what was before Mr Weir?" secondly, "Had he conducted a reasonable enquiry and if not, what more should he have done?" Thirdly, did he make up his mind bona fide?"—and they seem to have found that he did—and fourthly, "if the material did not justify him making up his mind in that way, why was that?" They should have explained that.

(The Employment Judge went on to hold) 'Further, it is clear to us that the Appeal Hearing was procedurally flawed as it is clear that the Applicant and the union advisers thought that this was an appeal and this appeal was being heard by the same person who originally dismissed the Applicant'.

That seems a very strange conclusion.............

*It is almost inconceivable that the union officers who had requested a **review** meeting would have attended on Mr Weir on the second occasion (the review meeting) but thought that this was an appeal, or that they would have pursued an appeal (in the strict sense) to the man who reached the original decision.*

It seems, from what is set out, so far as the reasons go, that it was of the Union's seeking that this second interview with Mr Weir took place and that what they asked Mr Weir to do was to reconsider his decision in the light of fresh information and arguments that they wished to lay before him, in particular the return of the £23.

So far as the reasons are given, there was really no satisfactory material and certainly no satisfactory explanation to support this conclusion that this was an appeal hearing.

And then the Tribunal says: 'at Para 15: no reasonable employer would have dismissed an Applicant who had been employed for 14 years with only minor conduct blemishes on his record in the way that the Respondents did without making a proper investigation and without making clear to the Applicant that he could appeal the hearing in a proper way. We therefore conclude that this was an unfair dismissal'.

It seems to us that the Tribunal were again short-circuiting matters and not making it clear what a proper investigation would have been; and with regard to the question of an appeal, this very matter had been raised before Mr Weir on 19 May and the matter, so far as could be seen, was made perfectly plain.

It seems to us that talking about making it clear to the Applicant that he could appeal the hearing in a proper way, would have been beside the point when he was represented by union officers.

In due course, being told by his union that they would not take the matter any further, Mr Daniel was apparently left without proper advice about the matter. Whose fault was that? one asks.

How could that possibly be attributed to the employers as unfairness, retrospectively?

We say that it seems clear to us, on reading this decision in a natural and we hope, fair and proper way, that here the Industrial Tribunal were not explaining properly to the employers why they had lost and, indeed, to the Applicant why he was successful.

Furthermore, it is pretty clear that that arises because the Tribunal were, indeed, putting themselves "in the shoes of the employer" and thinking about what they thought was reasonable after reviewing the evidence given to them. There was not a word (as there should have been) about what was before Mr Weir.

It was all about what evidence was given to the Tribunal and the whole emphasis should have been on what was in front of Mr Weir, to see whether he had acted fairly.

We also think that the Tribunal quite inadequately expressed the reasons for saying that the review by Mr Weir was an appeal in the strict sense.

Therefore, we cannot on reading this say that the Tribunal has set out adequate reasons, in an adequate way, showing that they had addressed their minds correctly to the matter and telling the parties how they had come to win or lose the case in front of the Industrial Tribunal.........

We ....think that the only proper course is to remit the matter to an Industrial Tribunal differently constituted.

It is quite clear that it would be embarrassing for this Tribunal to be asked to reconsider the matter in the light of our <u>criticisms</u>." (my emphasis).

As it is the Judge who drafts the decision and informs the lay members about the law, this was a clear criticism of this Judge, quite rightly. Her decision was a travesty and her behaviour at the tribunal hearing quite shocking.

Second Tribunal Hearing

At the second, freshly constituted Tribunal we had an excellent Judge and lay members and the good fortune that Mr Gordon, the full-time union official, gave evidence for the Company.

He explained why the union had not supported Mr Daniel either by putting in an appeal on his behalf or had not represented him at either of the Tribunal hearings or at the Employment Appeal Tribunal.

The Union had asked for the 'review' meeting heard by Andy Weir and no-one believed that this was the appeal hearing.

The original Judge had held it was entirely improper for the review meeting to be heard by the same dismissing manager. It was entirely proper as it was at the request from the Union for Andy to 'review' his decision. There was nothing unfair about that.

The second Tribunal accepted Mr Gordon's evidence without a single question being asked of him and they thanked him for attending. It is very rare for a union to refuse to act for its member no matter what they have done and then to give evidence for the employer at a Tribunal. That was the very high regard the union had for Andy Weir and their view of the egregious behaviour of Mr Daniel.

Our forensic document expert gave evidence that the handwriting on the anonymous note was an almost perfect match to the handwriting of Tracey.

On a scale of 1-5, the specimen of her handwriting had scored "4", the second highest score, for a match with the handwriting on the note sent to the union.

We were confident about the result.

This second Tribunal found the dismissal had been entirely fair. Finally, a job well done for a client who had not put a foot wrong.

A few years later, a well-respected and most congenial Regional Employment Judge met me in the corridor of the same Tribunal. He greeted me warmly and said he had some good news and bad news. *"The good news is that*

Mrs X is retiring" he said with a twinkle in his eye. He then added, *"The bad news is she's coming back part-time."* Oh well, you can't win them all.

After the case was over, I received a call from the SIO (Senior Investigating Officer) from the Serious and Organised Crime Command. He told me that dismissing Mr Daniel had seriously undermined a lengthy covert investigation into a major drugs ring. They had him under surveillance as he worked at the docks and was suspected of being a drugs runner for a major drug dealer in Essex.

Losing his job at the docks meant that Mr Daniel could no longer be kept under surveillance and the police had lost one of their important leads.

This was a most unfortunate consequence of his dismissal. It did however explain the Armani suit, expensive designer watch and gold jewellery I had seen him wearing at the first tribunal.

I suspected that at the time he must be involved in some illicit business, given his affluent appearance and cocky smirk on his face, 18 months after his dismissal and his alleged failure to get another legitimate job.

Chapter 16
Farid's Tale

Farid was a fraudster, who was not very clever, and like many fraudsters, he got caught. Stupidly he boasted to his work colleagues about what he was doing. They didn't like it and someone reported him to the Finance Director and Chief Executive.

The Americans call working for yourself or for another employer, whilst still employed by your primary employer, the euphemism *'external business interests'*. We call it *'moonlighting'*.

In the early 1980s, I acted for a well-known Pharmaceutical Company. Their Sales Director, Farid, was very successful. He won a lucrative contract with the NHS to manufacture and supply a range of prescription drugs and medicines as well as surgical equipment used in operating theatres.

But Farid was a 'bad lad'. He had been 'moonlighting', running his own business with his wife, Aisha, making over the counter (OTC) cold remedies and selling them to a chain of pharmacies in North London.

It worked like this. Farid's wife would call in and say her husband was "sick." He would take at least one week off work, more often two weeks, and be paid full sick pay. He would then return to work, apparently "better."

One day an anonymous phone call informed my client that Farid and his wife were at their warehouse in a Business Park in Wembley and if they were watched at this address, they would be seen "at work."

This anonymous caller and other work colleagues had got fed up with Farid boasting about what he was doing and getting away with. The anonymous caller also said if my client was to watch the CCTV from the back of their warehouse on a particular evening, they would see Farid stealing sacks of granulations, putting them in the boot of his car and driving away.

Sure enough, on the night in question, the CCTV cameras had caught Farid going in and out of the back of the warehouse carrying out large bags of product and placing them in the boot of his car. The products he was seen stealing included vitamin C and paracetamol—used in the making of OTC cold remedies.

The bags of product had been sequentially numbered so they could all be identified. Twenty bags had disappeared from the warehouse that night.

Farid had no legitimate reason to take any product from the warehouse unless of course he was making medicines for his own business.

I was told after this case was over that the anonymous informant was a night security guard whom Farid had annoyed, by not giving him enough of a bribe to turn the security cameras away from the back door of the warehouse.

Private investigators (PIs) were instructed to watch and film Farid's warehouse in Wembley. They filmed Farid and his wife on numerous days going in and out of this warehouse carrying bags of product out of the boot of his car and into the warehouse.

On the following days they were seen driving off in a white van to various Chemist Shops in North London. They went in to the pharmacies carrying bags of product and came out empty handed—except for payment of course. There was no suggestion that the owners of these pharmacies had any idea that these medications were not 'legitimate' and had been made from stolen product.

When Farid returned to work, he was immediately suspended.

During the investigation that followed he was asked whether he owned a pharmaceutical business with his wife and whether, whilst off sick, he had been making cold remedies and selling them to pharmacists. He denied everything.

He was informed of the allegations and was sent the CCTV footage from the back of the warehouse and that from the PIs. A company search was also undertaken and his cold remedy Company was found, registered to him and his wife.

He was required to attend a disciplinary hearing for suspected gross misconduct. He refused to bring a fellow worker or trade union representative with him even though he had a statutory right to do so.

During his hearing he lied through his teeth, denied any wrongdoing and said it was not him in the CCTV footage either at the back of the warehouse or in the PI's video footage of him.

He denied that he and his wife rented a warehouse at the Business Park in Wembley or were co-directors of a limited company, despite having been sent and shown the Company Search.

He was not believed and was summarily dismissed for stealing granulations belonging to his employer; for running his own business during working hours; for taking time off alleging he was sick when he wasn't—in other words lying – and for claiming sick pay when he wasn't sick.

He then brought a claim for unfair dismissal.

The Company search on the Companies House Register disclosed the details of Farid and Aisha's company. It described the company's activities as manufacturing cold remedies.

Farid was a devout Muslim so at the tribunal he swore on the Qur'an (spelt 'Koran' in modern English).

In cross examination I asked him whether he was a Director of the Ultimate Cold Remedy Company Ltd. He denied he was. I reminded him he had sworn to tell the truth and asked him again to confirm whether he and his wife were co-Directors of the 'Ultimate Cold Remedy Company Ltd'. Again, he denied that either he or his wife were directors of *"that or any other Company."*

I then showed him the Company Search, which listed him and his wife as Directors and asked him again whether he would continue to deny that this was his Company, based at the Business Park in Wembley.

The Judge intervened at this stage and advised Farid that he may have committed perjury and to consider his position. The Judge advised him that he could remain silent on the basis of the privilege against self-incrimination. This allows an individual, who is asked to provide an answer which would tend to expose them to a criminal charge, to remain silent and to refuse to answer.

Farid did not seem the least bit troubled and said he would answer my question.

I asked him, *"Would you agree that you have just lied under oath? You and your wife own the Ultimate Cold Remedy Company Ltd and you stole granulations belonging to your employer and have been using them to manufacture and sell cold remedies. We have CCTV footage which I can show you if you like. This is a very serious matter. Do you accept that you have lied to this Tribunal?"*

He replied, *"Yes"*—to my shock and surprise—and then added, *"but you are all Infidels so I have not lied to you. A lie is the truth for Infidels like you."*

184

The Judge then intervened and asked him to explain. Farid replied that telling a lie to nonbelievers was 'a truth' and that lying to infidels was permitted in the Qur'an.

The Judge replied that his explanation for lying in a British Court was unacceptable and that he had committed perjury for which he could go to prison.

Not surprisingly Farid lost his claim for unfair dismissal and was ordered to pay all my client's legal costs.

He was lucky that the Judge did not report him to the police for perjury and he escaped prosecution.

I learnt afterwards that the Qur'an does not permit lies to be told to non-believers. That was another lie by Farid.

He may have been referring to the doctrine of Taqiyya, a practice whereby an individual may be less than fully truthful, when they are reasonably afraid that the consequences of being fully truthful may place them in serious jeopardy by an oppressor.

In other words, if telling the truth is going to place their life or wellbeing at risk, they can say what they need to, to survive and stay safe.

Generally speaking, in Islamic law, necessity makes the forbidden permissible.

So, for example, while alcohol is generally forbidden for believers, if they have no choice but to drink alcohol in order to avoid grievous harm, they are permitted to do so. Taqiyya does not extend to lying on oath in an English Tribunal or Court.

Chapter 17
Faith's Tale

"Coo-ee —it's Stuee—I'm coming to get you," texted Stuart to Faith from his train late one night when he was very drunk.

Stuart was the Director of Menswear for a large chain of retail clothes shops in the UK. Faith was a 21-year-old young girl whose first job after leaving University was a graduate trainee at this retail company. Her first placement was in the Buying Office for Menswear under Stuart's ultimate management.

Stuart started sexually harassing Faith from the start of her employment, bombarding her with text messages in an attempt to get her to have sex with him. Unfortunately, Faith deleted all his messages as soon as she received them as she was so disgusted by them.

Let me paint a picture of Stuart. He was a very overweight, very unattractive 49-year-old gentleman who was always sweating and panting. In fact, describing him as a "sleazebag" and "sex pest" are probably compliments.

I do not know how he could ever have imagined that Faith would find him in the least bit attractive or want to have sex with him but that didn't stop him trying.

He used to call her into his office regularly, inviting her to have lunch or dinner with him.

One day, when she had only recently started at the Company, he called her into his office and told her to come over to his desk. He grabbed her hand and put it on his trousers over his erection. He asked her what she could feel and told her, *"I've got a hard-on. This is what you do to me."*

She immediately ran out of his office into the Ladies and burst into tears and vomited.

Faith told her parents what Stuart had done when she got home that evening. They advised her to report him to HR but Faith said she was too scared. She told her parents that Stuart would deny everything and that as this was her first job, she did not want to be dismissed within weeks of starting and labelled a liar.

So she remained at work.

Then late one night, a few weeks later, when he was very drunk, Stuart texted Faith to say, *"I will be passing the back of your house on the train and I will shout out of the window 'Coo-eee, it's Stueee, I'm coming to get you'. Please ring me. I want sex, sex and more sex with you. I can imagine you now lying on your bed, naked, with your legs open just panting for me. I'm 'coming' if you know what I mean......"*

Faith was terrified, didn't answer him, but this time she kept the text message.

Faith broke down the next day and told her parents what Stuart had texted her. Her father telephoned me and told me what his daughter was going through. I asked them to come to see me.

I knew what I wanted to do to Stuart if I ever met him—perform a 'Bobbit'—cut off his balls (not his penis as Mrs Bobbit had done to her husband). I reckoned I might need a magnifying glass and tweezers to find his 'tackle'.

Faith was very distressed when she came to see me. She used up a whole box of tissues in my office as she described the past few months of hell.

Stuart had clearly never heard that sexual harassment was unlawful—or if he had, he didn't care.

I advised Faith to put in a grievance about Stuart's behaviour, to HR. She allowed me to draft and send it on her behalf. I attached his last text message to the grievance letter.

Faith then resigned out of fear, disgust and distress at how Stuart had behaved towards her. She had only been employed at the Company for just over three months.

Faith told me she was terrified of him and did not trust the Company. She feared they would side with him.

The HR Manager, Melissa, dismissed Faith's grievance without even offering to hold a hearing with her. However Melissa did interview Stuart—allowing him a full opportunity to deny everything.

Melissa stated the usual nonsense, *"It's he said/she said. Stuart has denied everything. You have no eye witnesses and there are no emails or texts (except one) either from him to you or from you to him telling him to stop his alleged unwanted attention so I cannot make a decision that Stuart did what you say he did, or if he did, that it disgusted you and was unwanted.*

There is only one rather inappropriate text message from Stuart that you saved, for which he apologises and says he meant no harm. He says he was very drunk at the time and feeling very lonely. He has agreed to undergo equalities training. The matter is now closed and no further action will be taken."

There are few fundamental errors here.

Firstly Melissa stated the blinding obvious – of course she *"wasn't there"*. It is more often than not *'he said/she said'*. It was her job, just like a Judge, who is also 'never there' when the alleged incidents occur, to determine who, on the balance of probabilities, was telling the truth. She had to determine whether Faith or Stuart was telling the truth.

Secondly she should have asked herself how likely was it that Faith would make up these allegations and lie about such serious matters? It would be career suicide and for what motive? It was hardly likely to enhance her career.

Thirdly, the most common response from men who are accused of sexual harassment is to deny it and say, *"I didn't do it"*. Although once, a man accused of serious sexual assault/rape, on oath, when being cross examined by me, told the tribunal, *"She did it for the money."*

Melissa made the stupid mistake of requiring 'proof' that Stuart had been guilty of multiple acts of sexual harassment instead of weighing up the evidence and considering the likelihood of who was telling the truth. In any event one serious act of sexual harassment is sufficient to establish sexual harassment. It doesn't always have to be multiple acts following the person being told their conduct is unwanted.

There was "similar fact" corroborative evidence—Stuart's text message late at night. That alone should have condemned him. It was pretty clear from the wording of that text that it was not the first communication of that nature that Stuart had sent to Faith so that should have tipped the balance to making it more likely than not that he was guilty of the harassment complained of.

Then Melissa made another mistake, saying there were no eye witnesses. I have rarely, if ever, had a case where the man sexually harasses a woman in front of witnesses. Now that would be dumb.

Melissa also wrongly concluded that because Faith had not sent any emails or texts telling Stuart to stop his sex texts and his attention towards her, they were not *"unwanted"* - one of the legal tests to determine whether the conduct alleged amounts to harassment.

Stuart was several levels/Grades above Faith. He was a Director in a very senior position. Faith told me that she was very worried that sending emails telling him to stop, on the Company server, could be read by others. She could be disciplined or even dismissed for doing so.

Similarly she was worried that she could be accused of sending disrespectful emails to Stuart, about a highly sensitive matter, on the public server, or of libeling him, breaching confidentiality and possibly his data protection rights and right to respect for privacy. This Company reserved the right to monitor and read all emails on the work server.

She said she was also terrified of sending any texts to Stuart about his behaviour on her personal mobile, again, in case he called her a liar and dismissed her.

Faith did complain about Stuart's behaviour through the official formal grievance procedure when it got too much for her to bear - just before she resigned.

The Company's pathetic and wholly inappropriate response to her grievance made matters much worse.

The Equalities and Human Rights Commission's (EHRC's) Guidance on Sexual Harassment states, *"...... ineffective responses to harassment complaints compound the impact of the harassment on the individual."*

Melissa's responses saying there were no eye witnesses and no emails from Faith telling Stuart to stop his unacceptable behaviour, were wholly inappropriate and *'compounded the impact of the harassment'* that Faith had suffered.

I issued tribunal proceedings on behalf of Faith for sexual harassment and discriminatory unfair constructive dismissal against the Company and against Stuart for sexual harassment. We could not claim 'ordinary' unfair constructive dismissal because Faith did not have the required two years' service.

In relation to the absence of Faith explicitly objecting to the harassment, the EHRC's Guidance states, *"It is not necessary for the worker to say that they object to the conduct for it to be unwanted...In some cases, it will be obvious that conduct is unwanted because it would plainly violate a person's dignity... (but it is something a Tribunal will take into account if no objections have been raised).*

'If the harasser's purpose is to violate the worker's dignity or to create an intimidating, hostile, degrading, humiliating or offensive environment for them, this will be sufficient to establish harassment.........

'Unwanted conduct will also amount to harassment if it has the effect of violating the worker's dignity or creating an intimidating, hostile, degrading, humiliating or offensive environment for them, even if that was not the intended purpose."

The London North Industrial Tribunal heard the case. Faith was certainly not keen to go to a Tribunal hearing and explain how she had been treated – but she did.

Stuart was separately legally represented, because the Company ran its statutory defence, which in those days was they had taken *"such steps as were reasonably practicable to prevent the employee from doing that act."*

That was hopeless defence because the Company had done nothing to prevent harassment in their workplace. They had no anti-harassment policy. They had done no equalities training and the then owner was well known for sexually harassing female members of staff and condoned similar behaviour by other male Directors.

I had discussed with Faith what the best compensation award might be. I told her that as she had got another, better paid job within one month of resigning, she had in law mitigated her loss. She only had one month's loss of earnings. I said an award of six months' net pay would be brilliant, to include damages for injury to feelings.

Faith had been paid £22,000 a year gross, £1750 net at this Company. Compensation awarded by a Tribunal is always based on net pay as they have to put the employee back in the position they would have been in had the discriminatory acts or dismissal not taken place.

An element of compensation that can be awarded by tribunals for unlawful discrimination, in addition, is damages for 'injury to feelings'.

This is an award for the hurt, humiliation and degradation suffered by the employee and is considered separately from any claim for financial loss, such as loss of earnings.

Tribunals have a discretion as to what to award for injury to feelings, taking into account the 'Vento' bands, developed in the case of *Vento v Chief Constable of West Yorkshire Police* [2003] IRLR 102, Court of Appeal.

There are three "Vento" bands for damages to injury to feelings—lower band, middle band and higher band. The level of damages in each band usually goes up most years.

At the time of this case the lower band was £500 to £5000. This was for the least serious cases, such as where the discriminatory act is a one-off, relatively minor harassment or discrimination.

The middle band was £5000 to £15,000 and was awarded for serious cases, such as a serious one-off act of harassment or a lengthy but less serious acts of discrimination. This band also covers cases where the discrimination was relatively minor but led to the person losing their job.

The highest band in those days was £15,000 to £25,000—for the most serious cases, such as where there has been a lengthy campaign of discriminatory harassment which has a profound psychiatric effect on the victim.

I was therefore hoping for an award of £10,000 damages for injury to feelings (in the middle of the middle band) plus one month's net salary of £1,458.30, which was a month's loss of earnings before Faith found her new job.

On the first morning of the hearing, the Respondents' barristers asked if we could have a couple of hours before the hearing started, to discuss *"matters outside"*. That meant settlement talks – at last.

The Tribunal understood what that meant and agreed, saying they would read the witness statements and the documents and we should re-convene in the tribunal hearing at 12 noon. The Judge said he wanted to kept updated during the morning because he did not want to lose much time.

We went into our separate waiting rooms. Their Barristers asked me to join them in Counsels' waiting room and they made the first offer.

Twenty minutes later I went back into our waiting room and said to Faith, *"Please listen carefully to what I have to say. Their first offer from both Respondents is £25,000 gross."*

Faith however, remembering what I had told her that she might expect as the best offer said, *"That's amazing and so much more than I was expecting."*

I said, *"So sorry Faith you must have got very confused. I think you must have misheard what we discussed would be an acceptable settlement. I will go back and reject their **first** offer."*

I told Faith that this was just a *first* offer. I told her I knew how to negotiate so I would make a counter offer. I went back into Counsels' waiting room and said, *"Your first offer was insulting and we cannot accept it.*

"We will not accept a penny less than £30,000 from the Company (the maximum tax-free payment allowed by law) and £5,000 from Stuart. We also want a letter of apology from Stuart that I will draft, and an undertaking that the Company will give Faith a good reference when she needs one."

Half an hour later the Respondents' Counsel asked me to go back into their room and told me that both Respondents had accepted our counteroffer.

Faith was amazed and quite frankly so was I. They had not asked, so we had not disclosed, whether Faith had got another job. They may have assumed she hadn't because we said we wanted a reference. Just shows, the first rule is 'never assume anything'.

Faith accepted the settlement, signed the Agreement and withdrew her claim and it was then formally dismissed by the Employment Judge.

One month after the Tribunal hearing, Faith received even better news. Stuart had 'left' the Company. We assumed he had been asked to leave. An announcement was made that Stuart had *"resigned for personal and health reasons."*

When I looked him up on Google, his employment history was littered with resignations from former employments for *"personal reasons"* or *"health reasons."* I surmised that he was a serial sex pest who quite frankly needed medical treatment or castration, one or the other or both.

Chapter 18
The Fraudsters' Tales

Most fraudsters get caught because they are either stupid or they slip up and make mistakes or both. The employees in the cases I describe below were both stupid and made schoolboy errors as well as being dishonest.

George's Tale

George was a Director and shareholder in a very successful architect's practice in the UK. He was a qualified architect and long-time Director of the Firm and owned 30% of the Firm's shares. He ran one of their largest offices in the UK. He had been a Partner in the Firm for 22 years.

Then he had some bad luck. He met a girl many years his junior, got greedy and met me.

In the last year of his employment he would regularly either go AWOL for weeks at a time or ring in sick. On the last occasion when he 'went sick' for two weeks, he had the bad luck to be spotted by one of the Firm's employees, walking into a rival architect's office.

Intrigued as to why George would be visiting a competitor, this employee watched him and then followed him. George came out of this office clutching a file. He was followed to a private residence and was observed going into the property, walking round outside the property with drawing materials in his hand, talking to the owner. He then went back to the rival architect's office.

He was of course supposed to devote his whole time and attention to his employer's business and on this occasion he had called in 'sick'.

It was a clear and flagrant breach of his contract to work for anyone else or for himself at any time during his employment. In addition he had restrictive covenants prohibiting him for six months after he left from working for any competitor or for himself as an architect, or soliciting and dealing with clients with whom he had dealt, in the area of the country in which he had worked, in the 12 months prior to his leaving.

He also had fiduciary duties as a Director, to remain loyal at all times to his employer and work for the sole benefit of his employer and the shareholders.

The employee who had spotted and followed George reported what they had seen to Neville, the Chief Executive. Neville asked me to investigate what George was doing.

I hired a Firm of private investigators (PIs) to investigate George's activities. They rang the rival architects' Firm and managed to speak to a very helpful girl, Michelle. They said they had been left an old Victorian house by their Aunt who had died recently and the house was in total disrepair and in need of complete renovation. They asked if they had an experienced architect who could attend at the property that week.

She told them that George had been working for them on a freelance, consultancy basis for several years. When asked for how long, she said she wasn't sure for how long. She said that he would be free that week and would do the work for them. When they asked to whom they should pay the fees, Michelle told them to pay the fees to George and he would then pay the Firm their share as he worked as a consultant.

The PIs then followed George's car and discovered that he was living with a young, new employee from his office, Sharon. She had been a schoolfriend of George's daughter.

When HR looked into this girl's recruitment, they discovered that George had recruited her without going through any of the approved procedures. He had not obtained any references for her nor had he taken any interview notes. In fact, it appeared she had never even had a formal interview. I wondered exactly what kind of 'interview' George had given her.

He had not asked HR to send out her offer letter or a contract. George had drafted her contract himself, agreeing to pay Sharon a significantly higher salary than anyone else in the office at her grade. In fact she was the second highest paid employee in their office (after George). This was undoubtedly for 'services rendered'.

Upon doing a Company search it was discovered that a newly-formed, limited Company, 'S&G Architectural Co Ltd' had been set up, offering similar architectural services to my client. George and Sharon were joint Directors.

George and Sharon were both put under surveillance for a few days and the video footage was priceless. On one day when they both called in sick, they were followed to the Maidenhead Leisure Centre where, dressed in Lycra gym gear and wearing trainers, they stayed for two hours. After changing into more suitable clothing they then went off for a romantic dinner.

George had alleged, when phoning in sick that day, he had crippling back pain and could hardly walk and said he was bed-bound the entire day.

On the same day, Sharon called in sick alleging that she had a bad dose of flu and was also laid up in bed. Well, we know whose bed they would both have been laid up in if they hadn't been gallivanting round Maidstone.

Sharon was called into Head Office the next day and sacked. She did not even have six months' service, so she could not claim unfair dismissal.

George was immediately suspended and sent all the evidence we had—the statement of the employee who had reported seeing him at the rival architect's office, the video footage of Sharon and George out in Maidenhead during their sick leave; the telephone recording of Michelle reporting George's freelance work for them and the Company search showing he was the joint Director of S&G Architectural Co Ltd.

George was invited to a disciplinary hearing to face multiple offences of gross misconduct.

He held shares in the Company that were valued at a substantial sum. With some clever accounting by the Finance Director, including George's share of dilapidations of the office that he ran (the lease was coming up for renewal), the value of his shares was reduced to a much smaller figure.

Neville instructed me to offer George a leaving package including a substantial amount of money for his shares. I said, *"over my dead body. Please leave this to me"* and they did.

George was called to a disciplinary hearing. He accepted our invitation to have a solicitor to attend with him. We had already sent the solicitor and George the detailed allegations and all the evidence.

It was obvious that neither had not read the documents they had been sent because the solicitor started the hearing by saying, *"my client has done nothing wrong."*

I stopped him and addressed the solicitor and said, *"just one minute—we are running this hearing, not you.*

"We will be taking both of you through each of the allegations and the evidence that we have and we will be asking your client for a detailed explanation in respect of each allegation. A general statement your client has done nothing wrong will not work. So please ask your client to listen to each question and then he must answer it – not you.

"We have substantial proof of his gross misconduct. All the evidence was attached to the disciplinary invite letter that you were sent last week. Perhaps you have not read through it all yet." That soon shut the solicitor up.

The hearing took place on Zoom and George had not switched on his video at the start of our meeting. Apparently, he had always refused to do so during the pandemic.

I wasn't having any of that so I asked George to turn on his video. He pretended not to know how to do it but I said unless he turned on his video so that we could see him, I was ending the hearing and he would be required to attend in person.

I offered to tell him how to turn on the video. I said all he had to do was to click the video button which had a line through it, at the top or bottom of his screen and by some miracle that turned on the video.

He soon managed to find the video button and clicked it on so we could all see him. He was not a pretty sight. He was overweight and sweating heavily. He looked very nervous. It looked as though he hadn't washed or shaved for a week and was wearing a grubby, stained T shirt with holes in that was too small for him and boxer shorts.

He looked bleary eyed and half asleep, slurred his words and clumsily knocked over a large jug of water that he had on a table in front of him, all over the papers. I suspected he had been drinking alcohol before the meeting which was at 11 am. In fact I could see some empty beer cans on the table where George was sitting.

I told him we could have a Without Prejudice (WP) meeting ahead of or instead of the disciplinary hearing. There was a short break and after 10 minutes his solicitor said his client agreed to the WP meeting.

I said on a Without Prejudice basis that we were offering him a significantly smaller the sum for his shares than they were valued at and he could resign without notice and without facing any disciplinary or criminal charges or a civil action for damages. I said I needed his answer to our offer by 4pm the next day.

The solicitor said his client would need the next seven days to consider the offer.

I replied, *"I will say this once and once only. Our offer remains open until 4pm tomorrow. If it is not accepted by then, it will be withdrawn and it will not be put back on the table. A disciplinary hearing will go ahead next week. We will also start civil proceedings against your client for damages and will provide the police with the evidence we have of your client's criminal activities. We will bring a private prosecution if we have to.*

I will also be reporting him to the authorities for consideration for disqualification under The Company Directors Disqualification Act 1986."

The solicitor soon shut up and we ended that meeting. At precisely 3.22 pm the following day I received an email from George's solicitor accepting our offer.

We have no idea what happened to George or Sharon and quite frankly, who cares?

Lewis's Tale

Employees who tell lies about being sick, when they are working elsewhere, or worse still, if they annoy their neighbours while they're working illicitly, should not be surprised when they are reported and get caught.

I acted for an employer who had an anonymous tip off that Lewis, one of their managers, who had been 'off sick' for weeks with an alleged bad back, could be found building his new house in Ipswich.

This tip-off came from a disgruntled neighbour who lived next door to Lewis's plot of land. Peacocks living on Lewis's land had been going into his neighbours' gardens, eating their plants and flowers and making a dreadful din.

This neighbour got fed up with Lewis.

It was not difficult to find out where Lewis's new build was. It was in the days before data protection laws so I rang the Planning Department of Ipswich Council and asked for the address of a self-build plot of land owned by Lewis.

The planning officer was most cooperative and told me the address. The land was called "The Peacocks" and was located just outside the City. The planning officer also told me that they had been receiving complaints from a number of his neighbours about the noise and damage the peacocks were making to their gardens.

Armed with this information I instructed a Private Investigator to go to the address of the new build and video Lewis from the roadside. The video footage was brilliant.

For three consecutive days and then for two days the following week Lewis was filmed building his house. He was shinning up and down ladders carrying heavy planks of timber over one shoulder, building the rafters for his roof, sawing heavy planks of wood and using an axe to chop timber from tree trunks, hammering nails into the walls of the Conservatory that he had built and driving a digger, pile-driving the foundations for his swimming pool. He was also filmed carrying heavy hods of bricks up and down the ladder.

He looked fit as a fiddle to me.

We then called Lewis to 'a welfare meeting' at Head Office in London.

On the day of the 'welfare meeting', Lewis drove his car with his wife as his passenger, to the outskirts of London and pulled into a lay-by. The PI was right behind him filming everything.

Lewis opened the boot of the car, took out a back brace and crutches with apparent ease. He 'dressed up' in his back brace, putting it over his shirt instead of underneath.

He then leant into the back of the car from the driver's side and got out a neck brace, which he put on. He then twisted his neck and shoulders and threw the crutches into the back seat, swapped seats with his wife and she drove the rest of the way to his office.

The PI got to our offices first and showed us the video recordings. Lewis arrived a little later. Observed on the security cameras we could see Lewis "creaking" up the stairs on his crutches, very slowly, assisted by his wife.

We greeted him warmly and asked how he was. He said he had got worse not better and was in agony and most of the time he was in bed on strong painkillers. When asked what they were he said they were morphine patches, 30mgs of codeine and Diazepam.

Then we showed him the footage of him building his house and driving his car and stopping on the motorway.

Lewis first of all said the person in the footage wasn't him. When we showed him a close up of his face, he said it was his *"brother."* We told him we knew his only brother was in prison.

We asked him to describe his medical condition. He said he was *"in the most agonising pain, day and night."* He said he could not sit down on a chair or stand for longer than a few minutes because of the nerve pain and sciatica in his lower back and leg and he had to lie down on the floor.

We then asked him how he had appeared so mobile in the video footage, with no sign of pain on his face. He said, *"I can explain. I have Bell's Palsy and the side of my face you can see is actually paralysed."*

We told him we had already received his medical records and there was no mention of Bell's Palsy. I offered to ring his doctor there and then, to check if the medical notes had omitted this condition. He declined the offer.

When we asked him what he wanted to say about the video footage he uttered the usual excuse, *"you got me on a good day. I was laid up in bed for days before and after that video was taken."*

We told him the footage had been taken on three consecutive days and then two further consecutive days the week after. We said we had heard the same lame excuses before.

I told him we were not 'buying' his story. Prolapsed discs, which is the condition that he alleged he had, are not a fluctuating condition and it is a physical impossibility to do the work he had been doing with prolapsed discs and the excruciating pain that he alleged he had, necessitating back and neck braces, crutches and morphine patches etc.

The video had not been taken on 'a good day'. All his days had been 'good days' - but not for long.

I said we were calling the police reporting him for theft of sick pay when he was not sick.

Lewis looked at our HR Director, winked at her, shook her hand, and without saying another word, got up and legged it down the stairs and out of the office in double quick time, leaving his crutches behind with his wife trailing behind him. My client never saw him again.

Gregory the Thief

Gregory had been a valued and long serving hotel manager until one night he did a midnight flit. He took with him just over £48,000 in cash, stolen from the hotel safe and several bottles of whisky stolen from the bar.

As soon as Morag, my client and the owner of the hotel, discovered he had gone with the cash and whiskey, she called the police.

He was caught at Aberdeen Airport just about to board a plane heading for Buenos Aries. He was handcuffed and arrested by the police and taken to the local police station.

When his suitcase was opened, the cash, £48.004.40, was found along with several bottles of good whiskey. He was charged with theft.

The police told me that when Gregory was arrested and asked where the money had come from, he gave them the same two usual 'stories' that most criminals gave.

His first story was *"I won it on the horses."* When he was unable to say which horse he had put the bet on, how much he had put on, which horse had won, in what race and what the odds were, he changed his story.

He said he was mistaken and the money had been given to him by *"an uncle."* However, he was unable to give the name and address of this fictitious uncle or give any reason why this uncle had given him the money and why Gregory was flying to Buenos Aries with it.

The police told him that what was found in his suitcase was the exact amount that had been stolen from the hotel safe to which only the owner, Morag, and he had the keys.

Gregory was found guilty at the Sheriff Court in Aberdeen and sentenced to twelve months in prison.

My client eventually got her money back. She made sure that the next Hotel Manager was not able to open the safe without her being present as the second key holder.

She also placed CCTV cameras in the bar and in the back office and over the safe. She was not going to be cheated again.

Lawrence 'the Love Rat'

This next case involved a corporate client of mine who owned several Care Homes. Lawrence was the manager of one of their Care Homes and Shirley was the manager of another.

They had both gone off sick at the same time. In another anonymous tip off my client was told that Lawrence and Shirley were having an affair and that Lawrence might be found at Shirley's home on their mutual "sick day."

I instructed my trusted Private Investigator, Steve, to follow Lawrence on the day after he and Shirley had both rung in sick for the rest of the week. Lawrence was filmed driving from his home to Shirley's and going into her house. They

200

were both seen upstairs at her bedroom window. Shirley then drew the bedroom curtains.

About an hour later they both emerged. Lawrence drove Shirley in his car to their local train station and they both got on a train to London. They had a lovely day out, shopping, going to a matinee of The Lion King and then having a meal before they returned home in the early evening. Lawrence's wife returned home half an hour after he got back—perfect timing.

We called Lawrence to a disciplinary hearing, intending to call Shirley to her disciplinary hearing after his.

Because Lawrence was the most senior person at the Care Home and was not a member of a trade union, I advised my client to offer him the option of bringing his wife along as his representative. Employees have a statutory right to be represented only by a fellow worker or a trade union representative but not anyone else. Unaware of what was coming, he accepted the invitation to bring his wife with him. We knew she was an HR Manager.

I suggested that they might both like to watch some video footage, before we started the disciplinary hearing. Lawrence's wife was at first very indignant and protested loudly that her husband had done *"nothing wrong"* and added *"I can't understand why this farce is continuing."* She soon did.

We ignored her and showed them both into the board room, where there was a screen and projector. The PI's recording was switched on and they were left to watch it alone.

After only a few minutes all we could hear was shouting and screaming. Lawrence fled out of the boardroom closely followed by his wife. We never saw either of them again.

Shirley was then invited to her disciplinary hearing but she was much cannier than her lover. She chose not to turn up to her disciplinary hearing and resigned with immediate effect as soon as she received the invitation letter.

Shaun 'The Fraudster'

I used my trusted Private Investigator (PI), Steve, again, in another case for another corporate client.

Shaun initially rang in 'sick' and was 'off sick' for six months when I was instructed.

Shaun was a Stevedore. A stevedore is employed at the docks to load and unload ships. He claimed he had had a bad accident slipping on some oil on the dockside causing severe leg, back and neck injuries from this alleged accident. He put in a claim for personal injuries to his employer's insurers.

Full sick pay was paid by this employer where an employee was off sick with a work-related injury. This had been agreed with the unions. There were, as you can imagine, an unusually high number of 'work-related' injuries.

Being suspicious, because Shaun had already made two previous personal injuries claims in the past three years, I asked the Company's insurers if they would agree to pay for Private Investigators to verify if he was really genuinely injured. They were reluctant to do this so I instructed Steve on behalf of Shaun's employer.

Steve filmed Shaun from the pavement outside his house in order not to breach his right 'to respect for private life' under Article 8 of the Human Rights Act 1998.

It is important that PIs do not film anyone whilst on their private property or where they can expect their privacy. Such evidence will normally be ruled as inadmissible in the courts.

Shaun was filmed from the roadside, in his front garden, lifting a very heavy, full watering can above his head, watering his hanging baskets. He then walked round to the driveway of his house, visible from the road, pulled out the front seats of his Land Rover, hauled them on to a high shelf in his garage and cleaned out the inside of his Land Rover with a hoover.

He then hauled the seats down from the shelf in his garage, polished them and screwed them back into his car.

He then drove to a local park to take his dog for a walk. He was filmed bending over with ease, picking up a ball over and over again and throwing it and some sticks for his dog to chase after.

The HR Manager, Andy, instructed Shaun to come to a gross misconduct disciplinary hearing at their Head Office in Stratford, East London. Andy sent Shaun all the video footage that Steve had filmed.

Shaun said he could not attend any meeting at Head Office because he lived over 50 miles away on the Kent Coast and was in too much pain to come by public transport and was too badly injured to drive himself.

I advised Andy to tell him we would send a private taxi for him. Andy asked me if I had *"gone soft in the head."* I replied, *"you don't know who my taxi driver is?"* It was of course Steve.

Steve had a hidden tape recorder in his pocket and during the 50-mile journey in the taxi, he gained Shaun's confidence and got him talking.

Shaun blabbed that he had taken six months 'off sick', on full pay and had put in a personal injury claim. He admitted to Steve he had actually twisted his ankle when he had gone ten pin bowling one weekend. He said the insurance company had never previously checked on his injuries when he had put in previous claims for compensation. All they had asked for were his GP's medical records and as he put it to Steve, it was *very easy to fool my GP*.

Shaun was probably one of those 'heart-sink' patients. The doctor's heart sinks when they see Shaun coming through their door. He was a very frequent visitor to his doctor's surgery, asking for many 'sick notes' over the years.

In the taxi Shaun told Steve he was doing building and plumbing jobs whilst he was 'off sick'. Shaun also told Steve that his wife, who worked for Kent Council, was also taking time "off sick." She was running a local cleaning business. She received six months' full sick pay and six months' half pay from the Council.

When Steve rang me to tell me 'mission accomplished' he said that Shaun had given him a £5 tip because he had enjoyed talking to Steve so much. He asked me if he could keep the tip. I said, *"Of course."*

At the disciplinary hearing Shaun and his union representative were shown the video and were played the tape recordings in the taxi. The union representative told Shaun to say, *"no comment."* That wasn't very helpful advice.

Shaun was summarily dismissed, without notice or pay in lieu of notice. In the dismissal letter it was put to Shaun that if he had had a plausible explanation for what was seen on the video, he would have given one, but he didn't.

Andy sent the video and tape recording to their insurers who immediately declined Shaun's personal injury claim.

Shaun then sued my Client for unfair dismissal.

He and his union representative walked into the Tribunal, both using two walking sticks. The union representative had had a very bad car accident ten years earlier and was genuinely disabled. I had a sudden fear that the Judge and lay members might mistake the union representative for the Claimant and conclude that he was genuinely injured so I asked both men to identify themselves to the Tribunal Panel.

During my cross-examination Shaun kept forgetting which leg was allegedly injured and which leg had sciatica. Shaun kept pointing to different legs throughout my cross examination despite alleging that he had injured his right leg. This did not go unnoticed by the Judge or the lay members.

We then showed the Tribunal the video footage and played them the tape recording from the taxi ride.

There wasn't much the union official could say after that.

It did not take the Tribunal long to make a finding that the Claimant had lied about his alleged injuries, had made a false claim for sick pay and for damages for personal injuries and had committed gross misconduct. He was held to have been fairly dismissed.

The Judge gave the union official a stern warning about supporting claims that were so obviously fraudulent and made a wasted costs order against the Union for the legal costs of my client defending this claim.

My client then wrote up the case in its monthly newsletter and named and shamed Shaun on the front page. They made sure everyone knew that Shaun had received full pay for six months, while actually working for himself. The report included the fact that he had lied about being injured and had also put in a fraudulent personal injury claim for compensation.

They also reported that they had successfully sued Shaun in the County Court for all the sick pay that he had been paid. The Company got a County Court Judgement (CCJ) against him when he didn't pay. That would seriously damage his credit rating.

He got no sympathy from his workmates who worked hard for their wages.

My client hoped that others would be discouraged from doing anything like this in the future.

Michael – "Taking the Mickey"

Why employees think their employers will not check what they are doing when they go off sick has always been a mystery to me. In the days before LinkedIn and the Internet, there were Yellow Pages and local radio where people used to advertise their businesses. Michael really "took the mickey" but got caught.

He had taken several months off sick with a 'bad back'. It seemed to get worse not better despite the fact that he was supposed to be at home resting. But Michael had some really bad luck whilst 'off sick'.

The HR Manager, Maureen, was looking for a local decorator to do some work in her home so she looked up local decorators in her local Yellow Pages. Guess what?—'Michael Home Decorators' was advertised. She thought she recognised the address and sure enough, it was the same address as the 'Michael' whom her Company employed. He was supposed to be off sick with a bad back.

Maureen rang the phone number given in Yellow Pages, which was Michael's home telephone number and spoke to him. She disguised her voice and asked if he was free to do some decorating at her home, as soon as possible.

He offered to go around to her house the next day to give her an estimate to paint the whole house inside and out, which he did. Maureen's husband, Mick, showed him round while she went out shopping.

Maureen asked me to investigate and catch Michael skiving. So once more I instructed my trusted Private Investigator, Steve.

Steve rang Michael with a brilliant ruse. Steve said he had seen Michael's advert in Yellow Pages and said he had just started a new local minicab service and had recruited five drivers. He said he would need a decorator to paint his new minicab office.

In the meantime, he said he needed to get flyers distributed, advertising his new business. He offered to drive Michael around the town, for free, for the day, if he would distribute flyers for Steve's new minicab service and said Michael could advertise his decorating business at the same time. Steve said that as Croydon had double yellow lines all over town he would stay in the car and would ward off any traffic wardens while Michael distributed their flyers. Michael fell for it.

Steve said he would hire Michael to do the decorating that Steve needed doing and would ask for 'mates rates'. Michael leapt at the offer and had no suspicions he was being set up.

Steve and Michael set off the next morning in Steve's 'minicab'. They drove round the local Croydon area with Michael distributing flyers in local shops and houses for both their businesses or so he thought.

At lunchtime they stopped at a local pub for lunch. Steve then asked Michael for a favour. Steve said his drivers were starting a competition for the best photo of the month. They would all put in £5 each month and the winner would win £30. He asked Michael if he would lift a suitcase in the boot of the car, above his head, and smile, while Steve took photographs. He said he hoped his photos would win him £30 that month.

The suitcase was filled with heavy books and a couple of bricks. It weighed a ton. Michael said he was only too happy to oblige. He took the suitcase and lifted it aloft, like Britain's Strongman, for a couple of minutes while Steve took a series of photos.

The rest, as they say, is history.

Michael was invited to a disciplinary hearing and was summarily dismissed with no notice or pay in lieu. The Company then sued him for all the sick pay he had been paid. Michael never suspected that Steve was in fact a private investigator. He told some ex workmates he could not work out how he had been caught—not very bright then, was he?

Frank the Fraudster

Patience is probably not one of my virtues but in the next case, my impatience paid off dividends.

I had been asked to join an interviewing panel for a new Finance Director for a multi-million pound Housing Association in the UK. They were another corporate client of mine.

After a number of colourless and indifferent candidates a 'star' appeared - Frank. He was a young man in his mid-thirties. Frank said he was working for an Global Investment Bank but it was just after the 2008 world financial crash and he said he wanted a change from the rat race in the City.

He answered all the questions put to him superbly well. He had impeccable qualifications and had done his research on the Housing Association. He asked some very intelligent questions and gave some very intelligent answers.

At the end of his interview I asked whether he would be going back to work or going back home. He said it was only a 30-minute ride on the Underground to the Investment Bank where he currently worked so he would be going back to his office.

As soon as he had left we all agreed he was by far the best candidate. I said we should make him a conditional offer there and then before he was snapped up by another employer.

I looked on his application form for his employer's telephone number, waited an hour and then called the number ready to tell him the job was conditionally his.

The receptionist answered and when I asked for Frank ... she said, *"Frank ... hasn't worked here for the past seven months."*

When I asked why he had left she directed my call to the HR department. I explained why I was asking.

The HR Director told me Frank had been dismissed for theft of over £1,000,000 of client funds. He had left the Bank seven months earlier. They had not reported him to the police because he had paid back some of the money and the Bank had replaced the rest of the funds so their client had lost nothing. The Bank was acutely conscious of the reputational damage this would have caused had it gone public.

I then looked on Frank's application form for his home number, waited another 30 minutes and rang the number. Frank answered. I said who I was and that I was surprised to find him at home because he had told us he was returning to the office.

I told him I had telephoned the Bank with the intention of making him a conditional offer of the job but had discovered he had left the Bank after being caught stealing client funds seven months earlier. I said obviously we would not be offering him the job now.

He then shouted at me, very angry, that he had ticked the 'NO' box to the question, *"May we contact your current employer?"* He said I had breached his data protection rights—as if I cared. Actually, it was the Bank who had breached his data protection rights by speaking to me, not me.

I said in my impatience to call him to offer him the job I had not noticed his answer on his application form to that question. I said I was minded to contact the police because he was now committing a criminal offence under s.16 of the Theft Act 1968 attempting to obtain a pecuniary advantage by deception. He then promptly ended the call.

Intrigued at the name of person that he had given at the Bank as his referee, I called that number. It was a mobile number of a man who purported to be Frank's boss. He said his name was James … Head of Fixed Income. Well that's what he said. Of course, he wasn't Head of Fixed Income.

After this imposter had given Frank a glowing reference, I revealed who I was. I said that I knew Frank had left the Bank seven months earlier and the reason why and asked to whom I was really speaking. The young man admitted he was a junior trader who had agreed to give Frank a reference if he needed one.

I gave this young man a very sharp rebuke. The then Regulatory Body, the Financial Services Authority (FSA), had very strict rules about giving honest references concerning 'approved and registered persons', persons authorised to give investment advice.

James had breached the FSA Rules. He was also aiding and abetting a fraud and was lying, which in a Bank is a very serious matter.

James was really shaken and promised he would never do any such thing again. I told him I would check at another time and if he ever repeated his glowing reference, I would report him to the FSA and to his HR Director whose name and direct number I had. I don't think James ever did that again.

So my impatience for once paid off.

"We're Off to Ibiza"

Social media, Facebook, Instagram and LinkedIn, have proved invaluable to employers when their employees have posted photos of themselves and messages on Facebook and Instagram and information on their LinkedIn profile.

One of my corporate clients sponsored Brian for his part-time B Tech course at the local polytechnic. He was given Fridays off with pay and all his course fees and books were paid for by his employer.

One Friday his employer was very surprised when an employee came into the HR department with copies of Brian's Facebook and Instagram accounts from that morning. It showed photos of Brian and his girlfriend, with the caption, *"Here we are at Gatwick just about to fly off to Ibiza for the week. Got a cheap flight and a very good deal on the hotel."*

My client immediately phoned the Polytechnic to discover that Brian had not been attending his course all year. He had failed to register at the start of his second year. The company had 'reimbursed' him for the second year's fees and for the books for his course and he had been taking off every Friday being paid his normal wages. His employer believed he was attending College.

Of course his employer should have paid the fees direct to the College. This was an error they did not repeat.

The following Monday morning, Brian's mother phoned the company to say her son was *"very unwell with a tummy bug and wouldn't be at work for the rest of that week."*

When Brian returned to work the following week he was confronted with the Facebook photos and the evidence from the Polytechnic. He was asked why he had failed to register for his second year, what he had done with the money he had been given for the course fees and books and what he had been doing every Friday when he was supposed to have been attending College.

He laughed and said, *"More fool you. You didn't check what I was doing. So what are you going to do about it?"*

The HR Manager immediately suspended him and then called him to a disciplinary hearing. His union representative was informed. Brian failed to attend his hearing and no union representative attended either, so Brian was summarily dismissed, in his absence. He did not appeal.

The Company then successfully sued him for the salary he had been paid every Friday during that year and for the College fees and expenses paid for by the Company. They hoped that Brian would learn a lesson and not be dishonest in the future. We heard on the grapevine that he and his girlfriend had gone to Turkey to live and Brian had got a very good job as a labourer on a building site and was doing very well.

However back in the UK, Bill, Brian's uncle, who was also a shop steward at the same Company, had called the men out on strike in protest to Brian's sacking. Alan, the HR Director, called Bill for a meeting after the strike had gone on for four weeks. Alan told Bill that whilst his striking members were not being paid, his nephew was in full paid employment in Turkey, after being sacked entirely fairly for defrauding the Company.

Seeing the irony of this, Bill called off the strike and the men went back to work.

Chapter 19
Gaynor's Tale

Charities often employ many hundreds of staff working all around the world. Sometimes they get it wrong and this Charity certainly did.

It employed a very nasty deputy HR Director, Emma, and an equally nasty HR Director, Shirley. Both were white, bigoted and racist women. They also had a very weak and stupid, long-serving Chief Executive, Kenneth.

Gaynor was my client. She is a woman of colour and a single mother. She was a senior and experienced HR Business Partner and had worked at this Charity for several years, very successfully, until these two individuals came on the scene.

Gaynor was very well liked and respected by everyone who worked with her or met her. Then things all changed when Shirley and Emma were appointed.

Gaynor had had several serious medical conditions including shingles and two prolapsed discs, causing severe neck and back pain. These conditions had necessitated a number of spells off work during her seven years' employment.

In her last unhappy year she was harassed, denigrated and verbally abused by Shirley and Emma. Both women should have known better.

Apart from making fun of Gaynor when she came back to work after a very painful episode of shingles, they denigrated her work and referred to her, within her ear shot, as *"a skiver and work shy."*

Shirley told Gaynor that an offer letter she had drafted was *"complete rubbish and a disgraceful piece of work."* Shirley said their employment lawyer, Matt, had reviewed this offer letter and had said, *"Gaynor should be sacked for gross incompetence. She is not even at the level of a junior HR Business Partner and she has given very poor advice and cannot be trusted."*

I discovered later that Matt had never written any such thing. That was a lie.

Gaynor was then given a final written warning for logging on to the work server whilst off sick. She had been told not to log on *"for work."* She had in fact only logged on to retrieve the appointment made for her to see Occupational Health.

Occupational Health did not have Gaynor's personal email address so she had to log on to her work email so that she could see when her appointment had been made. She did not log on *"for work."*

Nevertheless, Shirley ignored Gaynor's explanation and gave her a final warning for *"disobeying a lawful instruction."*

On her return to work after her last spell off sick with shingles, Gaynor saw Emma pointing at her, and within her earshot, heard Emma saying to Shirley, *"I don't know why we employ people like her. They're all the same—lazy, work shy and always trouble. I think it's genetic.*

"They're always playing the race card if you dare criticise them or tell them their work needs to be improved. They think they are untouchable. They make me sick. But you have to give them a job otherwise they will pull the race card and cry 'racial discrimination'. I would sack her if I were you and do it now."

Shirley refused to allow Gaynor to work reduced hours for the first four weeks after she had returned from sick leave as recommended by their Occupational Health Practitioner.

Gaynor was feeling pretty wretched both physically and emotionally having heard the nasty things that had been said about her.

She was even more distressed when, during her first week back, she was ordered by Emma to offer a job to a friend of the Chief Executive without any interview or checking their references. Gaynor argued this was not right so Emma asked another HR Business Partner to do it and noted in Gaynor's file she had refused to obey her 'lawful instructions'. Of course they were not 'lawful instructions'.

When Gaynor made a complaint to Kenneth about how she was being treated by Emma and Shirley, he told her to go through 'the correct channels', which, he said, *"is not me."*

On my advice Gaynor lodged a formal grievance complaining of race and disability discrimination and bullying by Emma and Shirley. The grievance procedure required the grievance to be sent to Emma and Shirley's line manager—yes, you've guessed it —this was Kenneth.

Gaynor never received an acknowledgement of her grievance nor was it ever investigated.

She then went off sick again with work-related depression and acute anxiety, sleep disorder and suicidal ideation. She lost over 24 lbs in weight in a matter of a few weeks which she could not afford to do as she was rather skinny to start with.

Within seven days of going off sick, Shirley had bent Kenneth's ear to *"sack Gaynor."*

Stupidly Kenneth did not take advice from their employment lawyer, Matt. Instead Shirley instructed an external lawyer, Julie, from a local Firm where Shirley lived, whom Shirley knew personally. That was a really bad mistake and error of judgment.

Julie advised Kenneth to dismiss Gaynor for gross misconduct and gross incompetence by letter, without any investigation or disciplinary hearing—the basic principles of a fair procedure.

Kenneth followed this shocking and obviously flawed advice and dismissed Gaynor and her grievance in the same letter, drafted by Julie and merely signed off by Kenneth. There had been no investigation into Gaynor's grievance nor any attempt to put to Gaynor the entirely false allegations in the dismissal letter.

This dismissal letter referred to 39 alleged errors, incompetence and bad advice made and given by Gaynor. It stated, *"Prior to you going off work this last time, we had been managing serious concerns with respect to you on an informal basis and had taken the decision to formalise these with you. These were concerns which both Shirley and Emma individually and collectively held, and I believe that they did so in good faith and for valid and lawful reasons.*

Whilst you were off work, additional serious concerns arose with respect to you and your performance, your conduct and our ability to have trust and confidence in you.

Clearly, these would have needed to be raised with you and addressed properly and adequately (a) as part of our internal procedures and (b) in advance of any potential return to work (if any).

Yet, we have been unable to do so as we would have wished to, in view of the stance which you have resolutely taken.

We are now at the point at which we cannot continue to defer addressing these matters with you, many of which are, of course, already within your knowledge."

Gaynor had nothing to do with any of the 39 cases of alleged incompetence and gross misconduct. They were either matters for which other HR Business Partners had been responsible or just made up. We had no idea as we never received any supporting documentation in respect of any of the 39 errors etc.

One of the allegations made by Kenneth was that Gaynor had written an offer letter to a job candidate containing major errors, including the wrong salary and an offer of a bonus to which this candidate was not entitled. Gaynor had had nothing to do with the recruitment or appointment of this person nor had she anything to do with the offer letter that had been sent to that job candidate.

Kenneth's dismissal letter went on to threaten legal action, to sue Gaynor for alleged financial losses incurred by her employer, which they argued Gaynor had caused.

The letter continued, *"you will appreciate, these concerns are very serious, numerous and wide-ranging. Individually, they have cost us a substantial amount of money and, cumulatively, a very hefty one, as well as reputational damage, both internally and externally.*

As you already know, under the terms of your contract of employment with us, to the extent that you have caused us financial losses as a result, for example, of negligence and/or breach of contract on your part, we are able to directly recover those losses from you. Hence you have previously offered to compensate us directly in respect of one of the items of loss outlined above......"

This was entirely untrue. Firstly Gaynor's contract said nothing about paying to the Charity any monies for any losses sustained by the Charity caused by her negligence etc – not that she had been negligent. The only term about repayment concerned any loan if one had been made to her, which there hadn't been.

Furthermore Gaynor had never offered to pay for any of these alleged losses. She had no idea to what he was referring.

The letter went on, *"On behalf of the Charity, I expressly reserve its rights in these and all other respects.*

Objectively, your performance has been so poor as to amount to gross misconduct in certain areas.

There are clear conduct-related instances of gross misconduct where you have repeatedly failed to follow instructions, for example, and, essentially, gone about things in your own maverick and highly ill-advised way. We have then had to suffer the consequences of you doing so, as have a number of our employees, who have since left the organisation because of the way you dealt with them.

When you look at the picture which has developed, it is a stark one. It has inevitably led us to the point at which we have been forced to conclude that we have lost trust and confidence in your ability to function as an HR Business Partner or, indeed, within any role within our organisation.

We then have to consider alongside this the fact that, on 1st April, you lodged a grievance with me. This focused upon your line manager, the deputy HR Director, Emma and HR Director, Shirley, and their management of you.

Yet, when you look at the timeline of events, in actual fact, you and Shirley only spent a small amount of time at work together during the period in question, as a result of your numerous and, in many instances, long-term periods of absence. I am bound to say that, if anything, they both dealt with you rather leniently during the period that they line managed you, in view of the nature and number of issues which arose………

Both Shirley and Emma very much consider the allegations which you have made against them are malicious, false and in bad faith. Both have a strong reputation for promoting equality of opportunity and diversity within our organisation as a whole and our HR team in particular, including within the areas of race, ethnic origin and colour.

For my part, as you already know, I too consider the allegations which you levelled against me to have been spurious and malicious and made in bad faith. Where such false allegations are made, in bad faith, you could be disciplined accordingly, for gross misconduct, for which summary dismissal without notice or pay in lieu of notice would typically result.

I say this with direct reference to the contents of our Inclusion & Equal Opportunities Policy and our Dignity at Work policy (both of which I have enclosed for your information).

As to where we go forward from here, I am conscious that we have now spent a considerable amount of time and resourcing in getting to this point, including by way of my direct involvement in things. In spite of this, we essentially remain at an impasse whereby we find ourselves unable to agree any reasonable course of action going forward with you.

You have effectively refused to participate in any internal procedure, in which those you accuse (spuriously or otherwise) are able to defend themselves. This cannot be fair or proper."

Kenneth then dismissed Gaynor with these words, *"In view of your consistent deflection of blame onto others, and primarily individuals who have left the Organisation, it does, however, start to form a modus operandi.*

You have already taken the opportunity to put across your version of events in detail and in writing on multiple occasions whilst off sick, in addition to the explanations which you provided for things whilst at work.

I have listened to the version of events as relayed by Shirley and Emma too. I have also reviewed correspondence and documentation of relevance.

I have taken the decisions to reject the allegations lying at the heart of your grievance and summarily dismiss you on the basis of the concerns which I have identified in this letter.

I am dismissing you summarily, in view of the serious nature and number of the wide-ranging and long-standing, ongoing concerns identified, which you showed no willingness to learn from or improve upon.

I am satisfied that a lot of support and assistance have already been offered and, where applicable, provided to you but that, in view of your mind-set and approach, it failed to generate any improvement upon your part.

Given that these issues go to the very heart of your employment contract with us, and the fundamental terms incorporated within it, such as in respect of trust and confidence, I think that the most appropriate course of action is to terminate your employment summarily without notice or payment in lieu of notice.

I am mindful of the fact that I am taking the unusual step of making these comments without actually having had the opportunity to meet with you but I also think that the circumstances of this case have reasonably necessitated this course of events.

Your employment is terminated summarily, with immediate effect on and from today's date."

He gave Gaynor a right of appeal against the decision to dismiss her and the dismissal of her grievance.

Drafted by me, Gaynor sent in her letter of appeal. Accompanied by me, the appeal was heard by three members of the Charity's Management Board whom I would describe as 'nodding donkeys'.

They had not asked for or been given any 'supporting' documentation concerning the myriad of false allegations of misconduct and incompetence made in Kenneth's dismissal letter even though I had asked that the appeal panel should be given this.

Of course they couldn't be given any evidence, because there was none.

When I asked the Appeal Panel if they had read the ACAS Code of Practice on Disciplinary and Grievance Procedures and the Guidance on how to hold an appeal or indeed whether they had read their own Organisation's appeal procedure, they said 'No'.

They took eight weeks to find that they had 'seen' no evidence of gross misconduct so ordered Gaynor to be paid three months' pay in lieu of notice (taxed). That was the only positive outcome from the Appeal Panel.

They also held they had *'seen'* no evidence of discrimination so rejected that part of her appeal. They did not recommend reinstatement or re-engagement or compensation and said nothing about her grievance.

How they imagined they could *'see'* evidence of discrimination was a mystery to me.

They had been given many examples at the appeal hearing by Gaynor of the racial and other abuse that she had suffered. That was "evidence", so I was at a loss to know in what other form they expected to 'see' this evidence. The appeal panel had clearly just not been listening during the two hour long hearing.

I issued proceedings in the Tribunal for unfair dismissal, race and disability discrimination and victimisation. I named Emma, Shirley and Kenneth as Respondents as well as the Charity.

I advised Gaynor to send an email to Kenneth explaining she had no option but to issue proceedings for the way that she had been treated during her employment and in respect of her outrageous dismissal and unsuccessful appeal.

She added that she would much rather get her lawyer (me) to sit down with their lawyer, Matt, to reach an amicable settlement. I then sent Matt a letter asking him to engage in settlement talks.

Julie, to whom my letter had been passed, then responded with probably the rudest and most stupidly aggressive correspondence I have ever received. It backfired on her spectacularly. Being rude to the other side very rarely if ever achieves anything.

This is only part of her letter to me.

"Dear Madam

I have been instructed to act and advise ..... (name of the Charity). As you know I am not their regular employment lawyer. I have been instructed to deal with you and your client. Please read carefully what I have to say below.

In summary, having considered things very carefully with my client this week, the comments which I wish to make in response to you for present purposes are as follows:

1. *I see no point in corresponding with you about anything relating to a potential exit package for Gaynor.*

2. *But for us learning on Monday evening that Gaynor had gone to you for advice, I would have sent a compromise agreement out to her the following day. We consciously held off on doing so because various people at my Client's organisation are aware of you and your reputation.*

3. *There are times when it is appropriate to behave like a Rottweiler (with or without a handbag) and times when a matter demands a lighter touch. Clearly, it is for you to advise your clients as you see fit but I have to say that the way in which you have handled this matter is, in my view, staggeringly lacking in judgment and not in the slightest bit in Gaynor's best interests.*

4. *It suggests to me you are an 'ambulance-chaser' on a hefty "no win no fee" arrangement. I suggest this is how you act in all your cases, hence your name. Well let me assure you it won't work with my client—not with me acting for them.*

5. *If Matt had been acting for my Client things may have been a different matter but he isn't and I am.*

6. *Gaynor comes across as someone who is stressed and anxious and desperate to get matters concluded under a compromise agreement this week. That being the case, I cannot see how you could possibly have thought that getting her to send the email which she sent to my client's Chief Executive with all of its contents would achieve anything beneficial for her.*

7. *That is particularly the case when you have obviously decided to get her to make wholly unsubstantiated race and disability discrimination allegations for the very first time in what is a flagrant attempt to extort a higher settlement package out of my Client.*

8. *I do not respond well to that type of tactic and nor does my Client. Your letter directed to Matt of 5.52 pm on …[Date] was presumably designed to give 'a heads up' as to what was coming and to make my Client scared*

and to expedite the compromise agreement process. It has had precisely the opposite effect and you should have seen that coming.

9. *Furthermore, I note your assertion that Gaynor's e-mail to my Client's Chief Executive was a 'protected act' under s.27 of the Equality Act. With respect, it was an e-mail written in bad faith, to try to obtain more money for her to leave my Client's employment so s.27 doesn't work for her.*

10. *That being the case, you have not achieved your desired aim.*

11. *Firstly, it does not afford her the protection from the victimisation you allege she has suffered - which she is presumably trying to obtain in respect of it.*

12. *Secondly, the e-mail was not a genuine attempt to resolve a dispute between the parties, so none of its contents attract without prejudice privilege. It is open correspondence and admissible in full, such that any reader can readily ascertain the context in which those allegations were made and for what purpose.*

    Your tactic has not worked in the slightest and I think it is highly regrettable when such tactics are resorted to, particularly when an employee is in a weak position, as Gaynor is, as opposed to a strong one. Right now, my Client could easily take action against her to (amongst other things) recoup a large five figure sum from her in respect of financial losses it has incurred as a result of her acts and omissions. Instead, it has been trying to engage nicely in settlement talks with her, which you have, to date, this week at least, totally derailed for her.

13. *I have seen the contents of Gaynor's e-mail to the Chief Executive and it is completely without merit. How on earth anyone can investigate a grievance of alleged bullying, which arises from a performance management process, without looking at anything to do with that process or hearing anything that the persons involved in that process might wish to say is a mystery to me? It is absolutely risible. It's tantamount to saying that Shirley is not allowed to say anything in her own defence. That simply cannot be right.* (I had no idea what she was referring to as neither Gaynor nor I had ever suggested that either Shirley or Emma should not have a chance to respond to Gaynor's grievance.)

14. *With respect to your/Gaynor's demand for an urgent grievance hearing next week, plainly, that can't happen because Gaynor has already seen*

the occupational health report which has been issued this week, which your client has had since last week. It says that she needs to be afforded some prior notice of any such hearing. The fact that your client has said, on your advice, that she is prepared to go to a grievance hearing next week — you presumably think you know better than doctors. (In fact their own Occupational Health Practitioner had suggested an expedited grievance meeting as the grievance was at the root cause of Gaynor's mental health issues and once resolved, she could start to recover.)

15. *Furthermore, no-one can hear Gaynor's grievance without also hearing things from "the other side of the fence." That includes Shirley's comments on Gaynor because they are of direct relevance to her grievance in countering it.*

16. *As to Gaynor's threat that legal proceedings have been issued and therefore it is in everyone's best interests to agree a without prejudice settlement simply does not wash with me on any level.*

17. *As you know full well, litigation is a means of last resort, having first exhausted internal procedures. Presumably based on your advice, Gaynor "pulled the race card" for the first time late at night on Wednesday and in bad faith.*

18. *I sincerely doubt that she would feel able to give sworn witness testimony on the stand to the effect that she genuinely thinks that there is anything race-related to anything that Shirley and/or Emma have done. Irrespective of that, however, if she instigates proceedings on Monday, she will look wholly unreasonable and she will be in breach of the ACAS Code of Practice which requires a period of Early Conciliation –* something you have patently ignored. (This was yet another error on Zoe's part as I explain below.) *I can't see that she would stand to get any award from a Tribunal but, for the sake of argument, if she were to do so, she would suffer the full 25% reduction on any damages awarded.*

19. *Her employer has devoted a considerable amount of time, effort and money so far to trying to deal with Gaynor in a gracious manner. It is, however, fast reaching the end of the road with her. If she wishes to externalise her grievance, then she can by all means feel free to do so. If she does, that will bring their internal grievance process to an end because she will have elected to externalise it instead.* (This was also wrong because an employer can and often does hold its own grievance

meeting even after legal proceedings have been issued. The one does not preclude the other.) *I trust you have explained that to her fully. That being the case, my client will be at total liberty to push full steam ahead with its wider internal processes, with respect to the concerns which it has against her in the areas of (a) conduct, up to and including gross misconduct, (b) trust and confidence and (c) poor performance/gross incompetence.*

20. *Logically, my client had the right and took it to summarily dismiss her, without any notice or pay in lieu of notice.* (Even the Appeal Panel had held that she should not have been summarily dismissed as they could not 'see' any gross misconduct.) *If your client does not like that outcome, then she can by all means add that to her threatened litigation as well. Where, however, does that get her? Not where she would wish to be. As she will know, her employer does not hesitate to fight Tribunal claims like this and will take them all the way, as do I.*

21. *I have liaised with the Chief Executive this week in connection with the above and the high handed manner in which things have been dealt with by or through you this week. I have somewhat persuaded him that I think that Gaynor has done what she has this week, based on your advice alone, and for that reason only and as a reasonable and indeed, compassionate employer, I think that it should remain willing to consider the possibility of putting a compromise agreement back on the table for Gaynor subject to two provisos.*

22. *Firstly, that I deal with Gaynor directly. You will agree not to be any further involved.*

23. *Secondly, that the level of the settlement package, which her employer would otherwise have been prepared to offer will now be reduced to take account of the wasted time, effort and expense which your actions of this week have caused.*

24. *This letter does, therefore, represent an olive branch. If she would like to give me a call and reassure me that she (not you) is prepared to handle things in a reasonable manner going forward, then her employer and I will respond in kind and get the settlement agreement process back on track. That surely is in her best interests. Her employer is willing to settle the dispute with Gaynor in a reasonable manner and on a reasonable basis; not, however, at any cost.*

25. *Finally, in these circumstances, I have copied Gaynor in on this letter sent by email only.*

26. *She can then by all means progress things as she would see fit. The sooner she does this the better, particularly if she would like to even have the possibility of entering into a compromise agreement today.*

27. *As things presently stand, as you will appreciate, and should have explained to her when you set her off on the path which she is currently on, my time this week has obviously been spent on having to deal with things relating to my legal advice with respect to Gaynor instead of on the possibility of settlement for her. If I am to pause that work, and move back onto her agreement work, then I need to be assured that that is a sensible use of my time (and her employer's money)."*

That is only an extract of the venomous and vituperative letter I received.

Oh dear, oh dear, oh dear - this is a lesson in how never to write to the other side.

I immediately reassured Gaynor that this diatribe was a load of utter nonsense and she should ignore its contents and leave everything to me.

Gaynor was a clever young woman. She said she had every faith in me and agreed to leave Julie to me. Gaynor said she would not ever correspond with this ghastly woman, as Julie had suggested.

Julie had tried to cut me out of the picture because she knew Gaynor was distressed and vulnerable and she thought 'could be got at'. Julie had another thing coming. I wrote back to her saying,

"Madam

The contents of your letter are noted. It is not covered by the Without Prejudice privilege as it no way attempts to achieve a settlement and makes threats which would be regarded as "unambiguous impropriety". I therefore intend to adduce your letter in evidence in respect of any costs application that I may make.

Your letter is littered with factual errors but we can park that for the moment.

Gaynor remains my client and wishes to retain my services. Please direct all future correspondence to me and do not write directly to my client again.

You may be unaware or have ignored the fact that we went through the one month Early Conciliation procedure with ACAS but your client failed to answer any of the conciliation officer's calls or emails.

ACAS has kept records of all the calls and emails made and sent to your client. We have followed the ACAS Early Conciliation protocol to the letter. It is your client who has not done so.

Your client has admitted that it took the 'unusual step' of not conducting any investigation nor did they hold a disciplinary hearing—two basic tenets of a fair procedure. Never a truer word was written as it is a most 'unusual step' not to hold a disciplinary hearing in this day and age.

We will be asking for the full 25% uplift on compensation for unfair dismissal in respect of your client's failures in this regard.

My client's grievance was never investigated nor was she afforded a hearing. I will say no more - 'see you in Court'.

Yours faithfully
The Rottweiler with or without the Handbag."

I did not even attempt to respond to the other appallingly rude and untruthful things that Julie had written.

Two weeks later, Gaynor's employer suddenly, as far as I was aware, dis-instructed Julie and Matt came back on the scene.

Matt put in a holding defence of two lines to our tribunal claim, saying nothing 'was admitted' (a neutral statement) and they would be 'seeking to engage in settlement talks with the Claimant'.

Matt then asked me if we would agree to settlement talks and said their client would pay my legal fees to attend a Without Prejudice meeting with Gaynor. That was a significant change of tone, so of course we said 'Yes'.

We arrived at the settlement talks at Matt's office, to find only him attending on behalf of Gaynor's employer. Neither Shirley, Emma nor Kenneth attended. That was the first surprise but there was an bigger surprise in store for us.

I must say the refreshments laid on for us were quite magnificent – every sort of pastry you can imagine; smoked salmon Bagels; lavish fruit bowls, baskets full of sweets and chocolate; a full array of soft drinks and tea and coffee. I for one did not hold back.

In litigation one always has to be ready for the unexpected—but what happened in these settlement talks had never happened before or since.

Matt attended the settlement meeting with a well-respected female QC acting for his client. I alone acted for Gaynor (with Gaynor there as well).

These settlement discussions were a little like a Mediator-less Mediation. We met in a large meeting room and I summarised to the QC and Matt how Gaynor had been treated during her employment and the manifestly unfair and racist treatment she had received. I read out parts of the egregious dismissal letter with its false and defamatory allegations about Gaynor and their failure to hold any disciplinary hearing before dismissing her and her ludicrous Appeal Hearing and outcome.

I also noted their failure to address Gaynor's grievance and their unwarranted threat to sue her for substantial financial losses that Kenneth alleged the Charity had suffered as a result of Gaynor's incompetence and misconduct for which there was no provision in her contract and for which she had never promised to pay.

I also read out parts of Julie's disgraceful letter to me and said how that had made things much worse.

We then broke into separate rooms. Their QC said she would take instructions about an offer and would come back to see us once she had discussed this with her client.

When I asked from whom their QC was taking instructions, she said only from Kenneth, the Chief Executive, who was available by telephone to give her instructions.

Gaynor and I had a bet about what the first offer would be. I said it would probably be £30,000, the maximum tax-free termination payment allowable by law. Gaynor thought they would start lower.

Their QC came to see us after forty minutes speaking to her client and said, *"My client wishes to make you an offer which I am sure you will agree is a very fair one."*

I nearly fell off my chair when she told me what it was. In fact I asked their QC to repeat the offer. It was an amazingly generous first offer – many times more than we had discussed would have been accepted by Gaynor. For a split second I thought of asking for more but Gaynor was ecstatic with the offer and I too was very happy with the figure proposed.

I said we would agree to that offer if the figure was grossed up so that the sum offered was net of tax. In other words that would be sum in Gaynor's hands after tax, which the Charity would fund.

The QC returned after another 40 minutes and agreed to our request about the tax and told us that they had spent most of that time talking on the telephone to their finance people, as to what the grossed-up figure would be.

When Gaynor and I had picked ourselves up from the floor, we said we also wanted a good reference and a written apology from Kenneth. The QC returned to us after another 15 minutes saying they had agreed to both requests.

Gaynor had to agree that she would not disclose the letter of apology to anyone or publish it anywhere but she had no intention of doing this. She just wanted it to put on the wall of her home to reassure herself that she had done nothing wrong. Her self-confidence was at this point at rock bottom.

I drafted the apology and then it was printed on the Charity's headed notepaper.

Whilst I am not at liberty to share its contents I can say it was a grovelling and fulsome apology listing the things that Kenneth was sorry for, including apologising on behalf of Shirley and Emma for their unacceptable behaviour.

I didn't think that Kenneth would agree to my first draft but bless him – he did. A fax came back with his signed apology on their headed notepaper. The original was posted to Gaynor.

When an apology is given by an employer it is usually in mealy-mouthed language such as, *"We are sorry if you have been distressed and wish you well for the future"*. Worth nothing. This was gold dust and has never happened since.

I asked the QC if Matt would tell me why his client had just rolled over and had made no attempt to negotiate a settlement. She said Matt wanted to meet us again in the main conference room, with her and he would explain.

When we reconvened I first of all thanked Matt for the courteous and professional manner in which he had dealt with us—which I said was a welcome contrast to Julie. A wry smile came over his face when I mentioned her name.

Matt said firstly he wanted to apologise to me personally on behalf of his client for the appallingly rude correspondence from Julie. He thanked me for my considered reply. I said it was water off a duck's back but I thanked him for the apology.

I then asked if he would kindly tell me, on a strictly confidential basis, why they had immediately offered such a generous settlement rather than negotiate with us. I said we were delighted with the settlement and that Gaynor deserved every penny.

Then Matt dropped the bombshell. He told us that Julie had been disinstructed shortly after sending me that appalling letter. Matt had been instructed to settle Gaynor's claim without any argument about the payment. He was to offer a very generous sum to settle. He was then instructed to sue Julie's Firm for her negligent advice that Kenneth had relied upon in dismissing Gaynor.

Julie had advised Kenneth to do this without any evidence of any alleged poor performance or misconduct on Gaynor's part and without giving her a hearing. Julie had drafted the dismissal letter which Kenneth had just signed and sent. It had been her advice to dismiss Gaynor's grievance without investigating her complaints or giving her a hearing or a reasoned decision.

Julie had also advised Kenneth to threaten to sue Gaynor for the alleged financial losses that they falsely accused her of causing by her alleged negligent acts and omissions. Julie had advised this to 'frighten' and 'distress' Gaynor, making her feel even more vulnerable.

Matt asked if we would give our permission for the Compromise Agreement to be shown to Julie's Firm's professional indemnity insurers.

Matt wanted to show the insurers our agreement as evidence of the compensation that their client had had to pay as a result of Julie's negligent advice. I gave Matt a wry smile and said, *"Oh I think we can agree to that."*

Sure enough, proceedings for negligence were issued against Julie's Firm. I gave a witness statement about how the case had been handled and included her letter to me.

As soon as witness statements had been exchanged, her professional indemnity insurers settled the claim in its totality. The insurers repaid to the Charity the settlement sum and the fees paid to the QC and to Matt's Firm for the settlement talks which were no doubt hefty sums. They also reimbursed the Charity for the fees they had paid me to attend the WP settlement meeting. That was a result.

Shortly after the settlement meeting we heard that both Shirley and Emma had 'left' the Charity. Kenneth had 'retired early' on health grounds shortly afterwards but kept his pension.

What happened to Gaynor?

Gaynor went on to achieve great success in her future career and I am pleased to say she recovered from this horrible time. We are still in touch and I admire her greatly.

This was a great result all round in the end, but a very bruising episode for Gaynor—and a very unexpected turn of events. Gaynor showed great courage and great faith in me for which I will forever be grateful.

Chapter 20
Grace's Tale

Grace was a brilliant and very talented History of Art Graduate. She was also very beautiful. After leaving Cambridge she worked for a very successful Brand Imaging Company. Victor was the Co-founder and Chief Executive.

Victor was considerably older than Grace, a very talented man who had a thriving business. He fell madly in love with Grace but he was married with two children. He wanted to have an affair with Grace and told her he would divorce his wife and marry her but Grace wasn't having any of it. She wasn't interested in Victor as a lover or as a potential husband.

Victor had written Grace many passionate love letters and sent her beautiful drawings over three years trying to woo her – but everything he did failed. His love was unrequited and his letters went unanswered. Victor had studied Art at St Martin's College and was a talented artist.

Luckily Grace kept all his letters and drawings and they would have come in very handy during the litigation that we started had we not had the result we did.

Victor found out that Grace was saving to buy a house so he offered to help her to get on the property ladder by making what he called was a 'company loan'. However she discovered that the money had actually come from one of Victor's personal bank accounts.

This loan was never evidenced in writing. There was no paperwork describing it as a loan but Grace always intended to pay him back. She would never have accepted this money as a gift from him, until that is, he dismissed her unfairly and unlawfully. But read on.

Grace told me that she had decided enough was enough after three years of Victor trying to get her to go out with him and become his lover.

Victor however remained madly in love with Grace even after years of fruitless attempts by him to get her to love him. He even followed her when she went to work in one of their offices abroad, when she tried to distance herself from him.

When Grace eventually returned to the UK she met and married a lovely young man her own age.

Victor was bereft and madly jealous and when Grace fell pregnant with her first child, it was more than he could bear. When she emailed him to say she was returning to work after her maternity leave had ended, he emailed her to come to a meeting in his office.

He told her, *"You know how I feel about you. I cannot have you back—it is far too painful for me. You must find another job somewhere else. You must resign right now. Please collect your belongings and leave. You will be paid three months' pay in lieu of notice and any accrued holiday pay."*

It is unlawful discrimination not to allow a woman to return after maternity leave. It is also automatically unfair dismissal.

Grace came to see me and I advised her of her rights. Reluctantly she instructed me to sue the Firm for unfair dismissal and sex discrimination and Victor personally for sexual harassment (his unwanted pursuit of her for several years).

Grace was pregnant with her second baby by the time she would have returned to work and believed, probably quite rightly, that with a young baby just 12 months old and pregnant with a second child, not many employers would give her a job. This was the 1990s when life was particularly difficult for working mothers – it still is.

After we had issued proceedings Victor instructed a notoriously aggressive London Law Firm to act for him and defend the tribunal claim.

Their solicitor, Richard, was a pompous, aggressive, arrogant young man, who was rude and patronising to me and tried to bully me—not a clever thing to do. I say 'tried' to bully me. He didn't have a chance.....

He spoke as if he had silver spoon in his mouth and I was some ignorant lowly creature who was unable to understand words of one syllable. I knew exactly how to handle him.

He told me that Grace had no case and that she would lose in the tribunal and that if we continued with our claim, they would seek costs against her and/or me.

He told me that his instructions were that Grace had resigned. She had, according to Victor, come to the meeting and resigned voluntarily, stating her reason as *"having a young baby to care for and being eight weeks' pregnant with my second child I will be unable to devote sufficient time to my full-time job'*.

Richard told me several times that his client had very deep pockets and would throw any amount of money at this and that they would instruct the best leading counsel they could find. As if that frightened me.

I said, *"Sure—let your client spend whatever money he likes. You don't frighten me and neither does your client. It makes no difference to my client who you instruct. She has lost a superb job and her career for doing nothing other than being a woman and a mother.*

"We will see who the tribunal believes shall we? My client or yours? My client is a successful career woman, who wrote an email saying she was coming back to work. Your client in response called her to a meeting and told her she couldn't come back as it was too painful for him and she had to resign.

"In fact your client dismissed mine as she would not resign as he instructed her to. Your client told mine she had to get her personal belongings and leave. That's unlawful sex discrimination and unfair dismissal in my book. Bring it on.

"When the Tribunal decides that your client unlawfully dismissed mine, we will see what the tribunal makes of a dismissal without any lawful reason other than Grace had a baby and was trying to return to her job after maternity leave. I think that is automatically unfair dismissal and sex discrimination unless I'm mistaken. We will adduce evidence of the sexual harassment to which my client was subjected by yours."

"Nonsense" said Richard, *"I don't know what sexual harassment you are referring to. Your client resigned and said it would be best for all parties if she didn't come back because she couldn't devote her whole time and attention to her job, now she had a baby to care for and was pregnant with her second baby.*

"There was no dismissal automatically unfair or otherwise and no sex discrimination or harassment. Your client resigned of her own volition. In fact I believe my client tried to persuade her to stay and work reduced hours.

"My client is a very well-respected business man. He will be believed and your client will be trashed. Believe me."

I replied rather sharply, *"Well I don't believe your client and no tribunal will either. I see how your client wants to play this.*

"What if I told you that Grace had recorded their meeting when Victor told her she could not return to work because he could not bear to see her married to another man, with a baby and pregnant with her second child and she had to

resign and when she refused, he said 'you will have to leave. I cannot have you back. It's just too painful.'"

We didn't have a recording but this oh so clever and pompous man, did not know that or listen to what I had actually said. I heard Richard draw breath.

I continued, *"I dare say you will have seen the email that my client sent yours the afternoon after she had attempted to return to work. She wrote 'I was devastated today when you told me that I could never come back to work for you because it was too painful for you and that I had to resign. You dismissed me—I haven't resigned and that's not fair.'*

"Does that sound to you like she went to that meeting to resign?

"My client isn't greedy. All she wants is a reasonable settlement. It may take her a year or two to get another job as she is now pregnant with her second child—something she also advised Victor at her meeting with him. Now Grace will miss out on her second paid maternity leave even if she is lucky enough to find another job.

"I will make you a Without Prejudice Save as To Costs offer to settle. What about X years' salary and the bonuses she would have earned and we can call it a day?"

At that, Richard had the cheek to say, *"We will argue your client only wrote that email saying that our client had told her she couldn't return to work, after speaking to you and being told by you that she had lost her opportunity to return to work by resigning."*

I couldn't help laughing out loud and replied, *"Grace didn't even contact me for the first time until exactly a week after the meeting when your client refused to allow her to return. I have that first email of instruction from Grace which I will disclose if you persist in such a nonsensical and defamatory suggestion.*

"I will provide the metadata of that email that Grace sent to Victor showing it went from her computer that same afternoon and was a week before she even called me for the first time.

"I'm appalled that you would accuse me of such devious behaviour and I expect you to retract that accusation immediately unless you have evidence to support this defamatory allegation.

"I don't know who you think you are but I don't give you permission to speak to me like that. You have no business accusing me of dishonesty. You are rude and patronising and you are a bully. Well you and your client will be sorry.

"There are two ways to deal with me – politely, tactfully, respectfully and professionally or in a bullying, rude, sexist and patronising manner. I will leave you to guess which is the more successful way of dealing with me.

"See you in Court as they say. I'm ending the call now. Goodbye."

Perhaps they believed that Grace <u>had</u> recorded the meeting on her phone. I had only said *"What **if** I told you Grace had recorded the meeting"*—I didn't say she *had* recorded it.

This solicitor was not very bright.

Within a matter of days of this first call, Richard rang back to say his client had asked him to start settlement discussions. He sounded just as patronising and there was still that tinge of public schoolboy arrogance in his voice.

To say I was not particularly cooperative with Richard during our settlement discussions is possibly an understatement. I gave him a really hard time and made him sweat.

I would not budge from the original offer I made which was a substantial sum including salary and bonuses and all her legal costs. I doubled the legal costs, with Grace's permission, because I charge a success fee of 100% of the fees charged, when we achieve a successful outcome.

I made Victor pay this success fee because of the egregious way he had behaved towards Grace and the way Richard had spoken to me.

I stated that the salary part of the settlement had to be grossed up to leave Grace with the net compensation we wanted in her hands but I agreed the bonuses and accrued untaken holiday pay could be paid after deduction of tax and NICs.

I suspected Victor would want the matter settled as quickly as possible as he would not want his love for Grace (and his failed pursuit of her which I called sexual harassment in our pleadings) to come out in a public hearing.

I wanted this arrogant solicitor to learn a very valuable lesson—that he would get nothing from me by being rude.

The settlement on my terms was agreed within 48 hours. That was almost a record.

However, Victor had failed to tell his solicitor about all his unanswered love letters he had written to Grace or the money he had given her to help buy her house.

Grace kept all his love letters because Victor never asked for them to be returned. Grace had no intention of making his love letters public.

Legally, copyright in the letters and the notepaper upon which they were written, belonged to Victor. Victor clearly did not want to disclose to his solicitor anything about his failed and unwanted pursuit of Grace or that he had written love letters to her and had sent her numerous beautiful drawings and paintings, demonstrating his love for her, which was unwanted and unrequited.

Victor had also never asked Grace to repay the money he had given her as the rather large deposit for her house. In law that would almost certainly be deemed to be an irrevocable gift. However I had expected to see both those items featured in the Compromise Agreement – the money for the house, set-off against the compensation. But it was silent on both issues.

Once Grace had received her settlement and had transferred it somewhere safe, I had great delight ringing Richard to ask him what Victor wanted to do about all his unanswered love letters and beautiful drawings he had sent Grace over the years. I said I had expected there to be a term requiring these letters and drawings to be returned.

Richard's rather pompous and dismissive tone quickly disappeared as soon as he realised that I knew something he did not. He asked in a rather measured and a tad more respectful voice, *"What unanswered love letters and beautiful drawings?"* I told him to ask Victor and then ring me back.

He rang back to say his client did not know what I was talking about. And that, as they say, was that.

Grace gave me all his love letters and drawings for safekeeping and I still have them in my father's fireproof safe in my office. They would have been used in evidence had we had to go to Tribunal and had the claim not settled, as evidence of the sexual harassment we had pleaded.

I called Richard a few weeks later and asked whether there had been another omission in the Agreement as there was no mention of the money gifted to Grace to assist in the purchase of her house. I said that although this money was definitely a gift I had expected there to be a set-off in respect of those monies and was surprised to see no mention of this in the Agreement.

I asked Richard to check that point as I wanted to ensure that there would be no request to pay back that monetary gift, as Grace was now no longer employed by Victor.

I suggested Richard might think of informing his professional indemnity insurers because it seemed to me that there may have been negligence in his drafting of the terms of the settlement.

Again, Richard sounded thoroughly perplexed and asked, *"What money/gift for the purchase of a house?"*

I suggested he ask his client and then call me back. He never called back.

Chapter 21
Gunilla's Tale

On occasion, I have acted for men who have been falsely accused of sexual harassment. David was such a client. He owned a well-known beauty and cosmetics business. He specialised in high end face and body creams, make-up products and perfumes costing hundreds of pounds. He also employed make-up artists and had clients from all over the world mainly models, pop stars and film stars.

It was therefore a great shock to David when Gunilla complained to the HR Manager that he was in the habit of telling filthy jokes in front of her, full of sexually lewd content and sexual innuendo. She alleged it had created an intimidating, hostile, degrading, humiliating and offensive environment in which to work and she felt violated, degraded and distressed. That is the legal definition of sexual harassment which no doubt Gunilla had looked up on Google.

She had only been employed as an accounts clerk for a few months in the year 2000. David had told her on several occasions that her work was not up to scratch. She had, for example, more than once, sent the wrong invoice to a client, invoicing for significantly less than should have been charged. This resulted in David having to accept reduced payment from the clients who had received the right beauty products or services but the wrong invoice. This caused him to make substantial losses.

Gunilla had done this twice in the space of one month and had been given two written warnings that she had to take care to send the correct invoices out and to check the prices of the products and services and then re-check the invoice, before she sent it out. She was on a final written warning. The next stage was dismissal.

She resigned just before being dismissed after she had been very rude to an important client, a film star who had called to book a make-up artist for a film in Los Angeles. She had telephoned asking to speak to David.

David wasn't in when this client called so they asked when he would be back. Gunilla snarled, *"How do I know? I'm not his secretary. You people think we are all your servants. Call back if you want to speak to David and stop wasting my time."* With that she ended the call.

The client complained to David about how rude Gunilla had been. Gunilla must have realised she would be dismissed as that was the last straw so she resigned, complaining falsely to the HR manager she was resigning because of David's sexual harassment. She brought a claim against his Firm and named him as a Second Respondent, for sexual harassment.

She sold her story to the newspapers in advance of the hearing. The headlines on the first day of the hearing were, *"Boss's jokes turned the air blue—I had to quit my job."* There was also a photograph of Gunilla looking demure and tearful.

David was a quiet, unassuming and deeply religious man, happily married and very respectful of diversity and inclusion. He had an equality policy which gave women, ethnic minorities, people with disabilities and gay and transgender workers positive opportunities for employment in his Firm.

David instructed me to represent him at the tribunal hearing. Gunilla was unrepresented. I'm sure she thought that nice, unassuming and non-litigious David would just pay her off. Not likely with me acting for him.

At the hearing, I cross-examined Gunilla and put it to her that it was she and not David who told dirty jokes. She absolutely denied this. I asked her several times whether she had ever told dirty jokes at work but she repeatedly said, *"No I did not, but that filthy pig David did—all the time."*

I also asked her if she ever used swear words, the 'f' or 'c' words and other sexually offensive language at work but she denied doing so. I put it to her that David had had to warn her on numerous occasions not to use that kind of language. She denied everything. I did not take long cross-examining Gunilla.

I need to describe both parties. David was 5 ft 7 inches in height, slightly built, quietly spoken and rather shy. In contrast Gunilla was a six-foot American lady with a very loud voice and a filthy mouth. Every other word when she was at work was "fuck" this and "fuck" that and she used the "C" word to describe clients and her work colleagues.

David then gave evidence about Gunilla's language at work. He said he had had to warn her over and over again that she should not use these words at work but she didn't take any notice of him.

I asked David to tell the tribunal if he had ever told any inappropriate or lewd jokes at work. He said, *"Never. I never tell rude or lewd jokes, not at home or at work or at social events. I have a zero-tolerance policy for any form of lewd language or discriminatory behaviour or harassment or bullying. If I ever hear any of my children swearing they are told in no uncertain terms that it is not acceptable. They are good kids and they are respectful of my views."*

I asked him about the rest of his workforce. He said, *"I have a very stable, loyal workforce—many of my staff had been with me from the start of my business, for 25 years.*

"Their behaviour and language have always been respectful and polite. "There had been a very good atmosphere amongst my workforce until Gunilla started working with us."

I then asked David if he had ever heard Gunilla telling rude jokes at work. He said, *"Yes. I had to warn her on numerous occasions that her dirty jokes were unacceptable and she must stop telling them, at work. It was Gunilla who told dirty jokes and used filthy language, not me."*

The Judge asked David to repeat one of the jokes that Gunilla had told in the office. David was very reluctant and asked if he could write it down but the Judge said this was a public hearing and David should just tell it. David told this joke below. He said it was one of many risqué jokes that Gunilla had told.

The joke that David recounted for the tribunal certainly turned the air blue. I could feel the buzz of excitement in the hearing room. The Press who were sitting at the back of the room had a field day the next day and this joke appeared in the newspapers.

"A man, an ostrich and a cat walk into a Bar. The barman asks, "*What'll you have?*"

"*I'll have a pint,*" says the man. "*Just a Coke for me,*" says the ostrich. "*I'll have a scotch,*" the cat says. The cat then looks at the man and says: "*As long as you're paying.*"

"*Right,*" says the bartender, "*that'll be £12.75.*"

The man nods and reaches into his pocket. He pulls out exactly £12.75 without counting it, and then another £5 for the tip. He and the animals go and find a table.

Later, the three return to the bar. They order a cider, a ginger ale, and another scotch. Again, the cat isn't paying for any drinks. The barman says that will be £13.50, and the man pulls the exact money from his pocket without looking at it and gives the barman another £5 tip.

This goes on for a few rounds, with the barman naming the price, and the man not even counting his money.

The barman asked the man, "*How are you doing that? pulling out of your pocket the exact money?*"

The man explained: "*I went to a local discount shop and I found this rather dirty, dented lamp but I thought it might come in useful so I paid a £1 for it and brought it home. I was cleaning it up, and out popped a genie. The genie offered me two wishes.*"

"*Only two?*" the barman asked.

"*It was a discount genie,*" the man explained. "*So, for my first wish, I wished to be able always to pull out exactly whatever money I needed to buy whatever I wanted.*"

"*Well, that's clever,*" the barman said, thinking how stupid, as most people would have wished for a million pounds.

"*Yes,*" said the man, "*I thought so too at first, but then I made my second wish.*"

"*And what was that?*" the barman asked.

The man nodded towards his companions. "*For my second wish, I wished for a bird with long legs and a tight pussy.*"

The Judge looked over at Gunilla, asked me if I had further questions for David. I said "*No*".

The Finance manager gave evidence that she had heard Gunilla tell this joke amongst many other lewd and smutty jokes. She confirmed that David had never told a smutty or dirty joke nor did he nor anyone else use lewd or discriminatory language.

Gunilla asked no questions of either of our witnesses.

The Judge said that he and the Tribunal Members would adjourn to make their decision.

They came back an hour later and dismissed Gunilla's case. They held that she had not been sexually harassed by David and that it was she in fact who had defiled the atmosphere in the office with her lewd jokes and offensive and inappropriate language.

The Judge also commented that she had sold her story to the newspapers before the case had started. This could have derailed the hearing. If the lay members or the Judge had read about the case beforehand, (they said they had not seen her story that appeared in a tabloid newspaper), they might have been influenced against David without hearing the evidence. They would then have had to have recused themselves.

The Judge severely criticised Gunilla with the way she had conducted herself. He held that it was a unanimous decision that Gunilla had resigned before she almost certainly would have been dismissed and she had not been harassed.

It was she who had betrayed the trust of a respectable and good man—my client—and when there was a conflict of evidence, they preferred David's evidence to hers.

David was very pleased with the complimentary language which the Judge used about him in his Judgment. This is part of his Judgment.

"David is a man of integrity and honesty. He has run a good business for over 25 years with a loyal workforce We believed his evidence that he has operated a zero-tolerance policy for any form of discrimination, bullying or harassment.

"When there was a conflict of evidence between the Claimant and David, on every occasion we preferred David's evidence.

"We have come to the conclusion reluctantly that the Claimant has lied and has fabricated this entire claim because she knew she was at risk of being dismissed for poor performance and serious misconduct.

"We have come to the reluctant conclusion, given the weight of the evidence against her, that she has made malicious claims in order to obtain compensation to which she is not entitled.

"She even sold her story to the newspapers before this case started.

"We say now that if any Claimant does such a thing in the future, we may strike out their claim because of their unreasonable conduct.

"We are awarding all of the costs of this trial against the Claimant because of her unreasonable conduct throughout this entire claim and the hopeless claims that she brought."

The Judge had, before giving his judgement asked Gunilla about her means. Gunilla had boasted she was a wealthy woman with a substantial private income. We were awarded all the legal costs of defending the case.

The headlines the next day were, *"Woman who told dirty jokes loses her harassment case."* The newspapers then repeated all her allegations and the dirty joke that David had repeated at the hearing.

In the December of that year, I met the Judge at a Chamber's Christmas party and he said he had been rather amused by this case.

I replied that my client felt greatly complimented by the very nice things the Judge had said about him and now we couldn't find a doorway wide enough to get my client's head through.

Chapter 22
Hannah's Tale

For the second time in the space of a two years, I was acting for another employer and a man, both (falsely) accused of sexual harassment. The woman concerned in this case was Hannah. My client was Mr X and his Investment Boutique which we call Y.

This case took place when 'woke' language had not been heard of and there was a more relaxed attitude at how staff were spoken to and about. I doubt that the language used by Mr X would be used by him now.

[This case was the subject of an RRO until the promulgation of the decision. The RRO did not apply to Eire so it was reported there during the hearing.

After the decision was published, the Claimant (Hannah is not her real name) gave numerous interviews to the Press and parts of the evidence given at the tribunal and the decision were published in The Sunday Times and the Daily Mail. Nevertheless I am anonymising all of their names and am not reporting the date when these reports were published.]

After several months of Hannah making complaints and grievances about the level of her salary and bonus, she resigned and sued Mr X and his Firm, Y, for sexual harassment, sex discrimination and victimisation. Her unfair constructive dismissal and breach of contract claims were brought against the Firm only.

She was a very bright but emotionally damaged young woman and her career for some time afterwards was in tatters.

Hannah alleged she had been sexually objectified and humiliated by Mr X and that he had refused to pay her the bonus he owed her. The Tribunal found that the root of her differences with Mr X was her dispute over her salary and bonus.

She alleged that Mr X had abused her and treated her as a sexual object by referring to her, to a prospective client, *"as our tethered goat."* She described this as *"a sexual taunt, using me as a sex object and sexual inducement to the client."*

Mr X admitted that he had used that expression in respect of a deal they were putting together in which Hannah was the lead on that deal. She was an experienced and very astute venture capitalist.

He explained to the tribunal that the idiom *"a tethered goat"* comes from the use of a tethered goat left in a pasture or the Jungle as a lure or bait for hunters to shoot their prey, such as lions.

He had used that expression 'tethered goat' about a number of his male staff on other deals, including one of the other Directors, as a tethered goat. Mr X denied that this phrase had been used in a sexual way or had any sexual connotation.

Hannah also claimed that on one occasion a colleague had brought her new baby into the office. She claimed that when she held the baby, Mr X had remarked that the baby was fixated and looked amazed at the size of her breasts. Nobody else recalled the remark. The tribunal said they did not believe that Mr X had made such a remark.

On another occasion, Mr X's sister brought her dog into the office and had told Hannah and her work colleagues that the dog had stolen a bar of chocolate from her handbag. Hannah claimed that Mr X then said *"bitches love chocolate. You of all people should know that Hannah"*

The tribunal held that Mr X had made a similar remark, but it was '*innocent*' and not directed at Hannah.

Hannah also alleged that he had further denigrated her by referring to her as *"a piggy with her nose in a trough."* Mr X explained that he had referred to all his staff, males and females, as *"piggies with their noses in the trough"* when referring to them waiting for him to announce their bonuses each year.

These were not derogatory or sexist references about Hannah. This was just colourful everyday language that Mr X used about all his staff, men as well as women.

Hannah then alleged that he had told the rest of the staff that he was putting a red light outside her office at 'her time of the month' because she was then like a raging bull. This was also not true.

She had transposed the story that Mr X had told about his father, a successful businessman in Ireland, who had been in the habit of asking his secretary to put a red light outside his office every afternoon between 1 pm and 2 pm, so he could take his afternoon nap without being disturbed by anyone.

Hannah made numerous other claims of sexual taunts. She resisted all attempts to settle the case to avoid lengthy and expensive proceedings. She had rather foolishly instructed one of the major City Law Firms to act for her. That, as it turned out, was a ruinous and another very ill-judged decision.

The Sunday Times reported that, "for reasons not fully explained (Hannah) had hacked into the Bank's confidential data even downloading Mr X's bank details including his cash card pin numbers and details of his stocks and shares. In most big businesses alert to Data Protection legislation this would be treated as an act of gross misconduct."

Mr X would have dismissed her gross misconduct but what she had done was not discovered until several months after she had resigned.

It would also have disqualified her from any bonus she may have been entitled to.

As she was suing for sexual harassment and sex discrimination she would, if successful, be awarded damages for injury to feelings. We therefore asked for any medical evidence that she had suffered any psychological or psychiatric damage as a result of her allegations against my client.

She refused to disclose any medical records so we had to have a Preliminary Hearing where we were applying for an Order for disclosure of all her relevant medical records.

Our expert psychiatrist, Maurice, was so eloquent and persuasive, that in the waiting room before the hearing started, he persuaded Hannah to release all relevant psychiatric and psychological medical records just to him, to her Counsel and to our Counsel. We did not need to obtain an Order.

Her medical records contained some very sensitive issues. When our psychiatrist gave evidence about Hannah's medical history, the tribunal was heard 'in camera'. This is permitted under Rules of the Tribunal where sensitive matters such as a Claimant's sensitive medical records or national security are involved. The Press, members of the public and all the witnesses are required to leave the hearing room.

In an interview she gave to The Sunday Times after the case, Hannah said she *"objected"* to having her medical records disclosed, *"including notes from therapy sessions she underwent after the death of her father in 1999. She had talked about boyfriends, rows with her mother, stress at work and other private matters."*

Hannah alleged these medical records *"were used to discredit her as a witness and cast her as unstable."*

This was untrue but sadly medical records must be disclosed in a claim for damages for injury to feelings and sometimes medical records do disclose matters, such as those in Hannah's case, which are highly sensitive and which perhaps the Claimant wishes to keep confidential.

In a case such as Hannah's where she was claiming damages for injury to feeling, her employer was entitled to see her medical records to see how damaged she had been, as a result of the alleged harassment.

Evidence was given in the Tribunal that in a six month period Hannah had sent 3874 personal emails (57 per day on average) including jokes about orgasms and testicles, some to Mr X, her boss.

This, it was argued on behalf of Mr X, meant that she could not have been harassed or felt 'violated' (the words used in the harassment section of the Equality Act 2010) when he used the expression she was their "tethered goat" or other alleged sexist comments.

Hannah had also deleted, or so she thought, emails to and from her sisters that were recovered from the Company server that showed she had been planning to sue Mr X for many months.

She hired a PR firm before the tribunal to promote her case in the press. When the tribunal agreed early on that she that had not been paid the proper number of weeks' holiday pay, she told the waiting Press on the steps of the tribunal, *"We won, we won"* - somewhat prematurely to say the least.

Her legal team representing her refused to continue to represent her after the first week of the Tribunal. Some people speculated that they may have felt that she had a weak case having seen and heard the evidence. But the simple fact was she had not and could not pay the fees due to this Firm or to her Counsel.

Counsel's fees are required by the Law Society to be paid upfront to the solicitors. This would have left the Law Firm she had instructed liable for

Counsel's fees. The fees owed to her Counsel and her solicitors remained unpaid with a bill which was reported to be in excess of £280,000.

The Tribunal rejected all of Hannah's claims of sexual discrimination and harassment, some of which were out of time. Legal action for acts of discrimination have to brought within three months of those acts having taken place.

Her numerous claims of sexual taunts were rejected by the Tribunal saying that in most cases she had '*misread the situation*'.

The Tribunal did find she had been constructively dismissed but she was awarded nominal damages of £1, on the basis of her contributory fault.

It was also reported that she had falsely claimed she was too unwell to attend the remedies hearing and was 'bed-bound'. One of her former friends informed Mr X that she had misled the tribunal and had in fact been out on the Saturday night at a boozy dinner, drinking herself into a stupor and was still too hung over the following Monday to attend the tribunal.

In the 80-page judgment the Tribunal found her to be *"egocentric"* and *"manipulative and arrogant."* Amongst other things the Tribunal found Hannah to be *"self-centred"* and sometimes *"unreliable"*, *"an obsessive, manipulative and pathological woman."*

Mr X had documents that showed the same calculation for bonuses had been applied to Hannah as her male colleagues. As she had resigned half way through the year, she was not entitled to any bonus for that year.

Bonuses were not paid on a pro rata basis. The rules required employees to remain in employment until bonus payment day and not be under notice or disciplinary suspension.

Hannah had resigned before bonus payment day so was not entitled to any bonus.

The tribunal found that Hannah *"at all times"* failed to understand the system. She tried to put a value on her entitlement, without understanding how the scheme worked.

Hannah alleged nonsensically to the newspapers that the requirement to produce her medical records was *"to punish me because he refused to give me the bonus that he owed me. This was ageist because he could not believe that at my age (she was 33 at the time) I could do the deals I was doing.*

"He made up stories about me being like a raging bull at my time of the month and objectified me in a sexual way to clients. He is a dirty old man and should be locked up."

The newspapers reported her as saying that the Judge and panel members were biased and prejudiced against her and **they** were *"ageist and sexist."*

The headlines in one national newspaper were, *"Getting her goat— Investment Banker loses harassment claims. Tribunal accused of being ageist and sexist."*

The newspaper article repeated the Tribunal's Judgement of Hannah that she was *"egocentric"* and *"manipulative and arrogant."*

The Press described her living the high life, at one point earning €400,000 a year, spending money on designer clothes. The judgment described her as a woman who worked hard and played hard, who was frequently out six nights a week, sent copious emails — 1,500 in a limited search, revealing a social life of partying, drinking and a series of boyfriends.

They reported that the Tribunal described Hannah as *"driven by money, extremely ambitious and convinced of her self-importance, even though she had only a few years' experience. She sought legal advice three times about her salary."*

It said she also showed herself as calculating. *"She chose to bide her time with a view to getting her bonus and extracting five months' pay before leaving to do an MBA."*

The Tribunal found she had an *"inflated view of her importance and contribution"* at the company. The Tribunal said she *"tended to believe she had full knowledge of what was going on in the organisation at senior level, although she was still relatively young and junior."*

The judgment was also very critical of Hannah for taking a confidential list of contacts before leaving the company. She claimed she didn't realise the list was secret. However, the Judge found that her explanation was *"naive, self-centred and not convincing"* in claiming that she did not know that the list was confidential. The tribunal in other words believed she was lying,

It was a very sad decision for this girl who was bright and hardworking but very emotionally damaged.

After the tribunal ended the Law Firm which Hannah had instructed sued her for their unpaid fees. She had to sell her home to pay them. A very sad ending for a very sad and damaged young woman.

Chapter 23
Harriet's Tale

"What great waps you've got" slurped senior lawyer Mark, to Harriet, a more junior lawyer, when he was three sheets to the wind at the office Christmas lunch.

The Olde Wine Shades wine bar in Cannon Street, City of London, was the location for this next case of sexual harassment. This time I was back on the woman's side.

Harriet was a lawyer originally from South Carolina. She had re-qualified in the UK and had joined the legal team of an investment bank in London a year before the incident that sparked off her legal case.

The Legal Team consisted of all male lawyers, except Harriet. She definitely didn't 'fit in' with the laddish behaviour of these men, most of whom had been to elite English Public Schools and Oxbridge. They had a puerile sense of humour and found it impossible to respect women on any level.

They were in the habit of playing practical jokes on each other. For example, Archie, one of the other lawyers, had a receding hairline and was going bald. He was obsessed with his receding hairline and talked about getting a hair transplant.

One day, one of his colleagues rang him, pretending to be a hair transplant clinic offering a special deal. This colleague 'made an appointment' for Archie to attend a clinic in Harley Street for a free consultation. Archie went off to the clinic one lunch hour—only to find it was a hoax.

When it got to December of the year in question, the department had its Christmas lunch. Some of Harriet's male colleagues had decamped to the Wine Bar in the morning a few hours before lunch and been drinking a large amount of alcohol before the start of their lunch.

When Harriet arrived at 1pm, the official start time for lunch, some of her male colleagues were certainly the worse for wear.

One of the senior lawyers, Mark, who had been drinking for nearly two hours, thought it was amusing to say some prurient and impertinent things to Harriet including,

- *"What great waps you've got. ('Waps' is a slang word for breasts) Or is the right word 'baps'?"*
- *"How often do you 'barbecue with your husband and his mate?"*
- *"Do you 'barbecue' inside the house as well as outside?"*
- *"Did you get married at the age of 19 because that was the only way you would have sex with your boyfriend? You're both Catholics aren't you?"*
- *"Why not take your knickers off and I will give you a treat."*
- *"How many times have you had sex with your husband in one night?"*
- *"He's a lucky man having sex with you whenever he likes."*
- *"What's your favourite position—not missionary please?"*
- *"Are you a member of the mile-high club?"* (This is slang for people who have had sex on an aeroplane during the flight.)
- *"Do they call you ginger bush?"* (He was referring to her pubic hair. She was a natural redhead.)
- *"I bet you have a great bum crack. Get your knickers off and let's see."*

Mark then spilt a bottle of red wine all over the table and all over Harriet. She finally had had enough, got up and left the wine bar. When she got home she immediately made a note of what Mark had said to her.

When she looked up the slang meaning of "waps" and "barbecue" she discovered 'waps' meant breasts and 'barbecue' was slang for two men having sex at the same time with a girl, one of them having oral sex and the other having either vaginal or anal sex.

At the time Harriet realised it must have been some form of sexual taunt but she had no idea of those words' actual slang meanings.

When they returned to the office the next day, Harriet lodged a grievance against Mark as he had gone too far. She accused the Bank of *"a culture of bullying and harassment"* and Mark and the other males of having a *"puerile obsession with sex."*

In her grievance she said that Mark and his colleagues, having gone to Eton and Harrow and then all male Colleges in Oxford and Cambridge, appeared to be sex-starved and uncomfortable in a professional woman's company. She suggested they needed special training from an occupational psychologist to make themselves comfortable at work with professional women and equality and diversity training to understand how appalling and unacceptable their behaviour was.

Mark denied saying anything to Harriet of a sexual nature at the Christmas lunch. He and his colleagues all said they were too drunk to recall what had been said.

Harriet's grievance was dismissed with the decision recorded as '*not proven*'. This is a possible verdict in the criminal courts in Scotland but it is not an appropriate decision for a grievance. A grievance must be decided on the balance of probabilities, whether it is well-founded and upheld or dismissed.

Harriet resigned in disgust and instructed me to issue Tribunal proceedings against the Investment Bank and Mark for sexual harassment and constructive dismissal.

Both the Bank and Mark defended the claims—to start with at least.

The Bank argued its statutory defence that they had done everything reasonably practicable to prevent the harassment taking place and placing the blame, if the acts took place, on Mark, the Second Respondent. However the Bank denied that any sexual harassment had taken place.

Mark had to be represented by a separate solicitor and barrister because the Bank's lawyers would have been conflicted after raising this defence.

They both instructed well known London Law Firms, known for their aggressive style of litigating and two experienced QCs.

The statutory defence pleaded by the Bank was hopeless because they had done nothing to ensure that harassment had not taken place. They had done no equality training, had no anti-harassment policy and no disciplinary action had been taken in the past against men who had been the subject of complaints of harassment from other women.

You might think that I was rather devious in this case but it needed to be done. I call it being imaginative.

A tabloid newspaper wanted a photograph and some details about Mark to publish on the first morning of the case. Harriet had no idea where he lived but she had his mobile number.

So I called Mark the week before the tribunal hearing and said I was doing a survey for a national newspaper and if he was prepared to participate, his name would go into a hat for a Prize Draw of a free Sky TV subscription for life. He greedily accepted. So I asked him to tell me,

(1) His full name and address;
(2) His marital status and name of his wife and the names and ages of his children;
(3) His age;
(4) His occupation;
(5) The name of his current employer;
(6) His salary and bonuses; and
(7) The name of his daily and/or Sunday newspaper.

His answer to my last question nearly gave me away. He said he read 'The Sun'. I was so tempted to say, *"You don't **read** The Sun. You just **look** at photos of topless women on Page 3"* but I stopped myself in time.

I thanked Mark for answering my questions and said he would hear **if** he had won the Prize. I hope he isn't still waiting.

I felt that I had won the Prize as I was able to give the photographer and the journalist Mark's home address and some personal details. On the Friday evening before the first day of the hearing the following Monday, the journalists and photographers door-stepped Mark and took some great photos.

On the first morning of the hearing, there was Mark, on the front page of a tabloid newspaper, with his personal details, including his age, the name of his employer, the fact he was married with children and what he earned in salary and bonuses, which was a lot. He looked startled and rather guilty in the photos.

I wanted to make sure that Mark did not get away with his appalling behaviour and that he was named and shamed—and he was.

For a reason I have never been able to fathom, neither of the Respondents asked for a Restricted Reporting Order so the Press were free to name and shame.

The Press could hardly fit in the hearing room on the first day. They were all given copies of Harriet's witness statement which contained the lurid details of her allegations, including what Mark had said to her at the Christmas lunch.

That lunchtime and the next day the Press had more photographs of Mark on their front page. This time he was photographed as he was leaving the Tribunal looking like a guilty schoolboy. The newspapers reported Harriet's allegations as she had set them out in her witness statement.

Before the second day of the hearing started, the Bank and Mark's lawyers asked us to discuss a settlement—at last.

We asked the Judge for time to discuss matters. She knew this meant settlement talks and of course agreed.

After negotiating for nearly the entire second day we reached a fantastic settlement which included a good reference.

The Agreement contained stringent confidentiality clauses ensuring that Harriet said nothing about the details of the settlement. Some of her allegations had already been published in the newspapers including what Mark was alleged to have said at the Christmas lunch. They tied her up in a non-disclosure agreement (NDA) so she would not talk to the Press or the media in the future – but the damage had been done and the story was in the public domain.

Harriet also signed a standard clause in the Agreement that she had not received nor was expecting to receive an offer of employment elsewhere.

Neither the Bank nor Mark had had their chance to deny anything at the hearing.

The papers printed the fact that *"a substantial seven figure sum had been paid in settlement of the case."* At the end of their story it concluded *"the Bank and Mark were not available for comment."*

We hit the BBC and ITV News that evening. I was filmed outside the Tribunal saying, on behalf of Harriet, *"The case has been settled. It has been hugely traumatic for my client but it is now over. She does not wish to say anything else. My client wishes to thank you for your interest but now wishes to get on with her life and asks that you respect her privacy."*

The Press could not be told how much the settlement was for but as one journalist said, they would *'just make it up'*. They speculated the settlement was over £1,000,000. I have no idea how they reached that conclusion.

I don't believe Mark or his solicitors ever realised how his photograph or personal details got into the newspapers on the first morning of the hearing. They do now.

What happened to Mark? He had resigned from the Bank before the hearing at the tribunal started as he had had an offer from another Bank but when they read about the case, this offer was withdrawn. He was reported as saying he was *"unemployable"* and was *"planning to work as a van driver."*

A year later Harriet asked me to issue another claim against the same Bank and this time against the Head of the Legal Department. This was for victimisation. She had read a confidential reference that the Head of Legal had written about her, which she believed was not only untrue but malicious. It certainly was not in the terms of the agreed reference negotiated as part of the settlement.

However two days into this second hearing, the Respondents' QC disclosed a bombshell which was extremely serious and was news to me.

As soon as this was revealed I asked for an adjournment (this was disclosed late on Friday afternoon). Harriet disappeared and after trying to contact her all weekend without success I had to dis-instruct myself because I was now in an impossible position with a client who failed to disclose critical evidence to me and who was dodging me and wouldn't talk to me.

The newspapers reported that she withdrew her claim that the reference had been malicious and made an apology to the Head of Legal. I was out of the picture by now so I had no idea at the time what had gone on. Someone friendly to me at her Bank told me afterwards.

Apparently she had breached the terms of the settlement agreement unknown to me.

Harriet did not however withdraw her allegations in relation to the first claim the year before, that had been settled. It was reported that she paid part of the Bank's legal costs in respect of this second hearing.

Chapter 24
Henrietta's Tale

I am not averse to trying a little gentle 'persuasion' or rather I like to call it 'inducements' to settle on behalf of my clients who are suing their employers— it's the Rottweiler in me. As they say, 'my bark is worse than my bite'.

When I acted for Henrietta, the phrases, "Don't be a hypocrite" and "don't lie to your mistress or cheat on your wife" come to mind, concerning another of the directors of this Firm.

Henrietta had a very good discrimination claim for age and sex discrimination and unfair dismissal. She told me a great story about a Board Director which helped enormously in my settlement talks with him.

Henrietta was dismissed for not agreeing to retire early or resign after 33 years' service —because she was 50. This was after the age discrimination regulations had come into force, making age discrimination unlawful.

Alan, the new Chief Executive, told Henrietta that she was *"over the hill at 50"* and he wanted *"a fresh pair of eyes and new blood in my Boardroom."*

Henrietta had worked for this Company, a global high end luxury goods giant, since the age of 17. She had made an informed choice not to go to university, but to join this Firm's management training programme straight from school. She had worked in one of the stores during the school holidays and had been spotted as potential management material.

She had worked her way up from sales assistant to Director of Womenswear, by the age of 40. She was the first female Board member appointed in the 1980s.

After Alan was appointed Chief Executive, Henrietta fell victim to his appalling, discriminatory views about women who reach 'a certain age'. He wanted beautiful young women in his Boardroom and Henrietta did not 'fit in'. She was an elegant, dedicated, highly professional woman. Being the only woman on the Board, among older grey-haired men, this attitude was not just ageist but sexist too.

In December, exactly six months after Alan had been appointed, at Henrietta's annual appraisal, he rated her "Exceeds Expectations." That is the highest rating possible and less than 1% of the staff in the Firm were ever rated in that category.

When the appraisal was finished, Alan said to her, *"You were 50 last October. I think you've have been here too long and quite frankly you're getting stale.*

"I am being brutally honest. The rest of the Board agree with me. You are too stuck in your ways. The Board needs new blood, someone dynamic with a fresh pair of eyes.

"You can look for another role in the Firm for the next three months. If nothing suits you, you must apply for early retirement or voluntary redundancy. In any event I want you out of here by the end of March."

What Henrietta did not know was that Alan had his 38-year-old girl friend in mind to replace her. There were rumours that he had had an affair with this young woman when they worked together at a previous employer.

Henrietta had no intention of applying for early retirement or volunteering for redundancy or leaving her Board position. She ran their business in the Middle East and Asia, based in Singapore. She had planned to continue working until she was at least 65. She had a partner but no children by choice. The business was her life.

She and her partner lived in a luxury, rented apartment in Singapore, with a live-in Amah (housekeeper), cook and chauffeur all paid for by the Company. She travelled extensively throughout Asia and the Middle East, flying first class wherever she went.

She owned outright a fabulous Penthouse overlooking The Thames at Kew Bridge, which she used as her pied-à-terre when she and her partner came to London.

When Henrietta did not apply for early retirement or voluntary redundancy or resign, Alan instructed HR to dismiss her. She was duly dismissed but was given no reason.

She put in a formal grievance but the Firm's solicitor told her this would never be investigated or dealt with.

She was offered her pay in lieu of notice of one year's salary, which would be taxed and a small bonus taxed and her share options that had vested, which would also be taxed. She had several hundreds of thousands of share options that had not yet vested.

That was all that was offered in settlement. No ex gratia offer was made.

Her salary was nearly £500,000 gross a year and she had earned very good annual bonuses.

The Firm also provided several other valuable benefits such as private health insurance for her and her partner, a generous staff discount on any luxury goods she purchased from any of their stores worldwide and a non-contributory pension and all expenses paid whilst living and working abroad for the Firm. These extra benefits included memberships of several exclusive Clubs in Singapore and a healthy expense account for entertaining.

A non-discounted early pension was however only available if the member of staff had reached the age of 55.

Henrietta refused to accept the settlement offered and instructed me to negotiate a 'decent leaving package'.

She told me at her age and having only ever worked in this high end luxury retail organisation for the same employer, she was highly unlikely to get another job. If she did, it would certainly not be at the same grade or with the same remuneration package. She said her pension, if she took it early, would be heavily discounted.

To begin with Alan denied ever saying anything about wanting to get rid of Henrietta or that she was 'too old' to remain in the Boardroom. Of course this was nonsense.

I wrote to Alan in no uncertain terms saying we had evidence of what he had told Henrietta. She had been so upset after her appraisal meeting after he had told her she was now, at the age of 50, *"too stuck in her ways"* and would have to leave, that she rang her partner from her car that evening, telling him what Alan had said to her and saying she was too distressed go out for her birthday dinner.

I was invited to attend Head Office to negotiate a settlement. I negotiated with Gareth, the Head of Legal and the Company Secretary.

I told him they needed to pay Henrietta not only one year's pay in lieu of notice but substantial compensation for age and sex discrimination to compensate her for her future loss of earnings and damages for injury to feelings.

I argued she would suffer significant loss of future earnings up to the age of 65 (for the next 15 years) when she had intended to retire. She would also lose her future bonuses and additional share options that had not yet vested. In any new employment she would not be eligible for a final salary pension scheme as most of these schemes had closed by this time.

I told Gareth that Henrietta's dismissal, being because of her sex and age, was unlawful discrimination and they needed to compensate her accordingly.

Henrietta, like all long-serving Board members, had no up to date written contract. She only had the very first offer letter she ever had with her job title as "Sales Assistant". This was of course desperately out of date.

Before Alan's appointment, the former Chief Executive had been an honourable man and would have behaved correctly if Henrietta had been dismissed in this fashion in their day. But a different regime had taken over. Alan did not share their sentiments or their sense of honour.

Gareth saw he was going to lose the battle with me and did agree to be generous. He offered to pay several years' salary and benefits. Henrietta also had many thousands of vested shares worth at the time a considerable sum and many other thousands shares vesting in one and two years' time respectively, which Gareth promised to honour but it wasn't over the compensation that we nearly came to blows.

During her handover period of three months before she was forced to leave, Henrietta was given permission to fly round the world to say goodbye to her global clients, many of whom had become good friends.

She flew first class and took her partner with her on some of her trips. She also bought a few 'essentials' on expenses for her retirement, including a new top of the range laptop, a new Apple computer, a new iPad, the latest smartphone for her and her partner, 2 cases of Pol Roger Winston Churchill Champagne 2013, several cases of 20 year malt whisky and a diamond Oyster Rolex watch. She also bought herself a new BMW 7 Series. They were 'retirement' presents to herself.

Gareth told me that he could not agree to the majority of these 'business expenses'. They totalled nearly £200,000. He said the Inland Revenue (as they were called in those days) would never allow them as business expenses. He said if the Revenue audited her expenses, they would deem them to be benefits in kind and taxable and then they would go back at least six years reviewing her business expenses. He said, *"Henrietta would not want that."*

I agreed with Gareth and then got into my stride. Henrietta had told me some interesting things about Gareth.

"Do you know" I asked, *"about one of Henrietta's fellow Directors? The bastard has been having an affair for 17 years with his PA, Adrienne?"*

Gareth visibly blanched. I carried on.

"The bastard keeps promising Adrienne that he will leave his wife and marry her but of course he never will. I am told by a very reliable source that Adrienne got so fed up with his promises she threatened to call his wife and tell her what she and her husband had been getting up to for the past 17 years.

"To shut her up, this Director took Adrienne on an all-expenses paid 'business' trip to Singapore first of all. They had actually had dinner with my client and then they went on to Australia and back to the UK via Los Angeles.

"They flew first class, stayed in luxury hotels and enjoyed fabulous meals. This Director bought Adrienne some expensive jewellery and a Hermes handbag in the duty-free shops—all on company business expenses. I call it 'hush money'.

"I dare say if the Inland Revenue went through that Director's expenses— indeed all of the Directors' expenses—they would find all sorts of items submitted as business expenses over the years that weren't legitimate.

"In fact, if my client was reported or audited by the Revenue then I think it's only fair that I report all of the Board Directors to the Revenue as well as this bastard I'm talking about."

By this time Gareth had gone white as a sheet and was sweating profusely. Sweat was actually dripping onto the table. For a minute I thought he might be having a heart attack.

When he finally managed to compose himself, he mumbled, *"What...errrrr...can I do?"*

I helped him out. I told him he could sign off these expenses as legitimate business expenses. He was Head of Legal as well as Company Secretary and he had full authority to do so. He could make sure that if the auditors could not confirm this payment was a legitimate business expense, the Firm would indemnify Henrietta if the Inland Revenue ever audited these expenses and found that they weren't legitimate business expenses.

And that's what happened. Henrietta was paid for all these 'business' expenses and I had no need to report anyone to the Revenue - or to this 'adulterer's' wife - as if I would.

The settlement included multiple years' salary and pay in lieu of notice, the bonuses that Henrietta would have received over the next three years (which we guesstimated) and all her share options that would vest in the next three years.

She was also allowed to keep her staff discount card for three years. All her legal fees were paid to me in full—a not inconsiderable sum of money.

The compromise agreement (as it was called in those days) also gave Henrietta an indemnity if the Revenue ever audited her expenses. The Company would pay any tax demand, fines, penalties and interest on her behalf.

Gareth rolled over like a little lamb. Just shows what a little, gentle blackmail—I mean persuasion—can do.

Henrietta has a wicked sense of humour. We are good friends with her and her partner, now husband, as they got married shortly after her dismissal. Henrietta suggested that we could have some fun at the next Annual General Meeting (AGM).

I already had shares in this Company so I could also attend the next AGM with Henrietta. I notified Gareth that I had 'an item' for the AGM under any other business (AOB).

The Press were there with microphones and cameras to report on the Company's profits and future plans.

Henrietta and I got to the AGM very early so we had front row seats.

When it got to AOB, I put up my hand to ask a question. Alan and Gareth tried to ignore me until some other shareholders, near the back of the room, unsolicited, shouted out, *"there's a lady in the front row who wants to ask a question."*

Alan was then forced, very reluctantly, to allow me to ask my question. *"Yes, Ms Howard, what would you like to ask?"* He already knew my name before I had got hold of the microphone.

I stood up and stared at Gareth and at Alan for about ten seconds. Gareth went white as a sheet again. I then turned and faced the HR Director, Clara, who was also sitting on the platform.

I said, *"I encouraged my son to buy shares in your company with his Barmitzvah money because I told him you were an ethical employer. What have you got to say about the newspapers calling you and your HR procedures 'brutal' when you recently made a large number of staff redundant?"* I then sat down.

Gareth and Alan clearly thought I had come to the AGM to ask a question about Directors' expenses or worse still about a certain director's affair with his PA. I am not that cruel. Henrietta and I were just having a little fun at their expense.

The relief on the faces of Alan and Gareth was a picture. I thought they were both going to get down from the platform and kiss me—luckily, they didn't.

Henrietta told me another story about this Company. In her last year as a Director, the Board had appointed a well-known Firm of Management Consultants, to assist them in drawing up their Five-Year Plan.

These Consultants were charging eye-watering fees of £1,000,000 so you might have thought they would have come up with something spectacular—but "No"—the only spectacular thing were their fees.

For several months they engaged 'focus groups' and spoke to Regional Operations Managers, Retail Store Managers and sales assistants, asking what direction they thought the Company should go in over the next 5 years and what products were best-sellers and what new products should go into the stores.

These management consultants then addressed the Board with the 5-year plan. They wrote one word on the White Board—"FIT."

The entire Board looked mystified until one of the Management Consultants explained. The Board's Five-Year plan had to ensure that the products in their stores in the next five years were a good *"fit"* with the expectations and needs of their customers BUT the customers had to *"fit"* their shopping habits with the products that would be in their stores during the next five years.

Each Director in turn, like the Emperor's New Clothes, said, *"Fit"*—as if they knew what on earth they were talking about and that this was some magic word. That is, until it came to Henrietta. She addressed the management consultants so that her fellow Board members could hear their answer.

She said, *"Excuse me Gentlemen, am I the only person here having 'a fit', listening to this nonsense? Perhaps I am being a little dense here.*

"You are saying that after months of speaking to focus groups and talking to our Regional Operations Managers, Retail Store managers and sales assistants, our Five-Year Plan must ensure that our products 'fit' in with the expectations of our customers but our customers must 'fit' their shopping habits with the products that we put in our stores?"

Once this had sunk in, Henrietta turned to these management consultants and said, *"This is what you are proposing to charge us £1,000,000 for. Please leave the Boardroom and we will call you back in a few minutes."*

When they left Henrietta said, *"Gentlemen pull yourselves together. This is mumbo jumbo of the worst kind that I have heard in a long time. I for one am not voting to pay these people £1,000,000 and I will be quite happy to share my reasons with the City Press if these Consultants have the nerve to complain or sue us. It is an outrage and certainly not in the best interests of our shareholders."*

One by one all the other Directors came to their senses and agreed with her.

Henrietta told me that the fees that were actually paid to these Management Consultants were only a tiny fraction of the original £1 million. The Consultants never sued for the rest of their fees.

As you might imagine I milked my knowledge of Gareth's activities with Adrienne over the following years (funnily enough without ever having to mention her again). Whenever a dismissed member of staff came to me to negotiate a settlement I managed to get a very good deal for them.

When I could not get exactly what I wanted from the Director with whom I was negotiating, I just gave Gareth a call and he fixed it.

Many years later, one evening at around 7pm, I was surprised when my phone went and a rather wistful voice said, *"I just wanted to say goodbye to the Rottweiler with a handbag."*

For a moment I could not think who this was but then realised it was Gareth. He said he was phoning me from the Boardroom after his farewell drinks. He was a little melancholy or perhaps had a few drinks too many. He was retiring after 40 years at the Firm and he just wanted to say goodbye to me personally. He really was a gentleman at heart. I was very touched and wished him well.

Before you ask—I have no idea if he ever did the honourable thing and leave his wife and marry Adrienne. That would have been a question too far even for me.

I hope Adrienne isn't still waiting for him.

Chapter 25
Iris's Tale

It isn't only men who act in inappropriate and offensive ways. Occasionally, I have found women behaving badly too.

Iris was a clerk in the Sales Department of a corporate client of mine, based in Liverpool. She had used her work computer to write extremely lewd, personal emails to her lover, a lorry driver, whose employer was one of the firm's hauliers.

Using the Company's server for personal use was prohibited. The rules made it clear the company server was to be used for business only. In addition, using abusive, offensive, racist, discriminatory or inappropriate language in emails was also forbidden. Such conduct was an example of gross misconduct under the Company's Disciplinary Procedure.

Iris got caught like most dishonest and stupid people. A customer had called to say that he had placed an order for goods, by email, but the goods had never arrived. Iris swore that no order had ever been received from this client. A search of her computer was undertaken by the IT Department to see if they could find this client's order.

The email placing the order was found, just like the customer had said, but other emails, to and from Iris and Kevin, her lover, were also found that made even me blush.

Iris and Kevin had been exchanging emails describing in graphic detail what they liked doing to each other and how much they enjoyed their sexual relationship. 'Fifty Shades of Grey' had nothing on them (not that I have read 'Fifty Shades of Grey').

The emails included Iris telling Kevin that (these are actual quotes) –

a) *"I would like to smear whipped cream all over your body and then lick it off and lick it off your cock. I will make it hard and then I will jerk you off. You can stick your tongue up my cunt and make me come"*;
b) *"I can undress you and you can undress me and you could perform fellatio on me in your lorry"*;
c) *"We can phone each other when we are at home alone, undress, lie naked on our bed and then we can masturbate and give ourselves an orgasm and we can describe to each other exactly what we are doing."*

There were even worse more explicit messages than these but I think you can get the picture.

Iris was immediately suspended when these emails were discovered and charged with gross misconduct.

The Company asked me to present management's case on their behalf at her disciplinary hearing. She had been sent in advance of the hearing all the offensive emails that had been found.

At the disciplinary hearing I put it to her that she was the author of many *"salacious"* emails (my description). I also described them as depraved and vile and wholly inappropriate and unacceptable language. I said she was charged with breaching the Company's Equality, Dignity and Respect policy and the IT and Email policies, sending personal emails on the Company server.

Her reply to the allegation that her emails were *'salacious'* was, *"I don't think there's anything wrong with my emails and they were personal and private – not for anyone else to read."*

Quick as a flash I replied, *"Oh well that's all right then. If you don't think there's anything wrong with what you wrote to Kevin, I will send your emails to your husband and we will see what he thinks."*

At that, Iris ran out of the hearing and we never saw her again. I call that 'a win'.

Chapter 26
Pauline's Tale

Pauline was raped in the stairwell of her office, one evening, when she was working late. Her line manager, Charles, the Sales and Marketing Director, was also conveniently working late as well. The Firm Pauline worked for is a very successful worldwide pharmaceutical Company.

Charles had asked Pauline to stay late in the office that evening, knowing they would be alone and that everyone else would be going home at the normal finish time.

At around 9 pm, he told Pauline that they should both go home but said the lifts weren't working so they needed to use the stairs. When they got halfway down the stairwell, Charles suddenly pounced on Pauline, pushed her against the wall, tore off her shirt and bra, put his hand up her skirt, pulled down her tights and panties and then unzipped his trousers and raped her.

Shrieking and shouting and trying to get her arms free to hit him, she then tried to bite him. He told her that if she didn't stop struggling he would allege that she had assaulted him and he would call the police and she would be sacked.

He also told her that no-one would hear her screams and no-one would be coming to help her because he had had the security cameras in the stairwell turned off.

After he had raped Pauline, he zipped himself up and told her to keep her mouth shut and stay there for 5 minutes and not run after him or say a word to anyone. He then ran down four floors to the front door and left the building.

Pauline was in severe shock and distress. She walked down the stairs and without saying a word to the security man on duty and drove home on autopilot.

She immediately showered scrubbing herself clean and burned the clothes she had been wearing. She couldn't bring herself to report the rape to the police and she had good reason. When she was 12 years old she had been gang-raped in a park by school boys whom she knew.

When her parents reported this to the police, the male police officer interviewing her told her no one would believe her and that she should go home and forget about it. The police would not even agree to interview the boys whom she had named.

A few days after the rape in the stairwell Pauline called her estranged husband, who was a senior police officer and told him what had happened. He told her not to report the rape as it would be her word against Charles's and the CPS would almost certainly NFA it (take 'no further action') as there was no forensic evidence.

The following week after the rape at work, Pauline made a complaint to her union and they made a formal grievance on her behalf. Charles denied everything and said she was a fantasist.

Because she had not reported the rape at the time, nor had she gone to a hospital or police station, there was no forensic evidence. Pity she didn't take a leaf out of Monica Lewinsky's book and keep the clothing she had been wearing unwashed – but she didn't.

After months of waiting, with no finding about her grievance and the union telling her not to make a fuss, Pauline instructed me to issue a claim against the Company and Charles for sexual harassment.

She had been on sick leave having had a nervous breakdown from the date of the rape.

I wrote the equivalent of a letter of claim to the Chief Executive and copied in their Head of HR, highlighting the history of Charles's sexual harassment ending with the rape on the stairwell and Pauline's mental breakdown after her rape and six months' sick leave.

Charles had, before he had raped Pauline, previously sexually harassed and assaulted her on numerous occasions. Once he had tried to get into her car when she was in the Company's underground car park. He had grabbed at her breasts and at a zip in her trousers and had put his hands on her genitalia.

He had asked her to go out with him on numerous occasions and had made suggestive remarks, including the fact that she had separated from her husband so she *"must want sex with a man rather badly."*

He continually asked her about her dating habits and her sex life. On every occasion she batted back his remarks with rejections, *"I don't think that's appropriate"*, and *"Please stop—don't ask me those kinds of questions. I find them embarrassing."* But that didn't stop Charles.

Pauline told me that her one of her first jobs was as a civilian in the Metropolitan Police. There she had met and married a very handsome Detective Inspector. She was only 20 years of age at the time and he was 20 years older than her.

Sadly she discovered he was having affairs with many other women in the Force and although he begged her to stay and said he would stop his philandering, she finally had had enough.

She did leave him after 14 years of marriage although she never divorced him. At the time she instructed me she was living with a boyfriend.

I issued tribunal proceedings against the Firm and Charles for sexual discrimination and sexual harassment. I argued that although the rape had taken place over six months previously (there was a strict three-month time limit from the act complained of to present a claim) there had been a continuing campaign of discrimination, covering up the rape and failing to deal with her grievance and failing to proceed with any disciplinary action against Charles.

In any event I argued if the tribunal was not with me on that, it was *"just and equitable"* to extend the time limit in this case given the gravity of the offence and the severe mental health and trauma that Pauline had suffered since the rape.

She had not been mentally well enough to present a claim until now. She had in fact been admitted to a mental hospital during the six months after the rape. She was on very strong medication including paroxetine 40mgs. She had been diagnosed with post-traumatic stress disorder (PTSD) and had been referred to Dr Stuart Turner who headed The Trauma Clinic at 7 Devonshire Street in the West End of London (sadly the Clinic is no more).

At the time Pauline came to see me she had run out of Company sick pay and Statutory Sick Pay (SSP) and had just been called to a long-term sickness absence review meeting. This was almost certainly to terminate her employment.

The Company had bombarded her during her six months' sick leave with emails and letters and text messages but Pauline had been far too unwell to answer them. The Company had done this despite the fact that her psychiatrist had written to the then HR Director asking them not to correspond with Pauline as she was too ill to read their letters or to respond and was suicidal.

I asked her Consultant to write a letter stating she was too mentally ill to attend or participate in this absence review meeting. He sent a letter confirming this and said he would review her in another eight weeks.

In fact, when she first came to see me, she found it so distressing to repeat to me what had happened to her that she told me she was seriously contemplating jumping in front of a Tube train when she left my office.

I immediately rang a psychiatrist whom I knew, with her consent, and he persuaded her to be readmitted to The Nightingale Hospital in Lisson Grove, as an in-patient. The Nightingale Hospital is a private hospital treating serious mental illness, addictions, eating disorders etc.

After I issued proceedings, a date for the tribunal hearing was set within six months of our claim being presented. In those days we didn't have to wait for years to get a hearing date.

The Firm and Charles in their defence denied any sexual harassment or that the rape had taken place.

As the Tribunal date got near, just four weeks before it was due to start, we had a real piece of luck. Pauline's then boyfriend found the old mobile phone that she had used to text him on the evening of the rape. She had told him in text messages what had happened. The problem was the battery was dead and it was an old model and she could not find the old charger for this phone.

I took the mobile to a phone expert and he had a charger that fitted the phone and he charged the phone and found the texts.

They read, *"OMG Charles has just raped me. I am disgusted and shattered and cannot believe what he has just done to me. Please, please, please do not call the police or my doctor. The police won't believe me. Charles had the security cameras switched off and is bound to deny he touched me. He tore off my clothes, kept me in an arm lock, then unzipped his trousers and forced himself inside me, penetrating me against my will and then ejaculated all over my stomach. I feel so dirty and disgusting. I just want a good shower and forget it ever happened."*

Her boyfriend's texts in reply had tried to persuade her to call the police and be examined by a police surgeon or to go straight to a Hospital for a medical examination but Pauline refused to do either.

As soon as we were able to access these text messages, I disclosed them to the Firm's and Charles's lawyers.

The Tribunal hearing started and sitting opposite us were a male QC, male Junior Barrister and their instructing solicitor, a male Senior Partner of an aggressive London Law Firm, acting for both Respondents.

Sitting behind them were eight men, four men from the Firm's insurers, two assistants from the Firm of Solicitors representing the Respondents and the Company's new male HR Director who had only been in post for four weeks.

Pauline and I sat at the Claimant's table. We had no-one sitting behind us. I read out an impassioned and compelling Opening Statement. We had a well-known and respected female Judge who was also a QC whom I knew well. She was very moved. I could see tears welled up in the tribunal panel's eyes and Pauline started crying.

The Firm's opening Statement was a blanket denial of all the claims.

After the Tribunal had heard Pauline read out her witness statement and they had been taken to our documentary evidence, including the text messages sent on the night of the rape, there was a distinct change of mood from the Respondents' side.

On the morning of the second day, after my client had finished reading her witness statement but before Respondents' QC had even started his cross examination of Pauline, he asked if we could have the morning to discuss matters with us. The Judge agreed and knew what that meant.

Although the hearing room was full of the Press and TV and radio journalists, the case was the subject of an RRO so the names of none of the parties could be identified.

That didn't stop the newspapers from reporting the case. The headlines in the Evening Standard on the evening of the first day and the major National newspapers the next day all reported that explosive evidence was being given in the London North Industrial Tribunal (as it was then) which contained claims of serious sexual misconduct and rape of a female victim by a senior Executive of a global organisation. The Respondents clearly did not want any more to be published.

We went to our respective waiting rooms. After 10 minutes the Respondents' QC asked to see and said, *"I have an offer for you. I have a feeling this is my Clients' best offer."* He then quoted a ridiculously low sum that was wholly unacceptable.

I immediately said, *"That is merely the excess on your client's insurance policy. We are looking for a substantial settlement, not a paltry sum like that.*

Please go back and tell your clients and the insurers that they will have to do significantly better than that otherwise we are walking out of here and I will ask the Clerk to re-convene the hearing. Your clients have until 12 noon to make us an acceptable offer. I'm not waiting all day for a decent offer."

Their QC repeated, *"I have the feeling this is their best offer."*

I replied, *"Well, that's all right because you're not being paid for your feelings. You are being paid to get the best result for your clients. And you are quite wrong. That's their **first** not final offer. It's a try on. Tell them to remember who they are dealing with. I'm strong and determined to get the best deal for my client. I will do what I have to, to get a proper settlement and justice for Pauline.*

"They wouldn't have asked for time to settle this case to make one pathetically low offer. Please go back to say their offer is rejected outright. Tell them they must make us a substantially better offer otherwise we will see them back in the tribunal at 12 noon."

The QC went back to the Respondents' waiting room and came back to our room 30 minutes later and said he wanted to see me alone.

This QC had been described to me by some other barristers, before the hearing, rather cruelly as *"an employer's hack"* but it just goes to show how wrong people can be.

When their QC and I were alone he asked what I wanted to settle the case. I started by saying that his clients would be ruined if their names were ever made public and they would be named and shamed as soon as the decision was published. The tribunal had stated that they intended to take the final day of this hearing to make a determination and give us an oral decision.

I asked him, *"Do you know what your client's global marketing budget was last year?"* The QC said he didn't know.

I went on, *"it was in excess of £20,000,000 last year; all wasted if this has to go to trial. Your client will be trashed in a heartbeat. I have several journalists baying at my heels for this story and I am quite prepared, after the Tribunal case is over, to give them Pauline's story. There will be no non-disclosure agreement (NDA) then. The names of your client will be plastered all over the front page of the Daily Mail and other newspapers will also then publish the story.*

"A television Company wants to make a documentary featuring my client's story and how she was raped at work and how your client did nothing about it and allowed it to happen and allowed Charles to get away with it.

"I would imagine that this publicity would severely dent your client's marketing plans and severely damage its reputation. I don't think many clients will continue buying your client's products with the headlines they will receive if this doesn't settle and settle quickly on decent terms.

"My client has given her evidence and she is perfectly willing to let me cross examine your clients and then leave it to the Judge and the two lay members to decide this matter.

"We are seeking a substantial settlement as my client hasn't worked for over a year and will almost certainly never work again.

"If your client wants bad publicity, oh boy, we can give them that. I will make sure she is properly remunerated for the hell she has been through—either by your client paying her a proper settlement to set her up so she doesn't have to ever worry about money again or by selling her story after winning this tribunal case."

Their QC looked at me and said, *"You've got more balls than all those men in the other room. Leave this to me."*

Within an hour we had a settlement that Pauline was delighted to accept.

The new HR Director, Paul, then asked if he could see Pauline alone. I was very nervous about this meeting but Pauline agreed. Ten minutes later she came back into our waiting room with tears in her eyes.

Paul had told her he was devastated to learn what had happened to her and how the Company had so badly mishandled her grievance and had told her that, *"things will change when I get back to the office."*

I thought to myself '*Oh Yes, pull the other one*' but I did not share my doubts with Pauline.

Sure enough a week later Pauline rang me to tell me that she had received a phone call from Paul that Charles had been dismissed for gross misconduct, without a penny, not even notice pay and if they were ever requested for a reference for him they would say he had been summarily dismissed for sexual harassment and rape. In other words, he was unemployable.

Pauline went off to Australia with her settlement money, built herself a beautiful villa there and opened a restaurant. She is happily running a business she loves, with plenty of money to live on.

We have remained in touch by Skype and now Zoom. We often speak at around 10 pm UK time, 8am in Australia.

There are times when I have to bare my Rottweiler teeth and get ready to bite. Luckily no-one has dared test me but some, like Charles and his employer, have got awfully close.

The following extract is Pauline's own words, written to me when she knew I was writing this book.

"When I came to see you, Gillian, all those years ago, I was a wreck, not just mentally but physically as well. I know I was actually at the edge. I did not recognise myself because I had gained weight and had not been outside my house for a month. That day, you took charge immediately and acted without hesitation. You also believed me, which was what I needed at that moment.

I remember you being appalled at the way the Company had hounded me and you reassured me that they were at fault, not me; particularly that their internal process they put me through - it was meant to last 14 days and had extended to 6 months. They had written recorded delivery letters each week, sent emails, and texts both to my personal phone and work phone. I felt completely alone and hounded and that somehow this was all my own fault.

You immediately demanded their internal findings, and they delivered it. Once you got that you realised exactly what they had done wrong, and what a strong case we had.

Anyway, what I am saying is, I was at my weakest ebb, and you just went into battle. The true Rottweiler, but not just attacking the foe, guarding me and protecting me from what I felt was an onslaught of harassment.

On the day of the Tribunal, I remember as I walked into the hearing room I was so shocked by the amount of people we were facing that I swayed backwards. You put your hand on the small of my back and held me there, and whispered ***"you can do this."***

It was a powerful moment for me, that I recount to friends, because the inequity between us and them was so large that it caused a physical reaction in me. I will never forget how you went into battle for me and gave me the courage to fight and win. I will never forget what you did for me."

Chapter 27
Sean's Tale

I remember this litigant because his name was Sean Crooks and he certainly lived up to his name. He was crooked to the core and a terrible liar as well.

Sean had been employed by one of my corporate clients, a major Firm in the City. I say 'employed' advisedly and not 'worked for' because he rarely did any work.

He went absent without leave (AWOL) for over a year and failed to remain in contact. He never provided any medical certificates (now called Statements of Fitness) from his GP, despite alleging, in the one phone call he made during that year, that he had a bad back and that was why he couldn't come to work.

He was eventually dismissed for unexplained and lengthy absence from work and for failing to make contact and keep in contact with his employer.

He never attended his disciplinary hearing which was postponed three times and he was finally dismissed in his absence. His employer had gone to great lengths to try to contact him but he never replied to any phone messages, texts or letters.

When he was dismissed however, he miraculously received his dismissal letter, sent to his matrimonial home and via email to his personal and work email addresses.

He then brought a claim for unfair dismissal and disability discrimination. He alleged he had several severe disabilities and for most of his absence he had been homeless so that was the reason he had been unable to remain in contact with his employer.

He alleged he had '*Repeated chest infections, chronic bowel condition, lack of concentration, hives, poor sleep and disturbing dreams, loss of interest in everyday activities, disturbing, suicidal thoughts and suicide attempts*'.

This was news to his employer. Yes, he certainly had a vivid imagination. He never produced any medical records to back up this litany of ill health conditions that he alleged he had.

At the Tribunal he presented a witness statement that read like a fairy story. Here is part of it.

"Consistently increasing work stresses caused my symptoms to become more severe, and the remainder of the symptoms ensued.

On the 22nd December, I suffered a stress-induced breakdown at work and was subsequently signed off by my G.P.

I suffer from numerous chest infections, and extreme heartburn caused by stress and depression, and was prescribed antibiotics, Citalopram, and steroids.

In late March, I found myself unable to move, and felt as if my body had locked up. I attended A&E and was treated with an anticoagulant injection due to a suspected pulmonary embolism.

My mum and my partner had to take my two children as I was unable to look after, feed, or take them to school.

I suffer fatigue in the form of severe aching in my arms, chest, shoulders, neck, and legs, and due to chest infections found myself severely breathless, all of which amounted to me be unable to travel long distances, or walk for longer than 10 minutes at a time at an extremely slow pace.

Due to constant pressure from my employer by way of emails, phone calls, and requests, I felt increasing stress with regards to returning to work and made two unsuccessful attempts to return to work.

In the following weeks my depression worsened, my prescription was changed to Sertraline, I still could not look after my children or myself, I could not leave my house, I suffered from disturbing and suicidal thoughts.

By June I was able to attend counselling and my medication was increased, with the continued support of my G.P, my mum, my partner, and my counsellor, I was able to attend counselling sessions and do basic things like go to the shops which were 5 minutes down the road without having someone with me.

In July I was evicted from my home due to increasing financial difficulty and my landlord not believing my situation. I left a lot of my personal belongings at the property as I had nowhere else to go, or store them. I started staying with friends. My wife and children went to live with her mother and they wanted nothing to do with me.

My condition worsened and I became more suicidal and hopeless with low motivation, lack of concentration, continued bowel symptoms, heartburn, fatigue, and increasingly became aggressive and threatening in public and towards my friend and family.

I became homeless and slept rough for several months.

On 24th November I was dismissed—the letter arriving at my previous address and my wife let me know that this letter had arrived.

I appealed my dismissal and when this was rejected, I was affected by many of the aforementioned symptoms much the same or even greater than before.

In January (two months after I was dismissed) I refreshed my CV and attempted to pick myself back up. I found somewhere to live and applied for many jobs, and secured some interviews but was never offered a job.

I provided the contact details of my former employer as a referee as requested but a reference was refused and I did not get the job.

Following these events, I made two suicide attempts and was taken into A&E where I was treated by a psychiatrist and referred to the community mental health team."

His actual witness statement was many pages longer than the extract here and was full of nonsense about his alleged symptoms and his physical and mental health conditions.

I did a google search and discovered that his witness statement had been taken straight off the internet from someone else's Blog about their medical history. It was word for word the same account of ill health and medical conditions as this other person's Blog.

All his employer's letters trying to contact Sean, calling him to meetings and asking him to update them as to how he was and where he was, had been sent to the only address on file, his matrimonial home. He claimed he had never received any letters because his matrimonial home had been repossessed and he had been homeless for most of his year off sick.

When I cross-examined Sean, he alleged he had never received any voice messages or texts from HR because his mobile phone could not accept voicemail or text messages. He alleged these were extra services charged for by his mobile phone provider in addition to their standard charges and he had not been able to afford to pay for them.

After the first day of his hearing, I had not finished his cross-examination. During my journey home from the tribunal I called Sean's mobile phone provider to ask whether they made any additional charges for voicemail or text messages. They told me that they were all part of the standard package and no extra charges were made.

I then rang his mobile phone and left a message and sent a text, both of which were delivered. Sean even called me back later that evening when he heard the message I left. I said I would have something of interest to say to him in the tribunal the next day. I said I would see him in the morning and I ended the call.

That evening I checked his GP medical records because I recalled that there was an address on his medical records. I checked on Google and discovered that his mobile phone number was also registered to that address. It turned out to be a house that his mother owned which she rented out to tenants. This is where I discovered he had been living throughout his year-long absence from work.

Another Google search revealed Sean had started a company during this year of absence, called 'The Luxury Caribbean Christmas Hamper Company'. It was registered in Sean's name, at the address of his mother's house, from where he had been doing a brisk trade for over a year, according to his website.

A manager went round to this house early on the morning of the second day of the trial and asked the tenants whether Sean was living there. They confirmed he was living there and had been for over a year. They even showed the manager his bedroom. The tenant showing the manager round said, *"Sean is in the middle of a Court case and he has just left for Court."*

Sean had nowhere to go when I put this evidence to him the next morning. I told him I had found out about the house where he was living and discovered his Christmas Hamper business. I said one of our managers had visited his mother's house earlier that morning and he was here in the tribunal, ready to give evidence. I said I would disclose a print out of my Google search of his website selling luxury Christmas hampers.

The Judge said she did not need to hear or see anymore. She asked Sean if he would be challenging what I had discovered and he said, *"No."*

The Judge did not take long to dismiss his case. She was not very nice about Sean when she gave her judgement.

She said, *"The Respondent could be forgiven for being concerned about the Claimant's evasiveness. They were right, he was living somewhere. He was not* on the streets. That was still shrouded in mystery until hearing the evidence today.

Where there was a dispute in the evidence, I would say the Claimant was not a witness in whom we, the tribunal, had any confidence.

The evidence of the Claimant lacked consistency and credibility in relation to a number of matters. It was of concern that his witness statement stated that he was suffering chest pains on 16 May which was one reason why he could not attend an occupational health appointment. However, this was not corroborated by his GP evidence nor was it corroborated in the medical report produced by Dr H, the Company's psychiatrist who had copies of 'Sean's' medical records.

The Claimant also stated he was not in a mental good state on 11th October which is why he could not attend the first disciplinary hearing without being assisted by his mother. This again was not corroborated by the medical evidence.

The medical evidence provided by Dr H was clear that at that stage he was no longer suffering from a mental impairment. There was therefore no consistent evidence to support the Claimant's evidence that his mental health had not improved.

The Claimant's evidence as to where he was living at the time and his access to Internet and telephone services were similarly not credible or believable.

The Claimant was taken to many documents in cross examination in the bundle showing that texts and e-mails had been sent from his iPhone, which the tribunal took as corroborative evidence that he had a mobile phone available to him most of the time and he also had Internet access. There appeared to be no good reason for the Claimant to fail to keep in touch with the Respondent in relation to his home address and to report his sickness absence in a timely fashion which was a requirement in the Company Handbook.

The Claimant gave a number of incredible excuses for failing to attend work or communicate with his employer.

The Respondent showed extraordinary patience in their dealings with the Claimant and continued to attempt to accommodate his wishes, but despite their best efforts to accommodate his requests and objections, he failed to attend any hearings or return to work.

The Claimant's failure to attend the OH appointments cost the Respondent in respect of lost appointments and unused rail tickets that they had bought to assist the Claimant to attend the OH appointments and also in respect of a considerable amount of management time.

The Respondent appeared to do their best to accommodate the Claimant's objections by even offering to provide a taxi to take the Claimant to and from the OH appointments but none of the Respondent's efforts were sufficient to secure his attendance.

The Respondent appeared to go above and beyond the requirements of a reasonable employer to support and assist the Claimant while he was on sick leave to establish how long he was likely to be off sick so that they could reach an informed decision as to if and when he could return to work.

The Claimant failed to engage and the Respondent was entitled to conclude that he had engaged in what was described as 'delaying tactics'.

Similarly, the Respondent attempted to obtain a medical report from the Claimant's GP but the Claimant failed, without good reason, to sign the medical consent form.

The Respondent was therefore not able to obtain any up-to-date evidence of the Claimant's medical condition at the time of the dismissal hearing, through no fault of their own.

The failure to provide sick notes, failing to attend occupational health appointments and failing to sign consent forms was evidence of misconduct and the Claimant failed to show <u>any</u> credible or consistent reason for his failure to comply with the Respondent's reasonable requests..."

Not only did the Judge dismiss all his claims, she asked if we wanted to make an application for costs. We did and were awarded all our costs against him— £19,630. The Judge took into account Sean's undeclared income from his Christmas Hamper business.

Sean never paid and my client obtained summary judgement in the County Court. This resulted in a County Court Judgement (CCJ) against him. My client decided not to use the services of the bailiffs because, they reckoned, Sean would lie and say he had nothing of value to take and the bailiffs would leave empty-handed. Nevertheless, a CCJ affected Sean's credit rating and his ability to get credit.

His story, his failure at the Tribunal and the Order for Costs against him were splashed across the front page of the Company newsletter for everyone to read—to ensure that everyone knew what happens if anyone tries to cheat the Company.

Chapter 28
Kiaran's Tale

Kiaran was the Head Chef at a fine dining restaurant. If he had stayed the Head Chef, he would have been fine but he was promoted to become an Executive Director of the chain of fine dining restaurants, owned by Charlotte, another of my corporate clients. That's when everything went wrong for Kiaran.

One December Charlotte decided to check the expenses that Kiaran had submitted over the previous three months. Charlotte thought they looked suspiciously high.

Not recognising a Firm of solicitors whose legal bill for £50,000 Charlotte had authorised and paid, she telephoned the solicitors to query their bill. She discovered they were Kiaran's divorce lawyers. Kiaran was in the middle of divorcing his third wife and he had submitted his lawyers' bills as "business expenses." Charlotte had signed off these expenses without checking.

If that wasn't bad enough, in December that year I was in the hairdressers reading an old 'HELLO' magazine when I came across photographs of the wedding of the daughter of a celebrity that had taken place on a Saturday in September that year.

Lo and behold there were photographs in the magazine of Kiaran, with around 50 of Charlotte's staff, dressed in the uniform of Kiaran's private Catering Company, 'Kiaran, the Perfect Caterer'. Kiaran's private company was catering this wedding.

Charlotte also had a high end private catering arm in her Company and Kiaran would often work as Executive Chef for her private clients who used this service. It was part of his contract to do so.

The headline above the photographs in 'Hello' read, *"After the marriage ceremony there was a sumptuous banquet for 150 guests, catered by top chef [real name], in a marquee at the home of the Bride's mother."*

Kiaran's contract prohibited him from working in competition with Charlotte's business, even on his days off. He was not permitted to run his own rival catering business during his employment or for six months after it ended.

Kiaran's conduct was made worse not just because he was working for his own business, during a working day, but he had taken 50 of Charlotte's staff when they too should have been working in her restaurants.

When Charlotte checked, all 50 staff from five of her restaurants were supposed to have been on duty that day, but they had all called in "sick" as had Kiaran.

Not only was Kiaran running his own catering business in work time but he had charged the cost of the food, wine and champagne, cutlery, crockery, glassware, linens and florists' bills for this wedding to Charlotte's Company.

Kiaran had a nice little racket going on with the Food and Beverage Manager of a local luxury hotel near the restaurant where he worked. This manager stored all this illicit food, wine and equipment for Kiaran and received a nice 'kick-back' for doing so.

This initial review of expenses caused Charlotte to review all of Kiaran's expense claims over the previous three years. To her horror she found numerous fraudulent expense claims which she had signed off without checking. They added up to over £100,000.

To add insult to injury Charlotte had to deal with a very angry wine merchant whom Kiaran had told would get the contract for all the wine and champagne for the restaurant that Kiaran ran if he gave Kiaran twelve free cases of Cristal Champagne as a gift.

When these wine and champagne orders never materialised the wine merchant rang Charlotte, very angry, threatening to sue her for the cost of the champagne and for breach of contract. One bottle of Cristal costs over £250.

The food and wine for all Charlotte's restaurants were ordered centrally so this wine merchant was never going to be awarded the contract for Kiaran's restaurant.

This supposed deal with the wine merchant, his moonlighting with Charlotte's staff at this wedding and his fraudulent expense claims were discovered just before Christmas.

I rang Kiaran in Ireland where he had gone over the Christmas period and advised him of the investigation that was now taking place. I told him he was suspended on full pay under the Disciplinary Procedure and when he returned to

London in the New Year he would be sent the evidence of his alleged misconduct and given a date for his gross misconduct disciplinary hearing.

On 4th January around 11 am, I telephoned Kiaran on his landline at his home in Wargrave outside London. He answered the phone and I told him he would be called to a disciplinary hearing the following week. I had already couriered to his home that morning a large pack of documents containing the evidence upon which we intended to rely. He confirmed he had just received the pack of documents.

Around 12 noon the same day Charlotte received a fax. It was a private medical certificate from a doctor in Dublin stating he had seen Kiaran that morning and Kiaran was unfit for work for the next four weeks due to a bad back.

I called the doctor in Dublin immediately we received the fax and asked him to confirm that he had seen Kiaran that morning at his consulting rooms in Dublin. The doctor replied, *"I did."*

I told him that a miracle must have happened or perhaps there was a magic carpet flying between Dublin and Wargrave where Kiaran lives, because I had spoken to Kiaran that morning at his home in Wargrave.

The doctor went silent for a few seconds and then uttered those magic words *"to be sure"* and ended the call. Five minutes later we received another fax from this doctor saying he had made a mistake with the identity of the patient he had seen that day. It had not been Kiaran after all and the doctor confirmed he was withdrawing Kiaran's medical certificate immediately.

The next day Kiaran faxed his letter of resignation to take immediate effect, giving no notice and no reason. His contract required him to give 12 months' written notice if he wished to resign.

When Charlotte asked me to sue Kiaran for failing to give proper notice, I had to explain to her, very gently, that she had to show a financial loss in order to sue Kiaran for damages for breach of contract.

Rather than suffering any financial loss, as a result of Kiaran not giving notice, she was many thousands of pounds better off.

The pilfering at the restaurants had stopped; the exceptionally high withdrawals from the petty cash at Kiaran's restaurant had stopped; the false expense claims had stopped; the unlawful purchases for Kiaran's catering company had stopped; the staff had stopped going 'sick' in order to work for Kiaran's company and the replacement Executive Chef employed at Kiaran's restaurant was paid less than Kiaran's salary. In fact, Charlotte would be saving over £200,000 that year.

I did advise her that she could sue Kiaran for reimbursement of his false expense claims and the cost of the food and wine ordered and paid for by Charlotte's Company but used for Kiaran's Catering Company. However when I told Charlotte the costs of instructing forensic accountants and the fees for leading counsel and the time it would take to get to Court, she told me not to bother.

All in all, it was a rather good result in the end. Charlotte saved a fortune after Kiaran resigned.

Kiaran became a well-known TV Chef for a short time and then he opened his own chain of restaurants. Sadly, they all went into administration after only a couple of years. He was riddled with debt and went bankrupt.

Shortly after Kiaran left Charlotte's employment, she asked me to join her in Paris for a slap-up lunch, the following Saturday, at the Tour D'Argent, as her guest.

Never knowingly refusing a free lunch, especially at the Tour D'Argent, I said 'Yes please with pleasure." I was looking forward to our trip. She was taking her chauffeur-driven Bentley on the Channel tunnel train and then we were being driven to Paris.

Charlotte owned a lavish estate in the countryside in Berkshire and a number of beautiful houses in London. One of these was a Georgian house in Mayfair which she used as her office.

Charlotte was the first person I knew to have two mobile phones which constantly rang, and sometimes both at the same time.

Her office was filled with fabulous antiques and original Impressionist and Victorian paintings. One of her prized possessions was a Louis XIV desk which she had bought for €175,000 from an Australian antiques dealer in Paris, five years earlier.

Charlotte had decided to have the desk valued for insurance purposes and to her horror, she discovered that it was a fake, worth only around £1,500.

Her purpose in going to Paris, as I discovered the day before we were due to go, was that while we were having lunch, her 'hired mercenaries' were, in her words, *"going to get my money back and would be breaking that man's kneecaps as a reminder of me."*

Suddenly the prospect of a free lunch did not look very inviting and I made my excuses and cried off. I never did get my free lunch at Tour D'Argent.

Later the same year I did however get a free lunch with Charlotte. I had gone to see her about an employment issue she was having.

The previous evening Barry (my husband) and I had dined at one of her Michelin star restaurants. This restaurant is in the most beautiful countryside just outside London. It was a very hot night and after ten minutes, when we had sat at the table with no-one offering us a drink, I caught the attention of a waitress as she was passing. I asked her if she would kindly bring a bottle of still water to the table. As she sailed past, she snarled, *"No—I'm busy. You'll have to wait."*

Stunned by her rudeness Barry walked up to the Bar and asked the Barman for a bottle of water. He said, *"Certainly Sir. Let me bring it to your table."*

This same waitress was very slow and rude to us during service. She made us wait ages before bringing the menus. She forgot, to offer us any bread. She got my order wrong and then argued with me.

She brought me a lobster salad and when I told her this was the wrong order she argued that this was what I had ordered. I'm kosher so that was impossible. I had ordered a salad Niçoise. She clearly wasn't listening to my order nor did she write anything down.

Michael Winner where were you? He always made the waiter or waitress *"write it down."* He never trusted their memory when he was ordering at a restaurant.

The coffees this waitress brought at the end of the meal were cold and when we asked her to bring us hot coffees, she gave us a glare and a sneer, took the lukewarm coffees away but never returned with any hot coffees. By then we had had enough and asked for the bill.

When the bill came it had an 'optional' 12.5% service already added on. As her service had been shocking, we deducted the additional service charge and paid the rest of the bill. Barry left a nice tip for the Barman and for the chef and kitchen staff.

When we asked our waitress for Barry's jacket and my pashmina shawl, she threw them down on the floor and said in a loud voice, *"If you don't pay for service, you don't get service"* and walked off.

We were absolutely aghast. This was after all a Michelin star restaurant.

When I mentioned to Charlotte the following morning that we had been to this particular restaurant the evening before she asked me to tell her honestly what the food and service had been like. She added, *"I want to know because everyone is on their best behaviour when I visit my restaurants so, please tell me honestly—how was your visit?"*

Well, that was my cue to tell her about the lovely food but the very disappointing service from this waitress.

I told Charlotte how the waitress had behaved when we first sat down at the table, how she behaved during the meal and at the end of our meal after we didn't leave her a tip.

Charlotte looked at her watch and asked me if I was free for lunch. Another offer of a 'free' lunch was too good to miss so I said yes.

We were driven by her chauffeur to the same restaurant where I had been the evening before. We sat down at a table by the window, looking out onto the most beautiful gardens. Charlotte was right. Everyone was on their best behaviour and we were treated like Royalty.

She asked me to point out the waitress who had been rude to me the night before, which I did. I had no idea what was coming and nor did the waitress.

Charlotte called her to our table and asked the waitress if she recognised me. She said she didn't, so Charlotte introduced me. *"This is my Company's employment lawyer."*

The waitress looked at me and said rather petulantly, *"Well good for her—I still don't recognise her."*

"I'm not surprised you don't recognise this lady" replied Charlotte, *"you ignored her last night and used words I never want to hear in any of my restaurants.*

"When she asked for a bottle of water, you said 'No I'm busy. You'll have to wait.' You then brought her the wrong main course and argued with her when she pointed this out. You gave very poor service during their meal and then threw her husband's jacket and this lady's pashmina on the floor when they were leaving because they hadn't left you a tip because of your appalling service.

"Do you recall this lady now?"

The girl went red with embarrassment and said, *"Maybe."*

Charlotte then said, *"Well 'maybe' you shouldn't be working here. You will never have to see her again. You're fired"*—and pointed her finger at her, just like Lord Sugar in the TV programme 'The Apprentice'.

I was mortified. Whilst what she had done was quite out of order, I did not want her to lose her job. I begged Charlotte not to fire her and said I was sure she had learnt her lesson.

But Charlotte was not for turning. I felt less uncomfortable when this waitress returned to our table a few minutes later, after she had changed out of her uniform.

Looking daggers at Charlotte she shouted, so everyone in the restaurant could hear, *"you can fuck off and stuff your fucking job. I never liked your mean, stuck-up, nouveau rich customers who don't leave tips. I have worked long hours for a minimum wage and then get no tips because customers don't like the service after **they've** been rude and demanding. You can all go to hell. Goodbye."*

She then looked at the diners and shouted, *"and I hope you all get food poisoning. I wouldn't be surprised given the state of those kitchens."*

At that she walked out of the restaurant, never to be seen again.

We were stunned into silence for a few seconds and then Charlotte stood up, announced she was the owner and apologised for the waitress's appalling behaviour. She assured all the diners that the kitchens were meticulously clean and anyone who wanted to was welcome to inspect them right then.

Charlotte announced to all the guests dining at lunch, who had heard this ruckus, that the waitress had just been fired and lunch was on Charlotte. Now that's a clever businesswoman.

Chapter 29
Laurent's and Léon's Tales

There have been cases in which I have either acted for or against individuals who have had serious mental health issues.

Laurent, for whom I had the pleasure of acting, had a serious mental illness but was a delight to act for. Léon I'm sorry to say, was in my layman's opinion, 'a madman'. Luckily in his case, I was on the other side.

Laurent

Laurent was a young Frenchman, who unfortunately suffered from a 'delusional disorder'—a serious psychotic illness. He was only 29 years of age when he came to see me.

He had had paranoid delusions for many years but they had gone undiagnosed and untreated until he was seen by a brilliant Consultant Psychiatrist in London, Maurice. Laurent started taking medication for his illness and Maurice told me that he was hopeful that Laurent could be successfully treated.

Maurice recommended Laurent to come to see me for employment advice. His employers had told him they were considering dismissing him after he had been off sick for nearly a year. This was several years before the Disability Discrimination Act 1995. We might now have been able to argue that such a dismissal was potentially unlawful but in those days there was no protection for disability discrimination. To be frank, I don't believe that Laurent could cope with his stressful full-time job in finance.

Maurice told me that Laurent was not violent or dangerous but if he were to tell me about his deluded, paranoid thoughts, I should just agree with him and not argue or question anything as he believed they were real.

When Laurent came to my office, I warmed to him immediately. He was a really genuine, decent, charming young man with a devastating mental illness.

He told me why he could never go back to work. He said it was because he had invisible men living in his house and at his workplace and they stole his things. I said, *"Really—What do they steal?"*

Laurent said, *"Well, I will give you an example. When I come back to my house, every evening I always put my car keys in the same dish on the hall table. One morning I came downstairs and the keys had gone, vanished. These invisible men had stolen them."*

I said, *"I see. Have they done anything else?"*

"Yes" Laurent told me, *"They also live in my computer at work. I was writing a budget for my employer and I had finished part of it at the end of one day. I saved it and turned off my computer. The next morning, when I turned on my computer the document had gone, vanished, disappeared. These men had stolen my work and deleted it from my computer and destroyed it. I never ever found it."*

I thought to myself, that's funny—the same things had happened to me.

I said to Laurent, *"I know how you feel. I also always put my car keys in the same dish on our hall table when I come into the house. One morning I looked for my car keys and they weren't there. I went around the house asking my husband and two sons what they had done with my car keys, but they pleaded 'not guilty'. I couldn't find them and had to order another set."*

I didn't tell Laurent that I discovered what had happened to these car keys several months later. I picked up an empty Waitrose shopping bag and heard a clinking inside. I put my hand in and there were my car keys. They must have slipped out of my hand when I came home one day with my shopping. Without realising they had dropped into the bag.

I carried on telling Laurent that the same thing had happened to a document of mine in my computer. I said, *"the same thing happened when I was writing my first book. I had finished a Chapter and saved it (or so I thought) and turned off my computer. The next day I went to search for it and it had gone and I never ever found it."*

This was before WORD had an auto save function. I realised afterwards that I must have pressed the 'No' button in error when it asked me whether I wanted to save the document.

I phoned Maurice and asked him not to send me any more of his patients because *"I've got what they've got."*

Anyway, there was a happy end to Laurent's story. I advised him to resign from his job rather than be dismissed and to ask for a modest ex gratia payment and to use the following year to undertake his Masters.

He was allowed to resign and received an ex gratia severance payment.

He signed on for a postgraduate course at Imperial College and met a lovely girl on the course. They fell in love and a year later they were married. Laurent invited my family and me to their wedding on the Isle of Wight. It was a glorious occasion and it was joyful to see how well and happy Laurent was.

Laurent had been taking his medication which suppressed his paranoid delusions. He has led a very happy and successful life since and we have kept in touch.

Léon, The Mad Frenchman

Then there was Léon, the 'mad' Frenchman. He was, I believe, clinically mad, although I never saw a medical diagnosis to confirm my suspicions.

The HR Director of an investment Bank in London, Jenny, rang me, desperate, one day, and asked me if I would act for one of their Managing Directors, Tom. Jenny had heard me speak at an HR conference and had kept my contact details.

One of their traders, Léon, working on Tom's Desk, whilst still employed, was suing the Bank and Tom for racial discrimination. The Bank had tried to settle the case with Léon on several occasions before phoning me but he would not engage with them and refused every offer to settle the Bank had made.

His pleadings were extremely vague. He merely alleged that Tom had *'racially abused and harassed'* him.

His witness statement was equally vague. So off we went to the Tribunal.

As it was a racial discrimination case Léon had to give evidence first. He was unrepresented so the Judge suggested that he would ask Léon a few questions, to try to find out exactly what he was complaining about.

Léon told the Judge that on 11th March 2012, England had beaten France, 22-24, in Paris, in the Six Nations Cup (at Rugby). England had scored two very late penalties which they converted, which had given England an unexpected late victory over France.

Tom had come into the office the next morning and shouted, *"Victory over the French—again—they can't even beat the English at Rugby. Do the French ever win at anything?"*

Léon insisted that Tom was denigrating the French as a nation and racially harassing him as a Frenchman.

The Judge asked Léon, *"What was racist about those words and how had they harassed you?'*

"Surely", said the Judge, *"that was just an Englishman making a statement about a victory in a Rugby match?*

"Would you accept" asked the Judge, *"if England had lost and France had won, Tom would equally have come into the office the next day and said 'England can't even win a simple game of Rugby against the French. Do the English ever win at anything?'"*

Léon replied. *"No I don't—Tom's a blatant racist. He was referring to 'yet another French defeat'. This was a clear reference to the German occupation of France in the Second World War and the fact that some Frenchmen collaborated with the Nazis and it was the Allies who had to liberate France.*

"He was making out that we French were cowards then and are cowards now—always in defeat. That is racial harassment and it demeaned and degraded me as a Frenchman in the eyes of my English colleagues on my Desk."

The Judge asked Léon to repeat this allegation. The Judge was clearly bemused with Leon's reference to the Second World War and collaboration with the Nazis and asked me whether I had understood this allegation. I said I had not.

I did tell the Judge that Tom wasn't English. He was Irish and had been born and brought up in Dublin and had gone to Trinity College, Dublin. He had also played Rugby for Ireland. He did not 'fly the flag' for England.

Tom's witness statement explained that he was a great Rugby fan and he had expressed his delight that England had played well at the end of the match and had snatched victory from the jaws of defeat. His best friend, Tom Croft, had scored one of the late penalty goals so that was why he was particularly jubilant the next day.

Tom also explained that he was a great Francophile. He spoke very good French and had a holiday home in the Charente region, just West of Angoulême.

Léon went on to make even more fanciful allegations. He said the Bank had bugged his phone and all his calls were recorded and listened to.

Well of course his calls were recorded and monitored but his phone wasn't 'bugged'. All traders' calls were recorded and the Bank randomly listened to recordings of the traders' calls. All calls on the trading floor have to be recorded and monitored under the rules of then Financial Services Authority (FSA). This was so that clients' instructions could be verified in the event of a dispute and to ensure that no insider trading or other unlawful conduct by the traders was taking place.

The Judge dismissed Léon's case without anyone from the Bank or Tom giving evidence or being cross-examined. The Judge held there was no case to answer.

The Judge held that Léon had not put forward a prima facie case that he had been racially harassed. He held that the words used were not racist nor had Tom racially harassed Léon.

In fact, the evidence in Tom's witness statement (which the Judge had read and which Léon never disputed) was that Tom very much valued and liked Léon.

Tom had given Léon the highest appraisal rating and highest bonus that year of all the traders on his Desk and Léon had been awarded the Bank's Trader of The Year Award, nominated by Tom.

The Bank then made an application for costs. They disclosed the Without Prejudice Save As to Costs offers that had been made to Léon, including the offer of nearly $500,000, made on the morning of the hearing, which Léon had refused point blank.

The Bank and Tom were awarded all their legal costs—which totalled £140,000—virtually all were the Bank's legal costs, not mine, let me add.

After the hearing, the Bank held a disciplinary hearing and dismissed Léon for making malicious allegations of racial discrimination and for breaching the trust and confidence between employer and employee.

This time the Bank only made an offer to Léon of a payment in lieu of notice, which was three months' net basic salary. He accepted the offer and left the Bank. Mad or what?

Chapter 30
Miranda's Tale

Even after the #Me Too Movement started in October 2017, men have still continued to harass women in the workplace.

Miranda came to see me in 2019 very upset. She worked for an American company in their London office. Their headquarters are in Chicago, Illinois, USA. The company sold sophisticated software to large corporates and foreign governments, including spyware, virus and malware protection software.

Her boss, John Jr, was American and the Managing Director in the UK, living and working in London.

John Jr and Miranda had a stormy relationship right from the start. Miranda was their top salesperson in the UK and therefore earned a serious amount of commission and bonuses. John Jr actually earned less than she did as he was not responsible for any sales and he bitterly resented it. He also did not like her feisty, no-nonsense approach to him and others. She spoke her mind and said what she meant. She was not prepared to be bullied by anyone.

John Jr took every chance to demean and denigrate her. In meetings with her American colleagues, on video conferences, he would either ignore her, or speak over her or even worse make out that her ideas were his and he would talk about them as such.

He made fun of her but always in private. He would regularly call her *"Ice Maiden"* or *"frigid knickers"* or *"no knickers."* He would tell her on frequent occasions that he had *"pictured (her) naked, tied to a bed with handcuffs and shackles just waiting to be f...d."*

He would ask her very personal questions about her sex life. Miranda was a single mother bringing up her son on her own. John Jr clearly believed she was an easy target.

He would text her asking her if she had an active sex life, whether she went on dating sites to meet men and what dating sites she went on, whether she ever has 'one-night stands' and if she would like one with him and whether she had ever tried threesomes or lesbian sex.

She replied telling him to mind his own business and said if he continued to harass her, she would record all his conversations, report him to Head Office and would sue him.

He obviously thought she was joking because he took no notice of her protestations.

It all kicked off when he sent the most disgusting photoshopped photograph of Miranda and him, to all her colleagues in the London office.

The photo was of John Jr, with large sausages in place of his lips and his mouth wide open. The other was a photoshopped photograph of another woman's naked body, with enormous breasts, with Miranda's head, with a large sausage coming out her mouth.

A balloon coming out of John Jr's mouth was asking Miranda the question, *"Just think what you could do to me if that sausage was my prick? Who needs Botox?"*

Miranda had told him in her spare time she was training to become an aesthetic beautician (they give Botox and collagen treatments).

Someone in the office showed Miranda this photo which John Jr had posted on his Facebook page. The caption read, *"Just look at the woman who works for me. She's up for it."*—very foolish of him.

Miranda put in a grievance about John Jr's behaviour, about the fact that he regularly quizzed her about her sex life, had made disgusting comments about her, called her disgusting names and that he had sent this made up photo of her and him to her colleagues in the office and had posted it on Facebook.

John Jr did agree to take it off his Facebook page and then instructed HR to dismiss her grievance.

He alleged Miranda had encouraged him to send this photoshopped picture of the two of them and had initially said she thought it was funny. He alleged she had told him 'she fancied him' – in his dreams.

The Company dismissed her grievance with the words, *"this was harmless banter in the office. John Jr has accepted you were upset, after you had initially said you thought it was a good laugh, when he circulated the picture of the two of you round the office and posted it on Facebook. He removed it from Facebook* as soon as you asked him to. He says he has learnt his lesson and has promised not to do anything like that again. He has been reminded of our Equalities Policy. The matter is now closed."

I issued proceedings against the Company and John Jr for sexual harassment and against the Company for constructive dismissal as Miranda had resigned as soon as her grievance was dismissed.

She was so disgusted that John Jr had not stopped sexually harassing her ever since she started working for him. The final straw was the photoshopped photos of the two of them and his lies about her and the final straw was HR dismissing her grievance.

As soon as I sent the photoshopped picture and John Jr's filthy text messages to the Head of Legal and Compliance in Chicago and told him they would appear on the front page of several tabloid newspapers in the UK, he asked if I would not do that. He said they would like to settle the case if we would drop the Tribunal claim and agree to keep the matter strictly confidential.

After some interesting negotiation with me threatening to issue proceedings in the USA for millions of dollars, their legal counsel offered a substantial cash sum in settlement and the commission that Miranda would have earned during that year. She accepted their offer and happily completed her beauty training and set up her own business as an aesthetic beautician.

She did not have the stress of a Tribunal hearing or have to put up with any nasty bosses any longer.

The US Counsel was rather naïve. He told me right at the start of our negotiations that he was *"not a litigator. I am a deal-maker."* That meant there would be no fight in Court. That was a very foolish thing to admit to a seasoned litigator like me.

I thought to myself, *"Good—I won't even need to bare my Rottweiler teeth. He doesn't want a fight but I do because I am a litigator. I will fight tooth and nail to get the best deal possible for my client."* I believe I did just that.

Chapter 31
Nikki's Tale

Nikki Kingdon was Jeffrey Archer's last girlfriend before he was sent to prison for four years for perjury, on 19 July 2001. Sadly, Nikki died young, a few years ago.

This is a true story and the details below have been published so I am not changing the facts and I am using the real names of those involved.

Nikki instructed me to act for her to negotiate a fee with a national tabloid newspaper for her story about her short affair with Jeffrey Archer. This happened after her second divorce when she needed the money. Whilst I had never done anything like this before, I was willing to do this for her. It was a favour for a mutual friend who was her partner at the time.

I'm always prepared to try anything within my capabilities and I actually enjoyed negotiating with the Journalist to get the best deal I could for Nikki.

Nikki told me how she first met Archer and this was all published in the Daily Mail.

It was on 27th January 2001, when she met Archer. She was having dinner at a restaurant in London with her then third estranged husband, plastic surgeon Alan Kingdon.

Archer had, according to Nikki, been eyeing her all evening. She was a very attractive blonde, petite, slim lady, with no wrinkles, thanks to the skill of her then husband. Nikki was 48 at the time but looked around her mid-30s.

As she passed Archer's table, coming back from the Ladies, he handed her a paper napkin with his phone number written on it. So trite I know.

Nikki phoned him and they started seeing each other. She told me she was very flattered and intrigued by him. Archer took her to Le Caprice, a favourite restaurant of his, for their first date.

Archer had a table reserved for him in the corner of the restaurant whenever he dined there. According to Nikki, Archer told her that if anyone recognised him with her, they would probably think she was *"a PR girl for his publishers."* According to Nikki he promised to help her start her own business.

After dinner, they went back to his penthouse apartment overlooking the Thames.

He told Nikki he was going to South Africa six days later but he had cleared his diary for the rest of the week to be with her. They kissed and Nikki told me there was an instant chemistry. Archer made a second date for them later that week.

According to Nikki, when she asked about his wife, Mary, he assured her that he and Mary led completely separate lives and had had no sex life for a decade. He said he went to Cambridge every Sunday for lunch with her and that was their life.

On the fourth date Nikki told me she agreed to make love to Archer. Having resisted his advances for three nights, she said she succumbed on the fourth.

Apparently Archer preferred women in stockings and suspenders so that's what Nikki wore. Nikki told him if they were going to spend the next 25 years together, she wanted to know what he liked.

She saw Archer over the next two nights, making love after visits to the theatre and dinner.

On 4th February 2001 Archer flew to Cape Town to work on a new novel. He arranged for Nikki to fly out on Valentine's Day and, according to her, he greeted her with the words, *"Hello Heart, it's lovely to see you. I've missed you so much."*

The paparazzi discovered where Archer had gone and he and Nikki were photographed walking along a beach, hand in hand, paddling in the sea. The pictures were published in British newspapers. Archer told her she would have to move to a new hotel to avoid unwanted attention.

According to Nikki the holiday was ruined and with Archer's perjury trial in July of that year, she said she started to see a different side of him. Nikki left South Africa ahead of Archer.

On 18th March, the day Archer flew home, they met one last time and made love in a central London hotel.

According to Nikki, despite giving her the nickname 'Heart' and telling her he wanted to spend the next 25 years together, their relationship ended with sex in this hotel room, after less than two months.

After that they spoke twice on the phone. Once when Archer rang Nikki to tell her that Monica Coghlan, the prostitute at the centre of the libel case which had led to the perjury charge, had died in a car accident. This was a month before the trial. On the other occasion they spoke two days before his trial.

Nikki told me he seemed very confident he would get off the charges and they would just pick up their relationship.

However, Archer was found guilty of perjury and was jailed for four years. He started his sentence at Belmarsh, a Category 'A' prison, the most secure of prisons for the most dangerous prisoners convicted of very serious crimes.

He was then transferred to two other prisons finally ending up in Hollesley Bay Open Prison in Suffolk.

Nikki wrote to him in prison but never got a reply.

The Daily Mail wanted her story with photographs of them in South Africa. Nikki had photos that the Press did not already have.

After some tough negotiations with the Journalist involved, the newspaper agreed to pay Nikki a six figure sum, but she had to divulge intimate details of her love-making with Archer and provide hitherto unpublished photographs of them in South Africa, which she did. Actually the article was all rather anodyne.

Some of the photographs she gave the newspaper were of them both sunbathing in the garden of a private villa with Nikki topless.

The Journalist explained that payment was conditional upon publication. If a ground-breaking news story happened that knocked Nikki's story off the front page, there would be no publication and no payment.

Nikki's story was in fact published and the payment in cash was duly paid to Nikki in a brown envelope.

I did not ask for or receive any fee for negotiating this deal but Nikki did take me out to lunch to thank me—to Le Caprice.

I then saw another side of Nikki. She was a very sweet, lovely, rather naïve girl and the reason she had such a great figure was that she ate nothing. She ordered a salad and just pushed the lettuce leaves round her plate. I, on the other hand, enjoyed a hearty lunch.

Chapter 32
The Tales of Three Teachers

I have acted for several teachers during my career and for several schools.

Two teachers were falsely accused of serious safeguarding matters and they were cleared of all wrongdoing. In a third case the teacher did something very foolish and there was nothing anyone could do for him.

"She's looking at my willy"

Eloise was a teacher with 21 years' teaching experience. She taught in a private Preparatory School in South London. She had an exemplary record, was an excellent teacher and was loved by pupils, parents and staff alike. Her life was ruined by one little lie.

She had taken a class of ten 8-year-olds swimming with another teacher. Edward was the last little boy in the changing room after the swimming lesson. He was larking around and not getting changed. Eloise went into the changing room to hurry him up. The coach was waiting just for him before taking the children back to school.

As Edward came out of the changing room, he shouted, *"Miss Eloise was looking at my willy."*

The other teacher heard this and was duty-bound to inform the Head Teacher. Some of the parents heard about this as well and telephoned the school asking what was going on.

Eloise was suspended from School and the matter reported to the Local Authority Designated Officer (LADO). The LADO is responsible for investigating and managing all child protection allegations made against staff and volunteers who work with children and young people.

Edward was asked to attend a meeting at the School with the LADO and an appropriate adult, his mother, to tell the LADO what had happened. The Head Teacher and I were also at this meeting. I was advising the School.

The meeting started and the first thing that happened was that Edward's mother said, *"Don't believe a word Edward says. He's a terrible little liar."*

She looked at Edward and said, *"Tell this nice lady what you told me, Edward, and tell the truth. You told me you made up what you said about Miss Eloise. What you said about her wasn't true, was it?"*

Edward laughed and said, *"I said it for a joke. I didn't think Miss Eloise would get into trouble."* Then in a very worried voice asked, *"I'm not going to go to prison, am I?"*

The LADO reassured Edward he was not going to get into trouble if he told the truth. Edward confirmed that Eloise had not been looking at his willy and he had made it all up.

He said, *"She annoyed me. She came in and told me to hurry up and said I was holding up everyone else. I wanted to get her into trouble and pay her back."*

The LADO told the Head Teacher they would officially close the case and the complaint would be dismissed.

The Head Teacher immediately telephoned Eloise to tell her what had happened. However, whilst suspended, Eloise had had a devastating nervous breakdown. She said she could never return to teaching. It had been the worst weeks of her life.

Some of the parents had posted on Facebook that she was a paedophile and had no business teaching. 'Paedo' had been smeared on her front door in red indelible paint and her car had been trashed with the word 'Paedo' scratched on the side of the car. Some of her neighbours shunned her and some of her so-called friends disowned her.

The Head Teacher tried her best to persuade Eloise to return to school but she had been too traumatised and resigned. We heard later that she had moved out of London and relocated to Cornwall where she started her own pottery business. The school lost a brilliant teacher. I could see how vulnerable teachers were.

Edward's parents agreed to pay Eloise a term's salary in lieu of the notice that she was entitled to receive. They wrote a fulsome letter of apology to her, copies of which they sent to all the parents in the school.

Not a very happy ending to a very troubling time for Eloise.

When I was at school (centuries ago!), children tended not to be believed if they told tales about their teachers. They would get a clip around the ear or a slap on the hand or the leg with a ruler for good measure.

"They Did It for A Dare"

A few years after Eloise's case, I acted for a teacher, David, who taught at a private Catholic Girls' School in the Midlands. It was his first teaching job.

David was very good-looking—unfortunately for him. He was perhaps a little too good-looking for his own good. He was the Form Master for Year 8 - that is the Class for 12- and 13-year-old girls.

Many of the girls fancied him and teased him. One day in the playground five girls surrounded David. One of them, Rachel, went to hug and kiss him. Knowing this was getting dangerous David put his hand on Rachel's shoulder and gently pushed her away. He asked the girls to leave him alone and go elsewhere in the playground.

Rachel was furious. Half an hour later, the Headteacher, Andrea, called David into her office and suspended him. The five girls had alleged that he had gone up to them and had tried to hug and kiss Rachel and when she pulled away, he manhandled her and injured her shoulder.

David was mortified at this false accusation and was terrified that he would lose his job and that he would never be able to get another teaching job.

The mother of one of the other girls in Year 11, who had heard about the allegations, knew David and believed he was innocent. She called me and asked me to act for David and said she would pay my fees.

Andrea interviewed the five girls, all of whom backed up Rachel's story. Rachel by then was wearing a sling on her right arm and complained of pain and discomfort in her shoulder.

But Andrea had made a number of serious procedural errors.

Firstly, Andrea did not have an appropriate adult, such as a parent, with the girls at their interview so their statements would be inadmissible in any formal proceedings. They were all minors and it is mandatory to have an appropriate adult whenever a minor is asked to give a statement.

Secondly she interviewed all five girls together so she did not get independent accounts from each of them about what had happened. In fact, the ringleader, Rachel, did all the talking.

Thirdly Andrea compounded her errors by asking leading questions to the other girls after Rachel had given her versions of events. For example she asked, *"Do you agree that was what happened, just how Rachel has described it?"* The other four girls chorused, *"Yes."*

Andrea should have asked open questions such as, *"Please tell me in your own words what you saw, if anything, in the playground, between your form master and Rachel."*

Fourthly Andrea also failed to have a notetaker present at the interview with the girls. She did not take any notes herself at the time of the interview. She made some brief summary notes the next day but did not record the actual words spoken by any of the girls.

I wrote to Andrea pointing out all her errors. I asked if I could attend another meeting, with each girl separately, with an appropriate adult present and in Andrea's presence. I wanted to get to the truth and to do that I needed to interview the girls separately.

I said that allowing me to do so this would correct the serious procedural errors that had occurred when Andrea conducted the original interviews.

I explained in very respectful terms that if this went further and I was not allowed to interview the girls separately, I might have to report Andrea to the Teaching Council, in those days the Regulatory Body for teachers.

I said I would appeal on David's behalf to the Governors before Andrea made any decision about the complaint and would ask that she should stand down as Head Teacher.

I must have sounded convincing because Andrea readily agreed to my request for separate meetings with each of the girls, with a parent present, as the appropriate adult. A note taker would also be present at these interviews to take shorthand verbatim notes. This time the interviews would be done properly.

I started with Rachel, with her mother present as the appropriate adult. I realised I would need to handle this very delicate situation with kid gloves. I therefore lulled Rachel into a false sense of security by being nice to her and agreeing with her.

I said, *"Thank you for coming to this interview Rachel. You will of course be a vital witness at the Teaching Council's Professional Misconduct Hearing that you will be required to attend and probably at the Crown Court as well.*

"David will probably be charged with an attempt to sexually assault a minor and/or wounding with intent. You will be cross examined by David's barrister

who I am sure will be a very senior and experienced defence Barrister, possibly a QC, so think of this as your dress rehearsal.

"You will, of course, be giving evidence on oath, swearing on the Bible that what you say will be truth, the whole truth and nothing but the truth. I won't ask you now to swear the Oath on the Holy Bible but just imagine you have done this. Or would you like me to give you a Bible for you to swear the Oath."

Rachel shook her head and looked very nervous.

"No need to be nervous Rachel. If you are telling the truth you have nothing to worry about.

"I should advise you that perjury (lying) results in a term of imprisonment for the person who is found not to be telling the truth. That could be David if the Judge doesn't believe him and believes you."

I could see a look of horror on Rachel's face. I knew she was a devout Catholic so I continued, *"So let's imagine you have now sworn on the Bible to tell the truth."*

Rachel made it clear by her body language she was getting distinctly uncomfortable.

I continued, *"You are so lucky having David as your teacher, he really is very dishy. It must be lovely to have a handsome, charming young man as your form teacher. I would fancy him too."*

Rachel said, starting now to relax, *"Yes we all think he's very dishy."*

Then I said, *"I hear he is a great teacher too. Is that true?"*

"Oh yes" said Rachel, *"he's a great form teacher and the best English teacher we have ever had. He took us to see Shakespeare's 'Romeo and Juliet' at The Globe Theatre. It is one of our set plays for English GCSE.*

"He also took us to see the film "A wonderful Life" which we all thoroughly enjoyed. He's promised to take us on a School trip skiing next Winter."

"That's a shame" I said. *"He probably won't be here in the Winter Term as he is most likely going to be sacked from this School and struck off the Teaching Register—that is if you are believed. He will be banned from teaching for life.*

"Then he would almost certainly be prosecuted and if found guilty, he will be sent to prison for a long time and put on the Sex Offenders' Register for life. His life will be over. Teachers in this situation sometimes take their own lives rather than live with the shame."

"Oh No. He can't do that. That can't happen" cried Rachel, by now seriously alarmed.

I said, *"Oh yes this is the likely outcome, if you are believed. If this goes to the Teaching Council and they issue a Prohibition Order he will never be able to teach again in the UK. The police will probably ask the CPS (Crown Prosecution Service) to prosecute David and he would go on the Sex Offenders' Register for life."*

I could see Rachel stare at me with a look of horror on her face while what I had said sank in.

I then put it to her, *"Actually the incident you have described happened the other way around didn't it? You and your friends, all very mature girls for your age, surrounded David. Perhaps for a dare, you, Rachel, tried to hug and kiss him but he pushed you away, very gently, to avoid any physical contact. That's actually what happened isn't it?"*

I added, *"David did not do anything to you and save for a gentle push on your shoulder he did not manhandle or injure you in any way. He did not try to kiss you. You tried to kiss him and he tried very gently to get you to disengage from him. There's nothing wrong with your shoulder and you have no injuries caused by David or anyone else. That's the truth isn't it?"*

Rachel then went bright red and tears came to her eyes.

I said, *"What if I were to tell you we have several eye witnesses who were in the playground at the time all of this happened? Would you like me to call these witnesses?"*

There were other girls in the playground at the time who had been approached for a statement but they all said they had not seen anything.

Rachel then started to cry hysterically. I told her that she would not get into trouble if she told us the truth now and that it was very important, she did. I said that if she had told any falsehoods before, telling the truth now *"in the eyes of God"* she would be forgiven.

Knowing she was a Catholic who believed in confession I hoped that she would value forgiveness and telling the truth "in the eyes of God."

It worked. She broke down and admitted they had all fancied David and they had a bet to see who could kiss him first. They had planned it all—to surround him in the playground and for one of them to try to kiss him first. Rachel had picked the long straw and had therefore been the first to try to kiss David. She said he had not hurt or injured her.

Her mother looked daggers at her and said how sorry she was that her daughter had told such terrible lies.

I thanked Rachel and her mother for being frank and open now. I told Rachel that David would be very relieved that he could now come back to School without a stain on his character.

I asked Andrea if I could telephone David immediately to tell him he was exonerated and that he could come back to teach at the School. She said "Yes".

I let a mightily relieved David know that the girls had confessed what had really happened, that he had done nothing wrong. He was completely exonerated and he could go back to his teaching job.

Andrea then spoke to David and told him that there would be nothing negative or adverse on his record and that the allegations had been dismissed as completely false. She apologised for the distress it must have caused him.

Andrea then put her abject apology in writing to David for the trauma and distress that these false allegations must have had on him. She offered him counselling which he accepted.

David was very relieved at the outcome.

Andrea also wrote to all the parents at the School, without naming the girls, informing them that *"there had been a very serious misunderstanding, leading to a teacher being temporarily suspended. The teacher has been entirely exonerated. The teacher is innocent of all the allegations made against them and has done nothing wrong. The teacher concerned would be returning to School without a stain on their character. The teacher has the full support of the Governors and me. That is now the end of the matter."*

Andrea also spoke confidentially to David's class, as rumours had spread like wildfire about him. She then addressed the whole School at Assembly, explaining about the need to treat their teachers with respect and about the importance of telling the truth. She went on to describe a hypothetical case where lies had destroyed an innocent person's life. Most of the girls knew what Andrea was saying and why.

I was very impressed at how the School handled this matter after the initial mistakes that had been made. In fact, actually mishandling it to start with had worked in David's favour.

I was particularly impressed with the dignity and maturity with which David dealt with what must have been a very traumatic time for him. He was very lucky that the mother of one of the girls in his Class had faith in him and supported him.

Masturbating in the Changing room

In the third case in which I was involved, I was acting this time for a private Preparatory School in Surrey. The case involved Sam, who was a computer science and maths teacher at the school.

He had been seen masturbating in the male changing room of the local swimming pool whilst watching another young man taking a shower. Sam had gone back into the men's changing rooms, to go to the toilet, at the end of the swimming lesson, when he had been one of the teachers accompanying the pupils to their swimming lesson.

The man taking the shower had noticed what Sam was doing and had reported him to the Manager. He in turn reported this to Angela, the Head Teacher, as he knew the School where Sam worked.

I sat with Angela when she called Sam into her office. She said very sternly (in a voice you did not disobey), *"What do you think you were doing in the Men's Changing Room at the swimming pool? It has been reported that you were masturbating whilst watching another man take a shower. What have you got to say?"*

Sam went bright red and said he did not know what had come over him. He said he was gay but had not 'come out' and his parents would be mortified if they knew. They were strict Catholics. He said they would be appalled to learn what he had done in the changing room. He asked what Angela wanted him to do.

She told him, *"I will need you to resign with immediate effect. I am sorry but I will have to refuse to give you a reference for another teaching job. If I were to do so, I would have to explain the circumstances of your resignation. If you go for a non-teaching job, I will confirm your employment dates and job title and that you resigned and say nothing more. I can see you have learnt your lesson and you won't ever do anything like that again."*

Sam thanked Angela for her understanding, wrote out his resignation letter there and then and left the building.

Parents and pupils were told that Sam had resigned for personal and family reasons.

He got a good job very soon afterwards in a software company as a computer programmer and as far as I know he is doing well.

Chapter 33
Tomislav's Tale

Although this is a reported Employment Tribunal decision I have not used the Claimant's real name or that of the employer and some of the facts have been changed – to protect the innocent and the guilty.

Where do I start describing Tomislav? Well, he was probably 'mad' but again, that's just speculation on my part.

He was a Serbian National, who had come to the UK to work, in 2010. He had first found a job as cleaner for an insurance company and then got a job as a kitchen assistant with my Client, a major in-house caterer. He had trained to be a commi chef when he lived in Serbia.

Tomislav clearly had a problem accepting authority or respecting anyone in authority and he had a real problem with women. He abused women and did not respect them, whether they worked for the client or were his work colleagues or his manager.

Almost as soon as he started working for my client, in the staff restaurant of a large Accountancy Firm, Tomislav racially and sexually abused a female trainee who worked there.

The trainee was having breakfast in the staff restaurant when Tomislav went into the staff restaurant to clear up a spillage.

After a few minutes he walked up to the trainee and shouted, *"Stop looking at me. Actually you look very exotic. Where do your sexy looks came from? Japan or Thailand?*

"If you don't stop looking at me I will make some Kung Fu and Karate moves on you, so you had better watch out.

"Better still I could teach you some moves. It would mean close body to body contact but I bet you wouldn't mind that?"

The trainee ran out of the staff restaurant in horror and immediately complained to her HR manager. The trainee said she would no longer use the staff restaurant while Tomislav was working there.

The HR manager made a formal complaint about his behaviour, to his line manager, Elisabeth.

Tomislav denied the incident and alleged, falsely, that the trainee had told him she had been watching him and shouted at him he was 'a thief'.

The trainee denied calling him he was "a thief" but said she had seen him take soft drinks and a croissant from the counter and he was eating the croissant and was drinking a tin of Coca Cola whilst standing by the counter.

As Tomislav approached her, shouting at her to stop looking at him, she told him quietly that she was going to report him to his Manager for taking food and drink from the staff restaurant. Then Tomislav started abusing her before she could report him.

Tomislav was tall and heavily built. He was an intimidating figure. He had been a soldier in the Yugoslavian Army and had boasted to his fellow workers that he had enjoyed killing "dissidents" as he called them, some of whom were Kosovans who had once been his friends and neighbours.

This trainee was petite, 5 ft, 2", 8 stone in weight and only 23 years of age. Tomislav was 25 years older than her.

After an investigation, Tomislav's version of events was not believed and he was given a final written warning. The warning reminded him that his conduct was wholly unacceptable and that if he ever again made offensive, racist, sexist or any other inappropriate comments or made threats of any kind, to anyone, he would face dismissal.

He didn't stop. Five weeks later he abused his line manager, Elisabeth. He stormed into the staff restaurant one afternoon at 3 pm at the end of his shift. Some of the Accountancy Firm's Partners and support staff (the client) were in the restaurant.

Shouting in a very loud voice, Tomislav demanded to be paid expenses, in cash, for the dry cleaning costs of his uniform. The cost of dry cleaning of their uniforms was not covered by his employer's Expenses Policy.

Despite this, Elisabeth had kindly agreed to reimburse him through the expenses procedure. He however demanded that she gave him the cash there and then. She told him she could not take such expenses out of petty cash and tried to continue the conversation outside the staff restaurant but he would not budge.

She reluctantly had to carry on the conversation there. She told him quietly that she would have to claim these expenses herself via the normal procedures and then reimburse him. He became very angry and shouted at her that he wanted the cash now and if she didn't give it him now he would go directly to Human Resources (HR) and complain about her.

He left the staff restaurant for several minutes to get changed out of his uniform but then he came back. He started shouting at Elisabeth again that he had told her weeks ago he needed a transfer to a different site in London and that she had done nothing about it. He shouted that she was ignoring his disability and that she had called him a 'cripple'.

These accusations were entirely untrue. Elisabeth had no idea that he had any disability. He certainly had no apparent or visible physical or mobility issues and she had never used the word 'cripple' to or about him. This was pure fantasy on his part.

She told him that once she had sourced a suitable vacancy, he could apply for it. He shouted across the restaurant that she was 'a liar' and then left the restaurant.

This incident was very embarrassing. One of the Partners came up to Elisabeth to ask if she was all right because Tomislav had been so aggressive and unpleasant.

Elisabeth made a formal complaint to their Operations Manager, Eric. Tomislav in turn, filed a grievance against her, a tit for tat grievance, repeating the allegation she had broken her promise to transfer him to a new location and that she had called him a 'cripple'. Eric investigated both grievances.

He told Tomislav that there was nothing in his file about any disability. The Company had no knowledge whatsoever that he had any physical health issue—but by now the Company was having serious doubts about his mental health.

Tomislav told Eric that he was born with a spinal abnormality, scoliosis, which is a curvature of the spine. He said his doctor had told him he should "only work the early shift 0700 to 1500 so that I can get home in the afternoon to do my exercises." He said his previous employer had honoured this requirement.

Although this was not recorded anywhere in his file and no medical evidence had ever been produced to support this claim, Eric confirmed that Tomislav's original shift arrangement would remain in place.

The early shift was the most popular. All the other staff had to work on a rotating shift pattern, on the early, afternoon and evening shifts. Tomislav only worked on the early shift.

Elisabeth's grievance was upheld. She denied she had ever called him a *'cripple'* and accused Tomislav of aggressive behaviour and insubordination, made worse because he did it in the public view of the client.

Tomislav was given another final written warning for abusing Elisabeth and in public view of the client.

Don't ask me why he wasn't dismissed for this because he should have been. So now he had two concurrent final written warnings.

Then only a matter of weeks after the incident with Elisabeth in the staff restaurant, Tomislav made a further complaint. This time he complained that Elisabeth had not appointed him to the vacant role of Supervisor. He alleged this was because of her favouritism of a man called Terry. He alleged that she *"had the hots"* for Terry and that was why she had appointed him. She had worked with him in a previous job.

Tomislav argued this was unlawful sex discrimination against him. He was completely wrong. There is no sex discrimination where a person of the same sex is allegedly given preferential treatment—the comparison has to be with someone of the opposite sex. In any event this allegation was entirely untrue.

Neither Tomislav nor any member of staff had applied for this Supervisor post, even though it had been advertised on the notice board and Elisabeth had briefed all her staff, including Tomislav, about the vacancy and told them how to apply for it.

Because no-one internally had applied for the vacancy, Elisabeth had gone to contacts of hers outside the company. Terry was the only person who responded that he would be interested in the job. Elisabeth then went on holiday and it was Eric, the Operations Director, who had actually interviewed and appointed Terry in Elisabeth's absence. She had nothing to do with Terry's appointment.

Tomislav's grievance was again dismissed.

One week later Tomislav was in trouble again. He spoke to a Barista and a co-worker, Denise, in a shocking and most unacceptable way. He asked Denise what music she liked listening to. She said she did not have any favourite music and actually preferred watching sport and reading rather than listening to music.

He then told her that she should *"go and die somewhere."* This was particularly unfortunate because her brother had committed suicide two months earlier.

Distressed and totally traumatised by Tomislav, Denise walked out of the building and never returned. She wrote to Nicola, the Managing Director, complaining bitterly about Tomislav's behaviour.

Tomislav was pulled aside by Eric and told to attend an *'interview of concern'*. Tomislav was 'cautioned' never to say anything like that again. He was told to write a letter of apology to Denise. Tomislav denied saying anything to her and alleged that she had lied and *"abused her position to teach me a lesson."* A pity he never learnt any lessons.

Tomislav alleged that management's investigation was biased and said Denise had started the conversation and had shouted at him, *"foreign workers come here and take English people's jobs. Foreigners should go home."* Again, Tomislav was not believed.

Eric warned him to have a more *"positive attitude towards his colleagues"* but took no further action. This was despite the fact that Tomislav was not even half way through two final written warnings.

I asked the managers involved why Tomislav wasn't sacked by now? The managers involved realised, after this saga was all over, they had been far too lenient and had wrongly allowed Tomislav to remain in their employment far too long.

History then repeated itself. Tomislav applied for the job of Butler, working on the Hospitality Floor of the Accountancy Firm.

He passed the first round interview despite telling Eric that he could only work on the early shift and would have to leave work at 15.00. The Butler position required evening work as most of the hospitality and functions for clients took place in the evening. Despite stating this condition Eric put Tomislav through to a final interview. It came down to Tomislav and an external candidate (A).

The external candidate (A) was a much stronger and more able candidate than Tomislav. A's answers at his interview and his power point presentation were far better than Tomislav's and A was offered the job.

Seeing as Tomislav had been working on the Hospitality Floor at this Client's premises for nearly six months you might have thought he would have had a distinct advantage over an external candidate.

But No—Tomislav's responses at his second interview were very disappointing, vague and some were nonsensical.

The presentation that both candidates were asked to give was to include three challenges that could occur during service and to give solutions as to how they would deal with these challenges.

In his PowerPoint presentation Tomislav gave nine examples (not the three that were asked for) but gave no solutions.

At his interview his 'solutions' were shambolic. He cited as an example of a challenge, a guest with allergies and dietary requirements which were not known before the event. He said his solution would be *"not to interact too much with the guest."*

When he was asked how he would set up the hospitality floor for a VIP function, including a reception and sit down dinner, he said it was *"all imaginary—I haven't thought about it."*

When asked what music he would suggest for this VIP function, he said, *"a Caribbean-themed evening with a steel band during the reception and a DJ playing modern pop music throughout dinner."*

The rest of his answers were equally shambolic.

After Tomislav was told he had been unsuccessful for the role of butler, he asked Eric to move him to another site because he said he was too embarrassed and upset to continue working at that Site. So he was moved to another client, a Law Firm in the City of London.

Almost as soon as he moved Tomislav put in five new complaints which Eric had to deal with.

Tomislav's first complaint was that he had not been sent a birthday card. His employer sent every staff member a birthday card. Eric explained that his birthday happened to fall when he was off sick and it was an oversight that his birthday card was not sent. When this was discovered a second birthday card was sent to him, albeit a few days late.

His second complaint was that *"everyone had a vendetta against me."* As an example of this he said he did not have any birthday drinks after work.

Eric explained that birthday drinks were organised solely by the staff and because he had been off sick on his birthday, his colleagues did not organise drinks for him. There was no vendetta against him.

Tomislav's third complaint was that Chef did not give him the same food as other members of staff. He complained that he had seen another kitchen porter eating a pizza but this was not offered to him. He also complained that there was very little meat in Chef's pasties.

His fourth complaint was that he was not allowed to take soft drinks from the staff restaurant whenever he liked.

The catering and cleaning staff were only allowed to take bottles of water for free. No member of staff was allowed to take soft drinks or food from the staff restaurant as they were solely for the consumption of the client's staff and guests.

If Tomislav had been taking soft drinks, this was unauthorised and had been done without the knowledge or permission of his manager.

His fifth complaint was that he alone had been threatened with dismissal by Eric about smoking during his shifts.

No-one was permitted to smoke other than on their meal breaks and they had to smoke well away from their office building. Tomislav had been reported on numerous occasions standing right outside the main entrance, smoking, and not just on his meal breaks.

Eric had given a briefing to all the staff about the rules on smoking. He had not threatened Tomislav with dismissal and had not just targeted Tomislav with the reminder about the rules on smoking.

Eric dismissed all five complaints and told Tomislav that he must forget his imagined slights and move on in a more positive manner.

However, things came to a head over an incident with a trolley in the kitchen, a few weeks later. You could say Tomislav was *"off his trolley"*.

Tomislav had by now moved roles to work in the kitchen of the Law Firm. One morning he had taken the service trolley that had been set up for an interview that day with a potential new Head Chef.

Tomislav had taken all the items off that trolley—plates, cutlery, glassware, food and drink—and had just dumped them in front of one of the fridges. He intended to fill that trolley with cookies and pastries that he had taken out of the ovens, to take down in the lift to the staff restaurant.

The Deputy Head Chef, Jeremy, had instructed everyone, including Tomislav, the day before, that this particular service trolley would be out of use for the entire day the next day.

So when Jeremy saw what Tomislav had done, he instructed Tomislav to stop what he was doing, to put back onto the service trolley everything he had taken off and to use another trolley to take the cookies and pastries down to the staff restaurant.

Tomislav approached Jeremy in a very aggressive manner and pointed his finger in his face and shouted very loudly, *"sod off and do the fucking job yourself. Why don't you put the fucking things back yourself you lazy English pig? You and your staff are all fucking useless, lazy, stupid, bastards."*

With that Tomislav walked out of the kitchen and out of the building, without advising his supervisor where he was going or why he was walking out in the middle of his shift.

Walking out of your shift without permission or without an acceptable reason was regarded as gross misconduct in itself and so was his abusive and confrontational language and behaviour.

Tomislav was therefore called to a disciplinary hearing at which he was advised dismissal was a possible outcome. The Marketing and Sales Director, Ivor, was the hearing manager.

Tomislav faced numerous gross misconduct charges including refusing to obey a lawful and reasonable instruction, gross insubordination and aggressive behaviour and language to the Deputy Chef, using obscene language and walking out of the building during a shift, going AWOL.

One of those offences alone could have justified summary dismissal (without notice or pay in lieu of notice) but Tomislav was already on two live final warnings so dismissal was the next stage in the procedure.

When Tomislav was asked at his hearing for his explanations, his responses were farcical.

He argued that Jeremy had *"requested"* not *"instructed"* him to *"re-pack the service trolley and not to use it"* so according to Tomislav he had not disobeyed a lawful 'instruction'. He said this was because he had not yet received a revised contract so he was 'legally' still employed at the accountancy firm. According to Tomislav, Jeremy had no authority over him to give him any instructions or orders.

Tomislav had in fact been sent a letter advising him of his new, contractual place of work confirming that all his other terms and conditions remained the same. So he was not been issued with a new contract. Now Tomislav was a 'barrack room lawyer' as well as being a madman and a misguided barrack room lawyer at that.

Tomislav then said Jeremy *"often came in late for work."* Ivor challenged Tomislav and asked him when this was and why he thought this was relevant to the issues that he was being asked to answer.

Tomislav replied, *"I don't know if Jeremy <u>was</u> late or if <u>I</u> was late. If you were doing a thorough investigation, <u>you</u> should know. What are you asking me for?"*

Finally, Tomislav alleged that the trolley he was asked to use was *"unsafe because (he) had to push it over uneven ground and items could fall, spill or break."*

That, according to Tomislav, was a valid reason for him to refuse to use the particular trolley Jeremy had instructed him to use.

Tomislav couldn't even keep his mouth shut at his disciplinary hearing and started abusing Ivor. Tomislav accused Ivor of being a *"a Yes man"* and told him he knew he would never have a fair hearing and that he was being set up to be dismissed.

Tomislav's arguments were considered and rejected and he was dismissed by Ivor, for the following reasons.

"You consistently assert that you are in the right and that any problems you have experienced are either due to a "vendetta" against you or that other people are lazy and incompetent and confrontational towards you.

Having fully investigated your allegations I do not accept that any of your complaints are valid or that you have given any acceptable reasons for your conduct.

It is my view that you are clearly unable or unwilling to accept any accountability for your own actions. You seem unable to consider the feelings of your colleagues or control your own feelings.

In deciding on an appropriate penalty I have read your personnel file and see that you are already on two final live written warnings and have had a note of concern put on your file as well. You have a long history of upsetting your line manager, our staff and our clients.

Turning to the reasons I am dismissing you. In summary, the instructions given to you by Jeremy, the Deputy Head Chef were lawful and reasonable. You refused to obey Jeremy for no good reason and were intimidatory and aggressive towards him. You then walked out near the start of your shift for no good reason without reporting to your supervisor that you were leaving.

Any one of these charges warrants summary dismissal.

Your behaviour throughout the incident with Jeremy and during your disciplinary hearing with me now was confrontational and against the ethos of our business. We respect each other and work together in a collegiate manner to serve our clients as best as we can. You are unable to do this despite numerous warnings and chances to improve.

I am therefore making the decision that you should be dismissed. I do not however want you to be without funds so I am dismissing you with pay in lieu of notice."

That was particularly generous seeing that Tomislav had committed multiple acts of gross misconduct that warranted summary dismissal.

Tomislav appealed his dismissal to the Managing Director, Francis.

Francis actually went to the kitchen in question, asked for the trolley that Tomislav had been instructed to use, filled it with pastries and two full glasses of water and pushed it over the floor, to the lift and down to the floor below, to see if it was unsafe. It wasn't.

Not a drop of water was spilt. Francis also checked whether there had been any reports of this trolley being unsafe and there hadn't been. In fact all the trolleys were new, having been bought six months earlier.

Tomislav's appeal was rejected and he remained dismissed.

He then sued for unfair dismissal, disability and age discrimination and victimisation.

He represented himself. Counsel and I acted for his employer.

I wrote several letters to Tomislav urging him to get free legal advice about the lack of merit of his claims, from either his local Citizen's Advice or the Free Representation Unit (FRU). I warned him of the severe difficulties of his claims and that if he lost, we would make an application for costs against him.

At a Preliminary Hearing the Judge awarded a deposit order against Tomislav in respect of part of his claim. The Deposit Order required him to pay £500, on the basis that that part of his claim had little prospect of success.

If the deposit is paid, the Claimant is able to proceed with that part of their claim. If they succeed at the full hearing they get their money back but if they lose, they are at risk of a costs order against them. The deposit order is supposed to make a claimant think very carefully before proceeding and to deter them from proceeding with hopeless cases.

Poor deluded Tomislav ignored the Judge's warning to him about the significant weaknesses in his claim and paid the deposit. He would not drop that obviously hopeless part of his claim – in fact all his claims were hopeless. The trial then proceeded with all of his hopeless claims having to be defended by my client.

Tribunals do not strike out discrimination claims as they need to hear the oral evidence of the parties to determine whether discrimination has taken place. It is very rare that an employer will put discriminatory statements or confirm discriminatory acts, in writing.

We had to call ten (10) witnesses to defend all his complaints. They included a disability discrimination claim because of his congenital back problem. He never produced any medical evidence about any disability never mind a back problem.

My client disputed that Tomislav was disabled so there was even more reason for him to have disclosed to us any medical evidence – but he didn't.

Work colleagues who gave evidence at the tribunal stated they had never seen that he had any problem walking, running, pushing trolleys filled with crockery and items of food, bending, lifting or carrying.

Their evidence was that he walked quite normally without any stoop, limp or outward sign of pain. He never ever complained of any back pain and the only sickness absence he ever had was for *'stress at work'* when he didn't get the Butler role and on the earlier occasions when he received his previous disciplinary warnings.

There were a few light moments at the tribunal hearing. When he cross-examined Elisabeth and asked, *"Why did you call me a bully?"* she answered without hesitation, *"because you are a bully—you bullied me and several other women—and you were rude and horrible and bullied Jeremy, the lovely deputy head chef, which ultimately got you sacked."*

The Tribunal rejected his claim about not being appointed to the Butler position because of his disability.

They held, *"We accept the Respondent's explanation that the reason why the other candidate for the Butler position was preferred and the Claimant was unsuccessful, was that the other candidate performed much better at the interview.*

"The Claimant has therefore failed to establish that he was the victim of disability discrimination in respect of the Butler position and that was the reason for his failure to be appointed."

In relation to Tomislav's dismissal, the Tribunal summed up by saying, *"We find that this employer had a wholly acceptable reason for dismissing the Claimant. He had failed to comply with a request or instruction not to use the trolley and when approached about this by the deputy head chef, he was confrontational, rude and bullying. This was set against two extant final written warnings."*

"This employer had reasonable grounds for believing that the Claimant had committed the conduct alleged. Essentially, the Claimant denied being confrontational but accepted the other elements of the incident as put to him.

"The Claimant accepted he had behaved as alleged on the day in question. His lack of contrition, against the background of there being extant final warnings meant that dismissal was within the range of reasonable responses.

"The Tribunal could not say that in these circumstances no reasonable employer could reasonably have dismissed the Claimant. The effect of all of the above is that the complaints of unfair dismissal and age and disability discrimination and victimisation under the Equality Act 2010 are all dismissed."

And you might have thought that that was that—but oh no. After he lost his case, Tomislav stood outside his former workplace, in the middle of the road for several days, shouting abuse at Elisabeth and some of his other former colleagues.

He was heard to shout menacing cries of, *"I know where you live. I'm going to get you for this. Don't think you are going to get away this. You'll be sorry."*

He was not seen again—until that is, at the costs hearing, over two years later. That resulted in him being ordered to pay part of the legal costs to my client— only a proportion of the actual legal costs. We had asked for the maximum that a tribunal has the power to award, £20,000.

The Judge has to take into account the means of the paying party. Tomislav argued before the Judge he was heavily in debt and his current earnings did not even cover all his living expenses. He was therefore ordered to pay £4500, only a proportion of that maximum award.

When he offered to pay £25 a month my client rejected this offer and threatened to get summary judgment at the County Court. Faced with the threat of a County Court Judgement (CCJ) against him, he agreed to pay in full, getting a loan from his credit card company to do so.

Chapter 34
Xanthe's Tale

The wonderful thing about acting for Claimants is they give me information which I can use to our advantage.

On this occasion it wasn't anything bad. Xanthe gave me an insight into the character of an amazing man, her former employer, the well-known and colourful entrepreneur, the late Lord Tim Bell. He had been made a Peer in July 1998, a few months before I first met him. He sat in the House of Lords until his untimely death in 2019.

Tim Bell was the advertising and public relations executive, who played a central role in Margaret Thatcher's three successful general election campaigns. He inspired the famous advertising campaign in 1978 *"Labour isn't working."* He went on to be one of Mrs Thatcher's closest advisers for the rest of her life. They adored each other.

Tim co-founded, with Piers Pottinger, and ran the very successful Public Relations Consultancy, Bell Pottinger, for 28 years.

He told me one of his favourite mottos was, *"Why tell the truth when a lie will do?"*

He was a real character. It was an honour and privilege to know him and advise him but I first acted against him.

Xanthe is a very talented woman. She speaks fluent Russian and is an Oxford Alumni. She was recruited by Tim to work at Bell Pottinger, when she sat next to him at a dinner one evening. She impressed him so much that he met her the next day and offered her a job.

Xanthe has exquisite beauty, charm, wit and amazing intelligence. She is a most talented woman. She had worked in Banking before her job in Tim Bell's Firm. She had made many contacts and was friends with World Leaders and Crowned Heads of State. She still has these amazing contacts.

She became close friends with the late Mikhail and Raisa Gorbachev and helped organise Mikhail Gorbachev's 80th Birthday party at the Albert Hall in London, on 30th March 2011.

Xanthe instructed me after she had been bullied and racially and sexually harassed by Max, one of the Directors at Bell Pottinger. Max had made her life a misery shortly after she started working there. He had not approved of her appointment and became wildly jealous of her because of the clients she was bringing to the Company and all her contacts. Max was also a shocking sexist and racist.

It all got too much Xanthe and she resigned after a year's employment.

Xanthe was born in Greece but had come to the UK when she was a small child and settled in Oxford with her parents and sister. Her father was a Professor of Medicine at one of the Oxford Colleges.

Xanthe told me that Max had become unbearable to work with and had set her up to fail after she reported him for being a bully and stealing her clients.

He used to talk about her in her earshot, making racist and sexist remarks including, *"that Greek girl—all she does is flash her eyes and her legs at any male who looks at her. It's quite outrageous that she's working for us. I think Tim must have lost his marbles recruiting her. She's not even that good. I wonder what she gave Tim in return for her job?"*

This was a disgusting and completely false suggestion and a great insult to both Xanthe and Tim. Tim had spotted real talent – that's why he had recruited her.

One day Xanthe was travelling abroad for work to meet a client who would have given them a very lucrative contract. She left her luggage with her passport and money behind the reception desk that morning. When she came to leave for the airport in the early evening all her things had mysteriously disappeared, including her passport. She was unable to go on her trip and the contact awarded the contract to the other bidder who had turned up to their meeting.

The next day, the receptionist told Xanthe that Max had come down in the afternoon and had asked her to get him a coffee from the shop over the road and he said he would 'man' the Desk. We suspected that Max was our thief but of course had no proof.

Xanthe had to wait weeks to get a new passport.

After Xanthe had resigned, she instructed me to sue the Firm and Max, the man who had harassed her. We issued a claim for sex and race discrimination and harassment. Lord Bell asked to meet me to discuss a settlement.

Xanthe told me, *"He loves to be told how much people admire him and how well people think of him and he loves talking about himself. So just ask him to tell you about his career and how he started out and 'schmooze' him."*

This was the most brilliant piece of advice.

Xanthe waited for me at the Dorchester Hotel around the corner from the Bell Pottinger office, while I attended the settlement meeting with Lord Bell.

Xanthe had agreed she would be happy with one year's net salary (with the first £30,000 paid tax free). She was sure she would secure an equivalent job within a year.

When I arrived, Lord Bell was in the Board room on the top floor of their building. He was with his Finance Director, Mark.

Lord Bell was a chain smoker so even with all the windows open, there was a lot of cigarette smoke in the room.

As soon as I entered the Board room, Lord Bell and I both started our 'charm offensive'. He shook my hand and told me to call him 'Tim'.

I smiled warmly and looked into his eyes and said, *"What a real privilege and honour it is to meet you. I have admired you for many years."* I meant every word even though our politics were poles apart.

Tim was tall, good-looking with a lot of sex appeal and was exceptionally charming. He obviously liked and admired women, particularly strong women. He had a real twinkle in his eye. He smiled and said it was very good to meet me, that he knew of my reputation as a *'Rottweiler'* but that was fine because he *"had been likened to an untrained Alsatian, so I think we will get along well."*

After I sat down, he offered me a glass of champagne which I readily accepted. I then started my script which I had rehearsed. I had looked him up on Google so I knew a lot more about him than I had known before we met.

I said, *"I would love to know how you started your career and how you started your own Company. Do tell me all about your wonderful relationship and friendship with Mrs Thatcher with whom I know you have a great mutual love and respect."*

That was clearly music to his ears. He told me all about himself, how he had started his rise up the career ladder. He said he had talked his way from his first job as an office boy at the old television company ABC, working his way up the ladder through various advertising and marketing jobs to a job in a new Advertising Agency, Saatchi and Saatchi.

He had been spotted by Charles Saatchi, who had hired him to provide the front of house salesmanship and relationship-building—skills that Charles said he felt they lacked.

Charles Saatchi was rather shy but had a brilliant business brain. He told Tim that he had been appointed to schmooze the clients and that Tim *"was born to pitch."*

Then Tim told me some wonderful stories about 'Mrs T'. They are in his autobiography, *"Right or Wrong—the Memoirs of Lord Bell."*

Nearly 30 minutes later Tim stopped talking and said rather wistfully, *"I went to the University of Life. I have no academic qualifications to speak of. The only real talent I have ever had is charm."*

He certainly had that in bucket loads—he could charm the birds off the trees.

I said I was in awe of his achievements and that he had what most University students could never learn—innate talent, great charm and successful risk-taking ability. I said that was far more valuable and much rarer than a University Degree. I meant all of that as well.

I then said I hoped we could do business and reach an agreement. He asked what I wanted and I trebled the figure Xanthe and I had discussed. I said, *"my client will think very highly of you if we can settle on £X."*

He turned to Mark and said, *"Did you hear that? Xanthe will think very highly of me if we can agree that figure. I think that seems fair. I think we can agree that, can't we Mark?"*

Mark looked more a frightened rabbit caught in headlights than a Finance Director. Not daring to argue with Tim, Mark said meekly, *"Yes—if that's all right with you Tim."*

Tim then asked me, *"Now what about your legal fees. How much are they?"*

Not expecting him to offer to pay my legal fees, I hesitated for a millisecond and then gave him the figure for the entire time I had been advising Xanthe, including my success fee—a sizable sum. Tim said, *"Yes that sounds very reasonable. We will pay those as well."*

I hadn't actually thought of asking for my fees but I graciously accepted.

When I got back to the Dorchester to report back to Xanthe, I said, *"there's some bad news and good news."* I said I would give her the bad news first. *"Tim didn't go for one year's basic salary."*

"And now for the good news" I said. *"He went for treble of what you said you would accept. And to top it all, Tim has offered to pay all my legal fees so I can pay you back for all the fees you have paid me."*

Xanthe and I became firm friends after that.

Then I was paid the greatest compliment of all, a year later after my first meeting with Tim.

One Friday afternoon, when I was very busy, the phone went. A voice boomed down the receiver, *"It's Tim here."*

Knowing that Larry, my good friend, neighbour and a former actor, is a practical joker, I replied, *"Very funny, Larry. I am exceptionally busy at the moment so I'm not interested in your fun and games."*

The voice then said, *"No, this isn't Larry, this is Tim. I want to instruct you to act for me. I never want to have you on the other side again. You took me to the cleaners last time."*

I said, *"Yes Larry, really, I know it is you"* not expecting the voice to say it wasn't. But the voice repeated the message, *"No this isn't 'Larry'. It's Tim here"*

I then realised who it was and said, in retrospective rather foolishly, *"Oh you're that 'Tim'. I'm so sorry. How lovely to hear from you"*—as though Larry had the same first name, Tim, and I had muddled up the two men.

Tim had telephoned to ask me to act for him. He said, *"You took me to the cleaners when we met. I thought you were very smart and I said to Mark afterwards, I have at last met a canny lawyer whom I like. I want her on my side next time.*

"My lawyers are not as quick witted or as forceful as you. I need you now to help me sort out a very tricky case. It involves two forceful women whose PR business we bought several years ago. I would like them to exit the business and could only think of you to help me do this. Will you come over to my side?"

Without a hesitation, I said, *"Yes, I would be honoured to do so"* and from then on, I acted for Tim and we became firm friends for the rest of his life.

I learnt a lot about charm from Tim. It stood me in good stead when he was interviewed in July 2017 by Herbert Smith Freehills LLP (Herbert Smith) who were instructed by the then Managing Director, James Henderson, to be the independent investigators into the 'scandal' at Bell Pottinger.

This scandal concerned the contract with Oakbay Investment that Bell Pottinger had entered into with the Gupta brothers in South Africa, in early 2016.

The Gupta brothers had close connections with Jacob Zuma, the corrupt President of South Africa at the time. The negotiations for this contract had nothing to do with Tim. Three members of Bell Pottinger negotiated the contract with Jacob Zuma's son Duduzane Zuma, a friend of brothers Ajay, Atul and Rajesh Gupta, whose business interests spanned media, mining and computing equipment. Atul Gupta alone was ranked the seventh richest person in South Africa in 2016 with an estimated wealth of $773m (£600m).

Tim had nothing to do with this contract. He had merely gone on the first trip to South Africa, with Victoria Geoghegan, who worked in corporate communications at Bell Pottinger (whose father, Christopher had introduced them to the Gupta brothers) and Jonathan Lehrle, a partner in the geopolitical division. This was initially just to meet the Gupta brothers for the first time.

When Tim returned he immediately sent an email to James Henderson, the Managing Director, essentially saying not to touch this contract with a barge pole. Tim was ignored and the contract was signed for a fee of £100,000 a month.

Tim then had a serious stroke in April 2016 but he had had nothing to do with this contract since his return from South Africa at the beginning of the year.

The "economic emancipation" campaign that Bell Pottinger waged for the Guptas' company, Oakbay Investments, succeeded in stirring racial tensions in South Africa.

The scandal of this contract hit the headlines for days and in September 2017, it led to the eventual administration of Bell Pottinger after it was reported there had been *"an exodus of clients and increasing losses."*

Tim had by this time left Bell Pottinger and had started a new PR Agency, Sans Frontières Associates.

In July 2017 Tim agreed to be interviewed by Herbert Smith as long as I was permitted to attend with him. We arrived at Herbert Smith's offices just before 11.00 am and went straight into a meeting room.

There were three Partners, one of whom was the Senior Partner, three Associates, two Assistants and a trainee in the room, surrounded by a large number of lever arch files containing approximately 44,000 emails and documents relating to the Oakbay contract.

They had an old-fashioned double-headed tape recorder on the table as the interview was to be recorded.

We sat down and the Senior Partner switched on the tape, introduced himself and his colleagues and thanked us for coming. He asked Tim to introduce himself for the purposes of the tape.

The Senior Partner had meant Tim just to say his name and job title but Tim must have been thrilled to be given the floor. He gave us his life history. He spoke about his early life and how he had climbed up the greasy pole of business and then started at Saatchi and Saatchi, then how he had started Bell Pottinger with Piers Pottinger. He regaled us with his lifetime career and achievements, which were many.

Thirty minutes went by and Tim was still going strong. By then the lawyers were surreptitiously looking at their watches and staring at me willing me to stop him and start the interview.

When Tim stopped to draw breath, I chipped in and asked him very courteously, *"Is there any **particular** time that you need to leave Lord Bell?"* He replied, *"No I have all day."*

I corrected him immediately and said, *"I think you've forgotten, we both have another appointment in an hour or so. Perhaps we should let these gentlemen start the interview."*

At that the Senior Partner seized the moment and asked his first question. Rather cheekily they asked Tim what certain emails meant that he had only been copied into. He hadn't written them himself nor had they been sent directly to him. Many had been sent to other members of staff by his arch enemy, James Henderson, the then Managing Director of Bell Pottinger. Tim had just been copied in out of courtesy.

Tim started to say what he thought Henderson must have meant but I metaphorically 'kicked' him under the table to stop him. I interrupted and piped up, *"How can my client answer that? He didn't write the email. He was merely copied in. You will have to ask the author of that email. Please move on."*

The interview lasted three hours—the lawyers asking questions, Tim starting to answer them and me butting in, talking over him, telling the lawyers that Tim couldn't possibly answer that question.

In the end the interview finished at around 3.00 pm with the solicitors none the wiser from Tim, about the scandal and how the contract to advise the Gupta brothers had come about. They had been asking the wrong man. James Henderson was the man to ask, amongst others, but not Tim.

Tim was not mentioned as being responsible for any part of this scandal. Herbert Smith's Report concluded, *"We have seen evidence that the Bell Pottinger account team used other tactics in relation to the economic emancipation campaign which arguably breached the relevant ethical principles, including taking steps which might mislead or undermine journalists who were asking questions in relation to the campaign."*

In July 2017, James Henderson issued an *"unequivocal and absolute"* apology for the *"inappropriate and offensive"* social media campaign; a U-turn from the company's stance when it resigned the Oakbay business in April 2017.

Then, a spokesman for Bell Pottinger had said it had been the victim of a politically motivated smear campaign involving a *"number of totally false and damaging accusations"*.

Herbert Smith's report was said to have found that senior management did not know about the campaign, but that they had failed to put in place the appropriate safeguards that would have alerted them to what the staff were doing. Parts of the Report were reported in the Guardian on 5th September 2017 and later in the Huffington Post.

Tim was not aware of what had gone on. He sadly died on 25th August 2019 at the young age of 77.

I learnt much more about Tim at his Memorial Service when Lord Michael Grade gave a most moving, eloquent and amusing eulogy. Here is part of it. My very grateful thanks to Lord Grade for giving me permission to publish this.

"Tim enjoyed the good life, fine food, fine wine and fine clothes. But in the early days, he told me that his weekly salary didn't quite match his taste. Ever inventive, he persuaded his then flat mate, B, that they could find expensive clothes shops with names that sounded as if they could be a restaurant. So, in went the expenses, substituting lunch or dinner with a client for the clothes he had bought. This worked a treat until he was summoned to the finance director who said, "Tim I see you have eaten a mohair suit at Herbie Frogg." That was the end of him and his expense claims.

He told me that he was invited to pitch to the Prime Minister of Y. The country was anxious to raise its profile. Tim and his colleague S, duly arrived in the magnificent modern penthouse office of the Prime Minister, ready to present.

'Before we get down to business' said Tim somewhat wistfully, 'I just want to say on a personal note, that if you look out of that window to the hills beyond, that is where I spent the happiest few weeks of my life in a wonderful hotel on

my honeymoon. That is where I fell in love with your country and got to know and admire its people, and I am so moved to be here again.'

He then switched mood into the formal pitch, where the central idea was getting a Bond film shot in the country and/or persuade Formula One to stage grand prix there. He won the business.

Some months later, he and S were pitching to the Prime Minister of B. They had a similar brief—to raise the profile of B on the world scene. (Gales of laughter) Yes you are ahead of me ... In the Prime Minister's office Tim told me he had started by saying, 'If you look out of that window to the hills beyond, that is where I spent the happiest few weeks of my life in a wonderful hotel on my honeymoon. That is where I fell in love with your country and got to know and admire its people, and I am so moved to be here again.'

The formal pitch was getting a Bond film or a formula one Grand Prix to B.

The same routine went on a successful world tour, including winning business in (name of capital City) for the Prime Minister of D. Tim said it 'was a winning pitch, so why change it?' ...

Tim told me about a certain Conservative Peer, Norman St John Stevas, who was a dreadful name dropper. One evening when Tim was having dinner in the House of Lords with Lord St John Stevas during which he had not stopped namedropping Tim told me he had said, 'Norman—you have to stop namedropping' and he replied, according to Tim's version, 'I agree with you, as I was saying only this morning—to the Queen Mother' ...

Tim was pitching to an Arab Prince and was told to remove his shoes before entering the Throne Room for his audience with the prince. When the summons came to enter the Throne Room, he told me rushed forward in his socks, onto a highly polished marble floor and try as hard as he could he slid forward at a terrific pace and ended up in the Prince's lap. The Primce was very amused and said, 'Lord Bell, I have heard your client services are legendary, but you don't have to go this far.'

That says it all about the brilliant and much-lamented Tim Bell.

Chapter 35
'Tales of The Unexpected'

"What did you say?"

In one of my first cases in the mid-1970s, I acted for a train driver, Alan, at the Bristol Industrial Tribunal (as Tribunals were called in those days). This was a case where the Tribunal and I thought we had heard a most unexpected thing from my witness. Luckily she hadn't said what we thought she had said. We had all misheard her.

Alan had been dismissed by South West Trains without notice or pay in lieu, for going absent without leave (AWOL) on a particular shift.

He told me that his manager had been mistaken about the date. Alan **had** failed to attend for a shift one day when he should have been at work. He had gone to the races instead, but not on the day alleged. He had been driving his train on the day he was accused of going AWOL. His manager had mistaken the date that was all—but that counted for everything as it turned out.

Being the Rottweiler that I am, I took on Alan's case and sued South West Trains for unfair dismissal and wrongful dismissal, for his notice pay as he had been dismissed without notice or pay in lieu of notice.

Alan told me he could prove he had been driving the train on the day he had been accused of going AWOL because he had a witness, Edith. She was a little old lady who lived in Bristol. Her house lay behind the railway line on the regular route that Alan took. Alan said she would vouch for him that he was on duty driving the train on the day it was alleged he had gone AWOL.

I called Edith as a witness and asked her to tell the Tribunal how she knew that Alan was driving the train on the day it had been alleged he had not been on duty.

She spoke with a strong Bristolian accent and the Judge and I both thought we heard her say, *"I know it was Alan driving his train that day because I always stand at the bottom of my garden and 'every afternoon I 'ave my wicked way with him.'*"

I froze and the Judge halted the proceedings and asked me, "*What did your witness say?*"

I said that I had to confess I thought I had heard Edith say that, '*every afternoon (she) has her wicked way with him.*'

To everyone's relief Edith interrupted me, "*No, no my lover (standard Bristol speak), I said 'I stand at the bottom of the garden every afternoon and I 'ave my little wave with him.'*"

She said this in her strong Bristolian accent and we had all misheard her, much to the relief of everyone in the tribunal. It is amazing what you think you hear.

I then asked her how Edith knew it was <u>that</u> particular day that she had seen Alan. To my delight she said it was her birthday that day and Alan had slowed down the train to a stop and had thrown a bouquet of flowers over the fence into her garden and had sung "*Happy Birthday*" from his cab.

With that, South West Trains asked for an adjournment and settled the case.

"Don't Ask a Question…"

In these next two cases, I had not learned the important lesson of never asking a question in cross examination to which I did not already know the answer. You sometimes get an answer you're not expecting.

In one of my very first tribunal cases, I acted for Harvey, who had allegedly breached the company car expenses policy by claiming for private mileage when the rules stated only pay business mileage could be claimed.

Harvey's manager said in evidence that nine months earlier he had "warned" Harvey about the rules on claiming for petrol. Harvey had been caught most days doing a 30 plus mile detour on his way home to visit "*a friend*". She was not his wife.

The manager said he had actually shown Harvey the rules and had told him that only business mileage could be claimed and that he would be dismissed if he ever claimed for private mileage again.

His manager then caught Harvey claiming for private mileage nine months later and on that occasion, dismissed him.

Harvey brought a claim for unfair dismissal. This was in the days when Applicants, as they were called, only had to have six months' service to bring an unfair dismissal claim.

Harvey told me that he had never been shown a copy of the Company Car Expenses Policy and his manager had never "warned" him nine months earlier about the expenses he could and could not claim or that he would be dismissed if he claimed for private mileage again.

Harvey's manager admitted he had not put anything in writing nine months' earlier. *"Ah ah"* I thought *"I've got you now."* So to emphasise that it was impossible for Harvey's manager to remember what he had actually said nine months earlier, in my naivety, I said, *"I put it to you that you never used the word 'warning' nor can you possibly remember what you actually said nine months ago to my client."*

I thought I was asking the killer question next, *"If you have such a good memory, as you say, what did you have for lunch that day?"*

Quick as a flash the manager replied, *"I can tell you exactly what I had for lunch that day—cheese and an apple. I have the same thing every day."*

"I dare say" I replied and wished I had never asked.

"It's Black and White"

In this next case I was acting for Samantha, a senior nurse-manager in a Care Home. She had been dismissed for gross misconduct. I got an answer in that case I was not expecting when cross examining the HR Manager of the Care Home.

Her employer's case was that two agency nurses, on their first night shift in the Care Home, had witnessed Samantha hitting an elderly resident on her head, dragging her out of her chair in the TV lounge and carrying her off to her bedroom at 8.30 pm.

If true, Samantha had not only breached the rules about not abusing residents and the manual handling rules, (there were supposed to be two people to lift a resident) but also the rules relating to treating the Residents with dignity and respect.

Hitting a resident was obviously completely forbidden and was an act of gross misconduct in itself, for which summary dismissal was normally the penalty.

On the matter of the dignity of and respect to the Residents, they had the right to decide when they wanted to go to bed in the evening. This particular old lady was the last resident left in the TV lounge. It was 8.30 pm and the two nurses alleged that they saw Samantha strike the old lady hard on the back of her head and then shout at her to get up. Samantha had then allegedly 'yanked' this lady out of her chair quite roughly and carried her to her bedroom. They suggested that Samantha wanted to go to the rest room to have a sleep.

I put it to the HR manager, in cross-examination, that Samantha had only gently 'tapped' the back of the old lady's head to get her attention, as she was deaf and could not hear what Samantha was saying to her. This is what my client had said when giving her evidence.

I then suggested to the HR Manager that this could be a 'set up'—that the two agency nurses could have been sisters, living together and they could have gone home after their first shift and concocted the whole story.

This was a ridiculous suggestion on my part because I could not see what motive these agency nurses would have to make up such a story about Samantha after only their first night at the Care Home and I had no idea if they were sisters but I had to try to think of something.

The HR Manager turned me and said, *"Your suggestion is quite wrong. I know they are not sisters nor do they live together."*

Not getting the hint I ploughed on, *"And how do you know they aren't sisters?"*

She turned to me and with a wry smile said, *"Because one is white… and the other is black. We got one nurse from one Agency and one from another Agency They did not know each other before working for us and they do not live at the same address."*

I hadn't expected that answer. Hence the mantra—never ask a question in cross examination to which to do not already know the answer.

"Banker arrested, walking naked over London Bridge"

Not long into my employment law practice I read this headline in the lunchtime edition of the Evening Standard. That Banker was my client and it was definitely not what I was expecting.

The man reported in the Evening Standard was the deputy Managing Director of a Private Bank in the City of London.

Rachel, the HR Director, happened to know me because she had attended one year the Annual HR conference run by Barrister, Daniel Barnett and I was one of his Speakers.

Rachel telephoned me one lunchtime to tell me that John, their Deputy Managing Director, had been arrested walking naked over London Bridge and asked me if I would act for him in the disciplinary process that was to follow.

The background was that Rachel had been alerted by Security to several boxes that had been delivered to their offices from The Netherlands. They were addressed to John. Notices on the boxes read '*Private and Confidential. To be opened by the addressee only.*'

The Bank had a very clear rule that no private correspondence should ever be sent to the Bank and employees were warned that any and all correspondence whether it said 'Private and Confidential' or not would be opened.

When these boxes were opened, they contained a large quantity of illegal drugs, including cocaine, heroin and amphetamines, as well as hard core pornographic videos and magazines.

It transpired that John was a drug addict and to feed his habit he had been importing and selling drugs to a drug dealer in London to fund his addiction. He also sold illicit hard core porn videos and magazines to supplement his income. He had been spending over £5000 a week on heroin and cocaine.

He was under severe strain and he was high as a kite on cocaine that particular morning. He was also suffering from drug-induced schizophrenia.

When he realised he had been caught importing illicit drugs and porn videos and mags, he 'flipped'. He took off all his clothes, left them in the gentleman's lavatory at the office and walked stark naked over London Bridge.

He then started dancing and singing and got up on the rails of the Bridge and said he could fly and said he was going to jump off the Bridge.

Members of the public took photographs of him and someone called the City of London Police. He was arrested after a fight with the police whilst standing on the Bridge threatening to jump. He was eventually handcuffed and taken to the City of London Police Station, in Wood Street in the Barbican. A police surgeon examined John and had him sectioned immediately.

Rachel asked me to assist in drafting a statement for the Press who came buzzing round the office asking for the Bank's response about John's arrest and to represent him, in his absence, at his dismissal hearing.

John was able the following day to give me his informed consent to represent him but he had nothing worthwhile to say in his defence.

John was dismissed. There was little I could say at his disciplinary hearing. He was subsequently prosecuted and found guilty of importing illicit substances and illicit pornography. He was sent to Ashworth, a high security psychiatric hospital where he spent two years recovering until his release on parole.

I heard a few years later that he had died of an overdose. He had never been successfully treated for his drug addiction.

"Those were my verrrry worrrrds"

I once instructed Raymond Williamson, a solicitor from an Edinburgh firm, to represent a corporate client of mine, in an unfair dismissal case that took place in the Edinburgh Tribunal.

I had learnt my lesson about acting for clients in Scotland. I had previously acted for a client in the Edinburgh Tribunal. The Judge had asked me why I had come up from London to represent a Scottish employee and said, *"we have very fine advocates in Scotland Ms Howard"*. I felt very welcome.

I had also failed to understand the language spoken. The clerkess (as they are still called in Scotland) asked me if I had any *"productions"*. Not realising what she meant I answered I did and said how lovely of her to ask, I *"have two little boys aged 7 and 8"*.

The clerkess started to laugh and my client told me that *'productions'* meant *'documents'* in Scotland. I felt like saying, but I didn't, *"Well why didn't the clerkess say so?"*

So when I had my next case in Scotland I instructed Raymond Williamson to act for the Respondent.

He has now retired but he was a larger-than-life Scotsman and a brilliant advocate. He had a beautiful, sonorous voice and a lovely Edinburgh accent, a wicked sense of humour and very quick mind and tongue.

Counsel on the other side in this case, acting for the Applicant, was a lugubrious, windbag. He introduced himself as a specialist Advocate in landlord and tenant. We had no idea why he was acting for a claimant in an unfair dismissal case at an Industrial Tribunal in Edinburgh.

The case was only listed for one day and it should have been completed in one day but because of this very slow 'windbag', by lunchtime it was perfectly obvious we were going part-heard.

At the start of the afternoon session this 'windbag' stood up (everyone stays seated in a Tribunal but he obviously did not know the protocol) and waffled on and on and on, *"With the greatest respect my Lord (Tribunal Judges or Chairmen as they were called in those days, are addressed as 'Sir' or 'Madam')*

I will not finish with this first witness by the end of today. In fact I will probably need at least another half day with this witness.

"The evidence is taking much longer than we originally thought. I do not believe that my cross examination, with the speed it is going, will finish until tomorrow lunchtime at the earliest. Then the Applicant must give his evidence and be cross examined by my learned friend.

"At this pace I doubt my learned friend will finish with my client until the end of tomorrow or until sometime the following day. That will mean a third day for this case.

"Then we must have two hours each for our closing submissions, time for the tribunal to deliberate and give us your decision. If, as I am expecting, the Applicant succeeds in his claim, we then must argue about remedy and compensation.

"In my opinion we will need at least another three days. I don't know what my learned friend has to say?"

Raymond paused, took several seconds, looked at his 'learned friend', then looked at the Judge and the panel members and said in his slow, deep and deliberate voice, *"he's taken the verrry worrrds **out** of my mouth."*

I did not dare look up and how I kept a straight face I will never know.

Telling the Truth

Sometimes clients have taken my advice too literally when I have advised them *'to tell the truth'* when giving their evidence. There is a spectrum of truth beyond which one's client should never go.

This case was another very early case of mine, in the mid-1970s. Oh how I wish I had been as wise then as I am now.

My client was a recording company and their most famous recording artist was a popular Band who had failed to record their latest album on schedule, so revenues that year had dropped dramatically. Some administration staff had to be made redundant.

Sheila, who worked in their office in Leeds, had rushed into Harry's (her manager's) office when she heard that there would be redundancies and asked to be made redundant. Harry told me he couldn't believe his luck as he didn't then have to select anyone.

Two months after Sheila was made redundant Harry received her tribunal claim.

Harry was our only witness. He told me he was very nervous about giving evidence as he had never been to a tribunal before. In my naivety I said to Harry, *" there's no need to worry—just tell the truth."*

He took my advice literally and gave an answer at the tribunal that I certainly wasn't expecting.

Harry was giving evidence, explaining how Sheila had heard about the redundancies and had come to his office *"asking me for one."*

It came to my crunch question to Harry, *"So please tell this Tribunal why you made this lady redundant?"* and I pointed to Sheila.

Harry looked over at Sheila and with a completely straight face, turned back to me and said in his Leeds accent, ***"Well to be quite truthful luvvie (pause)— she were fat and ugly."***

I did not dare look at the Judge or panel members but in the words of Frazer in 'Dad's Army', I thought we were *"doomed."*

Out of the corner of my eye I could see the Judge and his panel members desperately trying to stifle their laughter. They had also looked over at Sheila and were nodding in agreement with Harry's cruel but accurate description of her.

However, I was able to retrieve the situation when I came to cross-examine Sheila.

Before the start of the hearing Harry had found out why Sheila had been so keen to be made redundant. She had recently taken out mortgage payment protection insurance that would have paid the interest on her mortgage and her credit cards debts if she was made redundant.

The salesman who had sold her the policy had not however explained the small print. Premiums had to be paid by the insured party for 12 months before the policy would pay out. Sheila had not paid the premiums for 12 months at the time she was made redundant so the insurance company refused to pay her out.

That was why Sheila had asked to be made redundant and had then sued her employer—to compensate her for the loss of her job that she thought she had insured in the event of her redundancy.

In theatrical mode I waved a blank insurance form in front of Sheila and told her, pointing to this form, that I too thought the salesman who had sold her that policy had been totally deceitful.

I said, *"You can hardly read the small print on this Policy. The salesman hid the details of the Policy from you, didn't he? He never told you that you had to pay the premiums for 12 months before the policy would pay you out? That was really deceitful wasn't it?"*

I put it to her that her dispute was really with the Insurance Company and not her employer.

To my relief Sheila fell hook, line and sinker. She smiled at me and agreed, *"Yes, he was a devious little man and tricked me into buying the Policy without explaining the conditions for paying out in the case of a redundancy. I assumed I was covered from Day one. **That's why I asked Harry to make me redundant.**"*

That was the admission I was hoping for.

"So do you accept that Harry did not unfairly selected you for redundancy nor was your dismissal unfair?"

She conceded that in light of the fact she thought she was covered by this insurance policy she had 'volunteered' for redundancy. Harry had merely responded to her request to be made redundant. There was nothing unfair about her selection for redundancy or her dismissal.

She carried on mouthing off about the devious salesman who had sold her the Policy and I let her continue ranting.

Luckily for me, my theatricals paid off. Sheila agreed to withdraw her claim and the tribunal then dismissed her claim.

She then went off to challenge the Insurance Company about their small print and their slick salesman. I have no idea if she succeeded. I reckon not.

"Four Fatal Words"

Another client, Violet, for whom I acted, also failed to understand when to say just enough and no more. Four little words were enough to prove fatal to her case.

I wasn't expecting her to say anything like what she added to her evidence, especially as I had briefed her on the questions I was going to ask her and she told me what her answers would be.

Violet was a young woman who had worked for a shoe concession at a major retail store. On 7 July 2015 a series of four coordinated suicide bombings took place in London, in three Underground stations and a double decker bus in Tavistock Square. The bombs killed 56 people including the 4 suicide bombers and 784 people were injured.

The staff and customers at the store at which Violet worked at one end of Oxford Street were evacuated and the Store was closed for the rest of the day. It reopened the following day.

Violet told me that she was so traumatised that she telephoned her employers the next day and asked if in future she could work at the store until lunchtime and then go home with her paperwork and work from home for the rest of the day.

She said she was having panic attacks thinking of travelling into London every day on the Underground during the rush hour, working all day in the store and then having to travel home again on the Underground in the rush hour.

She told me that working just half a day in the store and going home at midday to finish her paperwork would ease her panic attacks.

The next day, after her call to her employers, Violet received a letter from them '*confirming*' that they had accepted her resignation. The letter said they understood her concerns about being too traumatised to travel into London and that she would be looking for a local job instead. They sent a cheque for her notice pay and said her P45 would follow.

Violent immediately protested that she had not said she was resigning during her phone call but her employers were adamant she had. She therefore had to leave.

She instructed me and I advised her that if what she had said to her employers was correct, she had been unfairly dismissed so I sued her employers for unfair dismissal. I argued that by her employer not allowing her back to work, that was a dismissal in law. I denied Violet had resigned because they were Violet's instructions to me.

Before the hearing I asked Violet to recall as far as she could the actual words she had used to her employer in that phone call. I asked her whether she had said anything that could have led to them to believe she was saying she 'was resigning' and wanted to find a local job instead. She was adamant she had said nothing of the sort.

I told her I would ask her at the Tribunal to recall as closely as she could, the words she used in that phone call. She told me again she had said nothing about resigning or wanting to resign or wanting to get a local job.

I told her if she could just say "Yes", "No" or "I don't know" to questions put to her by the other side in cross examination or by the Tribunal, that's what she should answer.

As dismissal was disputed, the Tribunal had to determine whether she had been dismissed. So Violet had to prove she had been dismissed by her employer. She was the first witness.

I asked her to repeat to the tribunal as far as she could recall what she had said on the telephone to her employers the day after the bombings. She repeated what she had told me—that she had asked her employers if she could work until lunchtime every day at the Shop and then go home and work on her paperwork from home in the afternoons to avoid going home on the Underground in the rush hour.

I then asked her what I thought would be my killer question, *"Did you say you wanted to resign or that you were resigning or anything of that nature?"*

She said, *"No I did not"* and that would have been great if she had stopped there but then she added four fatal words, *"Well, not this time."*

I said, *"Thank you, Violet, that will be all"*. I had no intention of asking her to explain what she meant by that.

But the Judge had other ideas. He interjected, *"Would you explain what you meant by 'not this time?'"*

"Oh well," she said. *"I've had the wobbles before. On several occasions, I have telephoned my employers to say I don't think I can continue working in town and I am resigning and I will find a job locally.*

"On all the other occasions, my employer asked me to reconsider so I thought about it and decided I would not throw away a really good job that pays good money so I stayed.

"But this time I did not say that, so I was shocked when I received my employer's dismissal letter and my P45."

Unfortunately, given the history of phone calls that Violet had admitted to, and the very clear evidence of her employer as to what they said she had said on this occasion, the Judge ruled that they preferred the employer's version of the phone call *"this time"*. The Judge ruled that it was more likely than not that Violet had said she was resigning on this occasion as well. We came second that time.

"He called his wife a cabbage"

Never before or since I have been the angry target of so many cookery writers as I was when I acted for a client who had been sexually harassed and assaulted by her boss. Let's call him Martin.

In Martin's desperate attempt to get his leg over, he had told my client, Melinda (Mel), *"My wife's a cabbage. She's dull as ditch water. She's got fat and has gone right off sex. I love you, I want you now. I want to make love to you right now."*

When suing him for sexual harassment I pointed out to him in cross examination that he was a *"misogynist"* and that he had insulted his wife and her intelligence by calling her *"a cabbage"*.

Martin clearly had no idea what a misogynist was and replied to me, in his Brummie accent, *"Oy don't know what that word 'mis'... means luvvie. Whatever you said, I'm sure I'm one of them but Oy luv and reeespect moy woyfe."*

He clearly thought being called a misogynist was a compliment. I could hardly stop myself from laughing but I carried on with my cross examination wondering what other nonsense Martin might say.

I put it to him that calling his wife *"a cabbage"* was an insult not a compliment. I said it certainly did not denote any *'respect'* or *'love'* for his wife. I put it to Martin that cabbages smell after a few days and that calling a **person** 'a cabbage' meant they had such a low IQ they could be considered brain-dead.

He said he could not recall referring to his wife as a cabbage but disagreed that it was an insult. So I asked him, *"Well please tell the tribunal what positive and attractive attributes were you referring to if, as Mel alleges, you called your wife 'a cabbage'?"*

Martin was not a quick thinker. In fact, he showed himself up to be extremely stupid. He went completely silent and couldn't think of a thing to say.

I repeated my question but he just looked at as if I was speaking a foreign language and then said he *"would have been referring to moy woyfe's intelligence."*

Really……….. a popular attribution of a cabbage is intelligence?

After the first day the headline in several national newspapers was *"My bullying boss called his wife a cabbage."*

The newspapers then quoted my client's evidence, *"I was appalled at his cruel and disparaging remark….To me a cabbage is a vegetable which many people despise. It suggested to me that he despised his wife."*

Then a storm erupted in the newspapers. Cookery writers complained that my client and I had demeaned the noble and honourable cabbage by saying it smelt and had the attributes of low intelligence and that many people despised cabbages.

They wrote that the cabbage should not be demeaned or denigrated.

I agree entirely with those sentiments. I love cabbage in all shapes and sizes but I maintain that calling a **person** *"a cabbage"* is gravely insulting.

Cookery writers please take note.

A 'Lady of the Night'? Surely Not?

Another of my early cases involved a lovely lady in her mid-50s who instructed me after she had resigned and wished to claim constructive dismissal. She had objected to the office move from Maddox Street (off Regents Street, Central London) to Frith Street, in the heart of Soho. This was only a matter of just over one mile away but Frith Street was in the 'red light district'—the haunt of 'ladies of the night'. So she resigned.

I argued at the tribunal that this office move was not 'suitable' or 'reasonable' in my client's circumstances and that the new location fell outside the implied term of reasonable mobility.

I argued that my client was fearful if she had to walk to and from the office in Frith Street, she might be mistaken for a 'lady of the night'. I claimed that she had been constructively dismissed and had been made redundant because she was no longer required to work in her contractual 'place of work'.

Employers are entitled to require staff to work at a different location from their contractual place of work if it is a reasonable location and is within reasonable daily commuting distance. This employer argued that the relocation was reasonable.

I argued it was not reasonable location in the circumstances of this case because of where the office was moving to, in the heart of Soho. Ladies of the night waited in the street for gentlemen callers. These 'gentlemen' walked or drove slowly up and down Frith Street *'looking for a good time'*.

I argued that my client might not be safe and may be importuned by these 'gentlemen' as she walked back and forth from the office.

The Judge however wasn't convinced but I wasn't expecting what came next. He took one look at my client and turned to me and said, *"Oh No Ms Howard. Your client would **never** be mistaken for a lady of the night—no chance"*—and ruled that the move to Frith Street was perfectly reasonable in her case and dismissed her claims. And that was the end of that. I came second again.

'What's Wrong with a Bicycle?'

I had another similarly unfortunate experience with a Judge for another client of mine being required to relocate.

In this case the factory moved from just North of Manchester to several miles South of Manchester. My client told me the new journey from Prestwich, North of Manchester where he lived to Wilmslow in Cheshire, would require him to have a mile walk to the bus stop, to take a bus into town and then take another bus out of town and then walk another mile and a half to the new factory.

He reckoned the journey might take him as long as an hour and a half each way so he resigned and claimed constructive dismissal and a redundancy payment.

I explained to the Judge that the journey my client would have to make to the new location was not *'within reasonable daily commuting distance'* and that the journey would require walking over three miles, taking two buses and an excessively lengthy travel time.

The Judge peered over his half rimmed spectacles and with a booming voice said, ***"And what's wrong with a bicycle? The journey to the new location is perfectly reasonable if he used a bicycle."***

I wasn't expecting the Judge to be a bicycle fanatic. We came second again.

"18 Inches"

I was asked by an Investment Bank, in 1990, to give a talk to some traders (all males) on sexual harassment in the workplace. They had been in the habit of shouting *'old tart'*, *'old slag'*, *'I bet she could do with a good fuck'* and many other crude and unpleasant things whenever a woman came on to the trading floor.

One of the traders even had the cheek to go up behind me when I was walking on the trading floor, farted behind me, slap my bottom and shout, *"Watch out the old tart is coming."* I really resented being called *'old'*.

I said to that young man, *"Old tart eh. Well you are coming to my workshop on sexual harassment. So you will see what this 'old tart' has to say to you then"*.

In general, the behaviour by traders in the City in those days was ageist, sexist, racist and disgusting, actually quite intolerable by today's standards but that was then.

I ran the workshop about what the law and their employer required in terms of equality and diversity, emphasising tolerance of gender, race, sexuality etc and what was acceptable and unacceptable behaviour and language.

I gave what I thought was a robust and hard-hitting talk to this group of traders, giving examples of sexual and racial and homophobic harassment, including examples of their appalling behaviour towards women.

I picked out the young man who had called me *"an old tart"* and described what he had done and I asked them to think how they would have felt had this happened to their mothers/sisters/girlfriends/wives/daughters?

I also explained the Bank's new Dignity and Respect Policy. My talk lasted two hours.

After getting the traders to answer case studies, at the end of my talk I asked each trader to tell me what one lesson they would take away from my talk. The trader who had called me an old tart put up his hand and winked at me and said, *"18 inches"* and everyone started laughing.

I said, *"I beg your pardon."*

He replied, *"you know—women are 'pussies' and we have to stand 18 inches away from them to give them some personal space - if you know what I mean"* and he winked at me again and carried on laughing.

I did not think that was in the least bit funny and said, *"Right, you are coming for a week to the Gillian Howard School of Correction and believe me you won't think that's funny."* That soon shut him up.

The Language of Judges

I always expect Judges to speak in formal and dignified language and I have been rather surprised when they have occasionally said something unexpected.

One evening I had the great pleasure to be sitting next to the late Lord Peter Taylor, former Lord Chief Justice. We were discussing the lack of training for Judges.

Judges used to be appointed to the Bench and just thrown in the deep end without any training in how to be a Judge. Often a civil practitioner would be appointed to the Criminal Courts knowing virtually nothing about the criminal law. Somehow they managed.

I asked Lord Taylor how he learnt to 'judge' whether a defendant was guilty or innocent or whether a claimant in a civil case had a strong claim and was telling the truth and whether the defendant was telling a fairy story.

He turned to me and said (to my great surprise) in his very pukka voice, *"You will have to excuse my language my dear but I find out who the shit is and I make sure the shit loses."*

I thought, *"Oh it's as easy as that."*

That's Wit

At another legal dinner, in 1996, a very witty and clever QC was asked to give the welcome speech to the three honoured guests—Lord **Tom** Denning, Sir **Richard** Scott and Lord **Harry** Woolf.

Lord Denning had been a Law Lord and then returned to the Court of Appeal as Master of the Rolls.

Sir Richard Scott had been a Law Lord sitting in what was the House of Lords, the highest Court in the land (before it changed its name to the Supreme Court). At the time of this dinner Sir Richard Scott was Vice-Chancellor and Head of the Chancery Division of the High Court.

Lord Harry Woolf had just been appointed Master of the Rolls. He went on to be Lord Chief Justice and retired in 2005.

The QC welcomed these three guests and then turned to the rest of us and pointed at each of the Guests in turn and said, *"Isn't it amazing—nowadays, any Tom, Dick or Harry can make it in the legal profession."*

Now that was real wit.

Barcelona 'Won'

At another legal dinner, this time on 16 February 2011, it was the night that Arsenal was playing Barcelona in the UEFA Champions League. Many of us were listening to the scores on our phones during the Dinner. Barcelona scored an early goal and it looked like defeat for Arsenal.

The Master of the Rolls, as he was then, Lord David Neuberger, got up at the end of the dinner to give a Speech. He started by saying, *"I know many of you will want to know the final score of the match between Arsenal and Barcelona tonight. I can tell you—Barcelona 'won,'"* and he paused. There was a large communal groan but then he continued, *"Arsenal two."*

The cheers were deafening. Arsenal had scored twice in five minutes, very late on in the second half, as they staged a comeback, to beat the Champions League favourites, Barcelona.

There Are No Secrets in the City

In 2006, I acted for a team of 17 proprietary traders working in Bank A who wanted to jump ship and move to Bank B. Their problem was they all had post termination restrictions preventing them from working in competition for another Bank in proprietary trading, for six months, after they left Bank A.

Bank B was so keen to have them, they employed them, with a sign-on bonus and a guaranteed bonus at the end of the first year and agreed to pay them all for six months to stay home and do nothing during their restricted period. Their contracts of employment with Bank B, which they all signed, also contained similar post termination restrictions.

I had worked with Bank B's in-house counsel to agree the terms for the employment of my 17 clients. Bank B agreed to pay my fees as well. Their Counsel and I got on very well.

The 17 traders duly left Bank A and would have sat at home twiddling their thumbs until the 6-month restricted period had ended until something most unexpected happened.

Two months into that six-month period I received a call from one of the two co-heads, Robert. He told me they had all been approached by Bank C to go to work for them. Bank C had said *'write your own ticket'*. This meant they could name their price.

So, with even higher salaries and more lucrative guaranteed bonuses having been offered, they wanted to breach their contracts with Bank A and B and move to Bank C.

Robert had the nerve to ask me to call Bank B's lawyers and tell them that my 17 clients would not be starting employment with them after all, but, in breach of their restrictive covenants, they would be going to work for the rival Bank C.

I declined the request to tell Bank B anything and told Robert that he had to do his own dirty work. He had to call Colin, the Head of Fixed Income at Bank B, with whom the traders had been negotiating, and tell him the bad news.

Robert called me back an hour later to tell me that he had had the conversation with Colin. I asked what he had said. Robert told me Colin had said, *"fuck the lot of you. I already knew what you were going to do."* I certainly wasn't expecting that.

I asked Robert how on earth did Colin know? Robert said, *"The City leaks like a sieve. No-one can keep anything secret."*

The team moved to Bank C. Bank C threatened Bank B that if they made a fuss, Bank C would close the line of credit that had been extended to Bank B, which was $460 million. Bank B went very quiet.

I am still mystified at how the Financial world works. It seems to me to be smoke and mirrors.

But then something else unexpected happened. Irony of ironies, a year later, in 2007, Bank C bought Bank A and transferred the team to … guess where? Yes, back to their old Desk at Bank A. Merry go round or musical chairs or what?

'Scoops'

I threatened to sue one of the tabloid newspapers twice in the space of a year. Once was for the dismissal of one of their Deputy Editors. The dismissal wasn't actually unfair but what did that matter? The other time it was for defamation.

After both cases were settled very amicably and very well for my clients, the Managing Editor, John, asked me out to lunch because he said he was intrigued to meet me.

The reason for the dismissal of the Deputy Editor was that he had been passed copies of some of Princess Diana's diaries that had been stolen from Kensington Palace. Instead of passing them to his newspaper, he had sold them for a very high price to a salacious tabloid Sunday newspaper. When it was discovered what he had done he was dismissed.

I persuaded John to pay this Deputy Editor a handsome settlement despite the fact that his conduct was clearly gross misconduct.

The second threatened legal action was over the slander of a well-known Celebrity in the music business. His agent had shouted across a dining table, in the presence of other guests, *"you like inviting little boys on to your boat, don't you?"* Not only was this untrue but it implied by innuendo that my client was a paedophile.

The Agent had shouted this on the same day, 16th January 2003, Matthew Kelly had been reported in the newspapers and the radio and TV News, as having been arrested for allegedly sexually abusing teenage boys. That allegation was wholly untrue and Matthew Kelly was released a month later, without any charge for these alleged offences, quite rightly.

Someone at the lunch where my client had been defamed must have given the 'story' to a journalist because John's newspaper had repeated the defamatory statement about my client at the end of the continued reports of the arrest of Matthew Kelly, on the front page of the newspaper.

The innuendo was clear—that my client was a paedophile. I believed the newspaper had no legitimate defence in repeating these false allegations about him. There was no defence of public interest or justification or fair comment.

Again, I had very little difficulty in persuading John to pay a handsome sum in compensation to my client and to assist us in getting the article taken down from the internet.

During the course of a very lively and delicious lunch with John, I asked him about the scoops he had had when he was a journalist. He told me about two.

The first was at the time that Prince Andrew was dating Sarah Ferguson (Fergie). There had been a rumour that on 19 February 1986, on Prince Andrew's 26th birthday, at Floors Castle in Scotland, he had asked Fergie to marry him. The rumour was that he had presented her with a bespoke engagement ring featuring an oval-cut Burmese ruby surrounded by 10 diamonds.

The paparazzi were desperate to find out when Buckingham Palace would be making the formal announcement of their engagement.

So, on Friday 14th March 1986, the paparazzi descended on the late Ron Ferguson's home at Dummer Down Farm in Hampshire. The paparazzi camped outside the gates all weekend hoping that Major Ferguson would leave his house during the weekend and they could ask him to make a statement about the rumours of the engagement.

He failed to appear until late on Sunday afternoon when he sped out of the gates in his Range Rover and drove off down the country lanes so fast no-one could catch him.

The rest of the paparazzi realised they couldn't catch up with him and they all dispersed back to London, except for John that is. He told me he decided as he was there, he would drive round the country lanes to see if he might be able to spot Major Ferguson at some later time that evening.

Hours later, around 10 pm, John was passing the local village pub when he saw Major Ferguson rolling out of the pub very much the worse for wear. There was no way he could drive himself home. John wound down his window and offered him a lift back to his house. Major Ferguson gratefully accepted.

During the journey John said (knowing Major Ferguson was very drunk), *"Major Ferguson, I must apologise to you on behalf of my fellow journalists and photographers for ruining your weekend. I promise we will leave you alone as* soon as we know when your daughter's engagement will be announced by the Palace."

Not realising a trap had been set, Major Ferguson replied in his rather drunken stupor, *"Oh yes, Ginger Bush (his vulgar name for his daughter) and Andrew, those two—thank goodness you lot will leave me alone after Wednesday."*

John dropped Major Ferguson home and rang his newspaper straightaway. The paper had the scoop on their front page on Monday morning, with the headline **"Palace to announce Andrew and Fergie's engagement on Wednesday."** Their engagement was duly announced by the Palace on Wednesday 19th March 1986.

John's second big scoop was after the Provisional Irish Republican Army (the IRA) had bombed the Grand Hotel in Brighton in the early hours of 12th October 1984, during the Conservative Party Conference.

Denis Thatcher was badly injured. Mrs Thatcher narrowly missed being injured. Everyone wanted a photograph of Mrs Thatcher's bombed out Suite but the police had cordoned off the hotel and no-one, including the Press, was allowed anywhere near.

John was walking along the Promenade on the Sunday morning and met the Hotel General Manager, whom he knew quite well. They got talking about the bombing and Mrs Thatcher's Suite being wrecked. The General Manager let slip that he had taken a number of 'unofficial' photographs of her Suite after the bomb had gone off but he had nowhere to get the photos developed or printed. It was Sunday and none of the print shops were open in Brighton.

John could not believe his luck. He said very innocently, *"Oh don't worry about that. I know where I can get those photos developed for you—just give me your negatives and I will get the photos back to you tonight."*

Naively the General Manager thanked John and handed over his films. John rushed back to London, got the films developed and had copies of the photographs couriered back down to Brighton to the General Manager.

The following morning John's newspaper had a fantastic scoop—the front and inside pages were full of photographs of Mrs Thatcher's bombed-out hotel suite and of Denis Thatcher being stretchered out of the wreckage.

The other newspapers were convinced that a police officer must have been bribed to allow John back into the hotel to take the photos. They had no idea what innocent little ploy had allowed John to get those photographs.

"Adversary or Ally?"

It has happened several times in my career that unexpectedly I have had the pleasure of being asked to act for 'the other side' after I have sued them.

A few years ago a corporate client introduced himself to me in this way by email.

*"**SUBJECT LINE** - From adversary to ally?*

Hi, I had the unfortunate experience of being temporarily pitted against you several years ago. You won't remember me but I remember you.

I run a company in [X City] and one of our former employees retained you in some capacity to deal with an issue regarding him leaving us. I now have no recollection of what that was about.

Anyway, it was all resolved…I can't even recall exactly what happened but I do know that my lawyer at the time, knowing that you were on 'the other side' advised us to throw the towel in…not what I'd wanted to hear from him as I felt I had a strong case…but such was your reputation that this suggested itself as the most appropriate course of action.

So, looking at your website now and seeing that you are still in practice and act for both employer and employee, I wondered whether you'd be interested in helping us address a current issue with an ex-member of staff? I have copied in Margot, my business manager, who is aware in more detail of the history of this matter. If you are interested in helping, please get in touch with either of us. Thanks in advance.

Best regards"

When I replied that his email had made me laugh out loud, and I would be delighted to act for him, he wrote back, *"Glad to see I can make even a Rottweiler smile:)"*

Now that's what I like to read.
My email to him when I had acted against him all those years ago was quite scary. It read:

"**From:** Gillian Howard

Sent: November … 15:04

To: < >

Subject: RE: MY CLIENT, A

By email only:

Dear Sirs

RE: YOUR THREATS TO SUE FOR BREACH OF CONTRACT/COPYRIGHT/DATA PROTECTION ETC

I act for A who has now gone on a planned year's trip round the world and has no further access to his personal email address. Please direct all future correspondence (if any) to me.

I am in receipt of all your emails, including the latest email of today at 10.12 am. Your threat of legal action for breach of contract/ breach of copyright and breach of your Data Protection rights, is wholly misplaced as I am sure your lawyers will advise you.

My client has done nothing wrong. You have no evidence whatsoever that he downloaded documents containing your patented items and gave them to a rival Firm. He absolutely denies any such conduct on his part.

You have obviously checked his email account at work and you are most welcome to have access to his personal email account – the log-in details I have. My client gave them to me for this purpose,

He has not stolen or misused or disclosed any of your confidential information or trade secrets for which you own the copyright, as you have also alleged.

You have not suffered nor will you suffer any financial loss as there has been no breach of contract or breach of your intellectual property rights etc, as you allege. My client is entirely innocent of all of your accusations. He did not send any material belonging to you to his personal email.

He owns the intellectual property of certain documents on his personal email as he has designed some entirely new products for which he has applied for a patent.

For the avoidance of any doubt, he did not transfer any of his intellectual property rights in those products to you for which he is seeking the patent. These products are not in any shape or form the same or in the same category as your products and he did this work in his own spare time.

We have now given you a satisfactory and full explanation and we regard this correspondence to be at an end.

If you persist in sending any more emails threatening legal action including injunctive relief and damages, we will take the necessary action to stop you in the future, including bringing a claim for defamation if you make public your false allegations or assumptions about my client. They are scandalous and without foundation.

My client's reputation is very important to him in his future career in the beauty business, which is worth millions.

Please show this letter to your lawyers and please tell them their letters frighten no-one. They are *'a mere puff'*. If you care to look me up I'm not scared of anyone.

Wishing you and your business every success in the future.

Yours faithfully
Gillian Howard"

I was therefore surprised and delighted when the Managing Director of this Company told me that his former solicitor, a senior partner in a nationwide Law Firm, was so intimidated by my reputation that he had advised him to end the matter rather than to start any litigation with me, as soon as he saw it was me on the other side.

Now that's what I like to see – the other side frightened before I've even started with them or shown them my Rottweiler teeth.

This Managing Director had contacted me because he was being sued by an ex-employee and that same Employment Partner he had instructed in the earlier matter, had told him to pay off the ex-employee rather than fight the case at tribunal.

This was the first Employment Tribunal claim this Firm had ever had in over 20 years – they are a very good employer.

This Managing Director remembered my robust approach when I was acting against him five years previously and how scared this Partner was of me. So he asked me to defend this claim on his behalf – which I did.

I instructed a brilliant barrister, Mark Stephens, and although we couldn't scare off the other side, together we defeated the claims of this ex-employee and won the case.

This poor woman has been misguidedly advised by her solicitor she had a good case. She didn't.

We were also successful in securing some of our client's legal costs against the Claimant's solicitor for his really shocking behaviour and then his barefaced lies.

I only had to bare my Rottweiler teeth a little to scare the living daylights out of this solicitor and within minutes of my letter advising him that we were going for costs against his Firm, he rolled over and paid the costs we were seeking immediately into my client's bank account.

Lies, Lies and More Damned Lies

Possibly the worst serial liar I have encountered was this solicitor acting for the lady in the case above. I gave him the nickname (rather cruelly) 'Big Ears' after I had googled a photograph of him. I will leave the readers to guess why.

My nickname for him could also have been *"big mouth"* and *"stupid liar"* given his multiple, stupid lies.

The first pathetic and stupid lie was on the Claimant's first Schedule of loss. The Schedule of Loss sets out the Claimant's losses in terms of their future earnings, and any state benefits that have been received whilst they have been out of work and their earnings if/when they start a new job.

On the first Schedule of Loss, 'Big Ears' purported that the Claimant had not found any new work since her dismissal over 12 months earlier.

Unlike me, he had not checked his client's LinkedIn profile. This clearly stated the name of her new employer and her new job title, a job that she had secured in the same month in which she had been dismissed.

So when I challenged 'Big Ears' and pointed out the omission of her current earnings in the first Schedule of loss, I asked him for an explanation. He replied in writing that this was his *"client's error"*. That was a big fat lie albeit at the time I did not know that and I took his statement at face value. After all solicitors aren't supposed to lie.

I let that pass and he re-drafted her Schedule of Loss for a second time, showing her earnings from this new job but seeking a ludicrous amount of money for damages for injury to feelings (over £50,000).

In the event neither Schedule of Loss was needed because the Claimant lost her all claims at the tribunal.

However at the tribunal hearing, when the matter of her failure to declare truthfully details of her new job was put to her, she denied that it was *'her error'*. Her evidence was that she had given 'Big Ears' all the details of her earnings from her new job and it was he who had failed to include it on the first Schedule of Loss.

As 'Big Ears' did not attend the Tribunal (we discovered afterwards he was on a *"no win no fee"* arrangement) her evidence had to go unchallenged. It was pointed out to the Claimant that his email alleged it was her *"error."* The claimant said that *'was a lie'*. Oh dear.

After the Claimant lost all of her claims, we made an application to the tribunal for wasted costs against her solicitor. I had warned her solicitor that we would be seeking costs, in a Without Prejudice save as to costs offer to her of a small nuisance payment, on two occasions, the last time being three weeks before the hearing.

I had told him that the prospects of his client winning her claims were nil. I explained the law and what she had to prove in her discrimination claim and pointed out the documentary evidence that showed her case was bound to fail. I made her a nuisance offer to withdraw her claims. 'Big Ears' refused that Without Prejudice offer within less than an hour of me making it.

That turned out to be a very foolish decision of his because our Counsel disclosed that offer to the Tribunal when making our application for costs.

At that point the Claimant sacked 'Big Ears'. She then disclosed to the Judge and to me several emails to and from 'Big Ears'. Two emails showed that she had in fact disclosed her new earnings to Big Ears before he had submitted her first Schedule of loss. So he was lying when he wrote the failure to disclose her new earnings was his *"client's error"*.

Other emails from him showed a ludicrous assessment of her chances of winning her case. I am sure 'Big Ears' believed that my client would make an increased offer and he would then receive one third of that better offer. He was sadly mistaken.

This woman's claims would never have been successful as documents we had disclosed, proved.

After we received the written reasons for the decision (which the Judge said at the start of giving his oral decision was going to be *"unpalatable to one of the parties"* and it was), I emailed 'Big Ears', attaching all the emails that his former client had sent to the tribunal and to me, inviting him to make an offer towards the costs.

Nine minutes after I had sent my email, I received a very odd out of office message stating he was *'on leave'* for the next 7 days, not returning until the following Friday. Out of office messages normally bounce back to the writer of the email almost immediately an email has been sent—this one didn't. This was another lie by Big Ears as I was about to find out.

Being suspicious I called his mobile and he answered. He told me he was now *"out of the office"* and he had *"no access to emails or to any client files"* and he was therefore *"not in a position to respond to your invitation to make an offer to settle your application for costs."*

Not believing that either, I called his office a few minutes later and guess who answered the office phone. Yes it was 'Big Ears'.

When I announced who I was, he purported that he was *"just leaving the office"* and said he was *"away for the whole of next week"* and slammed the phone down. This was on a Friday afternoon.

The following Monday I called his office and spoke to a very helpful assistant solicitor (Millie). I said I wanted to consult 'Big Ears' on matter. That wasn't a lie – I did.

She told me he was in an Employment Tribunal that day but he would be back in the office the following day, Tuesday. I asked her if he was on leave that week and she confirmed he wasn't.

She asked me if I lived locally and if I wanted to make an appointment to come into the office to see him the following day. I said I would call back. I made an attendance note of that call as soon as I put the phone down.

Not surprisingly when I emailed the Tribunal later that week giving our non-available dates for the costs hearing and making it clear I was pursuing 'Big Ears' for all the costs as a result of his *'unreasonable conduct'* he immediately made an offer to pay the costs, which we accepted.

'Big Ears' must have realised the game was up. He paid my client within 5 minutes of me accepting his offer.

Lies and deception were clearly not easy for an amateur like 'Big Ears'. He was very lucky that I did not report his conduct to the Solicitors Regulatory Authority (SRA). I had better things to do than waste my time but in my view he is clearly a serial liar.

I felt very sorry for the unsuccessful Claimant. She had been given terrible legal advice and not knowing any better she had followed it.

This unsuccessful Claimant emailed me shortly after the costs had been paid by her former solicitor and thanked me.

She wrote this email, which was very touching and was certainly not expected. She referred to me as 'dear Gillian'! That was not expected.

"Just wanted to send a quick email to say thank you for your help solving this matter. Thank you also for allowing us to move forward with our lives. There are a lot of lessons in this, dear Gillian.

Hopefully we will never need a solicitor again, but if we do - we know where to go. All the very best to you."

I was very touched and have that email on the wall in my office.

My Rottweiler Reputation Pays Off Again

I have sued a multi-millionaire entrepreneur, Peter, more times than he cared to remember but the first time I did so, I had an unexpected "win".

Peter had a reputation for being very quick-tempered, irascible and for using foul language much of the time. He was also, according to my clients, a dreadful bully.

My clients, all women, had over the space of several years, been dismissed by Peter when things went wrong and he needed to blame one of them, even though they were not at fault.

For example, he would insist that the following year would be a good summer so he would order the Head of Womenswear to over order their Summer stock. When the following year's Summer was poor and they were left with a lot of unsold stock he would blame the Head of Womenswear even though she had protested at his orders the year before and he would sack her.

My first client, Claire, a Director of Womenswear, was dismissed with no notice, along with another female Director. Claire's female colleague had instructed another lawyer. Claire had instructed me.

Claire told me she and her colleague had only been offered just a few thousand pounds more than their notice pay by Peter, when he dismissed them. There was no compensation for their unfair dismissal or the sexual harassment or bullying to which they had been subjected.

Claire had been a Director of one of Peter's companies for eight years and had worked for him for 22 years. She was on a six figure salary but was only on the minimum 12 weeks' statutory notice.

I asked Claire if she had Peter's private telephone number as I intended to call him and negotiate a decent settlement. She did. I called Peter on his private line.

He was at first rather bemused that I had got his private number and asked me why I was not dealing with his Finance Director, Ian. He was known to be mean and have a very bad temper.

Peter said he *"admired (my) Chutzpah"* at calling him direct and asked me what I wanted. I said, *"one year's gross salary and bonus for this year for my client."*

Peter told me that Ian would never let him pay out that kind of money through the business. So I said, being helpful, *"Well, you could send a personal cheque and Ian need never know. It was rumoured that you spent approximately €4,000,000 on your wife's 40th Birthday and you gave her a stunning party and she was a very happy woman. I'm sure you can write a cheque for the six figure sum I am asking for and make Claire a very happy woman as well."*

Peter laughed and said, *"I know you are called a Rottweiler and I will pay the cheque to get rid of you and so I don't have to pay my lawyers to argue with you."*

He added, *"if you act for any more of my staff please use my private number and call me directly. I don't want to pay for my lawyers to rack up their legal fees and for me to end up paying what I would have paid in the first place."*

When Claire's colleague found out I had done a deal directly with Peter, her colleague's solicitor had the nerve to phone me to ask for Peter's private number and to ask what I said to get such a good settlement. He had not been able to get any better offer out of Ian than had first been offered.

I told this solicitor, very politely, that if his client wanted a similar deal to Claire's I would gladly take her on as a client—and with that I ended the call.

Claire's colleague didn't instruct me and apparently all she received was the first offer made to her. Now that didn't sound to me as if her solicitor had done a good job for her.

I will fight tooth and nail for my clients to get them the best deal possible.

I used Peter's private number on several occasions over the years and we did deals without bothering his lawyers, as he had asked. I liked doing business with Peter.

An Unexpected Gift

My waspish tongue and Rottweiler reputation have come in very handy over the years. On one occasion it got my client and me a case each of Pol Roger Winston Churchill Champagne 2013, from my opponent, just because I asked for it—well it didn't quite happen like that. I had to bare my razor-sharp Rottweiler teeth first. I didn't expect my rather outrageous request to be taken seriously though.

A young and inexperienced solicitor, Sam, had annoyed me during negotiations to settle a rather juicy sexual harassment case against one of his clients, a major London Law Firm. I was acting for the woman, their former marketing manager, Juliet, and Sam was acting for the Law Firm. Sam's Firm was located well outside London. Sam soon got the measure of me after he had been rather too flippant.

He had been instructed by this London Law Firm, to settle the case. Juliet had been forced to leave the Firm because of the Senior Partner's sexual harassment of her. Let's call him 'Romeo'.

Romeo and Juliet had had a consensual affair for about two years but Romeo was married and when he had still not left his wife after two years, despite saying he would, Juliet finished the affair. Romeo was not prepared to let her go that easily. He bombarded her with phone calls and texts and even threatened to commit suicide if she would not continue the affair with him.

He was completely besotted with her and would follow her home, wait outside her house and then follow her when she went out in the evenings and at weekends.

Eventually she lodged a grievance to the Managing Partner of the Firm complaining about Romeo's behaviour, but her grievance was ignored.

After waiting for two months and nothing happening about her grievance, despite a weekly reminder by email from me, I advised Juliet to resign, which she did.

I issued proceedings against the Firm for constructive dismissal and sexual harassment. I joined Romeo as Second Respondent, suing him personally for sexual harassment. Sam from this Firm outside London was the poor unfortunate young solicitor instructed to deal with me.

Romeo's Firm did not want to "air their dirty laundry in public" and certainly did not want any other London Law Firm in the City to learn about this case.

I was on holiday when Sam first telephoned me to open negotiations. He made what I thought was a derisory offer and I told him so. I said he had to do much better than that and I made a significantly higher counter offer.

Sam then had the misfortune to say to me, *"that's an outrageous counter offer but I know how you negotiate. You are the Rottweiler with a Handbag."*

That was definitely not the right thing to say to me. I waited a few seconds and said, *"I don't think you know who you are talking to. I have a rule. I never continue a conversation with anyone who is rude or who tries to patronise me and that's what you have just done.*

"You have treated me as if I am some foolish little woman who doesn't know how to do her job. I can assure you I do. This Rottweiler eats men like you for breakfast.

"You would never have said anything like that to a man who was negotiating hard on behalf of his wronged client. I am sure you would have said or thought 'He's a tough negotiator. I wouldn't mind having him on my side'.

"But because I'm a woman you think it's appropriate to patronise me.

"Please remember that I am acting in a sex discrimination case for a woman who has been appallingly treated by your client's Senior Partner. I suggest you remember that and when you can have a respectful conversation with me, treat me as a professional person, instead of some silly little woman, apologise to me for your rudeness and come back with a much better offer, I am ending this call now. So I am now ringing off. Goodbye."

With that, I put down the phone.

I can only imagine what went on during the conversation that Sam had with his client. He was taking instructions from Stephen, the Head of Employment at the Law Firm who had instructed him. I know Stephen very well and like him very much. Their conversation must have been rather awkward as Sam relayed my comments to Stephen.

Forty minutes later Sam called me back. I'm sure Stephen must have briefed him what to say.

Sam started by saying, *"How can I apologise? I certainly did not mean to be rude or patronising. I know you have a great reputation and I wish to re-open the negotiations."*

Quick as a flash, meaning this as a joke, I said, *"Well if you're asking how you an apologise, I will tell you. You could send a case of Pol Roger Winston Churchill 2013 champagne to my client and to me. Then I may start talking to you again."*

Poor Sam, not having a quick (or any) sense of humour, replied, *"I certainly will. If a case of Pol Roger Winston Churchill 2013 Champagne will put matters right between us, it's yours and I hope you will now continue discussing settlement with me."*

Amused at this generous gesture I said, *"Of course I will Sam"* and merely repeated my rather outlandish counter offer. I said I hadn't changed my mind about the level of settlement I intended to ask for my client.

I think Sam was so relieved that I would continue talking to him he said, *"I will take instructions and get back to you."*

Within an hour Sam had telephoned me and said, *"my client agrees to your counter offer"*. I thought as much. We had a deal.

I immediately called Juliet to tell her the good news about the settlement and the case of Pol Roger Winston Churchill 2013 Champagne that I had negotiated. She said, *"That's wonderful. We can share the case of champagne."*

I replied, *"Share? I don't do sharing. I have negotiated a case each."*

I did not know that at the time of my call she was on Centre Court at Wimbledon at a crucial point in the Match. When I told her that I had got us both a case of Pol Roger champagne, she burst out laughing so loudly that I could hear other spectators telling her to hush.

To my amusement the Agreement actually included a term that her ex-employer would send us both a case of the champagne that I had asked for. The champagne duly arrived on time.

Now that really was unexpected. Never in a million years did I think my light-hearted quip would end up as a term in a settlement agreement.

I felt I had to ask Sam and Stephen to lunch. I took them both to 'Gordon Ramsay at Claridge's' (sadly no more). It was a fabulous restaurant in its day.

The waiter asked us if we would like an aperitif before lunch. I said, *"Yes please—three glasses of champagne but it doesn't have to be Pol Roger Winston Churchill 2013."* We all saw the joke.

My Waspish Tongue

My waspish tongue was put to good use in another case when I was acting for the employer this time.

At the time employees had only a three month time limit from the date of their dismissal to present their claim to a Tribunal. Since this case, there is a mandatory early conciliation period of up to 6 weeks which is added to the three-month time limit.

Unless there are rare circumstances *"where the tribunal is satisfied that it was not reasonably practicable for the complaint to be presented before the end of that period of three months"*, claims presented out of time will not be heard and will be struck out by the tribunal.

Cases presented out of time but allowed, are rare – for example where the Claimant is very ill in hospital in a coma, or physically or mentally unable to present a claim within the statutory time limit.

Even if a late claim is the fault of the solicitor and not the Claimant's, that will not be any excuse for a claim to be presented out of time. The poor Claimant is left only with suing their solicitor for negligence.

I was acting for an employer who had dismissed their employee for persistent lateness over a period of two years, despite several warnings. And yes, you've guessed it, that ex-employee then served his claim late, 29 days outside the then three-month time limit.

The Claimant argued at the preliminary hearing, which was to hear whether his claim should be accepted or struck out, that he had telephoned the Clerk of the tribunal ten (10) days after the three-month time limit had expired. The Claimant said that the Clerk had told him that it didn't matter when he presented his claim so he waited another 19 days and then served his claim.

He argued that he had been given the wrong advice by the tribunal Clerk and therefore as a matter of natural justice he should be allowed to bring his late claim.

The Judge turned to me and asked me what I had to say.

I said, *"The clerk did not give the Claimant the wrong advice at all. She gave him the correct advice. Once you have exceeded the three-month time limit and have not served your claim in time, it doesn't matter when you serve it. It is always going to be out of time. So the Clerk was correct in saying by the time the Claimant phoned the tribunal it didn't matter when the Claimant served his claim. It was always going to be out of time"*

The Judge through gritted teeth, trying to stifle his laughter, addressed the Claimant, *"Ms Howard is quite right. The Clerk did not give you erroneous advice. Once you are out of time—that's it. You are out of time.*

"You will only be permitted to bring a late claim if you can show it was not reasonably practicable to bring the claim in time.

"You have shown no reason why you failed to serve your claim in time and why it was not reasonably practicable for you to serve your claim within three months of your dismissal.

"You told me you had googled what unfair dismissal was.

"I too googled the same website that you did and read that it states quite clearly you have to present your claim within three months of your Effective Date of Termination. You didn't do that.

"I therefore accept Ms Howard's arguments that it did not matter, at the time you spoke to one of our Clerks, when you served your claim. It was out of time then as it was when you eventually did serve your claim 19 days after that call.

"The clerk did not give you the wrong advice. I am not extending time and your claim will be struck out."

I call that a win.

Another case of a late claim

It has never ever been my practice to wait until the last day or the day before the time limit expires for serving a claim or sending Grounds of Resistance (the defence for an employer).

In the old days we could use fax machines as there was no email or scanners or at least there was no facility to send any claims or defences online. It was either fax, in person or by post.

In another case I used my waspish tongue when another Claimant missed the three month deadline to present her case because her deadline was one day before Easter Friday.

She had posted her ET1 claim form, by recorded delivery, on the Wednesday, one day before the last day she could serve her claim which was the Thursday before Good Friday.

The ET1 form had not actually arrived in the Employment Tribunal office until the following Tuesday because it was not delivered the next day, on the Thursday (even though it was sent recorded delivery). The following day, Good

Friday, there had been no-one at the tribunal office to accept delivery of the recorded delivery letter nor was anyone there on Easter Monday. So the ET1 form was delivered and stamped with the date of the presentation of the claim form the following Tuesday, five days' out of time.

I looked up on the Royal Mail website about whether delivery of recorded delivery post was guaranteed the next day. The website stated *"99% of recorded delivery mail is delivered the next day."*

As I said to the Employment Judge, *"It's amazing how large that 1% is that doesn't get delivered the next day"*

She saw the funny side and ruled the Claimant had served her claim out of time. It had been *"reasonably practicable"* to present her claim in time and she had been foolish to leave it to the day before the final day for service to post her Claim Form. There was no 100% guarantee by Royal Mail that recorded delivery letters would arrive the next day. It said so on their website.

No Sense of History or Humour

I do expect lawyers on the other side to have some knowledge of history and have a semblance of a sense of humour but occasionally I am bitterly disappointed when my jokes fall flat.

I didn't expect a well-educated lawyer not to know his history but that's what happened here.

I was suing a French Bank with a Branch in London. Lorcan, a trader, was my client. He had knowingly and deliberately breached the trading and compliance rules and had been dismissed for gross misconduct.

However according to the Bank's Bonus rules Lorcan was still entitled to his bonus relating to the previous year, even though he had breached the trading rules and had committed gross misconduct. What he had done wasn't discovered until the day **after** bonus payment day.

The rules stated that as long as the employee is still employed and not under notice or disciplinary suspension **on** bonus payment day, they were entitled to their bonus.

Lorcan's wrongdoing was not discovered until 20th February, the day after bonus payment day (19th February) but Compliance, who discovered his wrong-doing somehow managed to get payroll to stop his bonus payment from going through to his Bank Account.

Lorcan was a day trader so he had to 'close' his positions by 4 pm each day whether his trades were up or down.

On this particular occasion he had kept his positions open for three days because the markets were going down very rapidly. He told me he *"was sure the markets would pick up."* His optimism was misplaced and the markets kept falling.

These open positions were eventually flagged to the Risk and Compliance Department on the morning of the third day, 20th February. Compliance immediately closed the positions. The Bank lost €4 million on these trades.

Lorcan was suspended on 20th February, faced disciplinary proceedings and was summarily dismissed on 5th March.

I then sued for Lorcan's bonus in the County Court in London. I didn't have the cheek to sue for unfair dismissal.

The Bank's witnesses, his line manager and the Head of Compliance were both French. They had to give evidence at the Mayor's & City of London County Court.

A week before the case was due to be heard, Peter, from a London Law Firm acting for the Bank, called me to see if we could settle the case. After a lot of argy-bargy, when I would not budge from insisting that Lorcan's full bonus should be paid, with Peter trying to offer increasing proportions of the full bonus, Peter said his client would agree to pay the full bonus.

Peter said he had heard I was the *'Negotiating Queen'*. I told Peter I knew his client would agree to the full bonus. I said I knew his witnesses would never give evidence and face us in Court.

Peter asked me why I was so sure, so I said, (half joking) *"because I haven't forgotten who won the Battles of Hastings, Agincourt, Crecy, Waterloo and Trafalgar—to name but a few."*

Peter went silent and then said, *"Pardon. I don't understand."*

"Never mind" I said, thinking to myself how ignorant he was about history and how sad he had no sense of humour.

I then said, *"well actually I will tell you the truth. I looked into my crystal ball. I can predict the future. That's how I knew."*

"Wow that's handy." said Peter. Oh dear, I thought, this man really was tiresome.

I suggested we got on with signing an agreement and doing the deal. This man had a serious sense of humour failure and was totally ignorant about History.

Then I realised who this 'Peter' was. He was the same lawyer who 15 years earlier had been the useless trainee in Alice's case (Chapter 3).

He had had no idea how to undertake a disclosure exercise or rather, he had been too lazy to do it. He hadn't been taken on by that Law Firm after he had completed his Articles (now called training contract).

I will never know to this day whether he recognised me. I rather suspect that he eventually did.

Getting It Badly Wrong?

Only once do I like to recall giving some advice to settle a claim and getting it dramatically wrong—but not to detriment of my client, quite the contrary. This is for me a truly memorable tale of the 'unexpected'.

Jim fought and won his race discrimination case against a major Investment Bank in the 1990s. It was widely reported in the Press including a leading article in The Independent.

Despite the Chairman of the Bank reportedly saying they did not accept the ruling of the Tribunal and they were *"considering their options"*, meaning they were considering an appeal – they didn't appeal because the decision was unappealable. There were no errors of law. The Tribunal had heard the evidence of the witnesses of fact and made their decision.

I am usually fearless (or ruthless) when negotiating settlements but in this case I gave advice to Jim to accept an offer of settlement made two weeks before trial, which luckily he did not take.

Jim was an African American, a Harvard graduate and a Director. He was a most handsome and charming client and very clever.

However he claimed he was hired as their *"token black face"*. He dealt mainly with private clients in Northern Europe.

A 'private client' is a wealthy individual as opposed to an Institution or Government. The individual typically, in those days at least, had £1 million invested with the Bank, though the minimum amount varied greatly, often with multi-million pounds of investments.

Alexander (not his real name) was Jim's boss. He told Jim, when he had applied for Equity Partnership, that he would never be made an Equity Partner because he was black. Alexander explained that their private clients in Northern Europe would not deal with a black Partner. Well this was in the 1990s.

Jim was fuming when Alexander told him this and made a formal complaint of racial discrimination.

Jim had previously complained that he had been a victim of racial discrimination. On one occasion he was told that one of his colleagues would be more suitable for a certain type of work because *"he talks and looks more like the people who would be coming from those areas (Northern Italy)."*

One of his former managers who had allocated a task to Jim, told him that *"it will be a great opportunity for you to dispel the notion that you people are lazy."*

After making this further complaint of racial discrimination about not being made a Partner, Alexander called him to a meeting, with HR present, and dismissed him, with no notice or payment in lieu of notice.

Jim alleged he was told that complaining that he was a victim of racial discrimination was regarded as not acting *'within the ethos of the Bank'*. He was regarded as disloyal and having breached the trust and confidence that the Bank had in him.

I issued proceedings for unfair dismissal, racial discrimination and victimisation.

The Bank denied all our allegations in their Grounds of Resistance and referred to our claim as a *'racial slur and a lie'*.

Two weeks before the case started, the Bank made a significant six figure offer to settle the case.

Jim was a trader (or as I call them *'informed gamblers'*) so he said he would take his chances at the Tribunal and he refused to take the offer.

In order to protect myself, I immediately wrote him a letter confirming my advice to take the offer, saying, *"In my opinion, you will not get anything like $XXX even if you win your case and the 'if' is a big if."*

The cap on compensation for discrimination had been only £8000 until the late 1990s. Just before Jim brought his claim the cap had been lifted and compensation for discrimination was in theory unlimited.

However Tribunals were not used to awarding large sums of compensation in discrimination cases and I feared that we would never recover anything like the settlement sum offered by his employer, from the tribunal, if we won.

Jim decided to take his chances so off we went to the Tribunal.

[Because there was no transcript of the evidence of the employer's witnesses and the case was heard 26 years ago, the cross examination of the Bank/s.

witnesses has been dramatised. So please read this as a piece of fiction – but it could have happened like this as far as I can recall.]

When it came to cross-examining Jim's boss, Alexander, I decided that if I was going to get him to admit what he had said to Jim about not being made an Equity Partner and then sacking him, I had to lead Alexander gently up the garden path. Aggressive cross-examination is sometimes not the way to lull the other side into saying what you want them to say.

I started my cross-examination of Alexander, *"I understand that Jim has the highest regard for you as I understand you have for Jim. Is that right?"*

Alexander answered, *"Yes, I have the highest regard for Jim. He is a remarkable individual. In fact a client described him to me as 'a clean player of the absolutely highest calibre'."*

I then asked, *"Have you ever known Jim to lie? Is he a fantasist? Does he make up conversations he has never had? Your employer in its defence has said that Jim has made up **'racial slurs which are untrue.'"***

Alexander replied, *"I have never known Jim to lie—never. He is straight as a dye. He is a man of utmost integrity. He is definitely not a fantasist. I have never known Jim make up conversations. He is a gentleman and I rate him very highly."*

Ah ah I thought, you have fallen right into the hole I was digging for you, with both feet.

I continued, *"That's exactly what I wanted to ask you about next—how you 'rated' Jim. I see you rated him on the highest appraisal score 'Exceeds Expectations', for the last three years. He was also awarded the highest bonus on his Desk for the last three years.*

"You scored him the highest score of '5' out of '5' in the individual categories —'leadership and motivational skills', 'communication skills', 'ability to work under pressure', 'ability to work on his own initiative', 'ability to gain new business' and 'team-working'.

"He has been your top fee earner for the last five years. That's right, isn't it?"

Alexander said, *"Yes."*

I continued (this was all going to plan), *"Well perhaps you would tell the Tribunal what are the criteria for promotion to Equity Partnership?"*

Alexander said, *"Well—they have to be scored '5 ie in the top band of appraisal ratings - 'exceeds expectations' for at least three years and have been rated "5' in several individual categories.*

"They have to have excellent 360^0 feedback from their peers and superiors. We also require excellent feedback from their clients.

"They have to be fully committed to the Bank, hardworking and loyal, be an outstanding motivational leader and demonstrate excellent leadership and communication skills. They have to be a top fee earner. They must have demonstrated they can work under pressure and on their own initiative. They must be a team-player. They also have to have demonstrated the skills and aptitude to gain new business and have a brilliant all-round track record."

I let that sink in and then said, *"So please tell the tribunal something. Why was Jim passed over for promotion to equity partnership? It seems to me from your rating of Jim for the past three years he has achieved all the requirements needed for equity partnership. So why wasn't he made an Equity Partner last year when he applied?"*

There was a long silence or at least it felt long, while Alexander realised that he had fallen right into the trap that had been laid for him.

Eventually he said, *"Because our private clients, the Northern Europeans, will not deal with an Equity Partner like him."*

Smiling slightly, I asked, *"What do you mean 'like him?'"* (knowing the answer.)

Alexander had nowhere to go. He muttered almost inaudibly, *"because he's black."*

"Sorry" I said, *"I don't think the Tribunal heard what you said. Would you please speak up and repeat what you just said."*

Alexander then boomed, *"because he's black and his clients told me they would never do business with a black Partner."*

"And that's what you told Jim isn't it?" I asked.

There was another long silence from Alexander. He knew that in the Bank's Grounds of Resistance this had been robustly denied he had said that. The Bank had actually threatened to apply for their costs against Jim for *"making up a wholly untruthful racial slur and a lie."*

Finally, Alexander answered—everyone was waiting—with just one word, *"Yes."*

The final question was a killer, *"And please tell the Tribunal why Jim was dismissed when he was such a brilliant performer and such a delightful and popular colleague?"*

Alexander told the truth. He said he had been ordered by his boss to sack Jim with no notice, no pay in lieu of notice and no hearing, after Jim had filed a grievance about not being made an Equity Partner because he was black (on my advice). He was also not given any right of appeal against dismissal – another requirement for a fair dismissal.

Jim was given no reason for his dismissal even though he had a statutory right for a written statement of the reason for dismissal and even though I had requested for one.

Jim had been devastated and wholly humiliated.

Alexander looked for several seconds at me and said. *"You know why. My boss told me he had to 'get rid of him'. My boss said 'He's trouble. He's complaining of being racially discriminated against. We don't want troublemakers like him.'"*

At that admission both Alexander and Jim wept.

I said, *"That is all my cross-examination Alexander but please stay there because the Tribunal may have some questions for you and your Counsel may have some re-examination."*

The Tribunal had no questions for him and neither did his Counsel who seemed pleased his cross examination had finished and he could leave the witness table.

As Alexander got up from the witness table he whispered to Jim, *"I am so sorry"* and I believe that was true.

Alexander was genuinely mortified that he had been made to bow to the racially discriminatory instructions and views of their clients and of his boss. These were acts of racial discrimination and were indefensible.

There is no defence or justification for discriminating because your clients tell you to do so, because they won't deal with a black person or a woman or someone of a particular religion etc.

Jim had then been sacked for complaining of racial discrimination - that's also unlawful. It is victimisation and there is no justification.

After that admission by Alexander it left the Bank nowhere to go.

The Tribunal had no difficulty in finding in Jim's favour and they upheld all of his claims.

The Judge asked Jim what his losses were. He replied that Equity Partners at the Bank at that time were earning $2 million a year. He said he had planned to stay at the Bank for five years as an Equity Partner and he would then have left.

So Jim said, *"the math is easy —5 x $2,000,000 is $10,000,000 so that's what I have lost."* So that's what the Tribunal awarded Jim in compensation.

As we were leaving the tribunal, slightly tongue in cheek, I said to Jim, *"You see, I was absolutely right. You didn't get anything like the offer the Bank made before the hearing from the tribunal."* Jim saw the funny side and said, *"Yes Gillian you were **so** right."*

He told me that he framed my letter telling him to take the Bank's offer and hung it on the wall of his office in Washington DC where he had made his home – next to a copy of the cheque for $10,000,000.

The story has a very happy ending—happier than even I could have expected.

Jim invested his settlement in shares in new technology start-ups and at the height of the dot-com bubble he sold his shares for many multiples of millions of dollars.

That was a great win and a great investment.

"What's Your Price?"

I think the words 'shocked' and 'totally unexpected' came to mind when for the only time in my life I was, knowingly at least, offered a bribe. This was offered by a foolish Union official, Bryan.

Bryan was representing Ron, a Chartered Surveyor, who worked for a Housing Association, one of my corporate clients. Ron was a Surveyor, responsible for inspecting the Housing Association's properties and authorising new central heating, new windows and virtually anything else that the tenants wanted—as it turned out, often in return for sexual favours.

These tenants were in the main young, single mothers on benefits and vulnerable adults some of whom had learning difficulties or had been victims of abuse.

Mary was a young, single mother who had escaped from an abusive relationship.

Mary made a complaint to Sally, the HR Director, that when Ron had come to inspect her windows, he had nestled up behind her when she had knelt on her bed to show him the mould on her bedroom window. He had whispered something very lewd about what he wanted to do to her—*"I want to fuck you up your arse first and then cunt fuck you and then I want you to take me in your mouth and suck me off until I come."*

She said she could feel his erection pressing against her and Ron would not let her go for a good few minutes.

Eventually he got off her bed and went into the kitchen. He picked up a pair of her knickers from the washing basket, sniffed them and made a disgusting remark about what he wanted to do to her without her knickers on—*"fuck you from behind and on top and then you are to kneel down and suck me off. That's if you want new windows."*

Not surprisingly, after a full investigation, Ron was invited to a gross misconduct disciplinary hearing, charged with sexual harassment and sexual assault. He was very lucky this tenant did not report him to the police.

We learnt from some of the other tenants that Ron would often attend their premises in the summer, dressed in very tight shorts and a T-shirt. The dress rules of this Housing Association, for men, in the summer, was a smart, short-sleeved shirt and long trousers. Shorts and T shirts were not acceptable business wear.

Ron's dress and appearance were clearly highly inappropriate but he wasn't sacked for his dress or appearance.

Other female tenants gave statements that he had offered them home improvements in return for various 'favours'. Some female tenants wrote to Sally after he must have told them he was in trouble, *"I love Ron. He was so good to me"* etc etc. I interpreted that accordingly.

The union official, Bryan, and Ron had arrived in the disciplinary hearing room, before Sally arrived. Bryan looked at me and said, *"What's your price?"*

I thought he was asking me about my fees so I replied, *"none of your business."*

"Don't be silly," he said, *"Everyone has a price. I'm asking what's yours?"* adding, *"to get Ron out of trouble?"*

I then realised he was offering me a bribe to advise my client not to dismiss Ron. I nearly fell off my chair. I remained open-mouthed and at that moment Sally arrived.

She asked me if anything was wrong so I told her that I had just been offered a bribe by Bryan to ensure that Ron got off without being dismissed. That went down like a lead balloon.

Bryan was requested to leave the hearing and he was reported to his union General Secretary. The hearing was postponed for five days while Ron found new representation.

Another hearing was held and Ron was dismissed in disgrace. He did not appeal. He disappeared without trace.

We never found out who employed him next. We would have written to any prospective employer to warn them about him.

The Housing Association paid Mary £10,000 as a settlement on account of Ron's behaviour. I never did get my bribe.

"He's Pulled a Flanker on us"

I used to act for an exclusive private Member's Club in London and dealt mainly with their HR Director, Hector. He was always extremely polite and professional so imagine my shock when I got back to my office one day to find a most unexpected voicemail message on my answer machine.

It was from the Director General of the Club, Major General Batten. In his extremely pukka voice, strained and obviously very upset, his message was, *"Hector has pulled a flanker on us. He's run off with all our money."*

When I called back to see what had happened, I was told that Hector had stolen around £500,000 from the Club's funds, over a period of several years. He had disappeared overnight taking the petty cash of nearly £1000 and the takings of over £5000 from the tills from the Restaurant, the Bar and gym.

His wife had called Major General Batten when Hector failed to come home the night before and that is how the theft was discovered.

In fact, Hector could not initially be contacted. He was reported to the police as a 'misper' (missing person). He was eventually tracked down using his wife's credit card that he had taken without her permission. He was arrested and taken to Holborn Police Station and charged with theft.

It then came to light that Hector was a gambler and had gambled away all his family's savings, had taken out a second mortgage on their house and spent that gambling and was in debt for nearly £1,000,000.

He had been stealing the Club's money for several years and the auditors had finally identified he was the thief. He had been notified of this the day he disappeared.

Poor man—he pleaded guilty at the Old Bailey and was sentenced to seven years in prison. His wife and family were evicted from their home and anything valuable was sold to pay off some of his debts.

The Club was not a preferred creditor so never got its money back. It had all been spent on Hector's gambling.

Don't Be Helpful to the Other Side

Some good advice to my witnesses has been not to be helpful to the other side. For example, it's not the employer's job to explain why the Claimant is alleging discrimination or unfair dismissal.

So if ever asked, *"please explain why the Claimant is alleging discrimination and/or unfair dismissal?"* I tell my witnesses that the correct response is to say they have no idea because the Claimant was not discriminated against or unfairly dismissed.

On one memorable occasion, when the HR Director, Freda was asked that very question, she forgot this advice. It has become a case study on how not to give answers in cross examination.

Freda was normally a level-headed and sensible HR Director but she completely lost it at the tribunal and gave evidence that none of us expected.

My client owned five private care homes in South London. Adebimpe (Adi), was the Deputy Matron of one of the Homes. She had been employed for 19 years originally as a nurse and then for the last three years as Deputy Matron. Adi was Nigerian by birth but had lived in London since the age of 3. She had trained to be a nurse here.

Matron had gone on leave, so Adi was 'acting up' as Matron of one of the Care Homes.

On the Sunday afternoon in question Adi left the Care Home 45 minutes before her shift ended, in breach of all the procedures. All but one of the eight care assistants also left early, after Adi had left. The only staff who remained at the Home was one care assistant, a domestic and a volunteer.

Adi did not report to the Director of the Homes that she was leaving early nor did she organise anyone to stand in for her. She was blissfully unaware that most of the other Care Staff had also snuck out early, after seeing her leave.

This left the Home in breach of the regulations about the requirement for the statutory number of care staff needed per resident.

After Adi and the other staff had gone home, one of the elderly residents, a frail 92 year old lady, fell out of bed. She called for help and no-one came until the domestic finally heard her shouting and came to see what was wrong.

Not knowing that she should leave someone with possible broken bones where they were, the domestic hauled the elderly lady up from the floor and dragged her into a chair. By this time the resident was screaming in pain because unfortunately she had broken her hip and should not have been moved.

The domestic then left the resident alone while she said she was going to call the care assistant for help. Alarmed at being left alone and in great pain and very frightened, the resident rang her son on her mobile phone.

Her son arrived to find only one qualified carer on duty. The domestic had vanished and the care assistant had not been informed of the resident's fall and no ambulance had been called.

The son had to call an ambulance and rang the Director on duty, William, who immediately came around to the Home. That is how my client found out that Adi and the other staff had left early that Sunday.

Adi was immediately suspended and an investigation carried out. She was then invited to a disciplinary hearing.

Her excuses for leaving early were that she had been on duty all week, had been working long hours, was very tired and had left early due to fatigue. She said she had no idea that the other care assistants had also left early just after her.

Before her disciplinary hearing, I checked Adi's rota. For the two days before the Sunday in question she had been on rest days. In the week preceding this particular Sunday, she had not even worked her normal 40 hours. She had only worked 36 hours.

Adi had no excuse whatsoever for what she did. It was gross misconduct and with no mitigating factors she was summarily dismissed. Her appeal against her dismissal also failed.

Adi then sought legal advice from a solicitor who represented her at the tribunal. She sued for unfair dismissal and racial discrimination.

I knew this might not be an easy case but I knew my client had followed a scrupulously fair procedure and Adi's colour, ethnicity and race had nothing whatsoever to do with the reason for her dismissal. Any white member of staff who had done what she did would also have been dismissed.

In her Grounds of Complaint, Adi argued that she had not been told in advance of the disciplinary hearing that she could be dismissed. She said she was only expecting a warning at the very worst.

The letter inviting her to the disciplinary hearing had not specified how serious the charges were and what the possible outcomes could be. This is something all employers *should* include in the disciplinary invitation letter no matter how obvious it may be.

She also argued that she had not been treated with any respect for the past year, by the new Finance Director, Emma and new HR Director, Freda, both white women. Adi said they were racists and had picked on her because she was black.

She argued that both women had specifically "set up her to fail" in order to dismiss her, by imposing new rules and procedures which they knew she would not understand or be able to follow.

These new procedures included a performance management and appraisal system which they had never had before, new health and safety rules, new drug control rules, new accounting rules, new rules for the collection of fees, new rules about not accepting gifts or money from residents and new petty cash procedures.

The new financial controls prohibited staff from taking tips or gratuities or gifts of any kind from residents or members of their family save at Christmas and the gift – not money - had to be less than £50 in value and declared to the Director. The staff were now also not allowed to accept payment for the resident's fees. Residents' fees had to be paid by Bank transfer directly into the Care Home's Bank Account and all extras also had to be paid by Bank transfer.

Emma had found that fees and petty cash had been 'going missing'. There had been disputes between residents or their families and staff as to whether or not the fees had been paid. Some families argued they had paid the fees in cash to a member of staff but that member of staff then denied they had been paid and no receipts had been given.

It was also viewed as potential bribery and unethical for staff to accept gifts or gratuities from the residents because of possible improper pressure on the resident.

Emma had put a stop to these practices that had apparently been going on for years.

Petty cash was now strictly monitored and every penny spent had to be accounted for, with receipts. All expenses had to be pre-approved and signed off by Emma.

The new safety measures that had been introduced included monthly fire alarm checks and annual fire drills in all the Homes. They had all been done, ad hoc previously, and in some years not all and very few records had been kept.

Adi argued these new procedures had all been introduced in order to get *her* out. She described Emma and Freda in her evidence as *"new brooms sweeping clean the Homes."*

Adi argued both women had wanted her out as she had heard through the grapevine they wanted a *"better and more modern image with better trained staff"* for the Homes.

Adi alleged that that meant they didn't want black faces around and they were just waiting for this opportunity to get rid of her.

It was probably true that Emma and Freda wanted modern practices and procedures and a better image for the Homes in a highly competitive market but this was not a plan to get rid of black members of staff.

All was going well at the tribunal until Freda was cross examined by Adi's solicitor.

He started his cross examination with his first question, *"Why do you think my client believes that she has been the victim of racial discrimination and a campaign to get rid of her under the new regime that you and the Finance Director implemented?"*

Instead of answering, *"I have no idea why your client should think that because it is not true,"* Freda said something I certainly wasn't expecting.

"Ah" she said, *"well, I can tell you why she might have thought that."*

Twenty minutes later, she was still explaining to the Tribunal about the new regime introduced by Emma and her and why Adi *might* have thought that the new procedures could lead to some of the longer-serving staff like Adi, not meeting the new performance standards or getting to grips with the new health and safety and financial rules.

Freda added that after training and re-training and a 'buddy' system and mentoring, it must have been clear to Adi that she might fail her first appraisal and receive *"Doesn't meet"* the requirements of the job.

Freda forgot to add the new procedures were *not* introduced in order to set Adi up to fail or to give the Home a spurious or unlawful reason to dismiss her.

The new performance management procedures had been introduced to improve performance and standardise staff performance to make the Homes more attractive to potential residents.

There was also fierce competition in London for good staff and these particular Care Homes had a very old-fashioned image, had difficulty recruiting good staff and had falling numbers of residents.

Freda told me afterwards that she just froze in the witness box, panicked and thought she had to answer the question. She said she just wasn't thinking straight.

In my re-examination of Freda, I asked her to go back to her answer about the allegation that all of the new procedures that she and Emma had introduced had only been brought in to dismiss Adi because she was black. I asked Freda if she wanted to add anything to what she had said in cross examination.

Freda was so terrified by this stage that she said *"No"*. Her evidence had been a disaster and I had nowhere to go and that was the end of re-examination.

The case was going really badly for us until it came time for me to cross-examine Adi. Then the tide turned.

I asked Adi, *"Please tell the tribunal what you expected to happen to you when you were invited to a disciplinary hearing, having left the Home early, with all but one of the care staff leaving early as well, without adequate cover?*

"As you know one of the elderly residents fell out of bed after you and the rest of the staff had left early. There was only one qualified carer on duty but she did not come to help this resident because the domestic had fled in terror. The lady had to phone her son for help and he had to call an ambulance. This resident sadly died in hospital six weeks later."

Adi was very flippant, *"Well, that was hardly my fault was it? I certainly didn't expect to be dismissed for leaving early because I was exhausted. The worst I thought I might get was a warning"* and then she added *"if that."*

Adi gave the impression she really did not understand the seriousness of what she had done or in fact that she had done *anything* wrong. There was certainly no hint from her that she would never do anything like that again and there was more than a hint of arrogance from her.

I asked Adi, *"Are you telling this tribunal that the new management procedures and financial controls, including the new appraisal procedures, the new drug control regime, the new rules on health and safety, the new rules banning the acceptance of gratuities from Residents and the new petty cash controls were all introduced in order to get rid of you, because you are black?"*

She said, *"Yes that's what I believe. Those two white women wanted to get rid of all us blacks and replace us with white staff to 'improve the image' —you know, they wanted 'people like you'"* and Adi pointed at the tribunal panel and then at me.

I waited until her words *"people like you"* had sunk in. I asked her, *"To whom are you referring when you say, 'people like you?'"* Adi went completely silent. I asked her again but she just refused to answer.

The Judge wrote down what Adi had said and I remained completely silent to allow that to sink in. The Tribunal Panel just stared at Adi for several seconds.

I continued, *"Do you accept that the Homes had been run inefficiently in the past? The rules had not been updated for years and there were virtually no financial controls in place. The health and safety rules were way out of date. There were no regular fire evacuation drills for the staff or residents nor was there any clear signage. The drug protocols were all out of date and potentially dangerous.*

"You are a qualified nurse so you must know that the former drug protocols did not meet the Nursing and Midwifery Council's (NMC's) requirements for the control and administration of drugs.

"You were still taking cash from relatives who were paying for the residents' fees until Emma changed the rules to allow only for direct Bank transfers or debit card payments.

"You also used to allow staff to accept gratuities and gifts from the residents and their relatives. This is regarded as improper and needed to be stopped.

"Would you agree that these were outdated practices that needed to be changed for the more efficient and transparent running of the Homes?"

Adi remained silent. I waited for her to answer but she refused to speak so I noted her refusal to answer and went on with my next question.

I asked, *"Would you agree with me that these new procedures were not introduced as a means to get you sacked nor were you sacked because you are black?"*

Adi didn't answer. I again noted her refusal to answer.

I asked, *"Please then explain to this tribunal why you think they were targeting you, as a black woman, in order to get rid of you?*

"Would you accept that if Matron, who is white, had done what you had done, she too would have faced dismissal?"

Adi didn't answer so I asked her again, *"Your pleadings quite clearly state that your dismissal was a sham, that you had been 'set up' and that the new management rules and new procedures were introduced to get rid of you because you are black.*

"Your pleadings state that your dismissal was unfair and racist and you were actually dismissed because Freda and Emma are racists and wanted to get rid of you because you are black.

"Please tell the tribunal on what basis do you say the new rules were introduced solely in order to get rid of you and there was no valid or fair reason to sack you and what was racist about your dismissal?"

Adi was silent and she refused to answer.

So I asked, *"Do you still believe that your conduct on that Sunday, with the appalling circumstances of that elderly resident's fall and subsequent death, the consequential reputational damage that occurred and the Regulatory investigation that followed, when you were acting Matron at the time, did not warrant your dismissal?"*

Adi was silent again. I said the tribunal was noting every silence and failure to answer my questions from Adi.

I then asked her, *"Please tell the tribunal if that elderly lady who had fallen out of bed had been your mother, how would you have felt about the acting Matron leaving her alone and helpless, possibly to die alone? You know she did die in hospital six weeks after her fall?*

"You know the Consultant on duty in A&E said that the mishandling of the resident after she fell out of bed and the delay in calling an ambulance possibly hastened her death."

Adi said nothing.

I carried on, *"Let me ask you another question as you are reluctant to answer any of my questions so far. How would you have felt if a deputy matron, acting up as Matron, who had done what you had done, had been allowed to come back to work in the Home, where your elderly mother was a resident? Would you have been prepared to keep your mother at that Home?"*

Adi looked at me and realised she had nowhere to go. She stuttered, *"I don't know. My mother is only 72 and in good health so I haven't thought about it."*

My final question was, *"In light of everything that happened that Sunday and bearing in mind there is an emergency number on the Board for you to phone* the Director on call, do you now regret what you did and would you do it differently if you had a second chance?"

Adi stared at me for some time and then said defiantly, *"I know what you're trying to do. You're trying to trick me into admitting I deserved the sack. I refuse to answer."*

I said, *"The Tribunal has noted you have refused to answer most of my questions so that will be all. Please stay there because the tribunal and your solicitor may have more questions for you."*

The Judge was particularly impatient with Adi. He asked her the same questions I had asked but got the same silent treatment. The Judge warned Adi that by refusing to answer his questions an adverse inference would be drawn. Adi remained silent.

Adi had done what I wanted her to do. She had damned herself by refusing to speak and answer my questions.

When I summed up, I asked the tribunal to find that *"my client had acted as any reasonable and responsible employer would have done."*

I asked the Tribunal the question, *"Would you trust your elderly parents in the care of this woman? She cannot or will not see, even now, that what she did was terribly wrong and thinks that a light reprimand is all that she deserved 'if at all' if I may quote her very words.*

"She has made untruthful statements and has made racial slurs about the new Finance Director and HR Director, two decent white women who were trying to do a good job.

"This is egregious behaviour on the Claimant's part as she knows those allegations of racial discrimination are untrue. She has made them purely to try to add weight to her otherwise wholly unmeritorious unfair dismissal case.

"She has clearly failed to understand the importance of her role or the seriousness of what she did or the regulatory nightmare that followed.

"The Local Authority had to be persuaded not to withdraw the licences of all five Homes. They were all very nearly shut down.

"There was also appalling PR damage as a result. The newspapers both National and local reported what had happened.

"Worse still we must not forget that elderly resident. She was left unattended for over 40 minutes, having been dragged off the floor with a broken hip by an untrained domestic and the last six weeks of her life ended in misery, distress and great pain. She was entitled to expect more than that and Adi failed her.

"The local newspaper named the Care Home and had put a photograph of Adi on its front page with the headlines '96-year-old Resident left to die after being left alone by this woman. Care Home under investigation'."

I asked the Tribunal to dismiss the allegations of racial discrimination because race had never been the issue and to find that the dismissal fell within the bands of reasonable responses that any reasonable employer could have adopted.

After listening to what I had to say and recalling Adi's poor and unconvincing excuses for her conduct that day, the tribunal overlooked Freda's shambolic evidence and found the dismissal to be fair and dismissed out of hand the allegations of racial discrimination.

I don't think Freda ever forgot that trip to the industrial tribunal.

"Foreplay"—It Ended with a Kiss

I was thinking of the Hot Chocolate song *"It started with a kiss"* but actually this case *'ended with a kiss'*.

I have conducted many settlement negotiations in my time but never one quite like this.

I was acting for Édouard, in a very acrimonious dispute between him and his employer. Édouard was a brilliant investment banker who had worked closely for 20 years with Henri, the Founder of the Investment Boutique. They had great mutual respect and admiration for each other.

Henri had retired and had handed over the business to his nephew, Eric. Édouard did not get on with Eric and they fell out spectacularly.

Édouard resigned and was owed millions of Euros in bonus payments, saved over 17 years. He had asked Henri to keep his bonuses in a separate bank account for him and to invest in the shares of this highly profitable Company.

After Édouard and Eric fell out spectacularly and Édouard resigned, he asked Eric for his shares to be sold. They were worth around €75,000,000. Eric at first refused to give Édouard any of his shares or the equivalent in cash.

I issued proceedings for breach of contract and Eric then offered Édouard €50,000,000 in full and final settlement.

Édouard asked me what I would say about the offer. I said, *"Happy Christmas."* Édouard replied, *"I am being screwed"*—so off we went to Court.

When we got to Court, the Judge having read the papers told the parties that this should never have come before him. He said it was a 'family and personal dispute' and we should go outside to try to settle.

After tortuous negotiations lasting several hours, we finally reached agreement—Édouard would receive the full €75,000,000 that he was owed.

But just before the agreement was signed, Édouard insisted that an extra term be added to the Agreement—that Eric must give him a kiss first before Édouard would sign the Agreement. I certainly wasn't expecting that – even from a Frenchman.

Totally bemused, I asked Édouard why he wanted a kiss from his deadly rival. He replied, *"Remember I said I was being screwed. Well before you get screwed you should always have some foreplay."*

This Frenchman had a great sense of humour.

Cross-Examination

Very occasionally there has been some memorable cross-examination when a witness for the other side goes spectacularly 'off-piste' and gives evidence that no-one is expecting.

There is an expression, "out of the mouths of babes." Well this came out of the mouth of a grown man.

I was acting for Fatima, a lecturer at a College of Further and Higher Education. I was suing the College and John, her head of Department of Modern Languages, for constructive dismissal, racial and sexual discrimination, harassment and victimisation.

Fatima was Muslin - that's relevant to this story. She was a great teacher and had not missed a day's work in the ten years she had been employed at this College. She described John as a 'racist, sexist pig'.

He had spoken about Muslim women to some of Fatima's colleagues within her earshot, saying:

- *"Do all good Muslim women have sex with their husbands whenever their husbands demand it?"*
- *"Do you agree that you should chop a Muslim woman's hand off in this country if they are caught stealing, like they do in her country (pointing to Fatima)? because I do."*

- *"They've got it right—Muslim women are stoned to death if they are caught committing adultery."*
- *What's the point of educating Muslim women? Most of them are stupid anyway and all they do is get pregnant and have babies for most of their working life."*

John then sent a grossly offensive cartoon to Fatima's colleagues in the Modern Languages Department and to others in the College.

The cartoon was of a Muslim woman being stoned to death, with her husband watching, and a bubble coming out of his mouth saying, *"Well that's one way to stop her going shopping."*

John had forwarded the cartoon from his work email with the words *"ha-ha—great cartoon."*

After Fatima made her complaint about this cartoon and the fact that John had circulated it, he refused to interview her for promotion to Principal Lecturer and refused to give her a salary increase that year, alleging that she was *"incompetent, lazy and not a team player."*

Fatima then resigned—she could not bear to work with John any more.

We sued the College for discriminatory constructive dismissal and religious and racial discrimination and John, for sex, race and religious discrimination and victimisation.

When it was John's turn to be cross-examined at the Tribunal hearing, I put it to him that he had expressed racist, religious and sex-stereotypical views of Muslim women and that he was a racist and a sexist bigot.

He looked at me and said, *"I am not a bigot"* and then added as an afterthought, *"but you know what foreign women are like?"*

I said, *"No. Please do tell me."*

"Well," he said, *"we all know that British women are frigid, Danish women are fast and loose and will shag anything whether it's got two or four legs and German women are fat, ugly and humourless. I could go on."*

"Please do" I replied.

"Well, the Spanish are a nation of stunning women who can't go to the bullfight dressed in miniskirts because their boyfriends and husbands (who are so macho) would have a fit. And then there's the siestas in the afternoon and the partying at night. The Spanish as a nation are lazy and loud.

"French women are snooty bitches and whores. They will shag anyone who asks them. They are rude and unhygienic. They don't shave anywhere or use deodorants and they are all snobs. French men think they are the world's greatest lovers. This is quite undeserved. The French deserve their reputation for their legendary rudeness.

"Italian women are all chatterboxes and bad listeners, interested only in the sound of their own voices. They are all good-looking and fashion-crazy until the age of 30 and then they go to pot. They grow into fat, ugly old hags—except Sophia Loren and Gina Lollobrigida—they are still gorgeous.

"No Italian ever pays their taxes and all Italian men live under the thumb of their beloved Mamma.

*"Russian women are beautiful but are crafty as hell. They are only in love with themselves, money and cocaine. They drink vodka and snort cocaine most of the day and once you get them drunk, they are anybody's. The Russians who have come to the UK are **all** crooks—Russian Mafia—they have brought their dirty money to London.*

"They have bought up all the fabulous properties in London and the Home Counties, making it impossible for us English to buy property any more. They are using England as a place to launder their money and this Government is doing nothing to stop them.

"Swedish women are frigid—they are not called Ice Maidens for nothing despite their reputation for believing in free love and all that. I think it must be the weather.

"Swiss women are just plain boring—they won't have sex other than in the missionary position—believe me I've tried."

I wish he had gone on longer but the Judge interrupted, *"John, I think you had better stop there. I think we have heard enough."*

The Judge turned to me and asked if I had any more questions, with an obvious hint for me to say *"No"*. I took the hint and said, *"reluctantly No Sir."*

I could have continued listening to John go on and on with his racist rant but the Judge had clearly signalled he had heard enough.

It took the Tribunal less than an hour to uphold my client's claims. Fatima was awarded a staggering sum in compensation for loss of earnings and damages for injury to feelings.

What Bad Luck

Sometimes ex-employees have really bad luck and none more so than Dr Black. He could never have imagined what was going to happen to him after his dismissal. He certainly wasn't expecting what happened next.

Dr Black had been dismissed from his job as Deputy Chief Executive of a Professional Scientific Institution, for falsifying his expenses, diverting the Institute's funds for his own use and taking bribes to give contracts to various 'favoured' contractors. A whistle-blower had informed on him.

It was discovered that the flat at the top of the Institution's Headquarters, normally used for visitors, had been used as Dr Black's 'love nest'. He had been having an affair with a young scientist and they had been having their love trysts in this flat in their lunch hours and after work.

Dr Black had bribed the security guards to ignore their activities in the flat and to turn the CCTV cameras away from the lift when they went up to the flat.

He had ordered a new £7000 Savoir bed and some very expensive Frette bed linen, beautiful Lalique vases, expensive soft furnishings and costly wallpaper for this flat. He had put all these items on the Building's refurbishment bills.

I acted for the employer and was instructed to offer Dr Black one year's pay in lieu of notice as the settlement when he was 'invited to resign' – which he did.

I drafted the agreement that he would receive his money in four, three monthly tranches. The agreement was that if he secured a new job during the year, he had to inform us and no further notice payments would be made to him. He would have mitigated his loss.

After the first three months, as far as we were aware, he had no new job and he was paid his first three months' pay in lieu of notice. Near to the end of the second three months he had not informed us he had secured new employment so I advised my client to authorise payroll to make the second payment at the end of that month. And here's where Dr Black's luck ran out.

Just before his second payment was due to be paid, I telephoned the Royal Opera House (ROH) for tickets for La bohème and was told that all the seats had been sold for the entire run.

Never one to take 'No' for an answer, I asked if I could speak to the Box Office Manager. I was put through and a distinctive voice boomed down the receiver, *"Dr Black here. How can I help you?"*

Well it wasn't his lucky day was it?

I said, *"Oh Yes Dr Black you certainly can help me. Fancy hearing your voice. Do you recognise to whom you are speaking?"*

He went very quiet so I helped him out, *"It's your favourite employment lawyer here, The Rottweiler with a handbag. I think your former employer will be very interested to know where you're working now."* The phone then went dead.

I immediately called my client and told them what had happened and asked them to instruct payroll not to make any further payments to Dr Black and to take him off the payroll.

When I called the ROH the next day I was told, *"Dr Black no longer works here."* The man had bolted or been pushed out.

Now I call that really bad luck and really bad timing—for Dr Black that is. I can sniff out a liar at 100 paces.

Sadly I never did get those tickets to see that production of La bohème.

Some Ridiculous Cases

There have been a handful of cases that should never have got as far as an Employment Tribunal.

Black Magic

One of the most frivolous cases that I should never have had to defend was the case of "Black Magic."

The Head of a Research & Development Laboratory, Martin, decided one year to ask his staff to bring a wrapped Christmas present to their Christmas lunch, as a Secret Santa.

'Secret Santa' is a tradition at Christmas where members of a group are randomly assigned a person to whom they give a modest gift—in this case it had to cost £5 or less.

Each member of the laboratory took a name out of a hat and they were responsible for buying and wrapping a gift for that person.

Martin had drawn out the name of one of his members of staff, Gloria. She happened to be black. Martin's wife Helen actually bought and gift-wrapped this present for Gloria. Helen had no idea about Gloria's colour, race or ethnicity.

All the gifts were put in a sack and one by one when their name was called, they were invited to pull out the gift and open it.

Gloria picked out her gift and opened it to find it was a box of Black Magic chocolates. Several members of staff thought this was hilarious and started sniggering. Gloria took great offence. She said she felt mortified in front of the other staff and brought a claim for racial harassment.

Luckily for my client, the Tribunal took the view that this was a thoroughly frivolous claim in the circumstances of how the gift was chosen and given.

The Judge dismissed Gloria's case at the end of the first morning but of course, the Press had a field day.

The headlines in the newspapers the next day read, *'Black Magic' chocolates sparks race row at X.*

Everyone's a Winner

This is another case that should never have ended up in a tribunal. This is the only case in over 40 years of practice when both parties ended up most unexpectedly being delighted with the tribunal's decision.

I was acting for Ahmed, a porter in a luxury block of flats in Hampstead, North West London. He decided one day that he was not going to wear his hat any more, which was part of his uniform.

The Managing Agent had appeared one morning and asked Ahmed why he was not wearing his hat. He said he did not like it and he was not going to wear it and then started shouting at the Managing Agent to 'get out of his face' – and worse. The Managing Agent promptly dismissed Ahmed on the spot, without any warning, hearing or appeal.

I told Ahmed that whilst the procedure was unfair, he would almost certainly not be awarded much, if any, compensation because he would probably be found to have contributed 100% to his dismissal. He told me he did not care about the money. What he wanted was a finding of unfair dismissal.

The Managing Agent, representing his employer, decided to defend the case despite not having followed a fair procedure because they didn't want to pay Ahmed a penny in compensation.

The Tribunal had little difficulty in finding the dismissal was procedurally unfair but found Ahmed was 100% at fault as predicted.

In terms of what is *'just and equitable'* to award as compensation, the Tribunal found that Ahmed deserved no compensation at all. All he was awarded was his basic award, which in those days amounted to a very small amount of money as Ahmed had only been employed for just over two years and was on a modest salary.

As Judgement was given, both parties looked very happy. That had never happened to me before or since nor had the Judge ever seen both parties smiling at his decision.

The Judge asked both the Managing Agent and me to wait behind before we left the hearing room.

He said that we did not have to answer but, *"This is a first. It has never happened that both parties seem very pleased with the decision of this Tribunal. Would you be willing to tell me why you are both smiling and seem so happy with our decision?"*

I said I would be happy to tell the Tribunal with the agreement of the Managing Agent.

I explained that my client wanted a finding of an unfair dismissal. He did not care about the money. It was a matter of principle for him. Quite what principle I found it hard to fathom. He had lost his job over a nonsensical principle.

In contrast his employers did not care that by a technicality, it was held to be an unfair dismissal. They believed there was no stigma in such a finding. The Managing Agent said there were thousands of unfair dismissal rulings every year. They did not want to pay Ahmed any compensation. They didn't have to, thanks to the Judge's ruling. So, both parties were happy.

The Judge said he wished this happened more often and sent us away - both of us very happy with his decision.

You get what you pay for

Patricia came to me for advice in the January of one year. She had been very badly treated by her male boss and could not stand his bullying and discriminatory treatment of her anymore and had resigned.

I drafted her claims against her former employer for unfair constructive dismissal and sexual harassment and sued her former boss as the Second Respondent.

After a few months of being unemployed and with no income she said she could not afford to pay the fees for Counsel herself but she had legal expenses insurance and she needed to use them. They had their own Panel of lawyers who were paid in those days £70 per hour. She asked me if I would do a no win no fee arrangement but I never enter into such an arrangement so I had to decline.

The No Win No Fee arrangement in my view compromises the lawyer as there are two clients – the client and the lawyer. The lawyer has a conflict between the interests of their client and their own interests.

I told Patricia I would advise her in the background for no fees but I could not remain on the record and she should use her legal expenses insurance, which she did.

Two weeks before the trial date she rang me in a terrible state. I certainly wasn't expecting to hear what had happened.

Her legal expenses lawyer had basically done no work. They had not even advised her to draft her witness statement.

Two weeks before the tribunal was due to start, these lawyers had received an offer of £1000 from Patricia's ex-employer and the lawyers had told her if she didn't accept the offer they would advise the legal expenses insurers, who would then refuse to cover her legal expenses any longer. These lawyers said her case was not worth any more.

She rang me and asked me to represent her at the tribunal and said she would borrow the money from her parents. I agreed to act for no fees and instructed Anna, a brilliant Counsel, to represent her at trial. Anna's fees were very modest as she too was incensed with how the legal expenses solicitors had behaved.

Anna and I worked for the rest of that week and all weekend on Patricia's witness statement and it came out rather well. We had to get up to speed with the documents and the other side's witness statements. The trial started the following Monday.

After brilliant cross examination by Anna of the Respondent's witnesses, they were crushed. All of Patricia's claims were made out and her boss appeared to be an arrogant, stupid, sexist misogynist.

The tribunal believed Patricia and found her boss to be *"an unreliable witness"* ie a liar.

The Tribunal awarded Patricia nearly £100,000 in compensation for her loss of future earnings and damages for injury to feelings.

I then wrote to the insurers' lawyers and told them of the stunning result from the Tribunal and that their assessment of Patricia's chances of success was clearly very wrong, that they were totally ill-informed and negligent in their advice to Patricia. I said they had let their client down really badly.

I said we would be suing them for negligence in respect of the legal fees that Patricia had to pay Counsel.

Within an hour these lawyers offered to pay Patricia for the entire fees she had paid. A cheque was sent the next day.

Patricia was thrilled with the outcomes – winning hands down at the tribunal, being awarded a very large sum in compensation and having her legal fees paid by the insurers instead of having to rely on her useless former lawyers.

Patricia took Anna and me out for a slap up lunch to celebrate.

The Case of the Headless Snowman

Perhaps one of the most unusual cases I have been asked to discuss on radio was the case of the headless snowman. This was on Nick Ferrari's Breakfast Show on LBC.

Warren was a bin man who was dismissed after he had kicked off the head of a snowman, in front of a three-year-old child. The child became very distressed and his parents went to the local newspaper with the story. It became headline news both in the national and local Press and on TV and radio.

Warren was dismissed for his aggressive behaviour in front of a young child, distressing the child and bringing his employer, the local Council, into disrepute.

Apparently, this little boy was even more shocked at what had happened because he used to wave to Warren and thought he was his friend.

Warren's feeble excuse for kicking the snowman's head off was that it had been "in the way" when he was emptying the bins.

Nick Ferrari asked me to explain on what grounds Warren's employer had dismissed him.

"Well," I said, *"there was this innocent snowman, standing idly by, minding his own business, not asking to have his head kicked off, when suddenly—off went his head."*

Nick Ferrari laughed out loud and said on air, *"Well you don't often hear those words being spoken by a lawyer—Gillian, thank you for that explanation."*

"Get Her Off"

There is always plenty of banter between Nick Ferrari and me. One morning on his show we were discussing bullying and he asked me if he banged the table with his fist and told his producer that he was a fool, always making mistakes, would that be bullying?

I knew there was friendly banter between Nick and his producer so I replied, *"Of course not Nick. That would be totally justified. I would say that was constructive criticism of your producer who should take notice."*

There was a pause and then Nick said, *"Ah my producer has just said in my earpiece 'Get her off. We're not having her on again'."*

"What a To-Do"

We all know that office Christmas parties can end in tears but you do not expect them to end in scandal or worse. No-one could have predicted what was going to happen at this client's Christmas party.

A corporate client based in the Midlands, hosted their Christmas party one year at the Town Hall. They invited local solicitors and accountants and dignitaries, including the Lord Mayor and his wife and the local Press.

All was going well until their Marketing Director, Tony, entered the party, very much the worse for wear, with his girlfriend, Mandy, the town stripper.

They both got onto the dance floor and started to strip. The Chairman of the Company tried to stop them and tried to get them off the dance floor and a fight broke out.

The Lord Mayor and his wife, who were both on the dance floor at the time, were hit several times by this drunken duo and the Mayor and his wife both ended up in hospital with some nasty injuries, needing stitches.

The police were called and Tony and Mandy were carted off to the police station and kept overnight in the cells. They were charged with being drink and disorderly and actual bodily harm, found guilty, fined £500 each and given suspended sentences and 100 hours' Community Service.

The newspapers had a field day. The day after the party, the national and local newspapers reported, *"Fight breaks out at Christmas party. Stripper in brawl with Lord Mayor and wife."* There were photographs of the fight as well.

Tony was summarily dismissed after Christmas for being drunk at a company event, fighting, causing serious injuries to guests and for bringing the Company into disrepute.

He then sued for unfair dismissal now that I was not expecting – the cheek of it.

Tony turned up at the Birmingham Employment Tribunal with Mandy in tow, both ready to give evidence.

The local and national Press had also turned up to capture the gory details and to print the names of all the people involved.

My client's instructions were to ask for an adjournment before the hearing started, to settle the case.

I asked the Judge if we could use the morning to engage 'in talks'. The Judge allowed us this time. We did a "deal" and paid Tony off but he bargained very hard. In the end we negotiated to pay him half his notice pay. The settlement was confidential so he could not tell the Press what monies he had received.

The press went away very disappointed but the headlines the next day reported, *"Town stripper's boyfriend wins substantial compensation for fighting at Christmas party."* I learnt from one of the journalists afterwards that if you read *"a substantial settlement"* in the Press it means anything over £15,000.

Unfair Dismissal—We Didn't Get the Sack....

One of the most bizarre claims I have ever had to defend for an employer was a claim of constructive unfair dismissal when two ex-employees resigned (former dockers), because their employer had not dismissed them.

I never expected a constructive dismissal claim from ex-employees arguing that it was unfair *not* to dismiss them. That's not normally pleaded in constructive dismissal cases. Constructive dismissal occurs where the employer has normally breached the implied term of mutual trust and confidence entitling the employee to resign.

Never before has it been argued that the employer had breached the term of trust and confidence for **not** dismissing these two men.

My client had inherited the men's terms and conditions when they took over a business at a London Dockyard. The collective agreements made with the unions and the former National Dock Labour Board gave these men greatly enhanced termination and redundancy payments.

My client had gone through a rigorous redundancy exercise and had decided not to make these two particular employees redundant. They were both 63 years of age, two years off the then mandatory retirement age of 65 for men. Their redundancy and termination payments would have exceeded their wages for the next two years. So it was cheaper just to keep these employees employed and pay their normal wages until they retired.

These two employees were incensed at not being made redundant as they would not be collecting a large six figure redundancy payment or pay in lieu of notice and would not be retiring early. They would have to work for their money for the next two years and would then just retire on their pension. So they resigned claiming constructive dismissal.

This case was heard at the (then) London Stratford Employment Tribunal. The Judge started at the beginning of the trial by turning to me and asked me if I could explain the Claimants' case. He said he and his Wing Members *"are mystified at this case Ms Howard. Are you able to explain to me in words of one syllable what this case is about?"*

This had never happened to me before or since but I was delighted to oblige. The two Claimants were not represented by either their union or a lawyer so the Judge thought I might have understood their case better than they did and would be able to explain it to the tribunal.

I told the Judge that this was the only case I had ever heard of where employees were complaining it was unfair not to have been dismissed.

I explained that these two men would have benefitted greatly from having been made redundant because of the enhanced redundancy payments in the collective agreement inherited from the National Dock Labour Scheme. Their redundancy payments and their generous termination payments would have exceeded their wages for the next two years. Because of the financial disincentive of selecting these two employees for redundancy, my client had decided not to dismiss them.

I said that these two men were very annoyed that instead of receiving a nice financial windfall at age 63 being able to stop work, they would have to carry on working for another two years. They would then only receive their pension.

They had misguidedly resigned and believed they could claim constructive dismissal.

I said my client was resisting this claim. I said we were seeking a strike out of their claim. I argued that there had been no unreasonable conduct by their employer and certainly no breach of any term of their contract nor of the implied term of trust and confidence. This was a nonsensical claim and a try on.

The Judge agreed. He turned to the two Claimants and told them very politely that they could not get off the starting block of showing they had been dismissed.

There had been no breach of contract or unreasonable conduct by their employer. Their resignation was a straightforward resignation and they had not been dismissed in law. Their claims were duly struck out before any evidence was heard.

This was a great result for my client who saved a large six figure redundancy payment for each employee.

'Talking About Sex...'

Sometimes I am invited to appear on TV and the radio to talk about employment law issues that arise in the news. As a lawyer I have to be prepared for the unexpected. On 14th July 1994 when I was invited on BBC News at Six, the unexpected happened and luckily, I was just about ready for it.

I was waiting in the Green Room to be interviewed live by Sue Lawley. The floor manager came to get me and said, *"Gillian I am really looking forward to hearing your interview."*

I thought that was strange as I was talking about a landmark European Court of Justice decision, *Webb v EMO Air Cargo (UK) Ltd (No 2)*, concerning pregnancy discrimination, that had been handed down that day.

I couldn't understand why the floor manager, a middle-aged man, would be looking forward so much to my interview about a pregnancy discrimination decision.

Anyway, I made my way to the studio and sat in the chair ready to be interviewed.

Sue Lawley introduced me, *"Tonight we are delighted to have Gillian Howard—an expert..... on sex education."* She then turned to me and asked me, *"Gillian what do you think about the Government proposal announced today that sex education should be taught by teachers in Primary Schools?"*

For a couple of seconds I was speechless and my brain was racing but I am used to thinking on my feet so without batting an eyelid I said, *"Well as a mother of two young boys I can truthfully say that I would welcome sex education to be taught by teachers in primary schools.*

"Let me tell you my own experience. After giving what I had thought was a simple and clear explanation about gay relationships to my 7 and 8 year old boys, I asked if they had any questions. My younger son, Ben, put up his hand and said, 'Yes Mum. I have a question—is Dad gay?' They obviously hadn't understood a word I had said.

"So perhaps primary school teachers trained to do this would do a better job than us Mums."

By then the floor manager had realised his mistake, having left the correct person for this interview in the Green Room.

The floor manager made frantic hand signals to Sue Lawley and instructions came through her ear piece to get me off the set as quickly as possible. I was not after all the expert on sex education. My interview was promptly terminated and I was escorted off the set.

The Producer then had to cancel both interviews, my interview about the landmark European Court of Justice case and the sex education expert's interview on sex education in primary schools.

The floor manager apologised to me profusely when I left the studio to go back into the Green Room. I said that it was *"all in a day's work."* My motto is *"Have mouth, will travel."* It's amazing how lawyers can blag their way out of trouble.

"You're the Expert... On Toilets"

But in this next case I was definitely not expecting this phone call.

Over 20 years ago my telephone rang and when I answered it, it was an HR Manager, Sandra, from a University in the Midlands. She told me that she had been given my name as the expert. I felt very flattered and asked how I could assist.

I wasn't quite so flattered when she told me what expertise she was ringing me about. That was unexpected. She told me she wanted to know about toilets.

A male lecturer with several years' service had turned up at the University at the beginning of term, dressed as a woman. He asked to be called 'Michaela' not 'Michael' and said he was going through the gender transitioning process and 'he' was now living as a woman for a year, before having the operation.

The question posed to me was, *"What toilet should s/he use?"*

The men with whom he worked complained they did not want a "woman" using their loos and the women said they would not accept a man using their loos because they did not want a man looking at them if they were changing their tights or talking about "women's things".

I asked whether there were any unisex loos and of course there were—they were the disabled loos.

In those days there was no anti-discrimination legislation on the grounds of gender reassignment so my suggestion that s/he should be asked to use the disabled unisex toilet seemed a sensible solution at the time.

Nowadays it would be considered highly offensive and wholly inappropriate.

Under the Equality Act 2010 gender reassignment is a protected characteristic and any form of discrimination including harassment is unlawful. The staff at this University would now be guilty of both discrimination and harassment – but not then.

Actually nowadays this issue would probably not arise because it is becoming increasingly common to see unisex loos in public places and in workplaces.

However 20 years ago Sandra was very pleased with my advice and thanked me for getting her out of a difficult situation.

It has always amused me how I had become known as *'the expert on toilets.'*

"Male Rape and Murder"

One of the daftest and most unexpected remarks from a Tribunal member came during a case in which I was acting for an employer against an ex-docker, Lamonte.

Lamonte was a very large black man, 6 foot 7 inches tall, weighing 20 stone. He had got into a fight with a white colleague, Tom, who was a mere lightweight at 9 stone and only 5ft 4ins in height. The argument was over cigarettes.

Lamonte had demanded that Tom hand over his cigarettes and Tom was having none of it. Lamonte had punched Tom a few times in the face and had then waved a metal scraper at him.

Metal scrapers are large tools used for scraping the insides of large empty barrels in order to clean them. They are 6 foot long and very sharp. They could definitely be regarded as offensive weapons and they are very dangerous in the wrong hands.

Lamont had been dismissed for gross misconduct, for aggressive, intimidatory and violent behaviour and for fighting on the dockside. He sued for unfair dismissal.

Tom told the Tribunal that Lamonte had threatened him with this metal scraper and had used the words, *"Fuck you. I'm gonna fucking kill you unless you give me them cigarettes."*

At that, the female Tribunal Member shrieked, *"Oh my G-d. He threatened male rape and murder."*

I had to explain to this Tribunal member that those words were common parlance amongst ex-dockers and were a mild form of abuse. They were no more than an expression of mild frustration. They certainly did not mean that there would be rape or murder.

The Judge said he understood that and told us that that kind of language was also common parlance at the Tribunal. He said only the previous week one of the clerks had called the Judge a *"fucking cunt"* when, by mistake, the Judge had knocked into him whilst they were passing the opposite way through a swing door, causing the clerk to drop the files he was carrying.

Well I wasn't expecting that revelation either.

'The Tale of Two Dogs'—Apologies to Charles Dickens

This case concerned an unexpected client for me, a dog called Paws. I suppose technically speaking the client was the dog's owner, Elise, but why split hairs? It caused me some mirth, but not for the dogs or their owners.

Elise, an American Banker and client of mine, was getting married in New York. She had arranged a wedding the day before hers, for her much beloved dog, Paws. They were both going to have Jewish weddings.

My 'client' Paws should have enjoyed his wedding but the bitch/bride to be, Dorothy (Dottie), got too frisky under the Chuppah. The Chuppah is the wedding canopy under which the Bride and Groom stand to be married.

Dottie went for Paws, her Groom-to-be and started biting him and everyone else standing under the Chuppah. Perhaps she had already been at the Kosher wine?

Unfortunately Paws bit Dottie back, rather harder than she had bitten him. In the mayhem that followed Dottie ran riot, barking and biting everyone in sight, which caused the other doggie guests to start fighting and then running off, with their owners having to chase after them.

This left Paws with no bride and no wedding but he was left with some rather painful injuries. He had also caused even more painful injuries to his bride-to-be.

Dottie needed to be taken to a vet to have an operation to clean up her wounds and be stitched. She was given painkilling injections and antibiotics. The vet's bill was over $26,000. Well, this was New York.

The doggie wedding disintegrated with tempers flaring amongst the human guests. Elise and Dottie's owner got into a serious altercation with some choice words being bandied around.

The doggie wedding-to-be finally ended up with no marriage for the doggie couple and they never saw each other again. The wedding that never happened nevertheless had to be paid for and someone had to pay the vets' bills.

The wedding had already cost $60,000, for the flowers, the cost of the Rabbi, the Cantor, the Chuppah, the photographers, the hire of the hotel ballroom, the Band and the drinks and food for the wedding guests as well as their owners.

A claim for damages for Dottie's physical and psychological injuries came to a hefty $20,000 as well as her vet's bills.

Sadly, Elise's Pet insurer refused to pay out anything. Elise asked me to sue Dottie's owner for her dog causing the riot and inflicting injuries on Paws.

However, I advised Elise to pay Dottie's owner for the damage and distress and the Vet's bills. I did not want this to end up as a $1,000,000 + law suit which could ruin Elise's big day.

Elise agreed to pay up. Luckily her wedding the following day went off without a hitch.

No Legal Advice Required

It is unusual and unexpected when clients don't receive legal advice when they come to see me. But it has happened a number of times during my practice. As Sir John Mortimer's Rumpole once said, *"I often think that knowledge of the law is a bit of a handicap to a lawyer."* In some cases I couldn't agree more.

When I was a postgraduate student, I worked as a volunteer at a Law Centre. A young lady came in one day, sat down in front of me and said, *"I want a divorce"*—just like that. I had just enough common sense to probe her further.

I asked her, *"Are you unhappy with your husband? Does he mistreat you? Does he keep you short of money? Is he violent or sexually aggressive or demanding towards you? Does he ignore you? Does he do nothing to help in the house? Does he drink to excess? Is he a gambler? Is he a serial adulterer? Has he said he doesn't want to have children?"*

I couldn't think of anything else that would make a woman want a divorce. I wasn't married at the time.

She answered *"No"* to all my questions, so I asked her why she wanted a divorce.

She told me that she was a newly married graduate, who had come to Cambridge with her husband. He had secured a job as a lecturer at the University. She had been unable to find a job.

They had bought a house on the outskirts of town, on a housing estate, where there was no public transport. Her husband took the car every day to College and left her alone all day, in these unfamiliar surroundings, far from her parents' home in Cornwall, with no friends in Cambridge. She and her husband had both gone to Oxford University.

She said she felt marooned on this Estate, with no job, no friends, no family nearby and no-one to talk to.

She had no children at the time, in contrast to most of the other women on the Estate, who had babies and young children. She said their only topics of conversation were babies, nappies, sleepless nights, breastfeeding, nurseries, schools, homework and what they were going to cook for their husbands' supper.

After listening to her tale of woe I said, *"You don't need a divorce. You need a car."* She looked very puzzled and asked me to explain.

I told her that she was clearly unhappy where she was living and was bored with no job. She was isolated and marooned on a housing estate, left with housewives and young mothers with whom she had little in common.

I told her she needed to get a job, even if it was part-time and suggested she apply to the Heffers, the University bookshop, in town. I knew they were advertising for part-time staff. She had already told me she had read English so this would be a perfect job for her. Heffers employed 'book sellers' not 'sales assistants'. There is a big difference.

I told her she could get a lift from her husband in the mornings to travel into Cambridge. She could then work in the bookshop and save up enough money to buy herself a little second-hand car. She would then be mobile, with a car and a job that she loved, earning some money. She would no longer feel marooned or sad. She would have an interesting job and would meet likeminded people at work and would make some nice friends.

She kissed me and thanked me so much for my "advice" and walked out of the Law Centre, happy as Larry, with her new life mapped out for her—with the added benefit that she would keep her husband.

I began to think that perhaps giving legal advice was not that difficult after all.

She Didn't Need *My* Legal Advice

I had another case where *my* legal advice was also not wanted. Early on in my legal career Claire came to see me with a letter in her hand, crying her eyes out. It was a letter before action (now called letter of claim) from her former employer's solicitors.

Claire had been employed by a hairdressers in North West London. She had left that Salon and had opened her own salon round the corner from her former employer, four weeks earlier. She had poached her former employer's senior stylist and the receptionist. Many of her clients had moved with Claire to her new salon.

This was in breach of her restrictive covenants that for six months after she left, she was prohibited her from opening, or working in, a competing business within a square mile. She was also prohibited from poaching 'key employees' ie the senior stylist, and was for the 6 months after she left, not to contact, or solicit for business or deal with the clients with whom Claire had worked during the 12 months prior to her leaving.

Solicitors for her former employer had written to Claire, threatening her with an injunction, demanding that she close her salon and pay damages for the lost income suffered by her former employer.

As far as I could see all these restrictive covenants in Claire's former contract were potentially perfectly reasonable and enforceable.

Claire had already signed a lease on her new salon, for a fixed term of five years, with no break clause that would have allowed her to terminate this lease on notice, earlier than at the end of the five years. There was also a prohibition on sub-letting without the landlord's prior written consent.

Claire had had expensive shop fitting done and she was doing brisk business.

The lawyer's letter demanded she shut the salon for the remainder of the six month restricted period and dismiss the stylist and receptionist.

Claire was desperate and asked me, *"What should I do?"*

Instead of answering her question I started telling her about the law and how the courts view restrictive covenants. I referred her to some of the cases and probably frightened her out of her wits about what could happen to her. I realised afterwards that I did not actually answer her question, *"What should (she) do?"*

My husband, Barry, a commercial property solicitor, who knew next to nothing about employment law, had by then come into my office to walk through to the kitchen and said *'Hello'*. He had heard a little of what I had been saying and interrupted me in full flow and asked Claire, *"Excuse me for interrupting but I specialise in commercial property. May I ask you if you have already signed a lease?"* She said, *"Yes."*

He went on, *"Well your former employer is a sole trader. Going to the High Court for an injunction and suing you for damages could cost her at least £30,000 just to get to the first hearing.*

"The letter is a warning but my guess is she has not got that kind of money to spend on uncertain litigation that she might not win.

"If you close your salon now, as the letter is asking you to do, you would be in breach of your lease and you would have to pay rent for the remainder of the term of the lease without any income coming in for the next five months unless you are able to sub-let the premises if your landlord agreed."

Claire confirmed to Barry that she needed the landlord's permission to sublet the shop.

Barry went on, *"So considering there is a greater risk to you in closing the salon and having to pay all that rent with no income, my advice is to carry on trading and ignore the solicitor's letter and they will soon get fed up and stop writing to you."*

Claire said to him, *"What brilliant advice. I cannot thank you enough for putting my mind at rest"* and off she went.

I put up my hand behind her back as Claire was walking out of the door, pointing to myself, mouthing, *"Excuse me. I'm the employment lawyer around here."* But Claire had already gone and was heading home, delighted with the advice that Barry had given her.

Claire telephoned me a few months later to tell me that she had done what Barry had advised her to do. She had not replied to any of the lawyer's two further letters that had followed the first one. By then five and a half months had gone by.

The restrictions had almost come to an end. She heard nothing more from her former employer or her solicitors.

Claire carried on trading very successfully.

A job well done then.

"Listen to Your Wife"

Years later I had another client who did not need any legal advice from me—he just needed a stern telling off from me for not listening to his wife's advice.

John was a main Board Director of a major global retailer in luxury goods. He came to see me very troubled. He was responsible for the lucrative property portfolio of all the freehold and leasehold properties in the UK and Europe.

A new Chief Executive, Luke, had been appointed and had told John that he was so impressed with him that he wanted him to take on the entire property portfolio worldwide.

John was already paid a very handsome basic salary with bonuses and share options, a non-contributory final salary pension and private health insurance for him and his family. He also had a substantial staff discount on all the luxury goods that this Firm sold. His overall remuneration package was substantial.

The new role offered to him, included all those benefits and a large rise in basic salary, a guaranteed bonus in the first year of 100% of his base salary and many more share options.

John told me he did not want a global role. He did not want to travel all over the world for a major part of the year and not see his family. He was happy with his UK/Europe responsibilities. He told me he had decided to resign rather than accept the new role that had been offered to him.

I asked him four simple questions.

Q. "Do you have a large mortgage on your 6 bedroomed house in Weybridge?"

He answered, *"Yes."*

Q. "Do you have any children and do they go to expensive private boarding schools?"

He answered, *"Yes. I have three children who all go to expensive private Boarding Schools."*

Q. "Do you have a job offer or even a promise of a job offer matching your salary and benefits?"

He answered, *"No, I haven't even started looking for another job."*

Q. "What does your wife think of you wanting to reject a major promotion and fantastic remuneration package and your suggestion of resigning without even having another job to go to?"

He looked at me and said with a quizzical smile, *"The answer to your last question, I assume, is the same as yours. She said 'Don't be such a damn fool. Pull yourself together'."*

I said, *"Well then, my advice is, to repeat your wife's words of wisdom and please excuse my very impolite language 'Don't be such a fool and listen to your wife'. There will be no charge for that excellent piece of advice."*

With that, John went off a happy man. No legal advice was needed there then.

An Unexpected Assignment

In the early 1980s, I was offered a contract with the Home Office to write a report on industrial relations amongst the uniformed prison officers and advise on how to improve industrial relations between senior management and the uniformed prison officers – members of the Prison Officers' Association (POA).

I visited many of the prisons in England and three of the secure hospitals, Ashworth, Rampton and Broadmoor.

The first closed prison I visited was Walton Jail in Liverpool. I had been "inside" before as I had visited a murderer in Leyhill Open Prison when I was an undergraduate at Bristol University.

He was a bank manager who had come home early one day and had caught his wife in bed with his best friend. This bank manager had gone downstairs, picked up a carving knife, gone back upstairs and stabbed both of them to death.

He then calmly put down the knife and called the police. He got a more lenient sentence because he admitted his crime immediately and showed insight and remorse. His fifteen year sentence was commuted to five years and he was out after three years on parole.

I found him a most delightful gentleman once I had got over the fact that he had murdered his wife and best friend. The French call it 'crime passionelle'. We call it murder.

At lunchtime the Governor of Walton Prison took me to the staff restaurant and we were served lunch by two young lads, 'trustys'—trusted prisoners. I asked the Governor if I could ask these trustys why they were 'inside'. The Governor said, *"Of course you may. They will be pleased to tell you."*

These two young lads told me that they had burgled *'posh houses on the Wirral'*. They had got in by breaking the glass in the French doors at the back of the houses and had stolen TVs and video recorders as those were easy to 'fence' in those days.

They told me they had carried out their 'swag' and had walked back to their Council flat but within half an hour the police arrived and arrested them.

I said, *"Well the police have very sophisticated detective devices nowadays so that's how you were caught so quickly."*

When the lads had gone, the Governor said, *"Oh no Gillian. I looked on the chargesheet. It was snowing heavily and those lads carried the stolen goods back on foot to their Council flat. The police just followed their footprints."*

So much for 'sophisticated detective devices'.

"We've Won the Lottery"

I advised a syndicate of six factory workers who asked me whether they had any legal obligation to share their Lottery winnings with a former work colleague, Joe. Their syndicate was one of three winners of the UK Lottery jackpot that week of £30,000,000—each winner scooping £10,000,000.

Joe had been a member of this syndicate but had left the Company literally the week before the Syndicate's big win. Having left the company Joe had not paid into the Syndicate the following week when they won the Lottery.

I told the Syndicate that as Joe had not paid for his share of the winning lottery tickets that week and was therefore no longer a member of the Syndicate, he was not **legally** entitled to a share of their winnings. **Morally** however, I suggested they might like to share their winnings with Joe.

The members of the Syndicate debated what to do but they all voted not to give Joe a share so they decided not to let him know about their win.

As they were talking about this, they heard that Joe was knocking at the factory gates asking for them.

It turned out that Joe had kept the same numbers as this Syndicate and he was one of the other two lucky winners. He had also won a share of the jackpot and had come to share his winnings with them. His colleagues were certainly not expecting that.

The Syndicate very rapidly changed their minds and told Joe that they had all agreed to share their winnings with him. Hmmmm.

'It happened to me'

You may not believe this but I was once the target of sexual harassment but this may not surprise you, it didn't end well for the man.

I had just come to London and was fiercely feminist and Socialist. At the time I was a member of the International Marxists and Communist Party. I had picketed at Grunwick, in 1976, in support of the Asian women who were striking for better treatment from their managers and equal pay with their male colleagues.

I was giving a lecture on employment law in the Autumn of 1997 when at lunchtime a Partner from one of the Big 4 Accountancy Firms asked if he could sit next to me. Not suspecting a thing I said 'Yes'. During the course of lunch he asked if I liked Opera as he had two tickets that evening for 'Salome' at Covent Garden. I said I loved Opera and had never seen 'Salome' so I was delighted to say 'Yes' when he asked me if I would like to go with him.

After the Opera he took me for dinner at a very expensive French restaurant, nearby, called 'Inigo Jones', sadly no more.

After the first course he said, *"Shall we go back to your place tonight or would you prefer to come back to my hotel?"*

Not believing what I had just heard I asked him to repeat what he had just said. So he did. He added, *"I've noticed you're not wearing a wedding ring so I have guessed you're not married."* I added *"Well I've noticed you are."*

At that I got up, walked out of the restaurant saying in the loudest voice possible, *"That dirty pig sitting over there has just asked me to go back to his hotel to sleep with him. I met him today giving a lecture at which he was in the audience. He thinks single women like me are easy prey. He's a married man and he's a dirty disgusting pig and that's insulting a pig."*

I turned round and shouted his name and pointed at him in case the diners wondered to whom I was referring.

Several women diners got up and clapped as I walked out and I hope I left this man shame-faced.

I never give anyone permission to harass, bully or be rude to me – and I started young.

There is a postscript – I did enjoy the Opera.

The 'Arkell Case'

I just love the story about the 'Arkell case'. It is an example of how some people respond to letters from respectable lawyers. Thank you Mark Stephens of Counsel for telling me about this case.

The case involved the satirical magazine "Private Eye." It was famous for being sued for libel. They often fought such cases and very occasionally successfully defended them.

Although there was no case here, this has become known as the case of *'Arkell v Pressdram Ltd'*. Pressdram Ltd is the legal identity of Private Eye.

On 9th April 1971, a brief and allegedly defamatory story about James Arkell had been published in Private Eye. A letter was sent by Mr Arkell's solicitors threatening legal action for libel.

As a result of Private Eye's reply, almost immediately Mr Arkell withdrew his complaint.

The magazine has since used this as shorthand when responding to threats of legal action, saying, *"We refer you to the reply given in the case of Arkell v. Pressdram."*

Goodman Derrick's Letter to Private Eye

29 April 1971

Dear Sir,

We act for Mr Arkell who is Retail Credit Manager of Granada TV Rental Ltd. His attention has been drawn to an article appearing in the issue of Private Eye dated 9th April 1971 on page 4. The statements made about Mr Arkell are entirely untrue and clearly highly defamatory. We are therefore instructed to require from you immediately your proposals for dealing with the matter.

Mr Arkell's first concern is that there should be a full retraction at the earliest possible date in Private Eye and he will also want his costs paid. His attitude to damages will be governed by the nature of your reply.

Yours,
Goodman Derrick & Co.

Private Eye's Reply

Dear Sirs,

We acknowledge your letter of 29th April referring to Mr. J. Arkell.

We note that Mr Arkell's attitude to damages will be governed by the nature of our reply and we would therefore be grateful if you would inform us what his attitude to damages would be, were he to learn that the nature of our reply is as follows, *"fuck off."*

Yours,
Private Eye

"My client was quietly grazing in the field...."

In my first year as an undergraduate law student we were taken to the Bristol Assizes to sit in at a criminal trial. The case involved a young shepherd lad accused of bestiality with one of his sheep. He had been caught having sex with one of his flock.

Prosecution Counsel stood up and opened the trial with these words, *"My client was quietly grazing in the field when suddenly the accused came from behind and stuck it in her. She did not give her consent to have sex with her...."*

The Judge glared at Prosecuting Counsel and told him this was a very serious case and the Judge would not have the matter trivialised or made a figure of fun. The Judge warned this Counsel he would find him in contempt of court if he made any other similar submissions.

We of course thought this was hilarious and marvelled at the wit of this Counsel.

"Excuses, Excuses"

Finally, I have read the most ludicrous excuses from employees when they have come into work late or have taken the day off and called in 'sick'. Here are some of the excuses employees and their doctors have given.

Excuses from employees for being late or absent from work:-

"Knocked the vicar off his bicycle"

"Dead cat"

"Knackered"

"Hangover"

"Sunburn"

"Ate cat food by mistake"

"Got locked in the lavatory"

"Found my husband in bed with another woman. Police were called. Spent the day and night in the cells"

"Had a lucky night and didn't know where I was in the morning"

"Accidentally glued the doors and windows—couldn't get out of the house"

"Locked myself inside the house and had to wait for the Fire Brigade to get me out"

"Stress—found dead spider in the bed"

"Uniform caught on fire"

"Ate too much birthday cake"

"Thought it was a Bank Holiday"

"Forgot the clocks went forward"

"Kicked by a llama, broke my leg"

"Sick parrot"

"Went to the beach, my GP said I needed more Vitamin D"

"Alarm clock didn't go off"

Reason for absence from doctors on Fit Notes:

"Ergophobia"—morbid fear of work

"Plumbum Oscillans"—swinging the lead—pretending to be ill rather than going to work

"Neurasthenia"—nerves again

"Paraskevidekatriaphobia"—morbid fear of Friday 13th

"TATT"—tired all the time

"NFG"—normal for Gosport

Glossary

1. **A v B [2003] IRLR 405;** the Employment Appeal Tribunal held that "serious allegations of criminal behaviour must always be the subject of the most careful investigation. While it is unrealistic and inappropriate to require the safeguards of a criminal trial, a careful and conscientious investigation of the facts is necessary…given the seriousness of the allegations … the standard of the investigation carried out by the employer (B) should have been to the criminal standard."

2. **"A mere puff"** first stated in the Court of Appeal in *Carlill v Carbolic Smoke Ball Company* [1892] EWCA Civ 1 The Plaintiff, believing Defendant's advertisement that its product would prevent influenza, bought the Carbolic Smoke Balls and used it as directed but she then caught the flu. The makers offered a £100 reward in their advertisement for anyone who caught the 'flu after using this product. The plaintiff sued for the £100 reward. The Court of Appeal held that the makers of the Smoke Balls could not be bound by the advert as it was not a binding offer capable of being accepted. It was a mere *'puff'* and lacking true intent.

3. **Adonis**—in Greek mythology, a youth of remarkable beauty.

4. **Adversarial system and inquisitorial systems.** In the adversarial legal system (eg. in the UK legal system) the barristers argue the case including the prosecution, who present the evidence that the police have gathered and the Judge makes a decision on the evidence presented to them. In comparison, in an inquisitorial system (e.g. in France) the Judge is involved throughout the process and actually steers the preparation of evidence. They are able to decide what evidence is admitted by both parties, before questioning the witnesses themselves and go on to make an informed decision on the outcome.

5. **'Air their dirty laundry in public'**—discussing unpleasant or private things in public.

6. **Alternative dispute Resolution (ADR) or Mediation,** refers to ways of resolving disputes between parties so that they do not need to go to court or tribunal.

7. **Aggravated damages**—granted rarely in Employment Tribunals. They are not awarded as punitive measure but are compensatory and are awarded for mental distress or injury to feelings caused by the manner in which or the motive with which the employer has behaved after the wrongful act, where the employer has acted in a high-handed or malicious manner.

8. **Assizes** were courts which formerly sat at intervals in each county of England and Wales to administer the civil and criminal law. In 1972, the civil jurisdiction of assizes was transferred to the High Court, and the criminal jurisdiction to the Crown Court.

9. **Associative disability discrimination** is the term that applies when someone is treated unfairly because either someone they know or someone they are associated with someone who is a disabled person under s.6 of the Equality Act 2010.

10. **Automatically unfair dismissal**—dismissals for which no service is required. Automatically unfair dismissals:—pregnancy, including all reasons relating to maternity; family, including parental leave, paternity leave (birth and adoption), adoption leave or time off for dependents; acting as an employee representative; acting as a trade union representative; acting as an occupational pension scheme trustee; joining or not joining a trade union; being a part-time or fixed-term employee; pay and working hours, including the Working Time Regulations, annual leave and the National Minimum Wage; Whistleblowing.

11. **BAME** – Black, Asian, Minority, Ethnic

12. **Barbecue—slang meaning**—where two men have sex at the same time with a girl, one having oral sex and the other having vaginal or anal sex; the shortened form BBQ in slang stands for 'Boobless Bitch Queen'.

13. **Barrack room lawyer** is a person who is not a lawyer but who likes to give authoritative-sounding opinions on subjects in which they are not qualified, especially legal matters.

14. **BHS v Burchell test**—this is a three-limb test which if the employer has satisfied, the tribunal must find the dismissal fair. The three limbs of the test are (1) whether the employer has a genuine and honest belief in their reason for dismissal; (2) whether the employer has reasonable grounds in their mind to sustain that belief and (3) whether the employer has conducted as thorough an investigation into the matter as was reasonable in all the circumstances of the case.

15. **Bobbit**—this was an incident in which Lorena Bobbitt severed her husband, John Bobbitt's penis, while he was asleep in bed, on June 23, 1993, in Manassas, Virginia, USA. The penis was subsequently surgically reattached.

16. **Brown envelopes** – this is slang for a bribe in cash that is often placed in a brown envelope so that it can be given anonymously to the person being bribed.

17. **Chutzpah** is Yiddish to describe someone who has overstepped the boundaries of accepted behaviour. Leo Rosten in 'The Joys of Yiddish' defines chutzpah as "gall, brazen nerve, effrontery". An example he gives is a man who murders both his parents and goes to Court and asks for mercy because he is an orphan.

18. **Civil Procedure Rules (CPR) 31.6** on Standard Disclosure state that the parties must disclose all relevant documents that (i) "adversely affect his own case; (ii) adversely affect another party's case; or (iii) support another party's case

19. **Claimant** – the individual bringing the claim;

20. **Compensation**—awarded as a remedy for unfair dismissal or discrimination or any other breach of the employment protection legislation.

21. **Conference (Con) with Counsel**—a meeting with the barrister who has been instructed to advise on or be the advocate in a case. This may be with a King's Counsel (KC formerly QC) who will represent the client at the hearing or a Junior Counsel.

22. **Counsel**—a Barrister.

23. **Court of Appeal**—can create precedent i.e. case law that has to be followed and is the second highest Court in England and Wales.

24. **Court of Session** is the equivalent of the Court of Appeal in Scotland.

25. **Cross-examination**—the formal interrogation of a witness called by the other party in a court of law in order to challenge or extend evidence already given. It can be aggressive or detailed questioning.

26. **Damages for injury to feelings**—compensation for the upset, distress or anxiety that a worker might have suffered as a result of discrimination. Awards for injury to feelings fall into three 'bands', lower, middle or highest band, called 'Vento damages' from the case which first described these damages. Vento damages are awarded depending on the severity of the injury suffered by the claimant.

27. **Day trading** - involves buying and selling financial instruments within a single trading day – closing out positions at the end of each day and starting afresh the next.

28. **Defendant**—in a civil court the person defending a Claim against them.

29. **Disclosure**—the duty to disclose all relevant documents to the other side

30. **'Door Step'** what the paparazzi do when they wait outside a person's home or office or other buildings hoping to get an interview from and photographs of that person.

31. **Employment Appeal Tribunal (EAT)**—the appellate tribunal from an Employment Tribunal decision—appeals lie only where there has been an error of law by the Employment Tribunal or where they have made a perverse decision or where the original Employment Judge has shown bias.

32. **Employment Judge**—the Judge in an Employment Tribunal

33. **Employment Tribunal (ET)**—formerly called Industrial Tribunal until August 1998 when they changed their name to Employment Tribunals. They were set up originally in 1964 to hear appeals from employers in respect of training levies imposed by the Industrial Training Boards. The jurisdiction of these tribunals was then extended to hear unfair dismissal cases under the Industrial Relations Act 1971. Since then their jurisdiction has been further extended to hear claims for all employment cases including unlawful deductions from wages; redundancy payments; discrimination, harassment or victimisation; breaches of the Working Time Regulations; Whistleblowing and claims under the Transfer of Undertakings (Protection of Employment) Regulations (TUPE). Employment Tribunals consist of an Employment Judge who is a barrister or solicitor with at least 5 years' experience (usually longer)

and two lay members, one appointed through the Confederation of British Industry (CBI) and the other through the Trade Union Congress (TUC). Since 2012 Employment Judges sit alone to hear single claims of unfair dismissal. In other cases, e.g., discrimination and whistleblowing claims a full three person panel normally sits.

34. **Evidence in chief**—evidence given by one party's witness to elicit from that witness all the facts supporting that party's case that are within the personal knowledge of that witness.

35. **Expert witness** - An expert witness is someone with specialised skills, knowledge, or experience who testifies in court about what s/he believes has happened in a certain case based on their specialised skills, knowledge, or experience. They are entitled to give opinion evidence i.e. Any evidence that lies within their expertise. In some cases, both sides will use expert witnesses who may reach different conclusions. The duty of the expert witness is to the Court and not to the party instructing them. So if an opinion of the expert does not support the party that has instructed them, they must still give their honest opinion whether it helps or harms the party who has instructed them

36. **Fiduciary duties**—Fiduciary duties are those which, as a director, reflect a relationship of trust and loyalty between the Director, the Company and shareholders. The expectation is that a director will act in good faith and in the best interests of the company. Fiduciary duties include the duties of care, confidentiality, loyalty, obedience, and accounting. Fiduciary duties also include the duty of a director to report any wrongdoing of others even if this would implicate the Director in the wrongdoing.

37. **'Focus group'**—is a group of deliberately selected people who participate in a facilitated discussion to obtain opinions and views about a particular topic or area of interest. They are used in market research in particular.

38. **"Fraud'**—is a "wrongful or criminal deception intended to result in financial or personal gain."

39. **"Getting the sack"**—means being dismissed. The expression came from the practice of tradesmen owning and bringing to work their own tools in a bag or a sack. It is known in France (since the 17th century) as 'On lui a donné son sac'. When their employers dispensed with their

services, they "gave (the tradesman) the sack." The Americans call this an MIT—a "Management-initiated termination."

40. **"Glass ceiling"** refers to the invisible barrier to success that many women come up against in their career. The glass ceiling effect is the pervasive resistance to the efforts of women and minorities to reach the top ranks of management in major corporations.

41. **GMC Rule 7 -** Once the GMC has reviewed a complaint about a doctor and found there may be a case to answer, an investigation will commence.

    After the investigation stage, the case is passed to case examiners. It is at this stage where the GMC will write to the Doctor (also known as a rule 7 letter). The rule 7 letter will outline the allegations made in the complaint and ask the doctor to comment. The doctor has 28 days to respond to this letter.

42. **Grunwick -** On Friday 20 August 1976 a group of female Asian workers walked out in protest against their treatment by the managers and the low pay they were paid in comparison to their male colleagues. They joined a trade union, APEX (Association of Professional, Executive, Clerical and Computer Staff). They began to demand that Grunwick should recognise workers' right to join trade unions in order to take up any issues the workers may have with the factory owners. After these Asian women spent a few months picketing outside the Grunwick factory, the cause of the Grunwick strikers was taken up by the wider trade union movement of the day. By June 1977 there were marches in support of the Grunwick strikers, and on some days more than 20,000 people packed themselves into the narrow lanes near Dollis Hill tube station.

    Grunwick operated a mail order service to develop photographs – there were no digital cameras in those days. People sent their film rolls by post and the workers at the Grunwick developed and printed them, then sent the photographs back by post. Because of this working relationship between the postal workers and the workers at Grunwick, the Union of Postal Workers supported the Grunwick strikers' cause and on 1st November 1977 the union voted to boycott postal services to and from Grunwick. Sadly the strike was defeated after two years but the women had made an important stand.

43. **Harassment** is defined in s.26 of the Equality Act 2010 as:

(1) A person (A) harasses another (B) if—

    (a) A engages in unwanted conduct related to a relevant protected characteristic, and

    (b) the conduct has the purpose or effect of—

    (c) violating B's dignity, or

    (d) creating an intimidating, hostile, degrading, humiliating or offensive environment for B.

(2) A also harasses B if—

    (a) A engages in unwanted conduct of a sexual nature, and

    (b) the conduct has the purpose or effect referred to in subsection (1)(b).

44. **Human Resources (HR)**—formerly known as personnel—(HR) is the division of a business that is charged with recruitment, training job applicants, and administering employee-benefits, compensation and benefits, advising on disciplinary matters and grievances and keeping up to date with employment law.

45. **'Insider dealing'**—is the illegal use of information available only to insiders in order to make a profit in financial trading. Insider dealing is the term given to the trading of stock or other securities, such as bonds or stock options, by people 'on the inside' who have access to private financial information about the company. This inside information specifically relates to information that, if published, would have a significant effect on the price of shares in a company. For example if an auditor or trader has inside information about a Company's accounts and the profits are good, the share price will go up. Those with inside knowledge could buy shares in advance of the profits announcement. However if the results are likely to be poor, they could sell their shares before the announcement and before the share price plummets.

46. **Inquisitorial system** is that applied by most European countries under civil law for example France. This means countries that derived their law from the Napoleonic or roman codes. This system demands a judge to investigate actively the case in front of them. The distinction between adversarial and inquisitorial system is that the adversarial system aims to get the truth through the open competition between the prosecution and the defence. The inquisitorial system is generally aims to get the

truth of the matter through extensive investigation and examination of all evidence.

47. **Judicial Mediation**—Judicial mediation is another form of Alternative Dispute Resolution (ADR). Employment Tribunals offer a judicial mediation scheme. It involves a trained Employment Judge bringing the parties together for a mediation at a private preliminary hearing. The Judge remains neutral and tries to assist the parties in resolving their disputes, which may include remedies which would not be available at a hearing before an Employment Tribunal (e.g. negotiating a reference or receiving a written apology etc).

48. **Judicial Oath** - "I, _____, do swear by Almighty God that I will well and truly serve our Sovereign King Charles the Third in the office of Employment Judge, and I will do right to all manner of people after the laws and usages of this realm, without fear or favour, affection or ill will."

49. **King's Counsel (KC) or Leading Counsel**—(previously Queen's Counsel – QC) refers to barristers and solicitors whom the King appoints to be a part of His Majesty's Counsel learned in the law. To achieve this status, a barrister must have practised law for a minimum of ten years and be recommended by the Lord Chancellor. Solicitor Advocates may also be appointed as KCs. They are men and women who are recognised for their skills in advocacy.

50. **Lay Members** of the Tribunal—two lay members sit on Employment Tribunals. one nominated by the Confederation of British Industry (CBI), and the other by the Trades Union Congress (TUC) or by a TUC-affiliated union.

51. **LGBT -** lesbian, gay, bisexual, and transgender.

52. **Letter of claim**—formerly known as a 'letter before action' sets out the details of the claim against a Defendant and they are obliged to respond. This is required under the Civil Procedure Pre-Action Protocols.

53. **Libel**—is the written form of defamation. Slander is the spoken form. For a statement to be defamatory it must not only be untrue but it must be malicious (i.e., the person making that statement knows it is untrue). It must also be published. Under the Defamation Act 2013 it must also have caused or is likely to cause serious harm to the reputation of the Claimant i.e., financial harm. There are several defences to

defamation—truth, honest opinion, publication on a matter of public interest; absolute and qualified privilege and retraction of the defamatory statement. There is absolute privilege to defame anyone (living) in the Houses of Parliament and in Court. Qualified privilege applies to any defamatory statement that is made where the person communicating the statement has a duty or interest to make the statement e.g., from one employer to another, in a reference.

54. **LIBOR** is the London Inter-Bank Offered Rate. This is the basic rate of interest used in lending between banks on the London interbank market and also used as a reference for setting the interest rate on other loans.

55. **'Magic Circle Firms'**—the Magic Circle Law Firms in London are Allen & Overy; Clifford Chance; Freshfields Bruckhaus Deringer; Linklaters and Slaughter and May. These five UK-based firms are considered to be amongst the most prestigious in the world. Although a rather old-fashioned term, the phrase 'the Magic Circle' has only been used since the late 1990s; before then, the prestigious law firms were called the "Club of Nine", and included Lovells (now Hogan Lovells), Norton Rose (now Norton Rose Fulbright), Herbert Smith (now Herbert Smith Freehills) and Stephenson Harwood. This group fragmented at the beginning of the 2000s, and now comprises the five that now make up the "Magic Circle", a term coined by legal journalists.

56. **Mareva Injunction**—A freezing order under Rule 25(1)(1)(f) of the Civil Procedure Rules 1998 (formerly known as Mareva injunction) is an interim injunction prohibiting a potential defendant in criminal or civil litigation proceedings from dissipating assets. Typically, such an injunction is sought to preserve a defendant's assets until a judgment can be obtained.

57. **Maternal wall of bias** occurs when colleagues view mothers—or pregnant women— as less competent and less committed to their jobs. This is a major problem for women's career advancement.

58. **Mediation**—Mediation is a process where a neutral (and trained) third party (the mediator) facilitates a discussion between the parties in a legal dispute to resolve the dispute before trial. It is an entirely voluntary process and absolutely confidential. Mediators have usually undergone specialist training—for example at the Centre for Dispute Resolution— CEDR.

59. ***Meek v City of Birmingham District Council*** [1987] IRLR 250 – *"The reasons given by Employment Judges .... is to tell the parties in broad terms why they lose or, as the case may be, win."*

60. **Mitigating your loss**—the duty to mitigate the loss is the obligation upon a Claimant, who sues their employer for compensation, to reduce their compensation by looking for another job. The duty is to take reasonable steps to reduce or stop their losses.

61. **"Moonlighting"**—refers to a second job in addition to an individual's regular employment undisclosed to the primary employer. The Americans call it "external business interests."

62. **National Industrial Relations Court (NIRC)** was created under the infamous Industrial Relations Act 1971. It was designed as a way to limit the power of the trades unions in the UK. It also heard appeals from the Industrial Tribunals.

63. **'Night of the Long Knives'** also called Operation Hummingbird was a purge that took place in Nazi Germany from June 30 to July 2, 1934. Chancellor Adolf Hitler, urged on by Hermann Goring and Heinrich Himmler, ordered a series of political extrajudicial executions intended to consolidate his power and alleviate the concerns of the German military about the role of Ernst Röhm and the Sturmabteilung (SA), the Nazis' paramilitary organisation, known colloquially as "Brownshirts."

64. **"Off his trolley"** – is a saying from the 1890s describing someone who is crazy or mad, someone who behaves oddly or has weird ideas.

65. **"Off-piste"**—saying or doing something unexpected or unplanned or deviating from what is expected.

66. **Out of character**—inconsistent with usual or expected behaviour

67. A **'position'** is a financial term to describe the amount of a security, asset, or property that is owned (or sold) by a trader or investor. They take 'a position' through an order to buy, hoping the market is either a bull or bear market. A 'Bull' market is one in which the price is expected to go up so they buy at a low price and hope the commodity or shares (equities) will go up. A 'bear' market is one where the price of the share or stock is expected to go down, so the trader either 'bets' that the commodity or equities will go down or sometimes they sell their equities or commodities a soon as the market starts to fall and then buys back at a much lower price hoping it is at the bottom of the market and then

waits for the market to rise again. That it how they make a profit. There are several reasons why a trader must close his position, one of them being that 'Stop' levels have been reached and the trade must be exited at a loss. A 'stop' level is the level of profit or loss falls to a specific percentage (%) level and is the loss at which the Bank requires the trader to close /sell one or all of their open positions.

68. **'Position Statement'**—in a Mediation provides an introduction to the dispute, sets the scene and describes key players. It can also set the agenda for the mediation by identifying issues that need to be discussed during the mediation.

69. **"Prima facie case"**—the initial burden of proof on the Claimant, to present enough evidence to create a rebuttable presumption that the matter asserted is true. The burden then shifts to the Respondent to disprove that their conduct was e.g. that the allegation of unlawful discrimination was an innocent act untainted by discrimination.

70. **"Promiscuous bundling and documentary carpet-bombing"**—A common trick by a Respondent or Defendant to overload the other side with thousands of irrelevant documents, meaning the Claimant and their lawyers have to plough through and read thousands of documents to find the few documents that are relevant for the case. This takes a huge amount of time and money. When these documents are served on the Court or tribunal and the majority of the documents are never even referred to, the Judges have referred to this practice as "promiscuous bundling and documentary carpet-bombing." Carpet-bombing is a military term when military planes make a devastating bombing attack that seeks to destroy every part of a wide area. Mr Justice Turner in Griffiths vs The Secretary of State for Health [2015] in another example of over-sized trial bundles quoted the Civil Procedure Rules. 1.3 and stated that "these rules impose a duty upon the parties to help the court to further the overriding objective and this duty is not fulfilled by promiscuous bundling and documentary carpet bombing."

71. **"Proofing a witness"** is the process of the lawyer speaking to a witness, usually in person, about the substance of their evidence, going through the person's witness statement and taking the witness to the documents referred to in their statement.

72. Proprietary trading ("prop trading") refers to a financial firm or commercial bank that invests for direct market gain rather than earning commission by trading on behalf of clients.

73. **'Protected act'**—under the Equality Act 2010. Making a claim or complaint of discrimination (under the Equality Act); Helping someone else to make a claim by giving evidence or information; Making an allegation that the employer or a third party has breached the Equality Act; Doing anything else in connection with the Act.

74. **Pukka**—means "superior"; "first class"; "elegant; "refined"; "good quality" etc. It is Hindi and Urdu in origin.

75. **Redacting a document**—the process of editing a document to conceal or remove confidential information or names of persons before disclosure.

76. **Respondent**—the employer who defends a claim in an Employment Tribunal.

77. **Restricted Reporting Order (RRO)**—The Employment Tribunals Act 1996, s.11, provides that the Tribunal may, on its own motion, or upon an application of one of the parties, make a restricted reporting order (RRO) in cases where sexual misconduct has been alleged prohibiting the names of any of the 'affected persons' who are listed in the Order, from being published or identified, until the promulgation of the decision of the Tribunal.

78. **Rule 7 letter**—once the GMC has investigated a complaint about a doctor and found there may be a case to answer, the case is passed to case examiners. It is at this stage when the GMC will write a letter to the Doctor, known as a rule 7 letter. The rule 7 letter will outline the allegations made in the complaint and ask the doctor to comment. The doctor has 28 days to respond to this letter.

79. **Sabbatical**—a period of paid leave granted to employees in certain industries including university teachers and journalists for study or travel.

80. **Safeguarding**—'Safeguarding' involves ensuring that children and young people are protected from harm, free from abuse, neglect and maltreatment. The Local Authority Designated Officer (LADO) manages allegations of abuse and gives advice and guidance to

employers and Organisations who have concerns about the behaviour of an adult who works with children and young people.

81. **'Salacious'**—having or conveying undue or inappropriate interest in sexual matters.

82. **Schmoozing**—Yiddish for talking with someone in a lively friendly way typically to impress or manipulate.

83. **Secondary Action**—Secondary action (or sympathy strikes as they are sometimes known) would occur if a trade union induces its members to take industrial action against their employer in support of fellow union members employed by a different employer where a trade dispute exists. Secondary action is rendered unlawful in the UK now following the repeal of the Industrial Relations Act 1971, by section 224 of the Trade Union and Labour Relations (Consolidation) Act 1992.

84. **Service requirement for unfair dismissal**—In 1971 under the Industrial Relations Act 1971 employees had to have one year's service to claim ordinary unfair dismissal. In 1985 the then Labour Government reduced this to 6 months' service. It then increased to one year's service in 1999. In April 2012 David Cameron's Government increased the service requirement to claim ordinary unfair dismissal to two (2) years and that still stands today.

85. **Settlement Agreement**—a legally binding agreement in which the parties agree terms—usually the Claimant agrees not to bring or to withdraw legal proceedings and the Respondent or Defendant agrees to make a monetary payment;|

86. **Similar fact evidence**—On occasion, evidence may exist that, for example, the accused has behaved in a similar way to that alleged in the instant proceedings. Although only evidence relevant to the crime or the claim is allowed in evidence, in certain circumstances such evidence of similar (albeit unconnected) incidents or facts may be admitted into evidence. In the law of evidence, there are conditions under which factual evidence of past misconduct of accused can be admitted at trial for the purpose of inferring that the accused committed the misconduct at issue; e.g., if a man is accused of being a paedophile having been arrested on Hampstead Heath after a complaint was made and the police find child pornography on his computer, that is similar fact evidence that

would be allowed to be produced by the Crown Prosecution Service in evidence.

87. A snuff video is a recording of a person being murdered on camera. It only counts if this is an actual murder, not a staged one.

88. **Summary dismissal**—dismissal without notice or payment in lieu of notice for an offence which strikes at the root of the contract i.e., something every serious.

89. **Tort**—is a civil wrong (other than breach of contract) that causes a claimant to suffer loss or harm, resulting in legal liability for the person who commits the tortious act. It can include intentional infliction of emotional distress, negligence, financial losses, injuries, invasion of privacy. Torts include negligence or nuisance or libel or slander. These cases are heard in the County Court or High Court depending on the remedy being sought.

90. **Triangulation**—Police rely on principles of triangulation to track down the phone. A mobile phone is able to communicate with three or more towers. Triangulation software can use the phone's signal strength from each tower to estimate the geographical position of the phone.

91. **Unfair dismissal**—ordinary unfair dismissal means dismissal for one of the five potentially fair reasons set out in s.98 of the Employment Rights Act 1996 for which employees need at least two years' service to bring a claim to an Employment Tribunal. There is a cap on compensation for unfair dismissal of a maximum of one year's salary or a statutory cap which is slightly increased each April. In 2022 it stood at £93,878 gross subject to deductions of tax and NICs, whichever is the lower.

92. **Vicarious liability**—liability imposed on employers—being held responsible for an employee's acts or omissions when they are acting in the course of their employment.

93. **Victimisation**—under the Equality Act 2010 is where the employer or another employee treats someone adversely and to their detriment **because** they have done a 'protected act'.

94. **Wasted Costs Order** is an Order made by an Employment Tribunal ordering the representative to pay the whole or part of any wasted costs of the other party.

95. **'Walter Mitty' character** is a person who fantasises about a life much more exciting and glamorous than their own.

96. **Without Prejudice save as to costs and subject to contract**—the parties to a dispute may enter Without Prejudice discussions or correspondence about an existing dispute, whether or not Court proceedings have already been issued. However, it must be noted that a communication can only be "without prejudice" there must be an existing dispute between the parties and the communication must contain a genuine attempt to settle the dispute. The words "save as to costs" allows the winning party to disclose the correspondence to the Court or Employment Tribunal in the event that the Claimant rejects the offer and loses their case or is awarded less than the Without Prejudice offer. In such a case, cost may be awarded against the Claimant who has lost. "Subject to contract" means until the terms of the agreement are agreed there is no binding agreement.

97. **Witness statement**—a statement prepared by a witness which stands as their evidence in an Employment Tribunal or Court with no evidence in chief being required by their Counsel. The exception is in Employment Tribunals in Scotland where witness statements are not used. Advocates in Scotland still have to examine their witnesses in chief.

98. **Works Convenor**—is the principal trade union representative within a workplace. Convenors are usually elected by the members often by a shop steward committee. They occupy the lead role in relations with management. It is often a full-time job—they are paid by the employer but undertake their union duties full-time. They frequently are given an office and other facilities such as a phone, computer etc.

CPSIA information can be obtained
at www.ICGtesting.com
Printed in the USA
LVHW022133210423
744988LV00001B/4